Mastering Statutory Interpretation

Carolina Academic Press Mastering Series
RUSSELL L. WEAVER, SERIES EDITOR

Mastering Administrative Law
William R. Andersen

Mastering Appellate Advocacy and Process
Donna C. Looper, George W. Kuney

Mastering Bankruptcy
George W. Kuney

Mastering Civil Procedure 2e
David Charles Hricik

Mastering Constitutional Law
John C. Knechtle, Christopher J. Roederer

Mastering Contract Law
Irma S. Russell, Barbara K. Bucholtz

Mastering Corporate Tax
Reginald Mombrun, Gail Levin Richmond, Felicia Branch

Mastering Corporations and Other Business Entities
Lee Harris

Mastering Criminal Law
Ellen S. Podgor, Peter J. Henning, Neil P. Cohen

Mastering Criminal Procedure, Volume 1: The Investigative Stage
Peter J. Henning, Andrew Taslitz, Margaret L. Paris,
Cynthia E. Jones, Ellen S. Podgor

Mastering Criminal Procedure, Volume 2: The Adjudicatory Stage
Peter J. Henning, Andrew Taslitz, Margaret L. Paris,
Cynthia E. Jones, Ellen S. Podgor

Mastering Elder Law
Ralph C. Brashier

Mastering Employment Discrimination Law
Paul M. Secunda, Jeffrey M. Hirsch

Mastering Evidence
Ronald W. Eades

Mastering Family Law
Janet Leach Richards

Mastering Intellectual Property
George W. Kuney, Donna C. Looper

Mastering Legal Analysis and Communication
David T. Ritchie

Mastering Legal Analysis and Drafting
George W. Kuney, Donna C. Looper

Mastering Negotiable Instruments (UCC Articles 3 and 4)
and Other Payment Systems
Michael D. Floyd

Mastering Partnership Taxation
Stuart Lazar

Mastering Products Liability
Ronald W. Eades

Mastering Professional Responsibility
Grace M. Giesel

Mastering Property Law
Darryl C. Wilson, Cynthia H. DeBose

Mastering Secured Transactions (UCC Article 9) 2e
Richard H. Nowka

Mastering Statutory Interpretation 2e
Linda D. Jellum

Mastering Tort Law
Russell L. Weaver, Edward C. Martin, Andrew R. Klein,
Paul J. Zwier II, Ronald W. Eades, John H. Bauman

Mastering Trademark and Unfair Competition Law
Lars S. Smith, Llewellyn Joseph Gibbons

Mastering
Statutory Interpretation

SECOND EDITION

Linda D. Jellum
PROFESSOR OF LAW
MERCER UNIVERSITY SCHOOL OF LAW

CAROLINA ACADEMIC PRESS
Durham, North Carolina

Library of Congress Cataloging-in-Publication Data

Jellum, Linda D.
  Mastering statutory interpretation / by Linda Jellum. -- Second Edition.
    p. cm. -- (Carolina Academic Mastering Series)
  Includes bibliographical references and index.
  ISBN: 978-1-61163-456-3 (alk. paper)
  1. Law--United States--Interpretation and construction. I. Title.
  KF425.J455 2013
  348.73'2--dc22   2013018729

CAROLINA ACADEMIC PRESS   ⌃
700 Kent Street
Durham, NC 27701
Telephone (919) 489-7486
Fax (919) 493-5668
www.cap-press.com

Printed in the United States of America

Contents

Table of Cases

Series Editor's Foreword

The Carolina Academic Press Mastering Series is designed to provide you with a tool that will enable you to easily and efficiently "master" the substance and content of law school courses. Throughout the series, the focus is on quality writing that makes legal concepts understandable. As a result, the series is designed to be easy to read and is not unduly cluttered with footnotes or cites to secondary sources.

In order to facilitate student mastery of topics, the Mastering Series includes a number of pedagogical features designed to improve learning and retention. At the beginning of each chapter, you will find a "Roadmap" that tells you about the chapter and provides you with a sense of the material that you will cover. A "Checkpoint" at the end of each chapter encourages you to stop and review the key concepts, reiterating what you have learned. Throughout the book, key terms are explained and emphasized. Finally, a "Master Checklist" at the end of each book reinforces what you have learned and helps you identify any areas that need review or further study.

We hope that you will enjoy studying with, and learning from, the Mastering Series.

-Russell L. Weaver
Professor of Law & Distinguished University Scholar
University of Louisville, Louis D. Brandeis School of Law

Preface

Preface to the Second Edition

This edition is dedicated to all of my students during the last few years, but especially to the students in the Connecticut University Law School's 2012 externship program in Washington, D.C. With their help and Professor Bernard Bell's willingness to share a problem he crafted, I have added a section to each chapter called Mastering This Topic, which is based on a running hypothetical involving an ordinance prohibiting vehicles in the park. I believe the new section will greatly aid your mastery of the subject.

I would also like to thank my research assistants, Ashley Turner and Dianna Lee, for all their invaluable help and great senses of humor.

Finally, I could not have made it through this very difficult year without the help of a few very special people: Professor Dorothy Brown, Professor Nancy Levit, Terry Smith, Esq., Mary Cullen, Yuichi Miyoshi, and my husband, children, and family members. Chris, camp is finally over!

Linda D. Jellum
Bethesda, Maryland
April 2013

Preface to the First Edition

This book is dedicated to my husband and children, who have not seen as much of me this year as they would have preferred, and to my parents, who have been there to guide and advise me for so many years.

I would like to thank the following for their insightful comments and helpful suggestions, endless review of draft chapters, and other assistance: Professor Michael Dimino, Professor Brian Slocum, Professor Steven Johnson, Professor David Ritchie, Professor Spencer Clough, Denise Gibson, Barbara Churchwell, Susan Wilson, Jamanda Turner, Chris Featherstun, Java Joe's in Hilton Head, and Mercer Law School (for research support). Each individual has made this text better with his or her involvement. Any remaining errors are mine alone.

Special thanks are due to my colleague and former co-author, Professor David Hricik. This project would have been infinitely more difficult without the foundation I gained from our earlier project. I also would like to thank Professor Russell Weaver for asking me to be involved in the Mastering Series and for supporting me in so many ways over the years.

Linda D. Jellum
Macon, Georgia
April 2008

Mastering Statutory Interpretation

Chapter 1

Introducing Statutory Interpretation

Roadmap

- Learn what statutory interpretation is and what it is not.
- Understand why most law works well.
- Identify your current inclinations.
- Understand "separation of powers" and its relevance to statutory interpretation.
- Learn how constitutional interpretation differs from statutory interpretation.

A. Introduction to This Chapter

Each chapter in this book begins with an introduction like this one, which will explain the purpose and organization of that chapter. So, let's get started. As you read this text, you will likely encounter new and unfamiliar words. There is a Glossary in Appendix B to help you learn the meanings of these new words.

This chapter introduces you to statutory interpretation generally — what it is and why lawyers should understand it. It then explains why laws, including statutes, generally work well and need little interpreting. But sometimes laws are unclear. This book describes the methods for interpreting unclear laws. To help you understand how to apply these methods, this chapter includes a challenging hypothetical. The point of introducing the hypothetical in this chapter is to help you understand what you bring to statutory interpretation before you master it. You don't come to this topic as a neophyte. Rather, you bring beliefs about the proper way to interpret statutes, the best role for judges and legislatures, and the use of legislative history, for example. This hypothetical will help you identify these beliefs before we get started. The book as a whole will help you analyze the soundness of your beliefs.

After introducing the hypothetical, this chapter turns to a number of topics that are related to statutory interpretation, including separation of powers, civil law systems, constitutional interpretation, and the Uniform Statute & Rule Construction Act.

B. Statutory Interpretation Defined

In the past, law was developed in the courts through judge-made common law. Issues arose, lawyers sued, and judges resolved the disputes. Law developed slowly in piecemeal fashion. Thus, if you were a lawyer practicing in the 1800s, your practice focused on reading and understanding cases. For example, assume that a client hired you to determine whether he could sue his neighbor for cutting down a tree located on the property border. To find the answer, you would study a number of cases to determine the law. You would analyze the facts and the holdings of these cases and compare the facts of those cases to the facts of your case. You would also look at the reasoning in the cases to understand why each case was decided the way it was decided. After all of this research, you could answer your client's question.

Today, the process is different. If the same client came to your office, you would not start by researching case law. Rather, you would check first to see if there was a local, state, or federal statute (or regulation) on point. Assuming you find one, you will need to understand what that statute says. Sure, you think, that is easy. I'll just read it. Not so fast. Even if the statute appears clear, it may not be. As you will learn, reading a statute's text is only the first step to understanding what that statute means. Because language is inherently ambiguous (for example, is "blue" a state of being or a color? Is dust a verb or noun?), interpreting statutes is more complex than it would seem. "In the end, much of our jurisprudential disagreement about how to interpret statutes represents a tension between our common law tradition and our democratic tradition." WILLIAM N. ESKRIDGE, JR., ET AL., LEGISLATION AND STATUTORY INTERPRETATION 17 (2d ed. 2006).

Statutory interpretation is the process of determining the meaning of a legislative act called a statute. But interpreting a statute is more than simply reading the language. Moreover, interpretation differs greatly from common law analysis. Statutory interpretation is different from common law analysis, in part, because the creation of the law is so different and, in part, because the reasoning is mostly absent; legislatures do not always include the reasons for enacting certain laws. Statutes are the product of a long, legislative process that includes competing interests. The final product—the statute—is a compromise arrived at only after a long, political, and often controversial, process. While process is never relevant to common law interpretation, process is often relevant to statutory interpretation. LINDA D. JELLUM & DAVID C. HRICIK, MODERN STATUTORY INTERPRETATION: PROBLEMS, THEORIES, AND LAWYERING STRATEGIES xxvii (2d ed. 2009).

Statutory interpretation is an art, not a science, a language, not a set of rules. Legislatures do not draft perfectly; ambiguity, vagueness, omission, and mistake are all common elements in the final product. Knowing how to interpret statutes in light of these imperfections will be critical to practice, because most of the work lawyers do today centers on statutes, whether federal or state. While interpreting statutes is not an exact science, there are canons (or rules of thumb) that guide interpretation. Recognizing the increasing importance of this topic, law schools around the country are adding statutory interpretation and legislation courses. "[A]cademic law is catching up with legal practice." ESKRIDGE ET AL., LEGISLATION AND STATUTORY INTERPRETATION, *supra*, at 2. Today, lawyers simply cannot practice law without knowing the art of statutory interpretation. Because statutes and regulations have proliferated, reading and understanding statutes is a basic legal skill and, thus, is essential to your success as a lawyer.

This book will help you learn the art of statutory interpretation. Because different scholars and courts use different approaches to statutory interpretation, this text cannot definitively explain how a judge or court will interpret a statute, but it will help you learn to make arguments for your client, speak a new language, and anticipate how statutes are likely to be interpreted. At the conclusion of this text, you should: (1) be familiar with the canons of interpretation, knowing how to use them and how to counter your opponent's use of them, (2) have an understanding of the various theories of interpretation judges use in interpreting statutes, and (3) be aware of the breadth of arguments that can be made about seemingly clear language. In short, this text will help you master the art of statutory interpretation.

C. Why Law Works Well Most of the Time

You may wonder why interpretation is necessary. After all, ordinary citizens obey laws every day. How is this possible if laws are so unclear? Most citizens do not have the luxury of hiring lawyers to help them understand the language of the law, nor do they have the time to study statutory interpretation in the detail you are doing. Yet, they are expected to know the law, whether they have read it or not, and conform their actions accordingly. And they do so more often than not. How can ordinary citizens know whether their actions conform to legal requirements if a lawyer has to read books like this to learn how to read statutes and take three years of law school to learn how to understand cases?

Simply put, many laws are intuitive and conform to societal expectations. Most of us do not need a law to tell us that killing, assaulting, or stealing from someone is wrong. We also understand that there may be times when doing one of these actions, though usually wrong, would not be wrong given the particular circumstances. While most of us do not need laws to conform our behavior to societal norms, some outliers and sociopaths may need laws to prevent, or at least allow society to punish, their behavior. Legislators write statutes (and judges make common law) to explain law clearly for the outliers and enforcers, to enable those in authority to punish wrongdoers, and to identify the boundaries of that law.

Let's focus on statutes. How do legislators explain law clearly? Legislators follow familiar patterns. Statutes are understandable both because they conforms much of the time to societal expectations but also because they have a familiar format. As one scholar recently noted, statutes resemble dictionary definitions. Lawrence M. Solan, The Language of Statutes 18 (2010). For example, the definition of the verb "lie" is "to make an untrue statement with intent to deceive." *Merriam-Webster's online dictionary,* http://www.merriam-webster.com/dictionary/lie (last visited May 17, 2012). If we unpack this definition, we see that people lie when they 1) make an untrue statement, and 2) have the intent to deceive. Let's compare the federal statute criminalizing perjury:

> Whoever ... having taken an oath before a competent tribunal, officer, or person, in any case in which a law of the United States authorizes an oath to be administered, that he will testify, declare, depose, or certify truly, ... and contrary to such oath states or subscribes any material matter which he does not believe to be true ... is guilty of perjury.

18 U.S.C. § 1621(1) (2012). If we unpack this definition, people commit perjury when they 1) take an oath promising to testify truthfully, and 2) state something material that they do not believe to be true. Do you see the similarity between this statute and the definition above?

When statutes conform to societal expectations and define conduct in expected ways, statutes generally need be less clear, for most individuals will follow the law without inducement. But when statutes do not conform to societal expectations or do not define conduct in expected ways, individuals and their lawyers fight back by holding the legislature to the precise words it used. For example, a statute that states "Whoever shall willfully take the life of another shall be punished by death" is probably both expected and clear enough. But a statute that requires individuals to pay thirty percent of their "income" to the federal government better define "income" very clearly.

Let's look at another example, one closer to home. Consider your commute to work or school. You leave your house, drive a car that meets state safety standards, fill it with the appropriate kind of gas, drive on the right side of the road, stop at stop signs, stay reasonably close to the speed limit, pay to park your car legally, and turn on headlights when it grows dark. Daily, like all other ordinary citizens, you follow laws without thinking about whether you are doing so. You may not follow the laws perfectly (note the speed limit example), but you will follow the laws well enough to help society run smoothly. Thus, laws generally work well.

From these examples, you can see that it is only the hard cases that wind up in court and only the toughest of cases that are resolved at the Supreme Court. Remember that fact because after reading this text, you will be warped into thinking that the language in all statutes is malleable and ambiguous. This is not the case. Let me be clear: Most statutes are clear and work well. But because language is imprecise—precision is impossible with a limited number of symbols representing a multitude of concepts—ambiguity and vagueness are unavoidable. When ambiguity and vagueness arise, the question becomes how should they be resolved? That is the question that this text answers.

D. Is an Ambulance a Motor Vehicle?

The question in this heading seems silly, to say the least. Of course an ambulance is a motor vehicle. But is it? You might be surprised to learn that very intelligent people disagree about whether an ambulance is a vehicle, at least within the context of a statute prohibiting "vehicles in the park." Indeed, this question is so famous and contentious that Justice Antonin Scalia and Judge Richard Posner recently had a very public falling out based, in part, on their resolution of this very issue.

Below is a hypothetical city ordinance that prohibits vehicles from entering a public park. This hypothetical is based on *McBoyle v. United States*, 283 U.S. 25 (1931). The issue before the Supreme Court in *McBoyle* was whether a defendant who transported a stolen airplane across state lines violated the National Motor Vehicle Theft Act, 18 U.S.C. § 408, which provided that "whoever shall transport or cause to be transported in interstate or foreign commerce a motor vehicle, knowing the same to have been stolen, shall be punished...." According to subsection 2 of the statute, "The term 'motor vehicle' shall include an automobile, automobile truck, automobile wagon, motor cycle, or any other self-propelled vehicle not designed for running on rails." While the Court acknowledged that the language of the statute was broad enough to cover an airplane, "in everyday speech, 'vehicle' calls up the picture of a thing moving on land." *Id.* at 282. The Court held that an airplane was not a motor vehicle. The decision sparked controversy.

After you read the hypothetical city ordinance and its "legislative history," you will be asked to consider some hypothetical scenarios and decide whether you, as a new prosecutor for the city, would prosecute the individuals involved for violating the ordinance. When you answer the questions, consider how, if you would prosecute, you would explain to a judge that the defendant's actions violated the statute. What might a defense attorney argue in response? Why? What materials do you find helpful, relevant, and appropriate to consider in making your decisions as a prosecutor? What materials do you consider unhelpful, irrelevant, or inappropriate to consider? Why? Does it matter which side of the argument you are on? You should think about how you would resolve these questions before you read this text and master statutory interpretation. This hypothetical will test your beliefs about statutory interpretation while you are still an ordinary citizen, albeit one already influenced by some legal training.

You will be tempted to skip this step; after all, no one will test you on your answers, and law school is time-consuming enough. But you will learn a lot from actually attempting the hypothetical questions and noting your answers in the margins. If you take the time, likely less than an hour at most, to jot down your answers to these questions, you will learn quickly how you naturally approach interpretation issues, a topic we explore in some detail in Chapter 2. Additionally, you will find your notes helpful as we return to this problem again and again throughout this text in a special section entitled: "Mastering This Topic." So much of interpretation is intuitive and happens without your conscious thought. As you learn the rules of thumb, the canons for interpretation, you will be tempted to think of these canons as legal rules. They are not! Legal rules are mandatory. The parol evidence rule is a legal rule. It prevents a party to a written contract from presenting extrinsic evidence in court if that evidence would vary the written terms of a contract. The parol evidence rule is not malleable; it applies in every case involving a contract and extra-textual evidence. In contrast, the canons of interpretation are not legal rules; rather, they are guidelines, suggestions, or even a legal language that lawyers and judges use to justify outcomes. As such, they are malleable, and for every canon that supports one party's interpretation, there is a canon that supports the opposing party's interpretation. Thus, know now that you are not learning law *per se*; instead, you are learning a new language, one that you do not master at your peril.

E. No Motor Vehicles in the Park: A Hypothetical[1]

A hypothetical local city ordinance is included below. Do not worry if you do not understand everything included in the problem at this point. Just do your best by reading the ordinance, the accompanying legislative reports, and the mayor's signing statement. Then answer the questions that follow, noting your conclusions and reasoning in the margins. You will want to come back to your conclusions as you begin to master the material in this text. Note any questions you have about the material. Later, you can see if this text helped you answer those questions. Assume as you think about this problem that this ordinance was enacted in the same way that federal legislation is enacted (which you will learn in Chapter 3) and that the methods for interpreting ordinances are the same as the methods for interpreting federal statutes (they mostly are).

1. Hypothetical Problem Materials

Assuming the following citation for the ordinance below: 27 P.P.C. § 120(B). Note that a marked-up version of this ordinance has been provided. (A marked-up version shows amendments made in italics and deletions in strike-though font. After the law is codified, the italics and strike-through are removed.)

An Ordinance
To Prohibit Motor Vehicles in Pioneer Park

Be it enacted by the Council of the City of Pioneer assembled,

(1) The short title of this ordinance shall be the Pioneer Park Safety Ordinance.

(2) No cars, motorcycles, or other motor vehicles may enter or remain in Pioneer Park, except as provided in section 3 hereof.

---

1. Bernard Bell graciously provided a modified version of this hypothetical to me. He describes how he uses the hypothetical in class in his article, Bernard Bell, *"No More Vehicles in the Park": Reviving the Hart-Fuller Debate to Introduce Statutory Construction*, 48 J. LEGAL EDUC. 88 (1998) (citing H.L.A. Hart, *Positivism and the Separation of Law and Morals*, 71 HARV. L. REV. 593, 607 (1958); Lon L. Fuller, *Positivism and Fidelity to Law—A Reply to Professor Hart*, 71 HARV. L. REV. 630, 663 (1958)).

(3) Motor vehicles may be used by authorized public groups:
   a. in maintaining Pioneer Park, and
   b. in placing barricades for parades, concerts, or other entertainment in
       Pioneer Park.
(4) Anyone violating this ordinance shall be subject to a $1,000 fine, pro-
    vided no injuries occurred. If any injury occurred, the fine shall be
    doubled.

Effective: August 15, 1998.

Public Parks Committee Report: March 7, 1998

Unlike other local parks, motor vehicles are currently allowed unrestricted access to Pioneer Park. This ordinance will address the recent concerns created by a spate of accidents in Pioneer Park. In two
of these accidents, a car struck a pedestrian and another struck a bicyclist on park roads. In the third, a motorcyclist drove off road and
hit a pedestrian. This ordinance thus bans all vehicles from entering
the park, except for vehicles used in park maintenance and in setting
up barricades to control crowds at park festivities and parades. All parades must be authorized before the ordinance allows the use of motor
vehicles to place barricades.

The Public Parks Committee recommends that the ordinance be
adopted. (Mark-up attached.)

Marked-up Version of Ordinance:

An Ordinance

To Prohibit Motor Vehicles in Pioneer Park

Be it enacted by the Council of the City of Pioneer assembled,

(1) The short title of this ordinance shall be the Pioneer Park Safety Ordinance.
(2) No cars, motorcycles, or other *motor* vehicles may enter or remain in
    Pioneer Park, except as provided in section 3 hereof.
(3) *Motor* vehicles may be used by authorized public groups:
   a. in maintaining Pioneer Park, *and*
   b. in placing barricades for parades, concerts, or other entertainment in
       Pioneer Park.~~, and~~.
   c. ~~Mopeds, skateboards, bicycles, and other such vehicles are exempt~~.
(4) Anyone violating this ordinance shall be subject to a $1,000 fine, pro-
    vided no injuries occurred. If any injury occurred, the fine shall be
    doubled.

Summary of the City Council Floor Debate: June 1, 1998

Debate was short and sweet. The majority of council members were in favor of the ordinance. Some discussion arose as to why bicycles, skateboards, and mopeds should be specifically exempted. For reasons that are unclear, that section was eliminated. An amendment was offered to include the word "motor" before "vehicles" in subsections (2) and (3). That amendment passed overwhelmingly. The effect on park revenue, noise, and pollution were briefly discussed. One member expressed concern that water-skiing be able to continue on Crockett Lake.

A vote was taken, with the ordinance passing.

Mayor Poordue's Signing Statement: August 14, 1998

This ordinance directly addresses the noise and pollution concerns that have increased in recent years and will make our public park much safer. The ordinance continues to allow boaters to enjoy water-skiing on the lake, but bans noisy, dangerous, vehicles. I am delighted to sign it.

2. Some Hypothetical Questions

Assume that you are a prosecutor for the city, it is your first day on the job, and you have been asked to review the following cases to decide whether to prosecute or dismiss the citations. How would you resolve each of them and why? Do you need any more information to decide whether to prosecute? If so, what information do you need?

1. An ambulance entered Pioneer Park to pick up and take to the hospital a man who had just suffered a heart attack. Did the ambulance driver violate the Pioneer Park Safety Ordinance (PPSO)? What about the man who suffered the heart attack?

2. A helicopter hovered over Pioneer Park for an hour. Was this a violation of the PPSO?

   a. What about a private jet that came in low over Pioneer Park as it approached the local airport?

3. A chapter of the local Veterans of Foreign Wars wants to put an Iraq War tank in Pioneer Park as a monument. Will this violate the PPSO?

   a. Does it matter whether the tank is operable?

   b. What if the city council had enacted an ordinance after the PPSO was enacted assisting the VFW in the purchase of the tank on the condition that the tank be used as a monument in Pioneer Park?

4. A teenager pedaling a moped without use of its motor entered Pioneer Park. Did the teen violate the PPSO? *yes*

 a. Does it matter whether the motorized portion of the moped was operable? *no*

5. Motorboats have been used on the lake within the park (Crockett Lake) for years. The city installed two jumps for water-skiers in 2001, and the city continues to maintain them. The jumps draw a number of water-skiers, and there is a summer competition that brings a lot of revenue into the city. Can motorboats be operated in Crockett Lake after the PPSO was enacted? *yes*

 a. If motorboats are okay, could someone use a car to bring a boat to the lake? (Assume that using some sort of land-based motorized vehicle is necessary to get a boat into the lake.) *no*

6. Celebration Inc. scheduled a parade in Pioneer Park. The organization failed to apply for the permit required to hold the parade. Celebration Inc. used a truck to place barricades for the parade. Has Celebration Inc. violated the PPSO?

7. Citizens for a Clean Pioneer Park, a group authorized to perform maintenance work, used a riding lawnmower to cut grass in Pioneer Park. Has CCPP violated the PPSO? *no*

 a. What if the president of CCPP drove into Pioneer Park to inspect the maintenance work performed by members of CCPP? Did the president violate the PPSO? *yes*

 b. What if Lawnworks Inc., a new group not yet authorized to perform maintenance work, used a riding lawnmower to cut grass in Pioneer Park? Have the Lawnworks employees violated the PPSO? *yes*

8. A police car entered Pioneer Park while it was chasing a car containing two people who had just robbed a bank. Have the officers violated the PPSO? What about the bank robbers? *yes*

3. More Hypothetical Questions

Assume that before you can provide the answers to the questions above to your boss, you learn that because of constant problems of interpretation that have arisen with respect to the Pioneer Park Safety Ordinance, and because the city council and the mayor cannot agree on a more detailed ordinance, the Commission of Parks (an agency) promulgated a regulation (you do not know whether formal or informal procedures were used) to interpret the PPSO regarding whether certain vehicles are permitted in Pioneer Park. Does this regulation change any of your answer to any of the questions above? Note your answers in the margins. The regulation provides as follows:

33 C.F.R. § 2300

(1) "Motor vehicle" in the PPSO means a road vehicle driven by a motor or engine used or physically capable of being used upon any public highway in this state in the transportation of persons or property, except vehicles operating wholly on fixed rails or tracks and electric trolley buses.

(2) Section 2 of the PPSO applies only to operable road vehicles (except that road vehicles may operate in Pioneer Park to the extent that they are necessary to transport boats to and from Crockett Lake).

(3) Section 3(a) of the PPSO permits vehicles to operate in Pioneer Park only if: (1) the vehicle is one that at least in part is directly used for maintenance, such as lawnmowers, cherry pickers, and road surfacing equipment, or (2) the vehicle is necessary to transport materials used in maintaining Pioneer Park and is primarily used for that purpose.

(4) Section 3(b) of the PPSO permits vehicles to operate in Pioneer Park only if the vehicle is operating in conjunction with erecting barricades or other traffic control devices for a parade, concert, or other event for which the event's promoters have a valid permit.

F. Separation of Powers & Statutory Interpretation

We now move from the hypothetical to a few other topics that relate to statutory interpretation, beginning with separation of powers. Separation of powers underlies all aspects of statutory interpretation. In Chapter 11, we learn about the role of separation of powers and agencies. Here, we examine separation of powers and its relationship to statutory interpretation more generally. While separation of powers does not inform the meaning of a statute *per se*, it plays a strong supporting role. Let's take a look at exactly how separation of powers affects interpretation.

Separation of powers is the concept that the powers of a government should be split between two or more independent groups so that no one group or person can gain too much power. Our federal governmental power is split among the legislative, executive, and judicial branches. No one branch is more powerful than any other. According to the U.S. Constitution, legislators make laws, while judges interpret laws. It "is emphatically the province and duty of the judicial department to say what the law is." *Marbury v. Madison*, 5 U.S. (1 Cranch) 137, 177 (1803). Were it so neat! A little history is in order.

England's system of government is very different from ours. In early English history, judges created law. The King and Parliament ran the country and only rarely enacted statutes to modify judge-made common law. The American system is based, in part, on the English system; thus, early American judges similarly developed law through the courts. In the nineteenth century, law developed almost exclusively in this way. Judge-made law, known as common law, was the norm. Statutes were uncommon; those statutes that did exist were private (meaning they applied only to specific individuals) not public (meaning they applied to all individuals). Legislators, who worked primarily part-time, were considered to be uneducated, unsophisticated, and subject to political pressure. Indeed, a holdover custom from these early days is that a bill must be read three times before it is enacted to ensure that any representatives who are illiterate know what they are enacting! Thus, in early American history, statutes were viewed with hostility and suspicion. Indeed, it was during this time that the judiciary developed the canon that statutes in derogation of the common law should be strictly construed (See Chapter 13). Also during this time, United States legal education was developing into its current form: the case method. The "inventor" of case method instruction, Christopher Langdell, believed that statutes were not true "law"; rather, he believed that only judicially created common law was worthy enough to be considered law. In the late nineteenth century, legislation's role began to change as legislatures became more prolific and legislation became more generally applicable.

Today, legislation is pervasive and detailed. For example, compare the Sherman Act, which was enacted in 1890, with the Patient Protection and Affordable Care Act (known pejoratively as "Obamacare" or the "Health Care Act"), which was enacted in 2010. The Sherman Act is a comprehensive and expansive act regulating federal antitrust activity, and yet it fits onto a single page. Congress left significant room for judicial development. In contrast, the Affordable Care Act spans 906 pages. Congress left little room for judicial development.

> Statutes like the Sherman Act, the civil rights legislation, and the mail fraud statute were written in broad general language on the understanding that the courts would have wide latitude in construing them to achieve the remedial purposes that Congress had identified. The wide open spaces in statutes such as these are most appropriately interpreted as implicit delegations of authority to the courts to fill in the gaps in the common-law tradition of case-by-case adjudication.

McNally v. United States, 483 U.S. 350, 372–73 (1987) (Stevens, J., dissenting).

As legislation proliferated, statutes began to abrogate common law. This evolution intensified during the New Deal when Congress began to solve social and economic problems through legislation. Additionally, as legislators became more skilled at their jobs, distrust of legislators started to fade. By the mid-twentieth century, the Supreme Court regularly heard cases involving statutes, and so statutory interpretation became increasingly important. Similarly, during this time, regulatory agencies proliferated. As more and more agencies drafted more and more regulations, agencies' authority to interpret statutes added to the debate.

Today, the dividing line between making law and interpreting law is blurred: Is implying a cause of action in a statute "making" or "interpreting" law? Some judges believe it is interpreting law, while others would say it is making law. A judge's theory of statutory interpretation is based in large part on that judge's view about the relationship between the judiciary and the legislature—or separation of powers. When judges decide cases involving statutes, judges fill gaps, resolve ambiguity, and identify statutory boundaries. Indeed, every case requires a judge to adopt one meaning and reject at least one other meaning. Because of *stare decisis*—the prudential consideration that similar cases should be decided similarly—that interpretation will have future application. Thus, it is simply wrong to suggest that judges just interpret law; rather, they act in concert with the legislature to develop law.

Yet legislative supremacy in this area is essential to our system of government. The exact relationship between the legislature and judiciary is at the heart of the statutory interpretation theoretical continuum. At one end of this continuum is the view that only enacted text of a statute is relevant to interpretation. This view elevates the role of the legislature at the expense of the judiciary. At the other end of the continuum is the view that either statutory purpose or legislative intent is most relevant. This view elevates the judiciary's role at the expense of the legislature. The truth, of course, is somewhere in the middle. "Where in the middle" is the basis of many scholarly articles and judicial debates.

Also today, the appropriate way to interpret a statute is far from settled. Indeed, statutory interpretation has become the focus of scholarly debate as experts disagree about the importance to be placed on the ordinary meaning of the text, the legislative history surrounding enactment, and the purpose of the statute. Justice Scalia can be credited, or perhaps blamed, for the reemergence of this controversy; he adheres to a strict approach to interpretation that ignores legislative history and unexpressed purpose. He has been credited with returning the Supreme Court to an approach, or theory, that brings the importance of the text of the statute to the forefront of interpretation. This approach is known as "new textualism." It and other various theories to interpretation will be explained in more detail in Chapter 2.

G. A Note about Civil Law Systems

Interestingly, the expansion of legislation in this country directly contrasts with the foundation of legislation in civil law systems, such as the one in France, where statutes are written to provide the basic outline for judicial interpretation and elaboration. Classifying legal systems into civil law and common law systems is complex. Generally, the U.S. legal system is understood to be part of the common law tradition. As noted above, it derived, adapted, and evolved from the English legal system, which was familiar to the British colonists who arrived in the New World. Although both countries use a common law system, our current approach to law is quite different—one obvious and very superficial difference is that few U.S. lawyers or judges wear wigs to court. But we share a common legal heritage with our friends in England, and that heritage plays a role in statutory interpretation, as we shall see throughout this text. Other common law countries include Australia, India, Canada, Hong Kong, Ireland, and Pakistan. (England)

Common law, however, is not the only legal system. Many countries in continental Europe and South America follow a legal system referred to as "civil" or "civilian law." Indeed, it is the most common legal system in the world, including most of the European Union countries, Brazil, China, Japan, Mexico, Russia, Switzerland, Turkey, Quebec, and Louisiana. Although based on a common foundation, civil law and common law systems differ in many ways. For our purposes, one important difference between them is the primacy they give judicial opinions versus statutes. For common law systems, judicial opinions are controlling. The common law system developed initially with judges deciding cases that became precedents. These precedents were eventually synthesized into legal doctrines (think of common law assault). Many of these legal doctrines have now been codified, but we still hear the echo of judicial doctrine in many of these common-law-turned-statutes. Moreover, in a common law system the opinions of appellate courts typically bind lower courts in the same jurisdiction which address similar issues.

In contrast, the civil law system typically starts with more abstract principles, which a legislature enacts as a code of laws. The role of the judiciary is to interpret and apply these legislative enactments. A civil law judge may have more latitude with interpretation and application of a statute than a common law judge because precedents may be non-binding and, therefore, are only (potentially) persuasive. In other words, the starting point and center of civil law analysis is the code (the statutes), not case law.

There are other systems as well, including Islamic Law and Socialist Law. This book, of course, focuses on the U.S. common law system and its approaches to statutory interpretation. However, it can be useful for you to remember that lawyers from other parts of the world may approach the statutory interpretation process quite differently.

H. Constitutional Interpretation Distinguished

Judges interpret language in documents other than statutes. Because the canons that you will learn in these pages are useful to anyone interpreting written language, you will find judges using the canons for more than statutory interpretation. For example, judges often interpret contracts and constitutions, both state and federal, and they use many of the same interpretation techniques to interpret these other types of documents.

However, there are some differences in interpretation techniques based on the text being interpreted, especially for constitutional interpretation. In Chapter 2, you will learn that judges approach statutory interpretation in a number of ways that academics call the "theories of statutory interpretation." Just like statutory interpretation, there are many theories of constitutional interpretation including textualism, originalism, strict constructionism, functionalism, doctrinalism, developmentalism, contextualism, and structuralism. For now, let's explore just two of these theories: originalism and textualism. Originalist theorists focus on finding the subjective intentions of the drafters of particular constitutional provisions. Originalists look for the meaning or understanding of the constitutional provision at the time the provision was ratified or amended.

In contrast, textualists or strict constructionalists focus on the literal meaning of a constitutional provision and reject claims that the text can mean more or less than what it expressly says. For example, former Supreme Court Justice Hugo Black claimed that the First Amendment's language that "Congress shall make no law ... abridging the freedom of speech" was clear: "No law" meant absolutely no law, not even laws imposing time, place, or manner restrictions. Strict constructionism appeals to those who wish for simplicity and determinacy. Today, the most fundamental disagreement among constitutional theorists is whether the U.S. Constitution is a living document, which is to some degree dynamic and able to change with a changing society or whether it is a document fixed as of a certain point in time, its origination. An important case in which these two different theories appear is *District of Columbia v. Heller*, 554 U.S. 570 (2008), in which the Supreme Court decided that the Second Amendment protects an individual's right to keep and bear arms. Justice Scalia, writing for the majority and taking a very textualist approach, noted that "[t]he 18th-century meaning [of the word "Arms"] is no different from the meaning today." *Id.* at 581. In contrast, Justice Breyer in dissent noted that he disagreed because "the District's regulation, which focuses upon the presence of handguns in high-crime urban areas, represents a permissible legislative response to a serious, indeed life-threatening, problem." *Id.* at 682. (Breyer, J., dissenting).

While it is not important that you understand what the various theories relating to constitutional interpretation, you should recognize that constitutional interpretation is similar to but differs from statutory interpretation in fundamental ways. For example, much of constitutional interpretation centers on discerning the intent of the Framers. Yet the Constitution represented a compromise of competing philosophical ideals. For example, the Framers made the legislature bicameral — meaning two houses — as a compromise between the big states, which wanted a legislative representation based on population, and the small states, which thought all states should be represented equally. How do you discern intent when the result was a compromise of competing interests? Another issue that affects constitutional interpretation is that, with all of the amendments, the Constitution was not drafted at one point in time; rather it was drafted during a 200 year time-frame. Language and culture changed tremendously during those 200 years. Moreover, the Framers did not always draft the new language. Additionally, ratification adds its own complexities. For example, the Twenty-Seventh Amendment, which deals with the compensation of members of Congress, was initially proposed in 1789, when there were only thirteen states. Yet it did not become law until 1992 when Michigan finally ratified it. Should the amendment be interpreted with the backdrop of 1789 in mind, 1992, or sometime in between? LAURENCE H. TRIBE, AMERICAN CONSTITUTIONAL LAW 5 (3d ed.). Thus, for many reasons, constitutional interpretation differs from statutory interpretation, but the two have a number of similarities.

I. The Uniform Statute & Rule Construction Act

Uniform Acts are proposed state laws that the National Conference of Commissioners on Uniform State Laws ("Conference") or another institutional actor drafts. The Conference was established in 1892 and is made up of lawyers, judges, and law professors. Members of the Conference draft laws on a variety of subjects and propose them for enactment within the states, the District of Columbia, the U.S. Virgin Islands, and Puerto Rico. The Conference has no legislative power; rather, the proposed uniform acts become law only when they are adopted in a particular state. Thus, proposed uniform acts serve as guidelines, or samples, for the state legislatures. The United States is a country with one federal system of laws and fifty or more state systems of laws. The purpose of the Conference is to help encourage uniformity across state lines, particularly in areas where state boundaries are essentially irrelevant. For example, the Uniform Commercial Code, which has been widely adopted among the states, unifies the law regarding the sale of goods. There are currently more than 100 different uniform acts, including one on statutory interpretation.

The Conference drafted the Uniform Statute and Rule Construction Act ("the Act") in an attempt to unify the process of statutory interpretation. The Conference approved the Act in 1993 and recommended enactment in the states. The Act represents a compromise among the various conflicting preferences in the field of statutory construction. For example, in Chapter 2, this text describes various theories, or approaches, of statutory interpretation, including textualism — which focuses on the text — and purposivism — which focuses on the text together with the purpose of the statute. The drafters of the Act claimed not to have adopted any theory. The Act does emphasize the primacy of the text, but it also recognizes non-textual sources such as legislative history from which purpose may be discerned. The Act thus takes a middle ground approach to this philosophical and academic debate. Additionally, the Act makes clear that its "rules" are not rules in the typical legal sense, but rather are simply a "hierarchy of values" for the interpreter to follow as the circumstances allow. Unif. Statute & Rule Constr. Act § 18 cmt. at 71 (West Supp. 1995). After all, statutory interpretation is not an exact science governed by legal rules; rather, it is an art: a patchwork of contradictory and competing canons.

To date, only the state of New Mexico has adopted the Act. However, the Act offers an easy reference guide and a succinct articulation of many of the canons we will be covering. Thus, this text often refers to relevant sections of the Act.

Checkpoints

- Statutory interpretation is the process of determining the meaning of a legislative act. It is a process governed by rules of thumb, or guidelines, not lawlike rules.

- Most of the time, laws work well because they regulate in ways we expect and with which we are familiar. It is the hard cases that wind up in court.

- Separation of powers — the idea that the powers of a government should be split between two or more independent groups — underlies all aspects of statutory interpretation.

- The common law system is only one legal system. Other systems approach statutory interpretation differently.

- Constitutional interpretation is similar to but differs from statutory interpretation in fundamental ways.

- Only New Mexico has adopted the Uniform Statute & Rule Construction Act, which legal experts proposed to make statutory interpretation more uniform among the states.

Chapter 2

The Art of Statutory
Interpretation:
Sources & Theories

Roadmap

- Identify the three sources of evidence judges use to interpret statutes: intrinsic sources, extrinsic sources, and policy-based sources.
- Examine the theories judges use to interpret statutes: textualism, intentionalism, imaginative reconstructionism, purposivism, dynamic interpretation, and Alaska's sliding scale.
- Explore whether theory really matters.

A. Introduction to This Chapter

This chapter will introduce you to the building blocks underlying statutory interpretation: the sources of evidence judges use to find the meaning of statutory language and the theories of interpretation judges use when approaching an interpretation question. While at first glance, this chapter may seem to be one designed for academics and theorists, it is not. Grasping the building blocks of statutory interpretation is essential for anyone wishing to make statutory arguments to a judge. Theory matters, but it matters in unusual ways. These sources and theories will enable you to "talk the talk," so to speak. You will not win your case simply because you mention the text to a textualist judge, but at least that judge will understand what you are saying. Thus, in this chapter, you will learn a new language, one with which you are likely already somewhat familiar.

B. The Art of Statutory Interpretation

In its most basic form, statutory interpretation is the art of discerning the intent of the enacting legislature, for it is the enacting legislature that has the constitutional authority to make law. Theoretically then, judges should interpret statutes as the enacting legislature expected or intended. But discerning an enacting legislature's intent is extremely difficult; how does one discern the intent of a group of individuals all having potentially different goals? One cannot simply contact the legislators after the fact and ask them what they intended to accomplish. Even if they were still alive, even if they remembered having a specific intent on the issue before the court, and even if they remembered accurately, such after-the-fact rationalizations are not considered valid evidence of the intent of the legislature as a whole.

Realistically, the idea that there is one, unified "meeting of the minds" is nonsense. While members of the legislature may share the goal of passing a bill to address a particular problem, rarely will all members have the same reason for passage or even the same expectations regarding the bill's effects. Rather, bills are the result of committee work and political compromise. A bill "emerges from the hubbub of legislative struggle, from the drafts of beginning lawyers, from the work of lobbyists who are casual about clarity but forceful about policy, from the chaos of adjournment deadlines." JACK DAVIES, LEGISLATIVE LAW AND PROCESS IN A NUTSHELL 307–08 (3d ed. 2007). Because of this enactment process, bills are filled with ambiguity, absurdity, lack of clarity, obscurity, mistakes, and omissions. Legislators rarely intend to be ambiguous, absurd, unclear, obscure, mistaken, or incomplete, but they often are.

Because of the difficulty of discerning legislative intent, judges have adopted a number of ways to resolve statutory interpretation issues. Some judges focus on the words of the text, believing that by giving words their ordinary, public meaning, the judge will best further the legislative agenda. Other judges focus on the stated or unstated purpose of the bill, believing that by furthering that purpose, they will best further the legislative agenda. And other judges focus on the piecemeal nature of the legislative process, believing that by comparing various versions of the bill and the legislators' statements accompanying the enactment process, they will best further the legislative agenda. Legal scholars have named these approaches the "theories of interpretation" and have exhaustively argued about which theory best accomplishes the goal of statutory interpretation. Lawyers are mostly oblivious to the differences in the theories and so approach interpretation questions based on the approach that is most intuitive to them.

So, you might wonder why this topic is in this text. After all, this is a text primarily for students and practitioners of statutory interpretation, not for academics or judges. Isn't theory something of interest only to those who have time to study such abstract ideas? The simple answer to that question is "no." Perhaps more than in any other area of law, understanding theory is critical to understanding statutory interpretation because theory drives every aspect of statutory interpretation. A judge's theory of interpretation determines what information a judge will consider when searching for meaning. For example, some judges will not look at legislative history or social context for meaning unless the text of the statute is unclear. To argue to one of these judges that the legislative history of the statute supports your client's position, you must first explain why it is necessary to go beyond the text for meaning. In other words, you need to learn to "talk the talk" of statutory interpretation. Indeed, you will likely lose your case unless you master this skill. Hence, this book covers theory early and in detail.

The theories are based around the three sources of information, or evidence, judges consider in construing statutory language: (1) *intrinsic sources* of evidence, (2) *extrinsic sources* of evidence, and (3) *policy-based sources* of evidence. These three sources are briefly explained below. The sources of statutory interpretation and the theories of statutory interpretation are interrelated but different. The theories, which we will study later, are based on the relevance of the sources.

C. The Evidentiary Sources of Meaning

To interpret a statute, a judge will look at a variety of sources of information, including intrinsic (or textual) sources, extrinsic sources, and policy-based sources.

1. Intrinsic Sources

Intrinsic sources are materials that are part of the official act being interpreted. The first step in the interpretation process for all theorists is always "Read the statute. Read the Statute. Read the Statute." John M. Kernochan, *Statutory Interpretation: An Outline of Method*, 3 DALHOUSIE L.J. 333, 338 (1976) (citing HENRY J. FRIENDLY, BENCHMARKS 202 (1967)). Clearly, the words of the statute at issue are the most important intrinsic source. But the words alone cannot be the only place a judge looks for meaning. Other intrinsic sources, such as the grammar and punctuation; the components of the act, including purpose and findings clauses, titles, and definition sections; and the linguistic canons of statutory construction may also be important to interpretation. All of these are intrinsic sources and are sources for meaning.

2. Extrinsic Sources

A second category of sources that judges may consider to discern meaning is the extrinsic sources—materials outside of the official act but within the legislative process that created the act. The following are examples of extrinsic sources:

- legislative history (statements made during the enactment process),
- legislative acquiescence (the canon that legislative silence in response to a judicial interpretation of a statute means legislative agreement with that interpretation),
- borrowed-statutes rules (the presumption that the legislature intended, when it borrowed another state's statute, to adopt the other state's judicial opinions regarding that statute in effect at the time), and
- agency interpretations (the presumption that the legislature meant to defer to the meanings agencies give to ambiguous statutes).

With the exception of agency interpretations, these sources are all intimately related to the enactment process. The use of some of these sources—such as deference to agency interpretations—is relatively non-controversial. The use of others—such as legislative history—is highly controversial. Historically, intrinsic sources were regularly used to aid interpretation, while extrinsic sources were used more sparingly. After the New Deal, this historical custom relaxed, and judges turned to extrinsic sources, especially legislative history, more readily. Today, as a result of the reemergence of textualism, consideration of extrinsic sources once again is more controversial.

3. Policy-Based Sources

Third, and finally, are policy-based sources. These sources are separate from both the statutory act and the legislative process. They reflect important social and legal choices derived from the Constitution, common law, or prudence. The following are examples of policy-based sources:

- the constitutional avoidance doctrine (the canon that if two reasonable or fair interpretations exist, one of which raises constitutional issues, the other interpretation should control),
- the rule of lenity (in a criminal case, the canon that if two reasonable interpretations exist, the court should adopt the less penal interpretation),

- the remedial and derogation canons (the rule that statutes in derogation of the common law should be strictly construed, while remedial statutes should be broadly construed), and
- clear statement rules (the presumption that in some situations, such as ones raising federalism concerns, Congress would not intentionally alter the status quo absent a clear statement to that effect).

Reliance on policy-based sources comes in and out of vogue. For example, the rule of lenity, which arises from constitutional due process concerns about providing adequate notice of penal conduct, has been relegated to a rule of last resort with society's current focus on penalizing criminals. Some state legislatures, such as California, have attempted to abolish the rule of lenity by statute; however, because the rule of lenity is derived, in part, from constitutional procedural due process concerns, these state legislatures have had limited success.

While it would be nice if the above categories were consistently defined in judicial opinions and academic circles, they are not. What one person calls a policy-based source, another might identify as an extrinsic source. Understanding exactly which category a source falls within is less important than understanding (1) that there is a breadth of informational sources available to judges, and (2) that some judges are more willing to look beyond intrinsic sources for meaning than others. What sources a judge will consider depends on that judge's theory of statutory interpretation.

D. The Theories of Interpretation

Do not expect anybody's theory of statutory interpretation ... to be an accurate statement of what courts actually do with statutes. The hard truth of the matter is that American courts have no intelligible, generally accepted, and consistently applied theory of statutory interpretation.

William N. Eskridge, Jr. & Philip P. Frickey, Introduction to Henry M. Hart, Jr. & Albert M. Sacks, The Legal Process 1169 (William N. Eskridge, Jr. & Philip P. Frickey, eds., 1994). This famous Hart and Sacks quote is still accurate today even though it is more than forty years old. But theory is relevant even if judges find it impossible to apply consistently. It is relevant because judges need a way to approach statutes to determine, among other things, whether to rely more heavily on the text and linguistic canons or on other, extra-textual evidence of meaning; whether to consider legislative history and if so, which history; whether to consider the unexpressed purpose of the bill; and how to determine the weight to give a source a judge will consider.

Judges interpret statutes in a variety of ways. These ways vary in their emphasis on the sources identified above. These ways are called the approaches to, or theories of, statutory interpretation; for our purposes, the terms are interchangeable. Adherents of the different approaches differ in what they believe best shows the intent of the enacting legislature and, thus, the meaning of the statute. They also differ about what role the courts and legislature should play in resolving statutory ambiguity. Simply put, adherents of the approaches differ in the willingness to consider sources other than the statutory text. For example, textualists believe that the text of the statute is central, while purposivists believe that the purpose of the statute is equally, if not at times more, important.

Judges can and do blend these approaches for a variety of reasons. A judge may generally prefer one approach, but find that for a specific case or even a specific issue, the preferred approach does not work. Hence, that judge may adopt a different approach or meld a variety of approaches. Additionally, because one judge, who may approach statutory interpretation in one way, writes an appellate opinion, and other judges, who may approach statutory interpretation differently, join the opinion, appellate opinions rarely exemplify consistency. The approaches that are described below are neither exhaustive nor exclusive.

Moreover, none of the approaches is perfect; each has its strengths and its weaknesses, its proponents and its critics. Perhaps because of the imperfections, the preferred approach has varied with time. An approach that dominated during one era often falls out of favor in the next. For example, early in American jurisprudence, judges preferred to look at the purpose of the statute; today, the text has gained currency. Debate over the appropriate approach has raged; indeed, the battle over the appropriate approach has left the pages of academic law journals and become center stage in judicial opinions and in legislative debates. For example, in *State v. Courchesne*, 816 A.2d 562, 587 (Conn. 2003), the Connecticut Supreme Court evaluated the various approaches and selected purposivism, an approach that focuses on the purpose of the statute. The Connecticut legislature disagreed, however, and, in direct response to that case, passed a statute requiring its courts to apply textualism. More recently, Justice Scalia and Judge Poser publically and contentiously debated the pros and cons of one form of textualism.

Below, the more prevalent approaches are explained in some detail, beginning with textualism.

1. Textualism

a. The Theory

As noted earlier, a judge's view of separation of powers affects interpretation. Textualists believe that a judge's role is to be faithful to the Constitution by protecting the power distribution identified within that document: The legislature has the power to enact laws, while the judiciary has the power to interpret laws. For enactment of statutes, the Constitution requires a specific process: bicameral passage and executive approval. Only the text goes through this process; thus, textualists believe that looking beyond the enacted text raises constitutional concerns. They "would hold Congress to the words it used.... [T]o do otherwise would permit Congress to legislate without completing the required process for enactment of legislation." Carol Chomsky, *Unlocking the Mysteries of Holy Trinity: Spirit, Letter, and History in Statutory Interpretation*, 100 COLUM. L. REV. 901, 951 (2000). Moreover, textualists believe that the text best shows the compromises reached during the legislative process.

> Textualists focus on intrinsic sources, particularly the text, to discern the public meaning of the language at the time it was used.

Textualism is a theory under which its adherents, textualists, look for the public meaning of the words used in the statute as of the time the statute was drafted rather than look for the legislature's intent. Textualists do so in a relatively linear fashion, turning from one source to the next source in hierarchical order until an answer is found. Of all the theorists, textualists examine the fewest sources, focusing primarily on intrinsic sources, especially the text and its relationship to the law as a whole.

Textualism is sometimes called the *plain meaning theory* of interpretation because textualism is based on the *plain meaning canon* of interpretation. The plain meaning canon instructs that the ordinary, or plain, meaning of the words of a statute should control interpretation. The plain meaning canon nicely matches textualists' interpretative goal of finding the public meaning of the statute. Specifically, textualists presume that the legislature used words, grammar, and punctuation to communicate this meaning. Thus, textualists will look at the text of the statute at issue (including grammar and punctuation), the act as a whole, the linguistic canons, and the text of other statutes (the statute in its legal context). Textualists are not completely text focused; they are willing to use dictionaries and the linguistic canons of construction — canons explaining how a normal English speaker understands words — to find the ordinary meaning of the language at issue. But textualists generally refuse to look at other non-text sources unless the language of the statute continues to be ambiguous or absurd. (See Chapter 4 for a discussion of both ambiguity and absurdity). In other words, only if intrinsic sources (and dictionaries) fail to resolve the meaning of the language will textualists then look beyond intrinsic sources for meaning.

Textualism comes in gradations. While all textualists, indeed all theorists, rely foremost on the text of the statute to discern meaning, the different forms of textualism differ in the willingness of their adherents to consider some of the non-intrinsic sources. For example, there are the "soft plain meaning" theorists—those who view the text as the primary, but not the exclusive, evidence of meaning. Soft plain meaning theorists are willing to consider legislative history and context in most cases. These theorists do not need a finding of ambiguity or absurdity to consider extra-textual evidence. Soft plain meaning is the oldest form of textualism, one that views the text as the central, but not as the solitary source of meaning. *See, e.g., State v. Grunke,* 752 N.W.2d 769, 775 (Wis. 2008) ("If the words chosen for the statute exhibit a plain, clear statutory meaning, without ambiguity, the statute is applied according to the plain meaning of the statutory terms. However, if a statute is capable of being understood by reasonably well-informed persons in two or more senses[,] then the statute is ambiguous, and we may consult extrinsic sources to discern its meaning. While extrinsic sources are usually not consulted if the statutory language bears a plain meaning, we nevertheless may consult extrinsic sources to confirm or verify a plain-meaning interpretation.") (internal quotation marks omitted).

Next are the moderate textualists. For moderates, the plain meaning canon controls. When the meaning of the text is plain, or clear, from the text, interpretation is complete; no other sources are consulted. When, however, the meaning is ambiguous or absurd, moderate textualists will consider other, intrinsic sources and non-intrinsic sources of meaning, including legislative history. Most textualists today are moderate textualists. *See, e.g., Fla. Dep't of Highway Safety & Motor Vehicles v. Hernandez,* 74 So. 3d 1070, 1074-75 (Fla. 2011) ("When the statute is clear and unambiguous, courts will not look behind the statute's plain language for legislative intent or resort to rules of statutory construction to ascertain intent. In such instance, the statute's plain and ordinary meaning must control, unless this leads to an unreasonable result or a result clearly contrary to legislative intent. However, if the statutory intent is unclear from the plain language of the statute, then we apply rules of statutory construction and explore legislative history to determine legislative intent.") (internal quotation marks omitted).

Moderate textualism is appealing, in part, because of its inherent simplicity: Examine the text with dictionary in hand, and then finish interpreting.

Turn to other sources only when absolutely required. But moderate textualism may favor simplicity over accuracy. One problem with the plain meaning canon is that language that seems clear to one person can be ambiguous or even mean something completely different to another person. For example, is a "buck" a male deer or a dollar? Is a "pig" an animal or a policeman? Is "dust" a verb or a noun? Is "bay" a body of water or a horse? Is a mosquito an animal? While textual context generally resolves which meaning was intended, litigation arises precisely because litigants and their lawyers disagree about the text's meaning. Theoretically, the plain meaning canon should never resolve an issue in any litigated case involving statutory interpretation unless one party is simply being unreasonable. If the meaning were that clear, the litigants would not be in court, paying huge sums of money to their attorneys to litigate the meaning of these clear words.

Moreover, the meaning of words can vary with context. For example, the word "assault" might mean one thing in a criminal statute and something completely different in a tort statute. Or the word "tomato" may mean one thing to someone making a salad and another thing to a botanist. Further, the linguistic capability of the readers (including judges) can affect meaning. For example, some readers understand the grammar rules, while others do not (consider the proper use of the word "which" and "that"). For this reason, non-textualists argue that other non-textual sources of meaning are essential to interpretation. The New Mexico Supreme Court put it this way:

> [Textualism's] beguiling simplicity may mask a host of reasons why a statute, apparently clear and unambiguous on its face, may for one reason or another give rise to legitimate (*i.e.*, nonfrivolous) difference of opinion concerning the statute's meaning.... [T]his rule is deceptive in that it implies that words have intrinsic meanings. A word is merely a symbol which can be used to refer to different things. Difficult questions of statutory interpretation ought not to be decided by the bland invocation of abstract jurisprudential maxims.... The assertion in a judicial opinion that a statute needs no interpretation because it is "clear and unambiguous" is in reality evidence that the court has already considered and construed the act.

State ex rel. Helman v. Gallegos, 871 P.2d 1352, 1359 (N.M. 1994). Thus, despite its intuitive appeal, the plain meaning canon (the very essence of moderate textualism) is imperfect. We will study more of its limitations in Chapter 4.

Finally, finishing our textualist continuum are the strict, or new, textualists. These are theorists who, like moderate textualists, also require ambiguity or absurdity to look beyond the text; but who, unlike moderates, refuse to look at

some types of non-textual sources, such as legislative history, legislative acquiescence, and unexpressed purpose. New textualists are unique in their refusal to allow any consideration of legislative history and unexpressed purpose.
They suggest that it is simply unconstitutional to consider anything that was
not subject to the enactment process outlined in the Constitution: namely, bicameralism and presentment.

The most famous proponent of new textualism is Justice Antonin Scalia,
who was appointed to the Supreme Court in 1986. He first articulated his new
approach in 1985–86 during a series of speeches in which he urged courts to
ignore legislative history, especially committee reports. Once he was appointed
to the Supreme Court, he brought his criticism of the Court's use of legislative
history into the Court's jurisprudence. *INS v. Cardoza-Fonseca*, 480 U.S. 421,
452 (1987) (Scalia, J., concurring). At that time, many members of the Supreme
Court regularly reviewed the legislative history to glean evidence of legislative
intent. Justice Scalia had a number of criticisms with this approach. Foremost,
Justice Scalia says that the concept of legislative intent is irrelevant to interpretation because the objective indication of the words is what constitutes the law.
For him, legislative history is irrelevant precisely because legislative intent is irrelevant. Additionally, he argues further that even if an interpreter were seeking legislative intent, legislative history would still be irrelevant in 99% of the
cases that reach the court, because even if the interpreter were looking for legislative intent, the interpreter would not be able to find it. "If one were to search
for an interpretive technique that, *on the whole*, was more likely to confuse than
to clarify, one could hardly find a more promising candidate than legislative
history." *Conroy v. Anskoff*, 507 U.S. 511, 519 (1993) (Scalia, J., concurring).

Justice Scalia has raised other concerns as well. He points out that legislators do not read committee reports, which staff often write, and thus, the reports cannot be relied upon as articulating the intent of a body that did not read
or write them. As Justice Scalia later wrote:

> The meaning of terms on the statute books ought to be determined,
> not on the basis of which meaning can be shown to have been under-
> stood by a larger handful of the Members of Congress; but rather on the
> basis of which meaning is (1) most in accord with context and ordinary
> usage, and thus most likely to have been understood by the *whole* Con-
> gress which voted on the words of the statute (not to mention the citi-
> zens subject to it), and (2) most compatible with the surrounding body
> of law into which the provision must be integrated—a compatibility
> which, by a benign fiction, we assume Congress always has in mind....

[I]it is natural for the bar to believe that the juridical importance of [legislative history] matches its prominence in our opinions—thus producing a legal culture in which, when counsel arguing before us assert that "Congress has said" something, they now frequently mean, by "Congress," a committee report; and in which it was not beyond the pale for a recent brief to say the following: "Unfortunately, the legislative debates are not helpful. Thus, we turn to the other guidepost in this difficult area, statutory language."

Green v. Bock Laundry Mach. Co., 490 U.S. 504, 529 (1989) (Scalia, J., concurring).

Professor Thomas Merrill coined the term "new textualist" to show that this "new" form of textualism differed from prior versions of textualism in that it was based on a strict view of separation of powers, ideological conservatism, and public choice theory. Justice Scalia's approach brought life back to textualism, which had largely disappeared, while simultaneously narrowing the sources that could be considered. Justice Scalia suggested it was no more than a return to the Court's pre-World War II approach. According to Professor Merrill, however, Justice Scalia's approach was a radical, not marginal, critique of the Supreme Court's approach to interpretation, especially its use of legislative history. It was a bold rethinking of the Court's role.

Justice Scalia initially gained a following for his new textualist approach and his criticism of the use of legislative history. Indeed, Judge Easterbrook of the Seventh Circuit has promoted a similar agenda. Frank Easterbrook, *Statutes' Domains*, 50 U. Chi. L. Rev. 533, 544–51 (1983). Justice Thomas is also a fan. And to be fair, Justice Scalia has radically altered the dialogue regarding statutory interpretation. While the other Justices have explicitly rejected Justice Scalia's suggestion that legislative history can never be relevant to statutory interpretation, the text-based approach has certainly gained currency. *See Wis. Pub. Intervenor v. Mortier*, 501 U.S. 597, 610 n.4 (1991). While the other Justices have refused to adopt his legislative history ban, some praise new textualism for limiting judicial discretion, increasing predictability and efficiency, encouraging more careful legislative drafting, and limiting inappropriate uses of legislative history. When judges and litigants are constrained to the text of statutes, they argue that meaning becomes more assured and litigation decreases. When legislative history cannot be considered as relevant to meaning, the cost of discerning meaning lessens and certainty increases. Finally, when legislatures are held to the words they use, they are more likely to choose those words with care. There is little doubt that the most important contribution of Justice Scalia and new textualism is the judiciary's renewed focus on the primacy of the text.

New textualism can also be faulted. First, it can be faulted for the unwillingness of its adherents to ever consider some sources of meaning, namely legislative history and unexpressed purpose. It makes little sense to prohibit all evidence generated during the legislative process simply because that evidence was not enacted. Non-textualists do not claim that legislative history is the statute, or even that, in any sense, it is law. While the text is authoritative and has the force of law, legislative history and purpose provide evidence of what that law means. In other words, legislative history and purpose can help illuminate the meaning of the words that do make up the law. In short, new textualists' refusal to consider legislative history or unarticulated purpose in any case seems rigid and simplistic.

Additionally, it is not clear why new textualists are willing to consult dictionaries and the linguistic canons, which similarly do not go through the legislative process, but are not willing to consult legislative history. While it might be a good idea for legislators to use dictionaries or the canons when drafting, there is no proof that they do so. If the Constitution allows judges to consider some non-textual sources, then why does it not allow consideration of all non-textual sources? What makes legislative history so untrustworthy? Moreover dictionaries are not the nirvana that textualists would have us believe. Sometimes a dictionary definition of a word differs from the ordinary meaning of a word, yet some judges rigidly adhere to the dictionary definition. For example, if a statute increases the sentence of anyone who "uses or carries a firearm" in relation to a drug offense, an ordinary reading of this language would suggest that a defendant must use the gun as a weapon to incur the additional penalty, not as an item of value to barter. But a dictionary definition of "use" is sufficiently broad to include bartering a gun for drugs. In *Smith v. United States*, 508 U.S. 223 (1993), the majority used the dictionary definition to find that the statute included bartering it for drugs, while the dissent strongly objected, noting that "[t]he Court does not appear to grasp the distinction between how a word *can be* used and how it *ordinarily is* used." *Id.* at 242 (Scalia, J., dissenting). Interestingly, Justice O'Connor, who is not a textualist wrote the majority opinion, while Justice Scalia, who is, wrote the dissent.

Regardless of his unwillingness to use legislative history, Justice Scalia properly returned judicial focus to the text of the statute as the starting point for interpretation. As a result of his and others' influence, the text of the statute has gained importance and, likely, will retain this importance in the years to come. But support for new textualism itself has waned in recent years, especially on the Supreme Court. Thus, in the remainder of this text, when the word "textualism" is used, moderate, rather than new, textualism is intended.

To summarize, textualism examines the fewest sources. Textualists will look at the text of the statute (including grammar and punctuation), the statute and laws as a whole, the linguistic canons, and the text of other statutes. The more strictly a judge adheres to the plain meaning canon, the less frequently that judge will look beyond these sources, the fewer extra-textual sources that judge will consider, and the less weight that judge will give to these other sources.

b. Textualism in the States

Although the Justices of the Supreme Court have wrestled throughout history with the appropriate approach to statutory interpretation, Congress has not chosen to provide direct guidance, though some scholars have suggested that it should. In contrast, many state legislatures have adopted statutes telling their judiciary how to interpret statutes. Not surprisingly, textualism is the most common choice. For example, as mentioned above, Connecticut has a textualist directive that reads as follows:

> The meaning of a statute shall, in the first instance, be ascertained from the text of the statute itself and its relationship to other statutes. If, after examining such text and considering such relationship, the meaning of such text is plain and unambiguous and does not yield absurd or unworkable results, extratextual evidence of the meaning of the statute shall not be considered.

CONN. GEN. STAT. ANN. § 1-2z (West 2012).

Colorado, Hawaii, Iowa, North Dakota, Ohio, and Pennsylvania also have textualist directives. COLO. REV. STAT. § 2-4-203 (2012); HAW. REV. STAT. ANN. § 1-15 (LexisNexis 2010); IOWA CODE ANN. § 4.6 (West 2011); N.D. CENT. CODE § 1-02-39 (2011); OHIO REV. CODE ANN. § 1.49 (West 2012); 1 PA. CONS. STAT. § 1921(b) (2012).

2. Intentionalist-Based Theories

Intentionalist-based theorists reject textualism for a variety of reasons. Before discussing the different intentionalist-based theories, a discussion of the underlying basis for these theories is necessary. Intentionalist-based theories are rooted in the belief that the policies an elected, representative body choose should govern society. For intentionalist-based theorists, it is the duty of the court to discern the intent of that representative body and interpret statutes to further that intent. Thus, intentionalist-based theorists attempt to understand the meaning of statutes by looking for the enacting legislature's intent.

Specific intent is the intent of the enacting legislature on the precise issue presented.

There are two kinds of intent: specific intent and general intent. Specific intent can be defined as the intent of the enacting legislature on the specific issue presented. For example, if a court had to determine whether affirmative action programs were allowable under a statute that says that "no person shall be discriminated against on the basis of race," a judge looking for specific intent would search the text, related statutes, and legislative history to determine whether the enacting legislature intended the word "discriminate" to apply to affirmative action programs that promote the hiring of racial minorities. So, if the legislative history for this statute showed that the legislators actually discussed affirmative action programs positively or negatively during, for example, the House or Senate debate, then a judge looking for specific intent would conclude that the legislature intended the word "discriminate" to include or to not include affirmative action programs, depending on the tenor of the debate. Thus, for a judge seeking specific intent, it matters whether the enacting legislature had a specific intent as to the language in dispute, in this case the word "discriminate."

In contrast, general intent refers to the overall goal or purpose of the legislature as a whole. For example, if we return to the discrimination statute in the last paragraph, a judge looking for general intent would search the text, related statutes, social context, and legislative history to determine whether the enacting legislature's purpose was to make society color-blind or was to improve the plight of racial minorities. In other words, whether the legislators actually thought about whether the word "discriminate" included affirmative action programs would not be the question for a judge seeking general intent. For a judge seeking general intent, it matters not whether the legislature had a specific intent as to the language in dispute. What matters is the goal, or purpose, behind the legislation.

> General intent is the overall goal, or purpose, of the legislature.

The two prominent intentionalist-based theories are (1) intentionalism, which focuses on specific intent, and (2) purposivism, which focuses on general intent. Each of these theories will be explored in detail below. A few of the less common, but related, theories will also be addressed.

a. Intentionalism: The Theory

Intentionalists, sometimes referred to as originalists, seek out the *specific intent* of the legislature that enacted the statute: What did that legislature have in mind in regard to the specific issue before the court when the legislature enacted the statute? To find specific intent, intentionalists start with the statutory language. But intentionalists do not stop with the text even if the text is clear, as a textualist would do; rather, intentionalists move on and examine other sources of meaning. Unlike a textualist, an intentionalist does not need a reason, such as ambiguity or absurdity, to consider sources beyond the text. In perusing other sources, intentionalists are looking for help in discerning the specific intent of the enacting legislature. Thus, intentionalists often find statements made during the legislative process and early draft versions of the bill enlightening. If these extrinsic sources demonstrate that the ordinary meaning was not what was intended, intentionalists will reject the ordinary meaning for a meaning that furthers the specific intent, as discovered in these other sources. Intentionalists will also examine policy-based sources.

> Intentionalists focus on the text and extrinsic sources to find the specific intent of the enacting legislators in regard to the language at issue in the statute.

Basically, adherents of the competing approaches differ regarding their view of the appropriate role for the judiciary when interpreting statutes. Intentionalists believe that their role is to be faithful agents of the legislature, working to ensure that the legislature's choices are implemented. They believe that examining sources other than the text helps constrain the judiciary and helps maintain its separate function—that of interpreting—by providing more information for a fully informed decision. Further, intentionalists believe that intentionalism furthers separation of powers because it protects the legislature's power to legislate from judicial interference. Judges must implement the *enacting* legislature's intent, not impose their own policy preferences.

Like textualism, the approach has strengths; but it too has weaknesses. For example, consider whether the Senate, a group of 100 individuals, all with different constituencies, can have one, unified intent. Some say not. Each legislator may have a unique reason for voting for a bill. For example, Title VII, which prohibits discrimination in the workplace, was a compromise of various competing interests: The liberal, Northern and Eastern legislators (who sponsored the bill) wanted to help black workers; the conservative Southern legislators wanted to ensure that black workers were not helped at the expense of white workers; and finally the conservative Midwestern legislators, the pivotal voters, wanted to limit government interference in business. With so many different interests, it is unlikely that each of these legislators would share a specific intent as to whether affirmative action programs should be allowed. The liberal Northern and Eastern legislators would likely have said "yes," while the more conservative Southern and Midwestern legislators would likely have said "no." Additionally, one might ask, whose intent matters: "[T]he 51st senator, needed to pass the bill, or the 67th, needed to break the southern filibuster?" WILLIAM N. ESKRIDGE, JR. ET AL., LEGISLATION AND STATUTORY INTERPRETATION 219

(2d 2006). In *United Steelworkers v. Weber*, 443 U.S. 193 (1979), the case in which this issue was addressed, the majority and dissent disagreed on whose intent was central. The majority focused on the liberal, Northern and Eastern legislators, while the dissent focused on the conservative, Southern and Midwestern legislators.

Of course, intentionalists respond to that criticism by arguing that a group can have intent. While the individual members may have different, private *motives* for their own actions, the existence of private motives does not necessarily eliminate the possibility that the group has a common goal or agenda. For example, consider a sports team as it takes the field, a political party as it enters an election, or the board of a company preparing annual strategy. The group's agenda and the members' motives might not be identical, but each group has one, overarching intent: to win. Intentionalism is thus less about the reality of always finding a unified intent and more about the *possibility* of finding one.

To find specific intent, intentionalists start with the text, but then commonly rely on legislative history in addition to the draft versions of the bill. Intentionalists' use of legislative history takes us to a second criticism of intentionalism: Some argue that legislative history can be manipulated to support any result a judge or a legislator wants. Judges may choose which legislative history might be relevant and reject contradictory history. As Judge Harold Leventhal used to say, "[T]he trick is to look over the heads of the crowd and pick out your friends." ANTONIN SCALIA, A MATTER OF INTERPRETATION: FEDERAL COURTS AND THE LAW 36 (1997). Additionally, legislators can manipulate legislative history; they may decide to add information to the legislative record to influence future litigation, although relatively recent procedural rules have abated this practice. Finally, legislative history is not subject to bicameral passage and presentment, the constitutionally proscribed process for enactment. Thus, even if a single, unified intent exists, the criticism continues, that intent should not be ascertained from anything other than the language of the statute, for it is only that language that goes through the enactment process.

Intentionalists do not ignore these criticisms. Rather, they accept the criticisms as valid but suggest caution, not wholesale rejection, of the use of legislative history. True, legislative history is not enacted law, and intentionalists do not claim it is. Rather, they claim that legislative history can offer insight into what some or all of the legislators may have been thinking when the law, which did go through the constitutionally prescribed process, was enacted. Because intentionalists wish to know what legislators were thinking, legislative history can be useful. For intentionalists, legislative history simply offers a fuller picture of the legislative process for a particular bill.

To summarize, intentionalism is an approach that is focused on finding the specific intent of the enacting legislature in regard to the language at issue in the statute. The approach focuses first on text (do not forget this!) and then on a review of the legislative history and unenacted versions of the bill, as well as all other relevant sources of meaning.

b. Intentionalism in the States

Interestingly, despite the criticisms of intentionalism, at least one state, New York, adopted intentionalism by statute. That state's statute provides as follows:

- Generally
  The primary consideration of the courts in the construction of statutes is to ascertain and give effect to the intention of the Legislature.
- Ascertainment of intention
  The intention of the Legislature is first to be sought from a literal reading of the act itself, but if the meaning is still not clear, the intent may be ascertained from such facts and through such rules as may, in connection with the language, legitimately reveal it.

N.Y. STAT. LAW § 92(a), (b) (McKinney 2012). The official comment explains New York's choice:

> Since the intention of the Legislature, embodied in a statute, is the law, in the construction of statutes the basic rule of procedure and the primary consideration of the courts are to ascertain and give effect to the intention of the Legislature.... So it is the duty of courts to adopt a construction of a statute that will bring it into harmony with the Constitution and with legislative intent....
>
> The intent of the Legislature is controlling and must be given force and effect, regardless of the circumstance that inconvenience, hardship, or injustice may result. Indeed the Legislature's intent must be ascertained and effectuated whatever may be the opinion of the judiciary as to the wisdom, expediency, or policy of the statute, and whatever excesses or omissions may be found in the statute. The courts do not sit in review of the discretion of the Legislature and may not substitute their judgment for that of the lawmaking body.

Id. cmt. a.

c. Imaginative Reconstruction: A Version of Intentionalism

As noted above, discerning the specific intent of the enacting legislature is often a difficult, if not impossible task. Moreover, limiting interpretation to a static point in time creates its own issues. For these reasons, in 1907, Dean Roscoe Pound urged courts to adopt "imaginative reconstructionism" as an approach for discerning the intent of the enacting legislature. Using Dean Pound's approach, a judge would try to imagine what the enacting legislature would have intended had the precise factual problem before the court been raised during the enactment process. As described by Judge Learned Hand:

> As nearly as we can, we must put ourselves in the place of those who uttered the words, and try to divine how they would have dealt with the unforeseen situations; and, although their words are by far the most decisive evidence of what they would have done, they are by no means final.

Guiseppi v. Walling, 144 F.2d 608, 624 (2d Cir. 1944).

To imagine what the enacting legislature would do, Dean Pound proposed that judges recreate intent by examining the available historical evidence, including the statute, with a sense of morality and justice to determine what the enacting legislature likely intended given the realities of today. Roscoe Pound, *Spurious Interpretation*, 7 Colum. L. Rev. 379, 381 (1907). This approach borrows from common law analysis and civil law practice in that the statute guides but often does not answer the question; rather, by using reason and analogy, a judge can apply the statute to situations the language does not explicitly cover to arrive at a just result. Imaginative reconstructionism is normative for it allows the judiciary to consider public policy when making interpretation choices. Using "practical reasoning," judges can adopt flexible interpretations based on current public norms. Justice Learned Hand was a proponent of this theory.

Not surprisingly, imaginative reconstructionism suffers from some of the same criticisms as intentionalism: Whose intent is reconstructed? Should unenacted information play any role in interpretation? While Dean Pound's approach has had some believers in academic circles, it garners little support among the judiciary.

d. Purposivism: The Theory

Purposivists believe that law, both generally and specifically, is designed to solve specific problems; thus, every statute has a purpose or objective for its enactment. Purposivists strive to discern and then implement this purpose. To do so, they will look broadly, but enacted purpose clauses and text are the starting points. Purposivists and intentionalists differ in what they seek by examining these extra-textual sources of meaning. As we saw above, intentionalists seek specific intent: What did the enacting legislature intend regarding the precise issue presented to the court. In contrast, purposivists seek general intent or purpose: What problem was the legislature trying to redress and how did it redress that problem? Once the purpose and remedy have been identified, purposivists interpret the statute to further that purpose as best it can subject to two caveats: judges should not give words (1) a meaning those words cannot bear, nor (2) a meaning that would violate generally prevailing policies of law unless the statute includes a clear statement to that effect.

Purposivism, also known as legal process theory, is perhaps the oldest form of interpretation. In the middle ages, detailed statutes were difficult to produce, and it was hard to develop and circulate multiple drafts. Copiers did not exist. Thus, early English legislators voted based on the general goal, or purpose, of the statute, not on the precise statutory language. To interpret statutes enacted in this way, judges focused on the spirit of the legislation rather than on the exact wording. Purposivism permitted this focus.

Like early English statutes, early American statutes were also very general. For example, the Sherman (Antitrust) Act, which was enacted in 1890, fits on only one page, while the Patient Protection and Affordable Care Act, which was enacted in 2010, is 906 pages long. In the past, the legislature drafted broad statutes to allow reasoned judicial development of a particular area of law. Because there was so little textual guidance, judges needed something other than the text to guide and to unify interpretation. Purpose provided that guiding and unifying factor. Judges could easily test their decisions by discerning which interpretation best furthered the statutory purpose. Thus, by focusing on the purpose of the statute, judges were better able to fit the statute into the legal system as a whole and make public policy coherent.

In the United States, purposivism made an early appearance in 1892 in *Church of the Holy Trinity v. United States*, 143 U.S. 457 (1892). In that case, a statute made it unlawful for anyone to import any alien into the United States to "perform labor or service of any kind." *Id.* at 458. Holy Trinity Church had hired a rector from England. *Id.* Despite the clarity of the text — rectoring is "labor or service" — the Court held that the statute did not apply because the purpose of the Act was to "stay the influx of … cheap unskilled labor.…" *Id.* at 465. Rectoring was not unskilled labor. Famously stating that "[i]t is a familiar rule that a thing may be within the letter of the statute and yet not within the statute, because not within its spirit nor within the intention of its makers," the Court rejected the definitional interpretation. *Id.* at 459.

After a lull, purposivism came back into vogue shortly after World War II, during a time of "relative consensus ... sustained economic growth, and burgeoning optimism about government's ability to foster economic growth by solving market failures and creating opportunities." ESKRIDGE ET AL., LEGISLATION AND STATUTORY INTERPRETATION, *supra*, at 727. The Supreme Court followed this approach, for the most part, throughout the 1950s and 1960s. By the 1970s, however, America was changing. Economic growth had faltered and issues relating to war, family, and government were much more controversial. Government became the enemy rather than the savior. Additionally, statutes became more complex and comprehensive. With those changes came a change in the judicial approach to statutory interpretation. Intentionalism garnered favor with such justices as former Chief Justices Burger and Rehnquist. Today, former Justice Stevens and Justice Breyer are two of the few remaining proponents of purposivism. To most judges, purposivism appears to be a relic from early statutory development that has little application in a world in which complex statutes are the norm. In this norm, there is a renewed emphasis on the importance and primacy of the text.

Like intentionalism, purposivism begins with the text but does not end there:

> There is, of course, no more persuasive evidence of the purpose of a statute than the words by which the legislature undertook to give expression to its wishes. Often these words are sufficient in and of themselves to determine the purpose of the legislation. In such cases we have followed their plain meaning. When that meaning has led to absurd or futile results, however, this Court has looked beyond the words to the purpose of the act. Frequently, however, even when the plain meaning did not produce absurd results but merely an unreasonable one plainly at variance with the policy of the legislation as a whole this Court has followed that purpose, rather than the literal words. When aid to construction of the meaning of words as used in the statute is available, there certainly can be no rule of law which forbids its use, however clear the words may appear on superficial examination.

United States v. Am. Trucking Ass'ns, Inc., 310 U.S. 534, 543–44 (1940) (citations omitted).

While intentionalists view themselves as faithful agents of the legislature, purposivists view themselves as "faithful agent[s] of a well-functioning regulatory regime." ESKRIDGE ET AL., LEGISLATION AND STATUTORY INTERPRETATION, *supra*, at 7 (emphasis omitted). For this reason, purposivists attempt to discern the evil or mischief the legislature meant to address when enacting the statute. To do so, purposivists are willing to examine text and legislative history, as well as other relevant sources, such as social and legal context. To a purposivist, a statute makes sense only when understood in light of its purpose: a rule without purpose is meaningless. For example, consider our hypothetical city ordinance prohibiting "vehicles" in the park. Is a non-motorized scooter a vehicle? To decide this issue, a purposivist judge might ask why the city council enacted the ordinance in the first place. If the council's purpose was to limit air and noise pollution, then "vehicle" should not be interpreted to include scooters. If, instead, the city's purpose was to increase pedestrian safety, then, perhaps, "vehicle" should be so interpreted. Thus, purposivists believe that knowing the evil, or mischief, at which the statute was aimed aids interpretation. Just as a reminder and in contrast, an intentionalist would look to see if the city council members ever discussed scooters in the legislative process or included them in a draft version of the ordinance, while a textualist would likely turn to a dictionary for the meaning of the word "vehicle." Note that in the hypothetical in Chapter 1, the word "motor" was added to the ordinance. From this fact, an intentionalist might conclude that non-motorized scooters should not be excluded from the park. However, an exemption for mopeds, bicycles, and other similar such vehicles was rejected. From this fact, an intentionalist might conclude that non-motorized scooters should be excluded from the park.

One benefit of purposivism is that it permits flexibility that the other theories do not. While purposivism and intentionalism are somewhat similar, purposivism has one advantage over intentionalism: Purposivists can interpret statutes in situations the enacting legislature never contemplated. "Purposivism … renders statutory interpretation adaptable to new circumstances." Eskridge et al., Legislation And Statutory Interpretation, *supra*, at 221. For example, in the hypothetical city ordinance prohibiting "vehicles" in the park, a purposivist judge could determine that the ordinance applied to electric scooters even though these "vehicles" may not have been around when the ordinance was adopted. But an intentionalist judge might have trouble with this issue because the city council could not have intended to regulate something not in existence when the ordinance was adopted. Therefore, purposivism allows for laws to change with technological, social, legal, and other advances — something true intentionalism is incapable of doing.

But there are criticisms of purposivism as well. The most troublesome aspect of purposivism is, of course, legitimately discerning a statute's purpose. Ideally, legislatures would include a findings or purpose provision in the enacted text of every statute. Unfortunately, they do not. Thus, judges often look for *unexpressed* purpose. To find such unexpressed purpose, purposivists consider the text, the legislative history, the legal history, the social context, and other sources. But these sources may not be conclusive. What then? Some legal theorists have suggested that to figure out a statute's primary purpose, a judge should posit various situations. In other words, a judge should start with the situations clearly covered and radiate outward. In doing so, courts should presume that legislatures are "made of reasonable persons pursuing reasonable purposes, reasonably." HENRY HART & ALBERT SACHS, THE LEGAL PROCESS 1378 (William N. Eskridge, Jr. & Philip P. Frickey eds., 1994). You can see why this approach might be concerning to a textualist.

There are other criticisms as well. For example, even if a purpose is discernible, there may be competing ideas of how to further that purpose: is affirmative action the best way to achieve racial parity? A related criticism of purposivism is that statutes often have more than one purpose, and these purposes can conflict. For example, one purpose of Title VII—which prohibits discrimination in the workplace—was to increase the number of African-Americans in the workforce. Another purpose was to make hiring and other work related decisions color-blind. Voluntary affirmative action programs further the first purpose but not the second. Is the fact that one purpose is furthered enough to sustain an interpretation? Purposivism does not answer the question of whether an interpretation is appropriate when one, but not another, purpose is furthered.

Similarly, a statute may have one purpose, while an exception to that statute may have a conflicting purpose. For example, the purpose of the Freedom of Information Act (5 U.S.C. §552 (2012)), is to encourage open government. But some of the exceptions within the Act, such as prohibiting the disclosure of personnel files, exist to protect individual privacy. If a judge interprets an exception, which purpose should control: the purpose of the Act or the purpose of the exception? In other words, should the judge interpret the exception in the Freedom of Information Act narrowly to better further the purpose of the Act as a whole or broadly to better further the purpose of the exception? Again, purposivism does not provide the answer to this question.

Finally, judges are constitutionally required to interpret statutory language. They are not appropriate policy-makers because they may not be elected and they are not expected constitutionally to perform this function. When judges make decisions based on their own policy choices, disguised as purpose, they aggrandize their constitutional power and intrude into the legislative arena.

e. Purposivism in the States

Purposivism is not a commonly chosen approach in the states. Indeed, the Connecticut Supreme Court tried to adopt purposivism, but the state legislature immediately overruled its choice, opting for textualism instead. Similarly, of the remaining states that have enacted statutory directives, most legislatures have chosen textualism. It is unclear why this is so, but perhaps it is due to the lack of legislative history materials available in many states and the fact that state judges are often more restrained in their approach to interpretation. Perhaps, as state legislative materials become increasingly available, this preference may be altered.

One state, Texas, does have a purposivist statute that provides as follows:

> In construing a statute, *whether or not the statute is considered ambiguous on its face,* a court may consider among other matters the:
>
> (1) object sought to be attained;
> (2) circumstances under which the statute was enacted;
> (3) legislative history;
> (4) common law or former statutory provisions, including laws on the same or similar subjects;
> (5) consequences of a particular construction;
> (6) administrative construction of the statute; and
> (7) title (caption), preamble, and emergency provision.

TEX. GOV'T CODE ANN. § 311.023 (West 2012) (emphasis added). But despite this clear legislative directive to look at all relevant information regardless of whether a statute is ambiguous, some members of the Texas judiciary refuse to follow it. For example, in *State v. Muller*, 829 S.W.2d 805 (Tex. Ct. Crim. App. 1992), the court said, "[W]e look to a statute's legislative history *only* if the plain meaning of the literal text of that statute is ambiguous or leads to highly improbable results." *Id.* at 811 n.7.

Similarly, a Georgia statute specifically directs courts to consider intent, purpose, and text when interpreting statutes:

> (a) In all interpretations of statutes, the courts shall look diligently for the intention of the General Assembly, keeping in view at all times the old law, the evil, and the remedy....
> (b) In all interpretations of statutes, the ordinary signification shall be applied to all words....

GA. CODE ANN. § 1-3-1(a), (b) (2012). Though acknowledging the existence of this directive, Georgia courts generally ignore it, preferring instead to apply textualism. For example, in *Busch v. State*, 523 S.E.2d 21 (Ga. 1999), the Georgia Supreme Court said, "If the words of a statute, however, are plain and capable of having but one meaning, and do not produce any absurd, impractical, or contradictory results, then this Court is bound to follow the meaning of those words." *Id.* at 23. In a later case, the Georgia Court of Appeals tried, but failed, to reconcile the court's use of textualism with the more purposivist directive of the statute:

> In construing a statute, our goal is to determine its legislative purpose. In this regard, a court must first focus on the statute's text. In order to discern the meaning of the words of a statute, the reader must look at the context in which the statute was written, remembering at all times that "the meaning of a sentence may be more than that of the separate words, as a melody is more than the notes." *If the words of a statute, however, are plain and capable of having but one meaning, and do not produce any absurd, impractical, or contradictory results, then this Court is bound to follow the meaning of those words.* If, on the other hand, the words of the statute are ambiguous, then this Court must construe the statute, keeping in mind the purpose of the statute and "the old law, the evil, and the remedy."

State v. Brown, 551 S.E.2d 773, 775 (Ga. Ct. App. 2001) (emphasis added) (citing GA. CODE APP. § 1-3-1(a)).

f. Dynamic Statutory Interpretation

An approach related to purposivism is dynamic statutory interpretation. Professor William Eskridge created dynamic statutory interpretation in 1994. It is not an approach that you will find referenced in an opinion or statute. Rather, it is one academic's ideal of what should happen in interpretation. Remember that intentionalist judges typically attempt to discern legislative intent as of the time the statute was enacted and that purposivist judges typically attempt to discern statutory purpose as of time the statute was enacted. The dynamic approach encourages judges to be more flexible and consider what the enacting legislature would have wanted when times and social moral values change. For example, let's return to the Civil Rights Act of 1964, which was enacted to prohibit discrimination based on race. It is highly unlikely that the Congress of 1964 would have approved of affirmative action programs; the statute was enacted to encourage a race-blind society. Yet, years after the Act had been in effect, discrimination was still the norm. The Act was not working. Should the Supreme Court interpret the Act in a way that would take this fact into account? Dynamic statutory interpretation would permit exactly that. In other words, even though no linguistic change had occurred since the Act's passage, the societal values of the interpreters (and society) had changed. Affirmative action programs were necessary to combat continued racism. In general, dynamic statutory interpretation allows judges to work in concert with the legislature to accomplish its goals as times and values change. Consider statutes enacted in the 1800s that criminalize sodomy. We would define this term very differently today. But note that a judge using this approach must identify the goals or purposes of the legislation. Thus, this approach is really a close cousin to purposivism.

Because it is so similar to purposivism, dynamic statutory interpretation shares some of the same criticisms. Notably, some critics view this approach as judicial power-grabbing, which violates the Constitution's separation of powers. Because of this criticism, dynamic statutory interpretation has made greater headway in constitutional interpretation than in statutory interpretation.

3. Alaska's Sliding Scale Approach: A Compromise

As we saw above, all of the approaches have shortcomings. For this reason, the Alaska judiciary rejected all of the above approaches (especially strict textualism) and created its own unique approach. This approach, the "sliding scale approach," blends textualism, intentionalism, and purposivism. It allows judges to consider a statute's meaning without first finding ambiguity or absurdity by applying a sliding scale of clarity. The sliding scale approach states simply that all evidence of meaning is relevant; however, the clearer the statutory language, the more convincing the evidence of a contrary legislative purpose or intent must be. *LeFever v. State*, 877 P.2d 1298, 1299–1300 (Alaska Ct. App. 1994). In other words, Alaska adopted textualism with a twist. Much like a sliding door that can be opened a little or a lot to control the airflow, the sliding scale approach allows a little or a lot of contrary evidence of meaning to flow into the analysis. The size of the opening depends on the clarity of the text: the clearer the text, the smaller the opening.

The Alaska judiciary considered moderate textualism but rejected it because that approach overly restricted the inquiry. Because words are necessarily inexact and ambiguity is inherent in language, other sources of meaning often prove helpful in construing a statute. Thus, even if the statute under consideration is facially clear, the legislative history can be considered because it might reveal an ambiguity not apparent on the face of the statute. *Anchorage v. Sisters of Providence in Wash., Inc.*, 628 P.2d 22, 27 n.6 (Alaska 1981).

Alaska's sliding scale approach has inherent appeal. The approach is a kissing cousin to the soft plain meaning approach; under the sliding scale approach, the plainer the text, the more convincing the contrary indications of meaning must be to trump the text. This soft version of textualism turns the plain meaning canon into a rebuttable presumption: the plain meaning will control absent convincing evidence that the legislature intended a different meaning. In many ways, this approach blends the best of the theories above, while avoiding the difficulties; the text is the primary, but not exclusive, evidence of meaning. But this approach shares many of the problems of textualism and, thus, is not the perfect compromise it may appear to be. To date, no other state has expressly adopted this approach.

4. Legislative Process Theories

In addition to the statutory interpretation theories discussed above, there are several theories that relate to the legislative process. For example, *pluralist theories* focus on the role special interest groups play in setting legislative policy. Interest group politics lead to "pluralism" — the spreading of political power across multiple political actors. The legislative process is one area in which conflicting interest groups' desires are resolved. Examples of special interest groups include political parties, churches, unions, businesses, and environmental organizations, among others. Interest groups can often accomplish what an individual cannot. Because there is strength in numbers, interest groups offer individual citizens the best possibility of meaningful participation in the legislative process. Theoretically, one benefit of a robustly pluralist system should be moderate, balanced, and well-considered legislation.

One pluralist theory is *bargaining theory*, which proposes that statutes are a compromise between various interest groups. Interest groups want a particular benefit or protection from government but often lack the clout to enact legislation absent support from other interest groups. Hence, interest groups work with other interest groups to increase their political power and get bills enacted; yet, in doing so, the groups must compromise their goals. Pursuant to bargaining theory, judges should focus on furthering the compromises that produced the necessary votes for passage of the compromise legislation. For example, if we again return to Title VII (the statute prohibiting discrimination in the workplace on the basis of race), the compromise necessary to ensure passage of that bill was that white workers would not be disadvantaged to remedy black workers' plight. Bargaining theorists would have interpreted the statute not to allow voluntary affirmative action programs because such programs disadvantage white workers even while helping black workers.

Public choice theory is another pluralist theory. Public-choice theorists rely on economics to explain legislators' behavior. These theorists believe that statutes are the result of compromises among legislators that come about as a result of private interest groups bargaining. These private interest groups seek the best result for their members without regard for others. Access to the political process is disparate: Business interests tend to be overrepresented, while the broad public interest and the less advantaged tend to be underrepresented. Thus, public choice theory helps explain the success of distributive legislation, legislation that rewards multiple special interests simultaneously. For example, tax bills that offer loopholes to many specialized groups or defense appropriation bills that send money to a variety of districts are both likely to be enacted for this reason. Under public choice theory, special-interest legislation and pork-barrel projects should enjoy limited support because very few special interest groups are rewarded. However, legislators may choose to support special projects for a variety of reasons, such as to gain political capital with other legislators for the future, to pay back special interest groups for financial or other support, or to increase the chances of reelection or movement within the party. Hence, contrary to intentionalist thought, public-choice theorists believe that there can be no single legislative intent; rather, each legislator may have a multitude of reasons for voting for particular legislation. Given the possibility of multiple reasons, public-choice theorists urge narrow interpretations of statutes. Additionally, these theorists suggest that judges should not fill in the statutory gaps because legislatures do not act for the public as a whole, but rather act to reward special-interest groups and maximize their own reelection potential. As for legislative history, public-choice theorists agree with new textualists that such history should be ignored when determining statutory meaning, because it shows nothing relevant. Legislation is a compromise of intentions; therefore, we cannot know exactly why legislators vote the way they do.

Public choice theory can be criticized for its skepticism. Not all legislators are opportunists looking for financial rewards from special interest groups; many are honest and have independent beliefs and goals that direct their legislative behavior. Thus, interest groups may be less effective at changing lawmakers' minds than public choice theory would have us believe. Finally, interest groups are better at blocking legislation than passing it, especially when legislation has low visibility. Hence, the theory may be inapposite for enacted legislation.

A second group of legislative theories, *proceduralist theories*, focuses on the legislative process and the political obstacles a bill must hurdle to become law. One such theory focuses on the "vetogates" of the legislative process. ESKRIDGE ET AL., LEGISLATION AND STATUTORY INTERPRETATION, *supra*, at 190. The legislative process is explained in Chapter 3. What you will learn when you study that process is that it is much easier to kill a bill than to pass one because of the many steps a bill must go through before it can become law; at any one step, the bill might be choked from passage. Vetogates are the chokepoints that can prevent a bill from becoming law. Some such chokepoints include the committee process, the conference committee process, and rules of procedure such as the Germaneness Rule. "Gatekeepers" are legislators that hold power at these vetogates. For example, a bill must be referred out of a committee (such as the Senate Judiciary Committee) to the full chamber (the Senate) before continuing the enactment process. The committee is a vetogate, while the members of the committee (especially the chair) are gatekeepers.

Vetogates are important for two reasons. First, gatekeepers can simply block a bill's passage at any vetogate. Second, courts often reason that statements gatekeepers made reflect the intent of the legislative body because the gatekeepers' support would have been essential to the bill's passage. But this reasoning may be flawed. Because these gatekeepers have such power, they can abuse their position. For example, the Alaska National Interest Lands Conservation Act altered the rules for access to all nonfederally owned land within the boundaries of the National Forest System. In *Montana Wilderness Association v. United States Forest Service*, 655 F.2d 951 (9th Cir. 1981), *cert. denied*, 455 U.S. 898 (1981), the question for the court was whether a subsection of the Act applied nationwide or just in Alaska. *Id.* at 953. Congressman Udall, a key gatekeeper at the time the bill was enacted, had claimed in the legislative record that the subsection of the Act applied only to Alaska. *Id.* at 956 n.9 (citing 127 Cong. Rec. 10376). However, other factors suggested that it was more likely that Congress intended the Act to apply nationally; thus, the court rejected the argument that Udall's comments showed Congressional intent to limit the Act's application to Alaska.

Another legislative theory, the *"Best Answer Theory,"* urges judges to interpret statutes to promote an "optimal state of affairs." Such a theory views judges as protectors of the minority, those individuals not in political power. Pursuant to this theory, a judge would likely find that Title VII did allow voluntary affirmative action programs because such programs would remedy employment practices that had had a disparate impact on a less powerful group, racial minorities. Allowing an employer to enact voluntary affirmative action programs, rather than wait for possible litigation, would promote harmony, lead to positive social change, and protect minority interests. Thus, in this example, promoting the "optimal state of affairs" would support allowing limited types of affirmative action programs.

E. Does Theory Matter?

Perhaps. But no one theory is better at discerning the "right" meaning than any other theory. "[T]here is no empirical way to show that one of these [theories] is 'better' than the others, in the sense that one [theory] more often than the others captures the 'true meaning' of a statute." LINDA D. JELLUM & DAVID C. HRICIK, MODERN STATUTORY INTERPRETATION: PROBLEMS, THEORIES, AND LAWYERING STRATEGIES 44 (2d ed. 2009). This is an important point for you will want to believe that your approach is right and that the other approaches are wrong. Only if we knew what the "right" interpretation was without applying a theory could we determine which theory most often leads to that "right" interpretation. But of course, we do not know which interpretation is right, nor do we even know what sources we are supposed to use to evaluate the correctness of any interpretation. Hence, the superiority of each theory will continue to be debated. In particular, academics love to debate the pros and cons of each of these theories. For example, in the famous hypothetical *Case of the Speluncean Explorers*, Professor Lon Fuller explored a hypothetical situation in which a group of explorers were trapped in a cave. Lon L. Fuller, *The Case of the Speluncean Explorers*, 62 HARV. L. REV. 616 (1949). While there, they killed one of their group and ate him to survive. After they were rescued, they were tried and convicted of murder. The statute provided simply: "Whoever shall willfully take the life of another shall be punished by death." A common law self-defense exception also existed.

Professor Fuller had each judge considering the explorers' appeal draft a separate opinion, using a different statutory approach to explore the role that morality should play within the law. First, Justice Keen, a textualist, voted to uphold the conviction. According to this Justice, law is wholly distinct from morality; if judges believe that the law is wrong, it is not appropriate to correct that law. Instead, the legislature should fix its mistakes. Similarly, Chief Justice Truepenny also voted to affirm because the judicial role should not be concerned with morality when the other institutions are more competent to evaluate morality. In this case, he believed the best result would be for the executive to offer clemency.

Justice Tatting withdrew from the case and refused to make any decision. For him, the tension between law and morality was unresolveable. Because he withdrew, the ultimate decision was a tie (two to affirm and two to reverse the conviction); thus, the divided court affirmed the conviction.

Justice Foster, who some have suggested was Professor Fuller in disguise, would have reversed the conviction. Using a purposivist approach, Justice Foster argued that the purpose of the murder statute was to deter wrongdoing. That purpose does not apply to the explorers because they killed their companion only as a last option to prevent the deaths of the others, and few persons facing death would be deterred by a criminal prohibition of conduct that would save their lives. He suggested that while law is not morality, the two are intertwined and cannot be separated as easily as Justice Keen believed. Thus, the judiciary should correct legislative errors and oversights not to supplant the legislative will, but rather to make that will effective.

Finally, Justice Handy also would have reversed. For him, law equals morality. Law should follow common sense and social norms. In this case, the public opinion supported acquittal, and Justice Handy argued that public opinion should be factored into the court's decision.

Despite the Speluncean Explorers hypothetical, the reality is that few judges rigidly adhere to just one theory. Even Justice Scalia admits, "I play the game like everybody else.... I'm in a system which has accepted rules and legislative history is used.... You read my opinions, I sin with the rest of them." Frank H. Easterbrook, *What Does Legislative History Tell Us?*, 66 CHI.-KENT L. REV. 441, 442 n.4 (1990) (quoting JUDGES AND LEGISLATORS: TOWARD INSTITUTIONAL COMITY 174–75 (R. Katzmann ed. 1988)). Professors Eskridge, Frickey, and Garrett best summed up the reality of today's doctrine:

> We do not think the Supreme Court has entirely returned to the pre-Scalia days and suggest the following generalities about where it is today. First, the text is now, more than it was 20 or 30 years ago, the central inquiry at the Supreme Court level and in other courts that are now following the Supreme Court's lead. A brief that starts off with, "The statute means thus-and-so because it says so in the committee report," is asking for trouble. Both advice and advocacy should start with the statutory text. Because the Court frequently uses the dictionary to provide meaning to key statutory terms, the advocate should incorporate this methodology as well.... Second, the "contextual" evidence the Court is interested in is now statutory as much as or more than just historical context. Arguments that your position is more consistent with other parts of the same statute are typically winning arguments. Similarly, as [one case] indicates, the Court today goes beyond the "whole act" rule to something like a "whole code" rule, searching the United States Code for guidance on the usage of key statutory terms and phrases.
>
> Third, the Court will still look at contextual evidence and is very interested in the public law background of the statute. If a statute seems to require an odd result..., the Court will interrogate the background materials to find out why.... It remains important to research and brief the legislative history thoroughly. The effective advocate will

appreciate that the presence of such materials in the briefs may influence the outcome more than the opinion in the case will indicate.

WILLIAM ESKRIDGE, JR. ET AL., CASES AND MATERIALS ON LEGISLATION: STATUTES AND THE CREATION OF PUBLIC POLICY 770–71 (3d ed. 2001).

While academics will continue rigorously to argue the legitimacy of the various approaches, few judges remain so dogmatic. Judges regularly mix approaches, fail to identify their approach, and even change approaches. Ultimately, judges want to further justice, not be dogmatically rigid. Professors Eskridge and Frickey call this *pragmatic theory*. "In deciding a question of statutory interpretation in the real, as opposed to the theoretical, world, few judges approach the interpretive task armed with a fixed set of rigid rules." John M. Walker, *Judicial Tendencies in Statutory Construction: Differing Views on the Role of the Judge*, 58 N.Y.U. ANN. SURV. AM. L. 203, 232 (2001).

To further their pragmatic theory, Professors Eskridge and Frickey developed their funnel of abstraction in which the various sources lay on one side of the funnel, while an indicator of abstractness runs along the opposite side of the funnel. Statutory text, which is the most concrete source of meaning, anchors the bottom of the funnel. Moving up the sources side of the funnel from the bottom are specific legislative intent, then purpose, and finally current social values or morality. ESKRIDGE ET AL., LEGISLATION AND STATUTORY INTERPRETATION, *supra*, at 250–51. Most judges do not confine themselves to the bottom of the funnel, but rather move up and down the funnel as various sources come into play. The funnel "reflects both the multiplicity of [sources] and the conventional hierarchy ranking them against one another." *Id.* at 250. "Easy" statutory interpretation cases are those in which all the sources point in one direction (or are at least neutral). *Id.* at 251. In contrast, the "hard" cases are those in which one or more sources cut directly against another, such as in *United Steelworkers v. Weber*, 443 U.S. 193 (1979). In that case, the text and specific intent pointed in one direction, while the purpose of the Act pointed in another.

Perhaps, as legal realists suggest, none of this theory stuff matters. The reality is that judges decide cases based on their own personal notions of justice and the underlying equities of the case. For this reason, you should not expect to win your case simply because you select a particular theory. To win your case, you must prove to your judge that a ruling for your client would be the just and right result. But knowing a judge's preferred approach can make your job easier. For example, if you are arguing before a purposivist, you would not talk about ambiguity and absurdity before discussing legislative history or context, as you must do if you are arguing before a textualist. Thus, the theories provide legal language and seemingly impartial reasoning to help you argue your case. In this world, the Ancient Greek aphorism "Know thyself" could be "Know thy judge's approach."

F. Mastering This Topic

Return to the hypothetical presented in Chapter 1 on page 9, regarding the city ordinance prohibiting vehicles in the park. You were asked to identify which materials you found helpful, relevant, and appropriate to consider in making your decisions as a prosecutor and which materials you considered unhelpful, irrelevant, or inappropriate to consider. If you have not completed this hypothetical already, take the time to go back and do so now.

Review your answers (which should be jotted in the margins). Do your answers indicate whether you found intrinsic or extrinsic evidence relevant? Did you prefer one type of evidence exclusively, find both relevant, or find one type of evidence more useful? What does your answer to this question tell you about the approach you likely prefer at this point of your studies?

When you were answering the questions, did you look to the text of the ordinance first? If the text did not definitely resolve the issue for you, where did you look next? Did you find yourself pulling out your smart phone and looking up words in the latest dictionary application or turning to the other materials provided? As you should know by now, the more you focused on the text and turned toward dictionary definitions, the more likely you prefer some form of textualism. If you refused to look at the "legislative history" completely, then you may prefer strict textualism, like Justices Scalia and Thomas. If you were willing to look at legislative history, but only when you had to, you may prefer moderate textualism. And if you looked at legislative history to confirm your understanding of the text, you may prefer the soft plain meaning approach.

If text was your starting point but not your ending point, you may lean towards intentionalism or purposivism. Can you determine which of these two better conforms with your answers? Did you find the legislative history more relevant to your interpretation process or the purpose for enacting the statute, namely safety. Were both relevant but one more so? Perhaps you are simply uncertain at this time. If so, do not let that concern you. To be honest, the more open you are to all of the theories and sources of meaning at this point, the easier it will be for you to master the art of statutory interpretation.

Checkpoints

- Understanding theory is critical to understanding statutory interpretation because theory drives every aspect of statutory interpretation.

- To interpret a statute, a judge will look at intrinsic sources, extrinsic sources, and policy-based sources of meaning.

- Intrinsic sources are materials that are part of the official act being interpreted.

- Extrinsic sources are materials outside of the official act but within the legislative process that created the act.

- Policy-based sources are extrinsic to both the statutory act and the legislative process. They reflect important social and legal choices derived from the Constitution or existing common law ideals.

- Textualism is an interpretative approach that relies heavily on the intrinsic sources to determine meaning.

- Intentionalism is an interpretative approach that searches all sources, particularly the legislative history, to discern the enacting legislature's specific intent.

- Purposivism is an interpretative approach that searches all sources to discern the enacting legislature's general intent or purpose.

- Theory matters, but justice and equity matter more.

Chapter 3

The Legislative Process

Roadmap

- Understand how a bill becomes a law.
- Learn about bicameralism and presentment.
- Understand the role of the various players in this process from legislators to the president.
- Identify the legislative history developed during the legislative process.
- Compare direct democracy processes.

A. Introduction to This Chapter

This chapter explains the basic process of enactment, focusing on the federal process. In addition to explaining the enactment process, this chapter also explains the role the various individuals in the process play, from legislators to lobbyists. Finally, as you learn how a bill becomes a law, you will discover the many ways that legislative history is created. We will return to this topic in Chapter 9, when we talk about the role legislative history plays in statutory interpretation. When you finish this chapter, you should have a basic understanding of how a bill is enacted, the importance of the constitutional processes of bicameralism and presentment, and the role that politics play. Let's start with process.

B. How a Bill Becomes a Law

First, this section explains the legislative process—the steps that a legislature takes to enact a bill; second, it identifies the legislative history developed along the way. This section explains the *federal* legislative process rather than the state process, but there are many similarities. Not all bills follow the path outlined here; for example, many legislatures have a shortcut for non-controversial bills: the consent calendar. Bills on the consent calendar are briefly explained to the members and then voted on. They do not go through the process described below.

The chart on the following page from LINDA D. JELLUM & DAVID C. HRICIK, MODERN STATUTORY INTERPRETATION: PROBLEMS, THEORIES, AND LAWYER- ING STRATEGIES 10 (2d ed. 2009), summarizes the legislative process. You may want to refer to it as you read the description of the legislative process in the remaining sections of this text.

As you read the description below, notice that the legislative process is not an easy one. Indeed, it is much easier for a bill to fail than to be enacted. The Framers of our Constitution chose this balance because "[t]he injury which may possibly be done by defeating a few good laws, will be amply compensated by the advantage of preventing a number of bad ones." THE FEDERALIST No. 73 (Alexander Hamilton) (Clinton Rossiter ed., 1961). Difficult passage promotes consistency, avoiding dramatic changes in the law. WILLIAM N. ESKRIDGE, JR. ET AL., LEGIS- LATION AND STATUTORY INTERPRETATION 79 (2d ed. 2006). Thus, in many ways, one might say that the purpose of legislatures is to kill bills not to pass them. This certainly seems to be true recently; as of late September 2012 (when Congress ad- journed), 3,914 bills had been introduced. Of those, only 61 bills, less than 2%, had been enacted into law. Unfortunately, 2012 was a particularly non-produc- tive year; the only other year in which Congress failed to pass at least 125 laws was 1995.

1. Legislatures & Legislators

a. A Bicameral Congress

Representatives pass federal laws, not citizens. While the Framers could have chosen a system that would have allowed citizens to enact law directly (and some states did make that choice), the Framers opted instead for a representa- tive system to better ensure that laws would protect all citizens, not just those in power: "Under such a regulation, it may well happen that the public voice pro- nounced by the representatives of the people, will be more consonant to the public good, than if pronounced by the people themselves convened for that purpose." THE FEDERALIST No. 10 (James Madison) (Clinton Rossiter ed., 1961).

Under the Articles of Confederation (which preceded the Constitution), the legislature was a unicameral body in which each state held one vote. But the larger states were not happy with the one-vote-per-state system. When the Framers drafted the Constitution, the legislature's structure was one of the most divisive issues of the Constitutional Convention of 1787. Ultimately, the Framers selected bicameralism, a system in which there are two chambers, or houses,

How a Bill Becomes a Law*

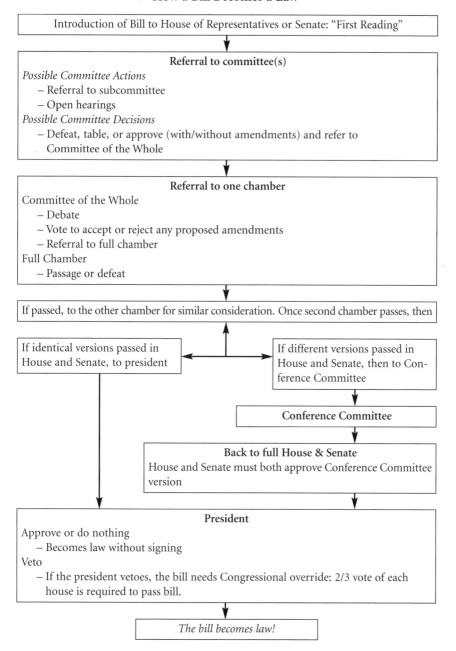

| Introduction of Bill to House of Representatives or Senate: "First Reading" |

Referral to committee(s)
Possible Committee Actions
 — Referral to subcommittee
 — Open hearings
Possible Committee Decisions
 — Defeat, table, or approve (with/without amendments) and refer to
   Committee of the Whole

Referral to one chamber
Committee of the Whole
 — Debate
 — Vote to accept or reject any proposed amendments
 — Referral to full chamber
Full Chamber
 — Passage or defeat

If passed, to the other chamber for similar consideration. Once second chamber passes, then

If identical versions passed in House and Senate, to president

If different versions passed in House and Senate, then to Conference Committee

Conference Committee

Back to full House & Senate
House and Senate must both approve Conference Committee version

President
Approve or do nothing
 — Becomes law without signing
Veto
 — If the president vetoes, the bill needs Congressional override: 2/3 vote of each
   house is required to pass bill.

The bill becomes law!

* Copyright Linda D. Jellum & David Charles Hricik. Used by permission.

constituting the legislative body. Although there is only one federal legislature, Congress, it is made up of two chambers: the House of Representatives and the Senate. The Framers chose bicameralism as a compromise: One chamber would represent public opinion (the House), and a second chamber would represent the views of the governments of the individual states (the Senate). State legislatures originally selected members of this latter chamber, who, as a result, were expected to be less susceptible to mass public sentiment. But today, citizens of the state they represent elect senators, just like representatives.

There are also fifty state legislatures, often called general assemblies. For the most part, the state legislatures are also bicameral, but Nebraska's legislature is unicameral. While this section will focus on Congress, its legislators and legislative processes, you should learn about the process in your state. It likely differs in some way from the federal process.

Because Congress is made up of two separate chambers, each has its own procedures, politics, and qualifications, all of which impact the legislative process. Because these differences affect interpretation, let's explore them for a moment. The Senate is the smaller of the two bodies. There are 100 senators; two for every state. In contrast, the House is much larger. There are 435 representatives; each represents a Congressional District made up of about 700,000 people. The number of representatives is currently fixed at 435 (Pub. L. No. 62-5, ch. 5, §§ 1–2, 37 Stat. 13 (1911)), although there is a bill currently pending to increase that number so that the District of Columbia can have representation. Each state is represented proportionally in the House based on that state's population. California has the most representatives: fifty-three, but every state has at least one representative. Currently, seven states have only one: Delaware, Montana, North Dakota, Vermont, South Dakota, Alaska, and Wyoming. In contrast, every state has two senators, both of whom represent the entire state. Senators serve a large constituency — constituents are residents of the state that elected the individual — with many varied interests. The Senate is sometimes thought to be more deliberative than the House because the Senate has fewer members. Because senators serve longer terms, they are more insulated from public opinion than members of the House. Both of these factors — size and term length — encourage collegiality and discourage partisanship within the Senate. In contrast, representatives are elected from smaller (approximately 700,000 residents) and more homogenous districts than senators. The House is generally the more partisan chamber.

> Although reelection and financial considerations are important to lawmakers, most are also motivated by the desire for status and reputation and the objective of affecting policy and the national agenda

in ways consistent with their ideological commitments. Empirical studies have found that a legislator's voting behavior is most related to her constituents' interests.

Eskridge et al., Legislation And Statutory Interpretation, *supra,* at 98 (citations omitted).

i. Legislator Qualifications

Not everyone can be a legislator. The Constitution requires that senators be thirty years old, citizens for at least nine years, and "[i]nhabitant[s]" of the state from which elected. U.S. Const. Art. 1. § 3. Similarly, representatives must be twenty-five years old, citizens for at least seven years, and "[i]nhabitant[s]" of the state from which elected. U.S. Const. art. I., § 2. There is no requirement that representatives actually live in the district they represent. These minimal requirements cannot be augmented. *Powell v. McCormack,* 395 U.S. 486, 550 (1969) (rejecting Congress's attempt to refuse to seat a representative who met these qualifications but was not trustworthy). Because neither Congress nor the states can alter or add to these Constitutional requirements, term limits imposed by many states on federal representatives in the 1990s were held to be unconstitutional. *U.S. Term Limits, Inc. v. Thorton,* 514 U.S. 779, 837 (1995).

Many things motivate legislators, including reelection. Representatives are up for reelection every two years (always in an even-numbered year). In contrast, senators are elected for six-year, staggered terms. Unlike the House where every representative is up for re-election simultaneously, only one-third of the senators are up for reelection at any one time. Because a senator's tenure in office is longer than representatives in the House, representatives may be more risk averse when it comes to passing new legislation than senators. Moreover, because it is considered more prestigious to be a senator, representatives from the House regularly want to "move up" to the Senate. The desire to move up may affect a representative's willingness to support unpopular legislation. Also, regular turnover negatively impacts the institutional memory of the House.

ii. Leadership

Politics matter, particularly in the House. Pursuant to the Constitution, approval of both chambers is required for legislation to become law. Indeed, the legislative veto, in which one chamber could unilaterally vacate decisions of the executive, was held to be unconstitutional because such a process allowed

Congress to act without following the "single, finely wrought and exhaustively considered procedures of Article I." *INS v. Chadha*, 462 U.S. 919, 951 (1983).

The party with the most seats in the House, the majority party, has the political power to get things done. The leader in the House is the Speaker of the House, whom the members elect. House rules and custom, not the Constitution, identify the powers and duties of the speaker. Thus, these powers and duties may change over time as one party attempts to expand or reign in the speaker's political power, which can be tremendous. The speaker has many powers that affect the legislative process. For example, the speaker has the power to control the order in which members of the House speak during debate on a bill. No representative may speak or bring a motion until the speaker permits. This rule gives the speaker tremendous power to control the course of the debate. Additionally, the speaker rules on representatives' objections arguing that a rule has been breached (called points of order), but the speaker's decision is subject to appeal, which the whole House resolves. Further, the speaker is the chair of the Steering Committee, which chooses the chair of the other standing committees; these standing committees are responsible for doing the preliminary work on all bills and, thus, hold tremendous power. The speaker also decides which committee should consider bills, appoints members of the Rules Committee, and appoints members of conference committees. All in all, the speaker has tremendous political power.

After the speaker, the majority party leader, also elected by his or her party, has the most political power. The majority leader decides which legislation members of that party should support and which legislation the membership should oppose. There is also a minority party leader who, not surprisingly, holds much less political power. Both parties also elect "whips," who try to ensure that the party's members vote as the party leadership desires. Representatives generally vote as the leadership directs because otherwise they may be threatened with reduced support for reelection campaigns, for pet legislation, and for committee chair positions.

Leadership is slightly different in the Senate; there is no speaker. Instead, the Vice President of the United States is the presiding officer, or president, of the Senate. The vice president is not a senator and does not regularly vote. But in the case of a tie, the vice president may cast the tie-breaking vote. For example, John Adams, the first Vice President and President of the Senate cast tie-breaking votes twenty-nine times (more than any other vice president). He voted to protect the executive's sole authority to remove appointees, and he influenced the location of the national capital. Because the vice president does not always attend legislative sessions, the duty of presiding often falls to the president *pro tempore*, usually the most senior senator in the majority party, who may choose to delegate this task to a junior senator. Similar to the House, the Senate has both majority and minority party leaders and whips.

b. The Important Role of Committees

Both the House and Senate operate via committee and subcommittee, each of which is responsible for a particular jurisdiction or subject area. House Rule X, clause 1 and Senate Rule XXV, clause 1 specify the permanent standing committees in the chambers. All legislators serve on one or more committees. Because there are so many of them, representatives often specialize. In contrast, because of the Senate's small size, its members do not specialize in the same way. Commonly, committees are broken into subcommittees, which do the messy work: hold hearings, take testimony, draft and amend bill language, and recommend whether to pass a bill on to the full committee. Not all committees have subcommittees.

While all bills do not reach the floor for vote, all bills that do reach the floor are first screened by the appropriate committee. While legislators are free to sponsor a bill that will be examined by any committee and advocate for that bill once it reaches the floor, in reality, legislators can most effectively influence the passage of bills while they are before the committee of which the legislators are members. Moreover, legislators will be most successful when chairing that committee or, at least, when having a majority of the committee members in their party. Because the party in political power selects the chair and members of each committee, it is difficult for the party not in power to enact legislation. Party loyalty is strong. Legislators who adhere to the party line are rewarded, while those who stray are penalized. Profiles in Courage, by John F. Kennedy, is a Pulitzer Prize-winning biography that details the bravery and integrity of eight United States Senators who suffered because of their decision to cross party lines. Hence, politics greatly influence bill passage.

c. Staffers & Lobbyists

It is not just legislators who make up Congress. Staff members surround each chamber. These staff members may also influence the legislative process; they may draft committee reports, write amendments to bills, and provide other relevant information.

Additionally, lobbyists, people who are generally paid to represent a particular point of view for a specific industry or organization, may also influence the legislative process. Interestingly, "[t]he term 'lobbying' arose from the practice of people waiting in the legislature's lobby to intercept legislators to at-

tempt to win them over to a particular position." RONALD BENTON BROWN &
SHARON JACOBS BROWN, STATUTORY INTERPRETATION: THE SEARCH FOR LEG-
ISLATIVE INTENT 130-31 (2002). Often, lobbyists draft bills, present information during hearings, craft amendments, advocate for passage, and argue against
passage. These non-legislator players also affect legislation.

Just how much of a role lobbyists should have is the subject of some debate. Lobbying is simply providing information to influence a lawmaker's
decision. If you have written your congress member to advocate a position,
you have lobbied. But *lobbyists* are paid experts in navigating the hurdles in
the legislative process; they are professionals hired to represent industries or
companies to influence legislation and policy. "Lobbyists inform lawmakers
about constituent preferences and interests; they inform legislators about the
effects of particular policies and problems that demand government solutions; they inform lawmakers about the preference of other lawmakers so
that proponents of policy change can successfully negotiate the vetogates of
Congress; and they inform the public about lawmakers' views and efforts regarding policies." ESKRIDGE ET AL., LEGISLATION AND STATUTORY INTER-
PRETATION, *supra*, at 197. Lobbying is increasing exponentially. Lobbyists
must register with Congress and regularly file reports disclosing the identity
of their clients, the issues for which they lobbied, and the amount of money
received for all lobbying efforts. 2 U.S.C. § 1603–04 (2011). "Lobbyists are paid
to further the interest of their constituency, not the public, and not other
industries. Lobbyists have both pernicious and beneficial influences on the
legislative process." JELLUM & HRICIK, MODERN STATUTORY INTERPRETATION,
supra, at 11–12.

Recently, lobbyists for the biotechnology industry influenced the record of
the historic House debate on Obamacare. The *New York Times* obtained emails
showing that the lobbyists drafted one statement for Democrats and another
for Republicans. These remarks were then printed in the extension of remarks
section of the Congressional Record under the names of forty-two different
members of Congress: twenty-two Republicans and twenty Democrats. While
it is not unusual for members of Congress to submit revised or extended statements for publication in the Congressional Record after the debate, it is unusual that so many of the statements matched word for word. It is even more
unusual to find clear evidence that the statements originated with lobbyists.
When asked in an interview about remarks added under his name, Representative William Pascrell Jr., a Democrat of New Jersey, said: "I regret that the language was the same. I did not know it was." He said his statement came from
staff members, and he "did not know where they got the information from."

For the full story, see Robert Pear, *In House, Many Spoke With One Voice: Lobbists'* N.Y. TIMES, Nov. 14, 2009, http://www.nytimes.com/2009/11/15/us/politics/15health.html?pagewanted=1&_r=2&hp&adxnnl=1&adxnnlx=1356177854-O fyR2geHJXzm3KGEGksiiA.

2. The Constitutionally Prescribed Process

a. Congress's Role — Bicameral Passage

Now that you understand the organizations and the players within each organization, let's turn to the legislative process. You must understand the legislative process to understand the role of legislative history. Keep in mind that behind the neat progression described below is an "often-chaotic process of lobbying by interest groups and of assessments by legislators of the public interest and of their own, sometimes less public-regarding needs (such as re-election)." ESKRIDGE ET AL., LEGISLATION AND STATUTORY INTERPRETATION, *supra,* at 3.

Congress holds two legislative sessions per year. Occasionally, an extra or special session is called. The first step in the enactment of a law is for one or more members of Congress to introduce a bill in one of the two chambers. Members of Congress often introduce bills on behalf of lobbyists because only a member of Congress can introduce legislation. Remember that lobbyists are people who advocate for the passage (or rejection) of bills that affect the interest of a particular group, such as an environmental advocacy group, not the public as a whole. Often, the lobbyists write the initial draft of the bill and then submit the draft to a legislator for introduction.

Proposed legislation is generally introduced as a bill, but some legislation is introduced as a joint resolution. For our purposes, there is little practical difference between the two. Concurrent resolutions, which both chambers pass, and simple resolutions, which only one chamber passes, are not used for this purpose because they do not have the force of law. Instead, concurrent and simple resolutions regulate procedure or simply express Congress's opinion on a relevant issue.

Generally, a bill can originate in either chamber, unless it is a tax or appropriations bill, both of which must originate in the House. One or more legislators must sponsor the bill. The main sponsor is responsible for moving the bill through the legislative process; hence, choosing sponsors can be critical. The chair of the relevant committee is often a good first choice because of the power that the chair wields in getting legislation passed. Having co-sponsors with varied political and geographical interests can also help ensure passage.

All bills go through several steps within each chamber. The first step is generally committee consideration. After a bill is introduced, the Speaker of the House or the presiding officer of the Senate (depending on where the bill originated) will refer the bill to the appropriate standing (meaning existing) committee or committees. Having the speaker or presiding member of the Senate refer one's bill to a supportive committee is helpful.

There are twenty standing committees in the House and sixteen in the Senate, each of which has a specified jurisdiction, such as foreign relations or finance. Standing committees consider, amend, and report bills that come within their purview to the full chamber. A bill may fall within the jurisdiction of more than one standing committee. Committees have extensive power over bills; most importantly, committees may block legislation from ever reaching the floor of the chamber. In addition to their legislative responsibilities, standing committees also oversee divisions of the executive branch.

To accomplish all of their objectives, standing committees may hold hearings, subpoena witnesses, and collect evidence. Each committee and subcommittee has one chair person and one ranking member; the chair is from the majority party, while the ranking member is from the minority party. The chair has extensive power over bills because the chair controls the committee's agenda. Thus, chairs can prevent a committee from ever considering a bill. Chairs used to be awarded by seniority. Today, the steering committee selects chairs. Chairs are often awarded to members who faithfully follow the party direction.

Committees have a tremendous impact on the future of a bill. Only one out of every ten bills referred to committee becomes law. Eskridge et al., Legislation And Statutory Interpretation, *supra*, at 72 (3d ed. 2001) (citing Burdett Loomis, The Contemporary Congress 156 (1996)). The committee chair decides whether to add the bill to the committee's agenda or to refer the bill to subcommittee. The chair also decides whether to hold public hearings on the bill. If public hearings are to be held, notice of the time and location of the meeting is published. Interested lobbyists and members of the public may attend; however, testimony is severely limited. Hearings are held, meetings occur, amendments may or may not be made, and finally, action is taken: The committee can vote to table the bill, amend (or "mark-up" the bill, see the hypothetical in Chapter 1), not report the bill, or approve the bill and forward it to the House or the Senate floor. A decision not to report the bill is the equivalent of killing the bill. If the bill is approved and forwarded to the full chamber, staff members prepare a committee report, describing the details of the committee's work. This report accompanies the bill to the floor; it may be the only part of the proposed legislation the voting members read, including the bill itself! The committee process is basically identical in both houses.

Assuming the bill is forwarded to the full chamber, the legislative process continues. The Senate and House vary somewhat in scheduling bills for a full chamber vote. In the House, the chair of the committee that is forwarding the bill to the full House must first ask the House Rules Committee to schedule the bill for floor consideration. The Rules Committee plays a strong role in the passage of a proposed bill because the Rules Committee passes the rules governing debate on each bill, such as the time allowed for debate, how that time is allocated to each side, and the scope of possible amendments. For example, the Rules Committee can choose to schedule "closed rule"—allowing no amendments to the bill,—"modified closed rule"—allowing limited amendments,— or "open rule"—allowing all germane amendments. The Rules Committee can recommend that consideration of a bill be expedited. The Rules Committee process provides another opportunity for derailment.

Assuming a bill is called up before the members of the House, the House must first vote on and debate the bill's rule. If the rule is accepted, the House dissolves into the Committee of the Whole. The Committee of the Whole is not a committee in the usual sense but is simply a committee consisting of all 435 members of the House, which follows simplified procedures to debate the bill. The Committee of the Whole was developed to expedite House action. It is the largest House committee and offers a forum for debating, considering, and perfecting proposed legislation. The Committee of the Whole debates the bill for an amount of time the House Rules Committee previously determined, usually one to several hours. Amendments may only be offered during this time. Debate and amendments must be *germane* to the bill being considered. Debate on proposed amendments is subject to the "five-minute rule," a House rule that in theory limits debate for and against an amendment offered in the Committee of the Whole to ten minutes, five minutes in support and five minutes in opposition. The Committee of the Whole may consider bills and amend them, *but it cannot pass a bill.* Instead, when the Committee of the Whole is done debating and amending a bill, "the committee rises" and reports its recommendations on the bill to the full House. Votes of the Committee of the Whole are not recorded; thus, legislators may feel free to vote as they wish without fearing political pressure or reprisal.

Assuming the bill is forwarded to the full House (the same individuals who just debated the bill as the Committee of the Whole), more debate may ensue. Eventually, debate concludes, and the House votes on the bill or recommits (refers) the bill back to the legislative committee from which it was reported. Referral back to committee generally means the bill dies. Voting of the full House usually takes fifteen minutes, but this time limit may be extended if the leadership needs time to "whip" its members into shape. For example, the 2003 vote on the Prescription Drug Benefit bill was open for three hours while the leadership worked to find the necessary votes for passage. Ties signal defeat for the bill; unlike the Senate in which the vice president breaks ties, there is no casting (tie-breaking) vote in the House. Unlike votes in the Committee of the Whole, votes in the full House are recorded; thus, representatives may feel somewhat less free to vote against the party line.

In the Senate, a different process ensues. First, the Senate does not have a rules committee. Rather, senate procedure is governed by a set of rules and by numerous customs and traditions. In many cases, the Senate will waive some of the rules by unanimous consent. Party leaders typically negotiate unanimous consent agreements before a bill reaches the floor. Any senator may block such an agreement; thus, while the majority party still has more power in the Senate, a single senator can, theoretically, singlehandedly kill a bill. In reality, such objections are uncommon.

Also, unlike the House, there is no committee of the whole in the Senate; rather, the full Senate can debate and amend the bill on the floor. Like representatives, senators may speak during floor debates only when the presiding officer permits. But unlike the Speaker of the House, the presiding officer of the Senate is required to recognize the first senator who rises to speak and, thus, has little control over the course of the debate. Moreover, unlike members of the House, senators may offer to amend bills at any time during floor debate. Sometimes senators offer amendments simply to kill a bill. For example, Representative Judge Howard W. Smith offered an amendment to Title VII, in part, to kill the bill. His amendment added sex to the topics protected from employment discrimination. He added this amendment, in part, due to his own commitment to equal opportunities for women, but also because he believed that the bill would then become so controversial that it would fail. His amendment was welcomed with laughter from his fellow representatives. Despite this greeting, the amendment did not have the effect he was after; the bill passed with the amendment intact (with a vote of 168-133).

Unlike the House, there is no germaneness rule in the Senate. There are few restrictions on what senators may say during debate. Moreover, there are no time limits: senators may speak for as long as they please. The Senate may adopt time limits by a unanimous consent agreement, but unlimited debate is generally protected.

To defeat bills and motions, senators may filibuster because the Senate rules allow unlimited debate of issues before the vote. A filibuster prolongs debate indefinitely: senators may use long speeches, dilatory motions, or extensive amendments to filibuster. Senator Strom Thurmond delivered one of the longest filibuster speeches in the history of the Senate when he spoke for more than twenty-four hours in an unsuccessful attempt to block passage of the Civil Rights Act of 1957. More recently, Senator Rand Paul spoke for thirteen hours to contest what he believed was the executive's policy on the use of drones against American citizens on American soil. Similarly, in the famous movie "Mr. Smith Goes to Washington," Jimmy Stewart stood on the floor of the Senate reciting the Declaration of Independence for twenty-three hours to prevent the Senate from voting on a proposed bill. Waiting for the senator to reach physical exhaustion is one of the two ways to break a filibuster. More commonly today, however, senators do not actually physically prevent voting, a threat is sufficient.

The primary way to defeat a filibuster is *cloture*. Senate Rule WWII, clause 2 currently provides that cloture can be invoked with the vote of sixty of the 100 senators; interestingly, when the Civil Rights Bill was passed, the rule required two-thirds (generally 67) of the voting senators. Because bipartisan support is almost always necessary to obtain cloture, it is rarely invoked. Indeed, since 1917, when the procedure was added to the Senate rules, cloture has been invoked successfully only twice. If it is invoked, debate does not end immediately; instead, further debate is limited to thirty additional hours. Eventually, the bill is voted on or sent back to committee. Votes are recorded. The Senate process is temporarily complete.

Once a bill has passed one chamber, it is less than half-way towards passage because both houses must pass the identical version of the bill and the president must approve it or a veto must be overridden. Once the first chamber passes a bill, it is *engrossed* and passed to the other chamber. The term "engrossed" is left over from a time when important documents such as statutes were copied onto parchment paper in large, clear handwriting. Today, bills are simply printed with a laser printer. The second chamber must pass the engrossed bill, no amendments or changes are allowed. If the second chamber passes the engrossed bill, the bill returns to the first chamber where it is then *enrolled*, signed, and transmitted to the president for approval or veto. The National Archives is the depository for the originals of all statutes.

Commonly, the second chamber will pass a similar, but not identical, bill (not the *engrossed* bill). Because the second bill is not identical, the two chambers must consult in conference committee, which is an ad hoc committee of select senators and representatives. Generally, the conference committee is made up of three to five members of each chamber, usually the senior members of the standing committees of each chamber that originally considered the legislation. Members of the minority party must also be included. The committee meets, discusses the differences in the bills, resolves those differences, recommends action, and writes a report analyzing those differences. While the conference committee is not supposed to substantially alter the bill language, in many cases conference committees have departed significantly from both the House and Senate versions.

Once the conference committee reaches a compromise bill, it submits the bill along with its committee report to the chamber that first passed the bill for approval. If that chamber approves the report, then it votes on the compromise bill. If the revote is favorable, the bill is sent to the other chamber, where the same process ensues. Once both chambers pass it, the bill is returned to the first chamber, enrolled, signed by members of both chambers, and sent to the president for approval.

b. The President's Role — Presentment & Signing

The final step in the legislative process is the president's approval or veto. If the president signs the enrolled bill, it becomes law. Once signed, the secretary of state files the act (it is no longer a bill).

If the president vetoes the bill, returning it to Congress with objections, the bill only becomes law if two-thirds of the legislators of each chamber vote to override the president's veto. Finally, if the president chooses not to act — neither signing nor vetoing the bill — the bill automatically becomes law after ten days (excluding Sundays). U.S. CONST. art. 1, 7. However, if Congress adjourns during this ten day period, then the bill lapses and does not become law. This lapse is known as a pocket veto. Because Congress is adjourned, it cannot override the president's veto.

If vetoed, the bill is returned to the legislature, often with a veto message. The legislature may override the president's veto only with a favorable, two-thirds vote from each chamber. Overrides are rare: Less than seven percent of vetoes are successfully overridden. ESKRIDGE ET AL., LEGISLATION AND STATUTORY INTERPRETATION, *supra*, at 76. Indeed, as of September 2012, there have been 2,562 vetoes (both regular and pocket) with 109 overrides (four percent). Interestingly, Franklin Roosevelt had the most vetoes (635); Harry Truman was second (250). In contrast, President George W. Bush vetoed ten bills, none by pocket veto, and President Obama has vetoed only two so far in his presidency.

The president must veto a bill in its entirety; the line item veto was held to be unconstitutional. *Clinton v. City of New York*, 524 U.S. 417 (1998) (finding the line item veto for appropriations bills unconstitutional). But note that forty-three states' constitutions allow governors the right to veto "items" in appropriation bills; "items" has been defined differently by each of the state courts. ESKRIDGE ET AL., LEGISLATION AND STATUTORY INTERPRETATION, *supra,* at 204.

Often, when a president signs legislation that that president does not like but does not want to veto, the president will include a limiting "signing statement." The president may also include a veto message when vetoing a bill. These statements may indicate how the executive intends to implement the law, which may make these statements very significant. More recently, these statements have been used to show disagreement for a particular bill or to narrow its effect. Chapter 11 discusses the role these statements play in interpretation. Here, we simply note that they exist as part of the process. There is no federal constitutional provision, statute, or case that explicitly permits or prohibits signing statements or veto messages.

Signing statements, which were once obscure, have become mainstream. The executive uses signing statements, in part, to take interpretive power away from the courts. Initially, signing statements were meant to give notice of the way that the executive intended to implement a law. President James Monroe was the first to issue a signing statement, in which he argued that the president, not Congress, held the constitutional power to appoint military officers. His was a non-controversial statement, which is why many believe that President Andrew Jackson, whose signing statement sparked the first controversy, was the first president to issue such a statement.

Under the direction of Attorney General Edwin Meese, President Ronald Reagan first considered whether these statements could be used to enhance the executive's influence over statutory interpretation. While working as an assistant attorney general for the Department of Justice under Meese, Samuel Alito, now Justice Alito, authored a memorandum entitled "*Using Presidential Signing Statement to Make Fuller Use of the President's Constitutionally Assigned Role in the Process of Enacting Law.*" You can find the memo here: http://www.archives .gov/news/samuel-alito/accession-060-89-269/Acc060-89-269-box6-SG-LSWG-AlitotoLSWG-Feb1986.pdf. In the memo, Alito argued that because bills require presidential approval in addition to approval by both houses to become law, "it seems to follow that the President's understanding of the bill should be just as important as that of Congress." *Id.* Alito suggested that signing statements should be used to "increase the power of the Executive to shape the law" and, further, "help curb some of the prevalent abuses of legislative history." *Id.* Meese then convinced West Publishing Company to include signing statements in the legislative histories section of the UNITED STATES CODE CONGRESSIONAL AND ADMINISTRATIVE NEWS (USC-CAN), stating that inclusion would assist courts in the future to determine what the statute actually means. Since 1986, signing statements have been published in USCCAN.

The use of signing statements is on the rise. In 2012, the Congressional Research Service counted the percentage of signing statements that contained "objections" to provisions of a bill being signed into law and concluded as follows:

> While the history of presidential issuance of signing statements dates to the early 19th century, the practice has become the source of significant controversy in the modern era as Presidents have increasingly employed the statements to assert constitutional and legal objections to congressional enactments. President Reagan initiated this practice in earnest, transforming the signing statement into a mechanism for the assertion of presidential authority and intent. President Reagan issued 250 signing statements, 86 of which (34%) contained provisions objecting to one or more of the statutory provisions signed into law. President George H. W. Bush continued this practice, issuing 228 signing statements, 107 of which (47%) raised objections. President Clinton's conception of presidential power proved to be largely consonant with that of the preceding two administrations. In turn, President Clinton made aggressive use of the signing statement, issuing 381 statements, 70 of which (18%) raised constitutional or legal objections. President George W. Bush has continued this practice, issuing 152 signing statements, 118 of which (78%) contain some type of challenge or objection. The significant rise in the proportion of constitutional objections made by President George W. Bush was compounded by the fact that his statements were typified by multiple objections, resulting in more than 1,000 challenges to distinct provisions of law. Although President Barack Obama has continued to use presidential signing statements, the Obama Administration has used the interpretive tools with less frequency than previous administrations — issuing 20 signing statements, of which 10 (50%) contain constitutional challenges to an enacted statutory provision.

TODD GARVEY, CONG. RESEARCH SERV., RL33667, PRESIDENTIAL SIGNING STATEMENTS: CONSTITUTIONAL AND INSTITUTIONAL IMPLICATIONS summary (2012).

As can be seen from this survey, all modern presidents use signing statements in this way; however, former President George W. Bush dramatically and mandatory provisions of the Act into advisory provisions.

President Bush's signing statement for H.R. 4986, the National Defense Authorization Act for Fiscal Year 2008

Today, I have signed into law H.R. 4986, the National Defense Authorization Act for Fiscal Year 2008. The Act authorizes funding for the defense of the United States and its interests abroad, for military construction, and for national security-related energy programs.

Provisions of the Act, including sections 841, 846, 1079, and 1222, purport to impose requirements that could inhibit the President's ability to carry out his constitutional obligations to take care that the laws be faithfully executed, to protect national security, to supervise the executive branch, and to execute his authority as Commander in Chief. The executive branch shall construe such provisions in a manner consistent with the constitutional authority of the President.

GEORGE W. BUSH

THE WHITE HOUSE,
January 28, 2008.

Rather than veto a bill, President Bush used signing statements to limit their reach; some argue that President Bush used signing statements much like a line-item veto (to limit the sections of an act he did not like). Remember that the Supreme Court held that the line-item veto violates separation of powers.

As noted above, President Obama has acted somewhat more moderately. While a presidential candidate, President Obama said that he thought signing statements were legitimate when used with "restraint" — for instance, to clarify how an ambiguous law should be interpreted. Since January 2012, he has signed twenty-nine such statements. He signs these statements when he believes a bill will impact his constitutional powers. For example, citing his role as commander-in-chief, he objected (1) to a provision that required thirty-day's advance notice to Congress before military exercises costing more than $100,000, and (2) to a provision that forbade him from putting American forces under a foreign commander as part of a United Nations' peacekeeping mission unless another military official signed off. Below is an excerpt from a lengthy and somewhat indignant signing statement from President Obama.

President Obama's signing statement on H.R. 1540

Today I have signed into law H.R. 1540, the "National Defense Authorization Act for Fiscal Year 2012.".…

The fact that I support this bill as a whole does not mean I agree with everything in it. In particular, I have signed this bill despite having serious reservations with certain provisions that regulate the detention, interrogation, and prosecution of suspected terrorists. Over the last several years, my Administration has developed an effective, sustainable framework for the detention, interrogation and trial of suspected terrorists that allows us to maximize both our ability to collect intelligence and to incapacitate dangerous individuals in rapidly developing situations, and the results we have achieved are undeniable. Our success against al-Qa'ida and its affiliates and adherents has derived in significant measure from providing our counterterrorism professionals with the clarity and flexibility they need to adapt to changing circumstances and to utilize whichever authorities best protect the American people, and our accomplishments have respected the values that make our country an example for the world.

Against that record of success, some in Congress continue to insist upon restricting the options available to our counterterrorism professionals and interfering with the very operations that have kept us safe. My Administration has consistently opposed such measures. Ultimately, I decided to sign this bill not only because of the critically important services it provides for our forces and their families and the national security programs it authorizes, but also because the Congress revised provisions that otherwise would have jeopardized the safety, security, and liberty of the American people. Moving forward, my Administration will interpret and implement the provisions described below in a manner that best preserves the flexibility on which our safety depends and upholds the values on which this country was founded.…

BARACK OBAMA

THE WHITE HOUSE,
December 31, 2011.

After the president has signed the bill, it is filed. Perhaps surprisingly, once an *enrolled* bill is filed, it is conclusively presumed to have been validly adopted—this rule is known as the *enrolled bill rule*. Some states follow the *journal entry rule* instead, which allows a court to determine whether constitutional requirements were met solely by looking at the journal entry. For example, under the journal entry rule, a judge could determine whether identical bills were passed, whether there were sufficient affirmative votes to override a veto, and whether a bill was subject to three readings (a holdover procedure from when some legislators were illiterate). However, because there is such a strong presumption that legislative acts are valid, the differences in the two rules are minor. Generally, courts will not entertain challenges to the legislative process of a particular bill. This rule (1) respects the division of labor among the branches by not allowing the judiciary to police the legislature's activity; (2) promotes stability by allowing citizens to assume that filed acts are law; and (3) promotes harmony by keeping the legislative and judicial functions separate. Arguably, a legislature could choose to ignore the constitutionally required process, knowing its choice will not be subject to judicial review, but legislatures rarely do so.

C. The Importance of Procedural Rules

Unlike the Federal Constitution, nearly all state constitutions require bills to include just one subject. This limitation is known as the *single subject rule*. For example, the Illinois Constitution provides, "Bills, except bills for appropriations and for the codification, revision or rearrangement of law, shall be confined to one subject." ILL. CONST. art. IV, § 8(d). Similarly, Pennsylvania's Constitution provides that "[n]o bill shall be passed containing more than one subject, which shall be clearly expressed in its title, except a general appropriation bill or a bill codifying or compiling the law or a part thereof." PA. CONST. art. III, § 3. Additionally, many state constitutions require the bill's title to identify the subject of the bill. To illustrate, Florida's Constitution provides, "Every law shall embrace but one subject and matter properly connected therewith, and the subject shall be briefly expressed in the title." FLA. CONST. art. III, § 6. Georgia's Constitution is similar: Bills shall not "refer[] to more than one subject matter or contain[] matter different from what is expressed in the title thereof." GA. CONST. art. III, § V, ¶ III. The term "subject," in this context, is liberally construed; the subject may be very broad. "Nonetheless, the matters included in the enactment must have a natural and logical connection." *Johnson v. Edgar*, 680 N.E.2d 1372, 1379 (Ill. 1997).

The single subject rule serves two functions: (1) to prevent lawmakers from burying a controversial subject in an otherwise popular bill, and (2) to increase the likelihood that legislators will know what they are voting for or against. The rule, thus, facilitates orderly legislative procedure, ensures that the legislature addresses the difficult decisions it faces directly while subject to public scrutiny, and prevents the passing of unpopular measures on the backs of popular ones.

While it is not common for state statutes to be struck down for violating the single subject rule, it does happen. For example, the Illinois Supreme Court invalidated a bill because it violated the single subject rule:

> [The bill] began its legislative life as an eight-page bill addressing the narrow subject of reimbursement by prisoners to the Department of Corrections for the expense of incarceration. As enacted on December 13, 1995, however, [the bill] had experienced an extraordinary growth, from 8 pages to over 200 pages. While the length of a bill is not determinative of its compliance with the single subject rule, the variety of its contents certainly is. Here, "An Act in relation to prisoner's reimbursement to the Department of Corrections for the expenses incurred by their incarceration" became a bill which created a law providing for the community notification of child sex offenders, created a law imposing fees on the sale of fuel, and enhanced the felony classifications for the possession and delivery of cannabis. This bill also created an exemption from prosecution for eavesdropping applicable to employers who wish to monitor their employees' conversations, amended the law to allow the prosecution of juveniles as adults in certain cases, and created the new crime of predatory criminal sexual assault of a child.... In sum, [the bill] amended a multitude of provisions in over 20 different acts, and created several new laws. By no fair intendment may the many discordant provisions in [the bill] be considered to possess a natural and logical connection. The enactment of [the bill] therefore violated the single subject rule.

Johnson, 680 N.E.2d at 516–17 (internal citations omitted). The court rejected the state's argument that all the topics related to one subject, that subject being "public safety." *Id.* at 517.

Because courts do not like the one subject rule, they generally interpret a single subject broadly, in part, to defer to the legislature. For example, in *Pennsylvanians Against Gambling Expansion Fund, Inc. v. Commonwealth*, 877 A.2d 383 (Pa. 2005), the court refused a single-subject challenge to a bill titled "regulation of gaming" even though the bill also established subject matter jurisdiction in the state's supreme court for the issuance of gaming licenses. *Id.* at 394–97.

Additionally, even when a court finds a statute to violate the single subject rule, courts have difficulty fashioning a remedy. While some courts have struck down the entire statute, other courts have struck just the offending sections of the statute. Arguably, the remaining statute was not what the legislature intended to enact, yet the legislature may well have wanted some law rather than no law at all.

There are other complications with the rule as well. The single subject rule applies equally to laws passed via initiatives and referendums (See Section D below). Drafters of these initiatives and referendums are typically less skilled in bill-drafting than lawmakers and, thus, these direct democracy laws are more often subject to attack for violating this rule. Given that the public often votes after doing little more than reading the title, some have argued that courts should apply the single-subject requirement more rigorously to direct legislation than to traditional laws. For now, however, courts do not apply the rule more vigorously. For example, in 2004, Georgia voters approved an amendment to its state's constitution that prohibited gay marriage. GA. CONST. art. 1, §IV, ¶1. The ballot measure read, "we adopt as the amendment's objective, reserving marriage and its attendant benefits to unions of man and woman." The Georgia Constitution required that ballot measures be limited to one subject. Suit was filed alleging that the ballot measure violated the single subject provision because it prohibited both same-sex *unions* and same-sex *marriage*. The lower court agreed. *O'Kelly v. Perdue*, No. 2004CV 93434, 2006 WL 1350171 (Ga. Super. Ct. May 16, 2006). Ultimately, the Georgia Supreme Court disagreed with the lower court's opinion that civil unions and gay marriage were different topics and upheld the amendment. *Perdue v. O'Kelly*, 632 S.E.2d 110 (Ga. 2006).

While the Federal Constitution does not include a similar rule, House and Senate procedural rules do exist to combat the problem of extraneous subjects being added to bills. The House has the *germaneness rule*—"no motion or proposition on a subject different from that under consideration shall be admitted under color of amendment." Rules of the House of Representatives, R. XVI, H.R. DOC. NO. 109-157, at 701. The Senate has a similar rule for budget bills only. Additionally, both chambers have rules that limit what can be added to appropriations bills. The appropriations limit exists because if appropriations bills are not passed, the government must shut down. Hence, legislators may be more willing to vote for a subject they otherwise would reject if it is attached to an appropriations bill. But internal rules can be and are waived, and courts are loath to enforce internal rules due to separation of powers concerns. The legislature and judiciary are co-equal branches of our government. Neither branch should be responsible for supervising the processes or deliberations of the other. A contrary rule would elevate one branch above the other. Thus, in *Des Moines Register & Tribune Co. v. Dwyer*, 542 N.W.2d 491 (Iowa 1996), the majority held that a statute that allowed the public to access a legislator's phone records was a nonjusticiable rule of proceeding rather than a reviewable statute on substance. *Id.* at 502–03. The court held that the rule was not subject to review.

D. Direct Democracy: The Referendum and Initiative Process

In contrast to the legislative process described above, about one-half of the states and many local governments allow their citizens to adopt laws or amend their constitution directly using the *initiative process*. Additionally, almost all states allow their citizens to reject laws and constitutional amendments proposed by their state's legislatures via a *referendum*. In this country, the initiative process is more common than the referendum process and is, thus, the more important process. Both of these processes are called direct democracy. Each of these two processes is somewhat different, but both have in common the notion that law should come directly from the people. Note that there is no similar process at the federal level, where the legislature drafts and enacts all statutory law.

The initiative process is available in twenty-four states (mostly the Western states). An initiative is a citizen-drafted statute or constitutional amendment placed on the ballot for popular vote. The process is relatively simple. First, someone drafts an initiative. After the initiative is drafted, the proponents of the initiative must obtain the requisite number of signatures by petition to have the initiative placed on the ballot. After the initiative is placed on the ballot, the voters either approve or reject it. This is the direct initiative process, in which the legislature and executive play no role. In contrast, some states require that initiatives be submitted to the legislature before being placed on the ballot. If the legislature fails to approve the measure or amends it unsatisfactorily, then the initiative proponents must secure more petition signatures to get the measure on the ballot. This is an indirect, as opposed to direct, initiative process because the state legislature is involved. One of the more well-known state initiatives was California's Proposition 13, which severely limited the ability of state government to increase property taxes. More recently, many states have had initiatives addressing the issue of gay marriage.

The referendum process is similar to the initiative process, but the referendum process is generally used to reject proposed legislation rather than pass new legislation. Almost every state allows some form of referendum process. There are two different kinds of referendums—popular and legislative. *Popular referendum* refers to the right of the voters, by collecting signatures on a petition, to refer specific legislation the legislature passed to the voters for approval or rejection. In contrast, *legislative referendum* refers to the ability of elected officials to submit proposed legislation or constitutional amendments to the voters for approval or rejection. Legislative referendum is constitutionally required for constitutional amendments in all states but Delaware.

As you can imagine, statutes that come about as a result of these direct voting methods present particular interpretation problems. If statutory interpretation is the art of discerning the intent of the enacting legislature (See Chapter 2), then whose intent matters when citizens draft a statute? Those courts addressing the issue have concluded that the voters' intent controls. *See In re Littlefield*, 851 P.2d 42, 48 (Cal. 1993); *State v. Guzek*, 906 P.2d 272, 284 (Or. 1995); *Lynch v. Washington*, 145 P.2d 265, 270 (Wash. 1944). But which voters: those who drafted the initiative, those who petitioned to get the initiative on the ballot, or those who voted for it? Many voters are unable to understand complex, lengthy initiatives. Should their intent really matter? Concerns that we may have about legislators actually reading bills should be multiplied in the initiative arena. Moreover, voters' opinions may be formed from media portrayals, whether by news or political advertising. Indeed, some courts have looked at these sources when interpreting initiatives.

Even assuming you can decide which group's intent matters, discerning that intent can be trickier than discerning the intent of a legislative body that leaves a voluminous historical record in one location. For this reason, at least one scholar has suggested that courts should focus on the sponsor's intent. Glenn Smith, *Solving the Initiatory Construction Puzzle (and Improving Direct Democracy) by Appropriate Refocusing on Sponsor Intent*, 78 U. Colo. L.R. 257 (2007).

At bottom, judges are skeptical about direct democracy processes: "[for] its lack of filters to calm the momentary passions of the people and its susceptibility to use by majorities to harm disfavored groups." Eskridge et al.,Legislation And Statutory Interpretation, *supra*, at 35. This skepticism can be seen in *Romer v. Evans*, 517 U.S. 620 (1996), in which the Supreme Court invalidated a state initiative that targeted gay individuals because the initiative was based on a "desire to harm a politically unpopular group...." *Id.* at 632.

E. Mastering This Topic

Return to the hypothetical ordinance provided in Chapter 1 on page 9. While the hypothetical involved a city ordinance, not a federal statute, it included information about its legislative process. Look back and see if you can identify this information on your own.

There are three areas to note. First, the hypothetical includes a committee report and a summary of the floor debates. For a judge willing to consider it, these types of legislative history may provide insight into meaning, whether the search is for specific or general intent. Some forms of legislative history are more relevant than others. In other words, there is a hierarchy of usefulness of legislative history, which you will learn in Chapter 9.

Second, the hypothetical included a marked-up version of the ordinance. Additions to the original text are italicized while deletions are crossed out. At the federal level, *italic* and ~~strike-through~~ text are used to indicate amendments to bills and can aid interpretation; knowing what language was added or deleted during the legislative process can be informative.

Finally, the hypothetical includes the mayor's signing statement. You may wonder how relevant executive signing statements are for interpretation. We will address this issue in Chapter 11. For now, consider what weight you think they should be given. Does the signing statement attempt to rewrite the ordinance or simply inform executive enforcement? You will learn that this is an area far from settled, but that, generally, signing statements are considered the least relevant "legislative" history. Keep in mind that the hypothetical, which is a teaching tool, includes more legislative process information than would be typical for a city ordinance or even a state statute.

Checkpoints

- It is far easier for a bill to fail than to be enacted.

- Congress, a bicameral body, is made up of the House of Representatives and the Senate. The legislative process begins when a legislator introduces a bill on the floor of either the House or Senate.

- A bill goes through a number of procedural steps before it is passed. The political party in power ultimately controls the fate of the bill.

- Both the House and Senate must pass a bill in identical form for it to be presented to the president.

- The final step in the legislative process is the president's approval or veto. If the president signs the bill, it becomes law. If the president vetoes the bill, then the bill fails to become law unless two-thirds of the members of both chambers override the veto.

- During the legislative process, legislative history is generated describing the bill's progress.

- About one-half of the states and many local governments allow citizens to adopt laws or amend the constitution directly using the initiative process. When laws are enacted via direct democracy, discerning "legislative intent" is very difficult.

Chapter 4

Canons Based on Intrinsic Sources: The Words

Roadmap
- Understand the plain meaning rule and its corollary, the technical meaning rule.
- Learn the difference between ordinary, definitional, and technical meaning.
- Learn how judges avoid the plain meaning rule by finding absurdity, ambiguity, scrivener's error, and constitutional questions.

A. Introduction to This Chapter

Finally, we begin the interpretation process. To do so, we start where all interpretation should start: with the text of the statute. In this chapter, you will learn that generally, judges assume that legislatures meant words in their ordinary, or plain, sense. Occasionally, but much less commonly, the legislature meant to use a word in its technical sense. For example, statutes are often written for lawyers, who have a technical understanding of the word "assault," and not lay persons, who have an ordinary understanding of the word. This chapter not only describes the plain and technical meaning rules but also describes the four situations when judges avoid these meanings.

B. The Intrinsic Sources

In Chapter 2, we learned that there are three sources judges use to glean the meaning of statutory language: intrinsic, extrinsic, and policy based. In the next few chapters, we will explore the relevance each of these sources has on interpretation. We begin with intrinsic sources, those sources that are part of the statute being interpreted. At this point, you should know that the words of the statute are of central importance to all judges regardless of theory. But the words are not the only intrinsic source. Grammar, punctuation, and the linguistic canons of statutory construction are also intrinsic sources. We will explore the words now, and we will explore other intrinsic sources in later chapters.

C. The Textual Canons: Words & Syntax

"We do not inquire what the legislature meant; we ask only what the statute means." Oliver W. Holmes, *The Theory of Legal Interpretation*, 12 HARV. L. REV. 417, 419 (1899). The language of the statute, including its words, grammar, and punctuation, is the starting point for all interpreters trying to find this meaning. "Unless a word or phrase is defined in the statute…, its meaning is determined by its context, the rules of grammar, and common usage." UNIF. STATUTE & RULE CONSTR. ACT § 2 (1995). Thus, your job as an advocate is to identify the statutory language at issue and then explain why that language means what your client wants it to mean. To help you do so, let's examine the plain meaning rule.

1. Looking for Ordinary Meaning

a. The Plain Meaning Rule

The first place to start in interpreting a statute is with the words. "The text of a statute or rule is the primary, essential source of its meaning." UNIF. STATUTE & RULE CONSTR. ACT § 19 (1995). To do so, you must first identify which words are at issue. While identifying the relevant language is generally easy, which language you identify may be outcome determinative. For example, two cases out of Florida interpreted the same statute under almost identical facts but reached opposite results because each court focused on different language in the statute. The statute provided that traffic citations "shall not be admissible evidence in any trial." *Dixon v. Florida*, 812 So. 2d 595, 596 (Fla. Dist. Ct. App. 2002) (quoting FLA. STAT. § 316.650(9) (2001)). In both cases, the defendants gave false information to an arresting officer, who entered the information on a traffic citation, which the defendants then signed using false names. Both defendants were arrested for forgery. At trial, the prosecutors offered the citations as evidence of the defendants' forgery (not the traffic violation); the defendants objected, citing section 316.650(9).

Despite the factual similarities, the appellate courts reached different conclusions because they focused on different language in the statute. In *Dixon*, the court held that the traffic citation was inadmissible because the language of the statute was clear: "*any trial*" meant every trial without exception. But in *Maddox v. Florida*, 862 So. 2d 783 (Fla. Dist. Ct. App. 2003), the court held that the statute did not apply because the ticket was not a "*traffic citation.*" Instead, it was "documentary evidence of Maddox's criminal conduct." *Id.* at 784. On appeal, the Florida Supreme Court agreed with the *Maddox* court, rejecting the interpretation in *Dixon*. *Maddox v. State*, 923 So. 2d 442 (Fla. 2006) (supporting its holding by identifying the purpose of the statute, reviewing other sections of the statute, and showing the absurdity of *Dixon's* plain meaning holding). As the appeal was pending, the Florida legislature amended the statute to allow citations to be admitted into evidence in subsequent forgery-related cases. 2005 Fla. Laws, c. 2005-164, §42. These two cases show that identifying the appropriate language can be outcome-determinative.

Typically, courts presume that words in a statute have their "plain," or "ordinary," meaning. This presumption is known as the *Plain Meaning Rule*. This text uses the term "plain meaning rule" to refer to the canon and "ordinary meaning" to refer to the ordinary use of a word. Be aware that the jurisprudence uses them interchangeably. Also, know that the courts do not clearly distinguish between the definitional, or dictionary, meaning and the ordinary meaning. There is a difference. The definitional meaning is the many ways a word might be used which dictionaries show, while the ordinary meaning is how a word is ordinarily used, which some dictionaries also note.

Judges do not always understand the difference between these two; consider this example. In *Smith v. United States*, 508 U.S. 223 (1993), the majority applied the plain meaning rule to decide whether a defendant who offered to exchange his MAC-10 (a gun) for two ounces of cocaine "*use[d]* ... a firearm" during a drug trafficking crime. The issue for the Court was whether bartering a gun constituted "using a firearm." The majority held that the meaning of "use" included trading the gun for drugs. *Id.* at 228–29. In so doing, the majority rejected the defendant's argument that the *ordinary meaning* of "using a firearm" was to use the firearm as a weapon. *Id.* at 229. The majority responded that "it is one thing to say that the ordinary meaning of 'uses a firearm' *includes* using a firearm as a weapon, since that is the intended purpose of a firearm and the example of 'use' that most immediately comes to mind. But it is quite another to conclude that, as a result, the phrase also *excludes* any other use." *Id.* at 230. The majority looked to dictionary definitions to find the definitional meaning of the word "use," then interpreted the word very broadly despite the rule of lenity. (See Chapter 13 for a discussion of this canon, which suggests that ambiguity should be resolved in a defendant's favor).

The dissent strongly disagreed and chastised the majority for failing "to grasp the distinction between how a word *can be* used and how it *ordinarily is* used." *Id.* at 242 (Scalia, J., dissenting). Most people would not say "use" when referring to bartering in this context. The dissent more accurately applied the plain meaning rule in this case by identifying the ordinary, as opposed to the definitional, meaning.

In a subsequent case interpreting the same word in the same statute, the Court held that "use" denoted active employment, not mere possession. *Bailey v. United States*, 516 U.S. 137 (1995) (holding that a defendant who carried a gun in the trunk of his car did not "use" a firearm within the meaning of the statute). Subsequently, and as a direct result of *Bailey*, the Court rejected a claim that a drug dealer who received a firearm for drugs "used" that firearm. *Watson v. United States*, 552 U.S. 74, 83 (2007). In so holding, the majority confirmed the correctness of its decision in *Smith*. Thus, one who barters a gun for drugs *uses* that gun, but one who merely receives a bartered gun in exchange for drugs does not *use* the gun. These cases show that the plain meaning rule, though appealing in its simplicity, does not always answer the question, especially when dictionaries are consulted. Dictionaries define words broadly; thus, definitional meanings will always be broader than ordinary meanings, which textual and other context limit.

Additionally, the plain meaning rule presumes, wrongly, that native listeners and readers of language understand words to mean the same thing the speakers intended. This presumption is inaccurate because words have multiple meanings. "[W]ords do not possess intrinsic meanings and cannot be given them; to make matters worse, speakers do not even have determinative intents about the meanings of their own words." Frank H. Easterbrook, *Statutes' Domains*, 50 U. Chi. L. Rev. 533, 536 (1983). Consider the word "blue." Blue is both a color and a feeling. If I say that I am "blue" today, likely I am saying that I am sad. But I may instead be pointing out that I am wearing blue clothing. Indeed, singers and poets take advantage of language's indeterminacy regularly; consider the song title, "Don't it Make My Brown Eyes Blue." Does the author mean blue in color, blue in feeling (sad), or both? While context often identifies which meaning is intended, context does not always resolved the ambiguity.

How does a judge find the ordinary meaning of words? In the past, judges might have perused legislative history to understand what the legislators believed the words meant. Most commonly today judges turn to their own understanding of a word's meaning or to dictionaries. Dictionary definitions are offered as relevant "not as evidence, but only as aids to the memory and understanding of the court." *Nix v. Heddon*, 149 U.S. 304, 307 (1893) (holding that a tomato is a vegetable not a fruit).

When a judge refers to his or her own understanding of a word to ascertain its meaning, the judge's choice appears subjective. But dictionaries lend an air of objectivity to the process. On the contrary, a judge's use of dictionaries is not objective; for example, which dictionary should a judge choose? There is no consensus about which dictionary to use, nor which era's dictionary to use. As for era, Justice Scalia, in his dissent in *Chisom v. Roemer*, 501 U.S. 380 (1991) (Scalia J., dissenting), indicated that a dictionary in effect at the time legislation was drafted would be appropriate. *Id.* at 410. But not all judges agree. Earlier editions of dictionaries do not account for changes in meaning over time. If the point of interpretation is to find the intent of the enacting legislature, this latter concern may not matter. But if the point is to find the ordinary meaning the audience would give the words today, it may be essential.

As for which dictionary, there is no consensus on one specific choice. Apparently, not all dictionaries are equal. In *MCI Telecommunications Corp. v. American Telephone & Telegraph Co.*, 512 U.S. 218 (1994), Justice Scalia, writing for the majority, identified a number of different dictionaries with similar definitions of the word at issue: "modify." While the majority of dictionaries suggested that modify meant a modest change, one dictionary, *Webster's Third New International Dictionary*, suggested that modify could mean either a modest or substantial change. *Id.* at 225–26. The Court rejected the latter definition and the appropriateness of that dictionary. *Id.* at 227. "Virtually every dictionary we are aware of says that 'to modify' means to change moderately or in minor fashion." *Id.* at 225. Justice Scalia cited widespread criticism of this dictionary when it was published for its "portrayal of common error as proper usage." *Id.* at 228 n.3. Apparently, Webster's Third was too colloquial to be considered authoritative for this Court. But if the point of statutory interpretation is to find the meaning an audience member would likely ascribe to the language as textualists argue, why is colloquialism not a good thing? This dictionary fight is simply a fight about the difference between definitional meaning and ordinary meaning. The ordinary meaning of modify is a modest change; while a definitional meaning of modify might include substantial change.

The use of dictionaries masks subjectiveness in another way. Dictionaries generally have multiple meanings for each word. Yet, the presence of multiple dictionary definitions is not alone enough to show that a word is ambiguous. The Supreme Court started down this road in one case when it accepted the argument that the presence of multiple dictionary definitions meant that the word was inherently ambiguous. *Nat'l R.R. Passenger Corp., v. Bos. & Maine Corp.*, 503 U.S. 407, 418 (1992) (stating that "[t]he existence of alternative dictionary definitions of the word "required," each making some sense under the statute, itself indicates that the statute is open to interpretation."). The Court quickly and correctly retreated from this unworkable definition of ambiguity in *MCI Telecommunications Corp.*, when it rejected an argument, based on *National Railroad Passenger Corp.*, that the existence of multiple dictionary definitions established ambiguity. 512 U.S. at 226. Had the Court adopted this definition every statutory word challenged in any future case would likely have been ambiguous, for it is rare, if not unheard of, for a word to have only one dictionary definition.

A second concern relating to the fact that words have more than one dictionary meaning is that there is no canon that says that the first dictionary meaning is *the* ordinary meaning. While the primacy of the definition may carry weight, it is not dispositive. "I cannot imagine that the majority favors interpreting statutes by choosing the first definition that appears in a dictionary." *Miss. Poultry Ass'n, Inc. v. Madigan*, 992 F.2d 1359, 1369 (5th Cir. 1993) (Reavley, J., dissenting), *aff'd on reh'g*, 31 F.3d 293 (5th Cir. 1994) (en banc). Without guidance as to which meaning to pick, how do judges know which of many meanings was intended? The choice of one meaning over another may mask subjectiveness.

Context helps to limit judicial discretion. Words often have different meanings in different contexts. Consider an example: The defendant "assaulted" the plaintiff. Is "assault" meant in its tortious sense, its criminal sense, or simply in its non-legal sense, meaning a violent attack? To determine which of these possible meanings should prevail, judges look to the statute's audience. For example, a Connecticut state statute required state boards of education to indemnify personnel who were harmed "as a result of an *assault*" while working. *Patrie v. Area Coop. Educ. Serv.*, 37 Conn. L. Rptr. 470 (Conn. Super. Ct. 2004) (citing CONN. GEN. STAT. § 10-236a) (emphasis added). The plaintiff had been injured when a student, without intending to hurt the plaintiff, jumped playfully on the plaintiff's back. *Id.* at 470. Under the statute, the plaintiff could only recover if the playful jump was "an assault." The plaintiff argued that the legislature would have wanted "assault" interpreted broadly to further the purpose of reimbursing school personnel for injuries that were no fault of their own. *Id.* Thus, plaintiff suggested that the term meant either an assault as defined in tort — freedom from the apprehension of a harmful or offensive contact — or as defined in that state's criminal law — an attempted but unsuccessful battery. Under either the tort definition or the criminal definition, any intent requirement would have been satisfied on these facts, for intent to harm is unnecessary under either legal theory. *Id.* at 473. But the court rejected both interpretations of the term. Instead, the court said, "The definition of 'assault' the plaintiff advocates forgets the audience the statute was aimed at — school administrators trying to meet budgets and run their schools and teachers concerned with their rights above and beyond workers' compensation." *Id.* Because administrators and teachers would more commonly think of an assault as being an intentionally violent attack (its non-legal meaning), the court held that in this statute "assault" meant an *intentionally* violent act. *Id.* Pursuant to this interpretation, the plaintiff could not recover for his injuries. Notice how textual context and audience were central to the court's holding in *Patrie*.

In another case interpreting the same word in a different statute, a different court interpreted the term "assault" to have its legal, tortious meaning, specifically freedom from the apprehension of a harmful or offensive contact. *Dickens v. Puryear*, 276 S.E.2d 325 (N.C. 1981). In this case, the word was contained in a statute of limitations regarding intentional torts. Using the non-legal definition in this context would have made no sense because the audience for statutes of limitations is lawyers and judges, both of whom would have a different understanding of the word "assault" than would laypersons. *Id.*

Thus, dictionaries can be useful guides to determining ordinary meaning, but they have limitations as well. First, their use can mask the subjectiveness of the choice of meaning; choosing a dictionary and then choosing one meaning over another are both subjective choices. Moreover, dictionaries may at times be ill-suited for determining the meaning of particular language in a statute because context is so essential to meaning. Despite these limitations, judges increasingly rely on both the plain meaning rule and dictionaries to determine meaning.

b. The Technical Meaning Rule

A word in a statute may have both a ordinary and a technical meaning. For example, as we just saw, "assault" can mean a intentionally violent attack— its ordinary meaning—or it can mean freedom from the apprehension of a harmful or offensive contact—a technical (in this case legal) meaning. While legislatures generally use words in their ordinary sense, occasionally, the ordinary meaning is not the one intended. Usually, courts presume that legislatures intended words to have their ordinary meaning because legislatures draft generally applicable statutes; however, sometimes legislatures intend words to be used in their technical sense. The technical and plain meaning rules work harmoniously to direct that "[u]nless a word or phrase is defined in the statute or rule being construed, its meaning is determined by its context, the rules of grammar, and common usage. A word or phrase that has acquired a technical or particular meaning in a particular context has that meaning *if it is used in that context*." Unif. Statute & Rule Constr. Act § 2 (1995) (emphasis added).

The technical meaning rule reflects the reality that most often the ordinary meaning was intended. Additionally, the rule allows for those few times when the ordinary meaning was not intended. Thus, the ordinary meaning will generally prevail when both a technical and ordinary meaning co-exist, absent any indication that the word was used in its technical sense. For example, is a tomato a vegetable—its ordinary meaning—or a fruit—its technical meaning to a botanist and linguist? Believe it or not, this issue was litigated before the Supreme Court! Confounding botanists around the world, the Court held that a tomato is a vegetable. *Nix v. Hedden*, 149 U.S. 304, 306 (1893). According to the Court, "The attempt to class tomatoes as fruit is not unlike a recent attempt to class beans as seeds, of which Mr. Justice Bradley, speaking for this court, said: 'We do not see why they should be classified as seeds, any more than walnuts should be so classified. Both are seeds, in the language of botany or natural history, but not in commerce nor in common parlance'" *Id.* at 307. At issue in *Nix* was whether a statute that taxed vegetables at a higher rate than fruits applied to tomatoes. Perhaps, unsurprisingly, the Court held that the statute did apply, and the Government got its money despite the canon that ambiguities in tax and tariff statutes should be construed in favor of the taxpayer. *Id.*

To determine which meaning was intended—technical or ordinary—a judge will look at two things: (1) whether the surrounding words are technical, and (2) whether the statute was directed to a technical audience. Illustrative of the first point (that surrounding words matter) is *St. Clair v. Commonwealth*, 140 S.W.3d 510 (Ky. 2004). In that case, the court had to determine whether the word "conviction" in a sentence enhancing statute was used in "its ordinary or popular meaning, [meaning] a finding of guilt by plea or verdict, [or] its legal or technical meaning, [meaning] the final judgment entered on plea or verdict of guilty." *Id.* at 569 (quoting 21A Am. Jur. 2d *Criminal Law* § 1313 (1998)). The difference meant life or death to the criminal defendant. Looking at the language surrounding the word "conviction" in the statute, the court held that "conviction" was meant in its ordinary sense because the legislature had used the phrase "*prior record of* conviction" and not "*judgment of* conviction." *Id.* at 563. Thus, in this case, the other words in the statute provided textual context for determining that the ordinary meaning was intended.

Illustrative of the second point (that audience matters) is *O'Hara v. Luchenbach Steamship Co.*, 269 U.S. 364 (1926). The statute at issue in that case involved the safety and welfare of those at sea. Because the act was directed solely to individuals and companies in the maritime trade, the Court construed the statutory language in its technical way, as it would be understood by those in the maritime trade. *Id.* at 370–71. Judges are not limited to audience and textual context, however, in determining whether the technical meaning was intended. Other indicia of meaning, such as titles, purpose, and legislative history, may also inform the court. We cover these other sources in later chapters of this text.

2. Looking Beyond the Ordinary Meaning of Words

a. Ambiguity

Sometimes the text of a statute is simply not very clear. The most common reason textualist judges look beyond the text for meaning is that the words are ambiguous. According to Dictionary.com, "ambiguous" generally means "open to or having several possible meanings or interpretations; equivocal: an ambiguous answer." *Absurdity Definition*, Dictionary.com, http://dictionary.reference .com/browse/am-biguous (last visited September 18, 2007).

Ambiguous words may be likened to op-tical illusions in that both parties legitimately claim to see — or in the case of words, un-derstand — the same thing in a different way. Consider the famous optical illusion to the right.

Do you see a young or old woman? Most people see the young woman first, but if you look at the picture long enough, you should be able to make out the old woman as well. The young woman's necklace is the old woman's mouth. The young woman's chin is the old woman's nose. The young woman's ear is the old woman's eye. They share the hair, fur, and feather. Anyone viewing the picture can legitimately say it is a picture of either a young or old woman. Both "interpretations" are legitimate because the picture is unclear, or "ambiguous," intentionally so in this case. Ambiguous words are similar to optical illusions; they have more than one legitimate meaning. Children love to joke using ambiguous words: For exam-ple, how did the baker get rich? She made a lot of dough! Or, why do you go to bed? Because the bed will not come to you. (I did not say they were good jokes!)

Jurisprudentially, ambiguity is not consistently defined across jurisdictions. One common articulation of ambiguity is that statutory language is "ambigu-ous if it is capable of being understood by reasonably well-informed persons in two or more senses." *State ex rel Kalal*, 681 N.W.2d 110, 124 (Wis. 2004). In other words, a statute is ambiguous when it has more than one meaning when applied to the facts of a particular case. For example, in *Church of the Holy*

Trinity v. United States, 143 U.S 457, 459 (1892), the Supreme Court had to interpret the word "labor." The statute could have included all types of labor or it could have included only unskilled, physical labor. The text of the statute alone (the word "labor" and its surrounding words) did not resolve the ambiguity, at least to the Court. Thus, the word "labor," in this context, was ambiguous. To resolve the ambiguity, the Court turned to other sources, namely the title and purpose of the act, to choose between the two possible meanings. *Id.*

In contrast, simply because a word has more than one meaning does not mean that the language is ambiguous. For example, in *Kalal*, an employer allegedly stole retirement funds from an employee. 681 N.W.2d at 115. A statute allowed the district court to bring a criminal action directly if the district attorney "refuse[d]" to issue the complaint. *Id.* at 114 (quoting WIS. STAT. §968.02(3) (2001–02)). The district attorney had told the employee that she "was free to proceed legally in whatever manner she believed necessary." *Id.* After being told this, the employee filed a motion for a criminal complaint, which the court granted. *Id.* The issue in the case was whether the word "refuse" required an explicit refusal or merely an indication of unwillingness to do something. *Id.* at 115. The court held that the language was not ambiguous, despite the two, reasonable choices, because the dictionary supported the second interpretation: an unwillingness to do something. Moreover, the second interpretation better furthered the purpose of the statute. *Id.*

Thus, although the "reasonable people disagree" standard is oft-articulated, it is inaccurate. This definition cannot be correct, because if it were, then ambiguity would be found in every court case involving a statutory interpretation issue. The litigants always disagree as to the meaning of the statutory language, and the judges often disagree as well. To accept the "reasonable people disagree" articulation, we would have to believe that most litigants, their lawyers, and many judges are not reasonable people. Instead, ambiguity more likely "means that there is more than one *equally plausible* meaning. In other words, it has to be more than just two *reasonable* interpretations—it has to be two *equally plausible* interpretations or some narrower standard." LINDA D. JELLUM & DAVID C. HRICIK, MODERN STATUTORY INTERPRETATION: PROBLEMS, THEORIES, AND LAWYERING STRATEGIES 94 (2d ed. 2009). This definition may be gaining ground. *Fla. Dep't of Revenue v. Piccadilly Cafeterias, Inc.*, 554 U.S. 33, 41 (2008) (stating that although both sides presented "credible" interpretations, there was no ambiguity because "two readings of the language that Congress chose [were] not equally plausible. . . ."); *Mayor of Lansing v. Mich. Pub. Serv. Comm'n.*, 680 N.W.2d 840, 847 (Mich. 2004); (stating that "a provision of the law is ambiguous only if it irreconcilably conflicts with another provision, or when it is equally susceptible to more than a single meaning.").

A judge's approach to interpretation might affect that judge's willingness to define "ambiguity" narrowly ("equally plausible") or broadly ("reasonable people disagree"). Possibly, a judge's desire to look beyond the text could affect this choice. A broader definition of ambiguity allows judges to review extra-textual evidence of meaning more readily, while a narrower definition constrains judicial review of such evidence. Hence, we might expect textualist judges to define ambiguity narrowly while non-textualist judges, if they define it at all, might choose a broader definition.

Note also that "ambiguous" means something different from vague, broad, and general, although judges use the term "ambiguous" to mean all three. First, ambiguity is not the same as vagueness. Vague means "not clearly or explicitly stated or expressed." *Vague Definition,* Dictionary.com, http://dictionary.reference.com/ browse/vague (last visited September 18, 2012). Vagueness means that the boundaries of meaning are indistinct. For example, if I say I want the report next week sometime, "next week sometime" is vague, not ambiguous.

Second, ambiguity is not the same as broadness. "Broad" means "not limited or narrow; of extensive range or scope." *Broad Definition,* Dictionary.com, http://dictionary.reference.com/ browse/broad (last visited, September 18, 2012). If I say that I want a ten to fifty page report, that range may be broad; but it is not ambiguous.

Third, ambiguity is not the same as generalness. "General" means "not specific or definite." *General Definition,* Dictionary.com, http://dictionary.reference.com/browse/general (last visited September 18, 2012). If I say I want a report on birds, the topic "birds" may be general, but it is not ambiguous. Despite these differences, however, judges routinely say that language is ambiguous when it is merely vague, broad, or general.

When a judge determines that language in a statute is ambiguous, that judge opens the door to extra-textual sources. Just which sources a judge will consider continues to be influenced by that judge's theory of interpretation.

b. Absurdity (The Golden Rule)

Sometimes, the ordinary meaning is not what the legislature intended. When a statute would be absurd if implemented according to the ordinary meaning, can a judge refuse to follow that meaning? The answer to that question is yes, pursuant to the absurdity doctrine.

The absurdity doctrine was first introduced in 1892 in the famous case *Church of the Holy Trinity v. United States,* 143 U.S. 457 (1892). The statute at issue in that case prohibited businesses from bringing anyone into the country "to perform labor or service of any kind." *Id.* at 458. The church had hired a pastor from England. Pursuant to the ordinary meaning of the statute, the federal government fined the church. A lawsuit ensued. The Supreme Court rejected the government's argument that "labor ... of any kind" was clear and covered pastoral services. Stating that "[i]t is a familiar rule, that a thing may be within the letter of the statute and yet not within the statute, because not within its spirit, nor within the intention of its makers," the Court found the statute absurd and looked to the legislative history of the Act. *Id.* at 513–14. That history, according to the Court, was relatively clear that the legislature intended the word labor to mean *manual* labor. The statute had been enacted to stem the influx of cheap labor from China. Thus, the ordinary meaning of the text could be ignored because that meaning contradicted the intent of the legislature. The *Golden Rule* was born.

The Golden Rule, or absurdity exception, is, thus, an exception to the plain meaning rule. This exception allows judges to look beyond the ordinary meaning of the text to extra-textual sources when the statute would be absurd if interpreted as written. If, after reviewing the extra-textual evidence, a judge determines that the legislature did intend the absurd result, then that intention should control. But if, after reviewing the extra-textual evidence, the judge determines that the absurdity was not intended, then the absurdity exception gives the judge the option to ignore the ordinary meaning. In essence, when a statute is absurd, a judge has a choice: interpret the statute pursuant to its ordinary meaning and make the legislature correct any unintended absurdity or interpret the statute in a way that eliminates (or at least diminishes) the absurdity. Judges generally choose the latter avenue because they assume that a legislature would not intend an absurd result.

To see how this exception works, let's look at an example. In *Public Citizen v. U.S. Department of Justice*, 491 U.S. 440 (1989), the Court invoked the absurdity doctrine to avoid the ordinary meaning of the Federal Advisory Committee Act. The issue in the case was whether a committee of the American Bar Association (ABA) was subject to the Act, which required disclosure and open meetings for all federal "advisory committee[s]." *Id.* at 446–47. "Advisory Committee" was defined in the statute as any committee "utilized by the President ... in the interest of obtaining advice or recommendations...." *Id.* at 451 (quoting 5 U.S.C. § 3(2)). Thus, pursuant to the ordinary meaning of the statute, the ABA was an advisory committee because the president routinely sought the recommendations of the ABA regarding judicial nominees.

Citing *Holy Trinity*, however, the majority refused to give the statute its ordinary meaning. Because the ordinary meaning of the statute "compel[led] an odd result," the Court searched "for other evidence of congressional intent to lend the term its proper scope." *Id.* at 455. According to the majority, the statute was enacted to cure two specific ills—namely the wasteful expenditure of public funds for worthless committee meetings and biased proposals by special interest groups. The Court thought it unlikely that Congress intended the statute to cover every formal and informal meeting between the president and a group rendering advice. Citing the absurdity doctrine, the Court held that the statute did not apply to the ABA despite the ordinary meaning of the words of the statute. *Id.*

Similarly, in *Green v. Bock Laundry Machine Co*, 490 U.S. 504 (1989), the Court rejected the ordinary meaning of the word "defendant" in Rule 609(a) (1) of the Federal Rules of Evidence. Plaintiff Green, an inmate, worked at a car wash while on work release. His arm was torn off by a laundry machine, so he sued the manufacturer. The manufacturer defendant wanted to make it known to the jurors that the plaintiff was an inmate in jail. Rule 609, as then in effect, required a court, when admitting evidence that a witness had been convicted of a felony, to balance "the probative value of admitting th[e] evidence [with] the prejudicial effect to *the defendant....*" *Id.* at 509 (quoting Fed. R. Evid. 609(a) (emphasis added)). In Green's case, there would have been no prejudicial effect to the defendant manufacturer in admitting Green's conviction into evidence, but it was tremendously prejudicial to him as plaintiff. The trial court allowed the information in, and Green lost. Green appealed all the way to the Supreme Court. While "defendant" ordinarily means any defendant, the majority held that that meaning would be "odd" because such an interpretation would deny a civil plaintiff the same right to impeach a witness that a civil defendant would have. *Id.* at 509–10. This interpretation would raise due process concerns; thus, the Court could have avoided this interpretation by turning to the Constitutional Avoidance doctrine (Chapter 13). Instead, the Court found the result to be absurd and perused the legislative history to conclude that the legislature more likely intended "defendant" to mean "criminal defendant." *Id.*

Unfortunately, absurdity, like ambiguity, is not consistently defined in the jurisprudence. Even in the case that spawned this exception, *Holy Trinity*, the Supreme Court never explicitly defined absurdity. Instead, the Court merely suggested that a meaning that conflicts with congressional intent would be absurd. In the cases identified above, the Court equated absurd with "odd" and "likely unconstitutional." Other courts have used different formulations. For example, in *Robbins v. Chronister*, 402 F.3d 1047 (10th Cir. 2005), *rev'd* 435 F.3d 1238 (10th Cir. 2006), the majority adopted *Holy Trinity's* broad definition of absurdity—contrary to congressional intent—while the dissent used a narrower definition—shocking to one's conscience. In that case, the Tenth Circuit reviewed an inmate's request for attorney's fees under the Prison Litigation Reform Act. The plain language of the Act capped attorney fees at 150% of awarded damages "[i]n *any action* brought by a prisoner." *Id.* at 1049 (quoting 42 U.S.C. § 1997e(d)) (emphasis added). According to the ordinary meaning of the text, the plaintiff, a prisoner, was entitled to only $1.50 in attorney's fees because he had won only nominal damages of one dollar in his civil case. *Id.*

The majority acknowledged that the language of the statute was clear, but it stated that where applying the ordinary meaning would lead to an absurd and unjust result that Congress could not have intended, the ordinary meaning need not control. *Id.* at 1054. Hence, the majority concluded, the statute was absurd because it would produce "an illogical result." *Id.* at 1050. According to the majority, Congress intended the Act to curb frivolous lawsuits brought by prisoners relating to the conditions and circumstances of their incarceration. *Id.* at 1052. Congress did not intend, or so the majority believed, to curb all prisoner litigation. In this case, the defendant had brought suit under 42 U.S.C. § 1983, alleging that the arresting officer had used excessive force while arresting him. "[I]t would be absurd to limit Mr. Robbin's attorney's fees merely because he happened to file his pre-existing constitutional claim while he was in prison." *Id.* at 1054–55.

The dissent did not dispute the ability of the majority to ignore the ordinary meaning if the result were indeed absurd. *Id.* at 1055 (Hartz, C.J., dissenting). Rather, the dissent disagreed that the result was absurd because, in part, the dissent defined absurdity differently. According to the dissent, a statute is absurd only when an interpretation "lead[s] to results so great as to shock the general moral or common sense." *Id.* The dissent also found the purpose of the statute to be different than that of the majority. The dissent believed that Congress likely did intend to limit prisoner litigation because prisoners have so much time on their hands, they often file frivolous lawsuits. The cap would encourage only those suits likely to lead to substantial damage recovery. Agreeing with this reasoning, the Tenth Circuit reversed the case on rehearing. *Robbins v. Chronister*, 435 F.3d 1238 (10th Cir. 2006).

Which opinion in *Robbins* had a more accurate definition of absurdity? Neither: The majority's definition of absurdity was so broad that it would essentially open the door for consideration of extra-textual evidence in almost every case. This broad definition might be appealing to non-textualist judges willing to look to extra-textual sources relatively readily, but less appealing to other judges. Yet the dissent's definition of absurdity is little improved. It sets a high standard — a result that "shocks the general moral or common sense" — one that will rarely, if ever, be met. The correct definition of absurdity must lie between these two extremes. Just where is not clear, and the jurisprudence is of little help. Most commonly, instead of defining absurdity, judges simply list other cases that have found absurdity, thereby suggesting that the instant case is like or unlike those in the list.

Use of the absurdity doctrine has waxed and waned over the years. It was a useful doctrine in the early years of textualism, in the late 1800s and early 1900s. Then it lost favor when the plain meaning rule fell out of favor. *United States v. Am. Trucking Ass'ns, Inc.*, 310 U.S. 534 (1940), launched purposivism back into the forefront. With the fall of textualism and the rise of purposivism, the absurdity exception proved unnecessary. Purposivists (and intentionalists) do not need a reason, such as absurdity, to examine extra-textual evidence of meaning. More recently, the absurdity doctrine has made a comeback. In 1986, Justice Scalia was appointed to the Supreme Court. Part of his mission has been to return the Court to a text-first analysis. As the Court has become more text-focused, the Justices have resurrected the absurdity doctrine.

Despite its nearly universal acceptance, the absurdity doctrine is not without criticism. Because the doctrine allows judges to avoid the ordinary meaning of a statute and look extra-textually for meaning, some suggest the doctrine allows judges to cross the border from interpreting law to making law:

> Where the language of a statute is clear in its application, the normal rule is that we are bound by it. There is, of course, a legitimate exception to this rule, which the Court invokes, citing *Holy Trinity Church*, and with which I have no quarrel. Where the plain language of the statute would lead to "'patently absurd consequences' that Congress could not possibly have intended," we need not apply the language in such a fashion. When used in a proper manner, this narrow exception to our normal rule of statutory construction does not intrude upon the lawmaking powers of Congress, but rather demonstrates a respect for the coequal Legislative Branch, which we assume would not act in an absurd way.... [However] the potential of this doctrine to allow judges to substitute their personal predilections for the will of the Congress is so self-evident from the case which spawned it [*Holy Trinity Church*] as to require no further discussion of its susceptibility to abuse.

Pub. Citizen v. U.S. Dep't of Justice, 491 U.S. 440, 470, 474 (1989) (Kennedy, J. concurring) (citations omitted). While Justice Kennedy might well have preferred to have eliminated this doctrine altogether, he faced an insurmountable hurdle given the breadth of prior precedent relying on it. Despite that fact, he tried to limit the doctrine's reach by defining absurdity very narrowly to include only "patently absurd consequences." *Id.*

Interestingly, the absurdity doctrine is the golden child of textualists. It is a doctrine that allows these theorists to avoid the results of the plain meaning rule, the golden child's twin, in those cases when it would be absurd to believe the legislature intended the statute as written. Yet, if textualists eschew looking for legislative intent, this exception seems odd indeed. Linda D. Jellum, *But that is Absurd! Why Specific Absurdity Undermines Textualism*, 76 Brook. L.R. 917 (2011).

There are two types of absurdity, only one of which should be the basis for an absurdity finding. The two types include (1) specific absurdity, where a statute is absurd only in the particular situation, and (2) general absurdity, where a statute is absurd *regardless* of the specific situation. To help you understand the difference between these two types, let's look at two examples. A statute that prohibits people from keeping wild animals as pets might be absurd as applied to a person who rescued an injured squirrel, which was exactly what the court held in *Ohio Division of Wildlife v. Clifton*, 692 N.E.2d 253 (Ohio Mun. Ct. 1997). But the statute as applied generally would not be absurd; for health and safety reasons, we do not want people keeping wild animals in their homes. Thus, this statute would be absurd in its specific application but not absurd in its general application. In contrast, a statute that burdened a civil plaintiff's ability to testify but not a civil defendant's would be absurd in all cases because it would likely violate the due process clause of the Constitution; the facts of any particular case would not matter. These were the facts in *Green v. Bock Laundry Machine Co.*, 490 U.S. 504 (1989). Arguably, cases of general absurdity should be much rarer and, thus, should be more deserving of the absurdity doctrine; however, judges generally do not seem to distinguish between the two types of absurdity, perhaps because the distinction is less bright-lined at times than these two examples suggest.

c. Scrivener's Error

A third way judges avoid the plain meaning rule is when the statute contains an obvious scrivener's error, or mistake. The *scrivener's error exception* to the plain meaning rule permits judges to correct obvious clerical or typographical errors. For example, in *U.S. National Bank of Oregon v. Independent Insurance Agents of America, Inc.*, 508 U.S. 439, 462 (1993), the Court corrected punctuation that had been misplaced in a statute. Similarly, in *United States v. Coatoam*, 245 F.3d 553, 557 (6th Cir. 2001), the Sixth Circuit corrected a cross-reference to the wrong subsection of an act. And in *United States v. Scheer*, 729 F.2d 164, 169 (2nd Cir. 1984), the Second Circuit changed the word "request" in a statute to "receipt" where the statute had erroneously provided that a certificate be furnished "upon *request* of the ... request." *Id.* The scrivener's error doctrine is a subset of general absurdity; Congress made a simple mistake, and so the court fixes it.

The scrivener's error exception is a narrow one and should not be used simply because the court believes an error might have been made. Rather, "[i]t is beyond [a court's] province to rescue Congress from its drafting errors, and to provide for what we might think … is the preferred result." *United States v. Granderson*, 511 U.S. 39, 68 (1994). Thus, in *United States v. Locke*, 471 U.S. 84 (1985), the Court refused to interpret "prior to December 31" as including December 31. *Id.* at 93. In that case, the Locke family needed to file papers to retain its right to mine gravel on federal lands. They were told by the relevant agency personnel that the papers had to be filed by December 31. *Id.* at 89 n.7. So the Lockes filed on that date. The agency then rejected the papers, claiming that the papers had to be filed on or before December 30.

The Court agreed with the agency because the language was clear and "a literal reading of Congress' words is generally the only proper reading of [filing deadlines]." *Id.* at 93. The Court explained when it had leeway to alter statutory text pursuant to the scrivener's error doctrine: "There is a basic difference between filling a gap left by Congress' silence and rewriting rules that Congress has affirmatively and specifically enacted." *Id.* at 95 (quotations omitted). While the phrase "prior to" was clumsy, its meaning was clear. *Id.* at 96. Luckily for the Lockes, the Court remanded on other grounds, and the Lockes got to keep their mineral rights.

The scrivener's error canon does not give courts *carte blanch* to redraft poorly written statutes to correct legislative "mistakes"; rather, it is a canon that allows courts limited authority to fix obvious drafting errors. Yet, despite the narrowness of this canon, occasionally, a court will correct a substantive error. For example, in *Shine v. Shine*, 802 F.2d 583 (1st Cir. 1986), the First Circuit used the doctrine to redraft a statute. In that case, the parties had been married and had separated. The defendant-husband was ordered to pay support independently from the subsequent divorce proceedings. Later, the parties divorced, but the divorce decree did not provide for either alimony or support. *Id.* at 584. The defendant failed to pay and eventually filed for bankruptcy. *Id.* The plaintiff-wife sought to have the support obligation declared non-dischargeable under 11 U.S.C. § 523(a)(5), which excepted from discharge any debt "to a … former spouse … for alimony to, maintenance for, or support of such spouse … in connection with a separation agreement, divorce decree, or property settlement agreement.…" *Id.* (quoting 11 U.S.C. § 523(a)(5) (1978)). If the debt were not dischargeable, the defendant would have to continue paying it despite the bankruptcy proceeding.

The issue for the court was whether spousal support obligations ordered by a court independent of a divorce proceeding or formal agreement were dischargeable. The text of the statute suggested they were not dischargeable, but public policy suggested they should be. Indeed, according to the court, these two public policies conflicted in the case: the policy of narrowly construing discharge exemptions to protect the debtor (*i.e.* let the debtor discharge as much debt as possible) and the long-standing policy of excepting spousal and child support from discharge to protect families. *Id.* at 585.

The court turned to the legislative history of the Bankruptcy Reform Act of 1978 to determine the purpose of the amendment. Early case law had interpreted the statute to include a "broad exemption for any liability for [spousal] maintenance or support." *Id.* at 586. During the amendment process in 1978, Congress changed the language in a "harried and hurried atmosphere." *Id.* at 587. The amendment limited alimony discharges to those "due, in connection with a separation agreement or divorce decree." Such language would not clearly include court ordered debts, likes the one in this case. In 1984, Congress corrected its error by amending the statute to specifically include the type of debt at issue in this case, but the amendment came too late to apply in this action. *Id.* at 588. Nonetheless, the court found this subsequent history telling. The court concluded that Congress made an error during the "harried and hurried" process in 1978, which Congress then corrected in 1984. *Id.* at 587. Using the scrivener's error doctrine, the court "corrected" the obvious drafting error and held that the defendant could not discharge his support obligation to the plaintiff. "While the wording of the statute may have given rise to some confusion, '(t)he result of an obvious mistake should not be enforced, particularly when it overrides common sense and evident statutory purpose.'" *Id.* at 588. (quoting *In re Adamo*, 619 F.2d 216, 222 (2d Cir. 1980), *cert denied*, 449 U.S. 843 (1980)) (internal quotation marks omitted).

This result is surprising for two reasons. First, there was no scrivener's error, yet the court used the doctrine to "correct" the statute anyway. Second, the court essentially applied a clear statement rule, requiring Congress to be clear when it wanted to limit spousal support. (See Chapter 13 regarding clear statement rules.) Few courts, especially today, are willing to redraft legislation so freely. Indeed, the legislative history in this case demonstrates that when Congress wishes to correct its mistake, it knows how to do so.

d. The Constitutional Avoidance Doctrine

A fourth way that courts avoid the plain meaning rule is the *Constitutional Avoidance Doctrine*. We will study this doctrine in detail in Chapter 13. For now, know that the doctrine allows a court to avoid the ordinary meaning of text when that meaning would likely raise serious concerns about the constitutionality of the statute. The doctrine directs that to avoid having to declare the statute unconstitutional, a court should adopt an interpretation that can be fairly discerned from the text but does not raise constitutional issues. Two seminal cases in this area are *Public Citizen v. U.S. Department of Justice*, 491 U.S.

440 (1989), and *Green v. Bock Laundry Machine Co.*, 490 U.S. 504 (1989), both discussed above.

In the first case, the Supreme Court construed the Federal Advisory Committee Act narrowly to avoid "formidable constitutional difficulties." *Public Citizen*, 491 U.S. at 466. The Act required advisory committees to file a charter; provide notice of meetings; open those meetings to the public; and make minutes, records, and reports available for public inspection and copying. *Id.* at 447. The issue for the Court was whether a committee of the ABA was "an advisory committee" when the Justice Department sought the committee's views on prospective judicial nominees. The Act defined "advisory committee" as any committee, board, commission, council, conference, panel, task force, or other similar group, or any subcommittee ... which is ... *utilized* by the President...." *Id.* at 451 (citing 5 U.S.C. § 3(2) (emphasis added)). Recognizing that the Justice Department and president did "utilize" the committee in a broad sense, the Court nevertheless rejected the ordinary meaning of the text because that meaning would raise a serious constitutional question: namely whether the statute "infringed unduly on the president's Article II power to nominate federal judges and [thus] violated the doctrine of separation of powers." *Id.* at 466. Rather than decide the constitutional issue, the Court adopted an interpretation that did not raise the issue and that was consistent with the purpose of the statute, even though the interpretation was at odds with the ordinary meaning of the text. *Id.* at 464.

In the second case—*Bock Laundry*—the Court rejected the ordinary meaning of the text of rule 609 of the Federal Rules of Evidence. Rule 609, as then in effect, required a court to balance "the probative value of admitting th[e] evidence [that a witness had been convicted of a felony with] the prejudicial effect to *the defendant*...." *Green*, 490 U.S. at 509 (quoting Fed. R. Evid. 609(a) (emphasis added)). While the ordinary meaning of "defendant" is any defendant, the majority held that the ordinary meaning would be "odd" because such an interpretation would deny a civil plaintiff the same right to impeach a witness that a civil defendant would have. *Id.* In other words, the interpretation would raise due process concerns. After reviewing the legislative history, the Court concluded that the legislature more likely intended the word "defendant" to mean "criminal defendant." *Id.* at 509.

Thus, ordinary meaning generally controls. Judges routinely use dictionaries to find the ordinary meaning. However, if the statute was designed for an audience that has a technical understanding of the words, then the technical meaning should control instead. Sometimes, the ordinary meaning is unclear because the words are ambiguous. When ambiguity is present, judges look extra-textually to determine which of two or more equally valid meanings was intended. Finally, in addition to the technical meaning rule, there are three other situations in which judges may avoid the ordinary meaning of words: (1) if the ordinary meaning of the text is absurd, however absurdity is defined; (2) if there is an obvious scrivener's error; or (3) if the ordinary meaning would raise constitutional questions. In the next chapter, we continue our exploration of the intrinsic sources of meaning, turning to grammar and punctuation.

D. Mastering This Topic

Return to the hypothetical ordinance provided in Chapter 1 on page 9. The first question that was asked was the following: "An ambulance entered Pioneer Park to pick up and take to the hospital a man who has just suffered a heart attack. Did the ambulance driver violate the Pioneer Park Safety Ordinance (PPSO)?" How should you, as prosecutor, attempt to answer that question?

The first step in the interpretive process is to identify the language at issue in the statute or ordinance. The answer to this question is easy, for we already told you that the language at issue is "motor vehicle." Keep in mind that it will not always be so easy to identify the language at issue.

Next, let's apply the plain meaning rule. What is the ordinary meaning of motor vehicle to you? It is unlikely that a dictionary definition popped into your head. Likely, a picture of a car or truck came to mind. A car or truck is a prototype of the category of motor vehicles. It is a prototype that most English speakers would think of. Most people think in prototypes when thinking of categories. Consider the word furniture. What popped into your mind? A chair? A couch? A bed? I bet that a lamp did not pop into your head. But you are likely willing, when you think about it, to concede that a lamp could be considered furniture. What about a bathtub? At some point, the prototype is beyond the boundaries of the category. When the prototype is close to the boundaries of the category, interpretation becomes harder. You likely had to think about whether a lamp was furniture; perhaps, you had to think about whether a bathtub was furniture. Ordinary meaning is about finding prototypes and similarities between the prototype and the instance to be interpreted. Is an ambulance like a car or truck? Yes; it is nearly identical to them. Hence, ordinary meaning would suggest that an ambulance is a motor vehicle.

What about definitional meaning; did you take that approach? Perhaps you opened your dictionary to find the definitional meaning of motor vehicle? Notice that you likely had to look up each word independently. Does meaning change when you join two words having multiple meanings? Let's assume the definition of "vehicle" is the following: "any means in or by which someone travels or something is carried or conveyed; a means of conveyance or trans-port...." *Vehicle Definition*, Dictionary.com, http://dictionary.reference.com/browse/vehicle?s=t (last visited May 2, 2013). Does an ambulance fit within the definitional meaning of "vehicle"? It seems pretty clearly to be something in which people are carried, and it has a motor; so, yes: an ambulance fits within the definitional meaning of "motor vehicle."

Thus, if you apply the plain meaning rule, whether you look for ordinary meaning or definitional meaning, you should find that the ordinance prohibits ambulances from driving within the park to pick up heart attack victims. There-fore, the driver should be fined, right? Does this outcome seem odd to you? Do you find yourself squirming, knowing you will have to fine the driver, who was only doing his job? Perhaps there is a way to avoid the results of the plain meaning rule. Let's see if any of the exceptions to the plain meaning rule apply.

First, is there an applicable technical meaning of "motor vehicle"? No. Even if a technical meaning existed, this ordinance was written for the general pub-lic, not a specialized audience. Thus, even if "motor vehicle" had a technical meaning, it likely would not apply here.

Second, is there ambiguity? Are there two equally plausible meanings of the words "motor vehicle," one that would include an ambulance and the other which would not? Simply put, no. There is no ambiguity. An ambulance is a motor vehicle, as we saw above. The term "motor vehicle" may be vague, broad, or general, but it is not ambiguous. Let's skip absurdity for the moment.

Third, is there a scrivener's error? No. There is no typographical or cleri-cal error.

Fourth, is there a constitutional question that should be avoided? No. The ordinance does not raise constitutional questions.

Finally, is there absurdity? Ah ha! That must be it. But let's see if the ab-surdity doctrine is truly satisfied. How would you define absurdity? If you de-fine absurdity as "shocking to one's conscience," then this situation likely does not fit within your definition. If, instead, you define absurdity as meaning an "odd result" or "contrary to legislative intent," then this situation likely fits within your definition of absurdity. It seems highly unlikely that the city coun-cil intended to prohibit ambulances from coming into the park to rescue crit-ically ill people, especially if it is a very large park (it does include a lake after all). Moreover, the ordinance was enacted to promote safety in the park. Does-n't rescuing a heart attack victim promote safety? Of course, the statute is ab-surd because it leads to an odd result in this case that is likely contrary to legislative intent. But is it?

Remember that there is at least an argument that the absurdity doctrine should not apply to instances of specific absurdity. This is a case of specific, not general, absurdity because generally, the ordinance makes sense; keeping cars and trucks out of the park promotes pedestrian and bike-rider safety. So, generally, the statute is not absurd as applied in the majority of cases. But in this case, safety would be promoted by allowing the ambulance to come into the park. The city council did not make a drafting mistake, the council just did not think through every possible scenario. The absurdity doctrine should not apply.

However, many interpreters will cling to the absurdity doctrine for the simple reason that applying this ordinance to the ambulance driver seems counter-intuitive or odd, and absurdity is the only legitimate way, assuming we apply textualist methods, to avoid the ordinary meaning of this ordinance. While purpose and legislative history may help avoid this counter-intuitive result, textualists will not look at these extrinsic sources absent a reason. Absurdity is the only legitimate reason to avoid the ordinary meaning of the text in this case.

At bottom, if you self-identified as a textualist, you should have been willing to fine the ambulance driver and make the city council amend the ordinance to explicitly exclude ambulances (and any other vehicles you decided not to prosecute). If you self-identified as either of the other theorists, this analysis may have seemed very formalistic, simplistic, and unnecessary to you. Your turn is coming.

Checkpoints

- The language of the statute, including its words, grammar, and punctuation, is always the starting point for interpretation.

- Typically, courts presume that words in a statute have their "plain," or "ordinary," meaning. This presumption is known as the "Plain Meaning Rule."

- Ordinary meaning differs from definitional meaning. Dictionaries often assist a court with determining the definitional meaning.

- A word or phrase that has acquired a technical or unique meaning in a specific context has that meaning if the word or phrase is used in that context. This exception to the plain meaning rule is known as the "Technical Meaning Rule."

- The most common reason textualist judges look beyond the text for meaning is that the words are ambiguous, meaning that they are capable of being understood by reasonable people in more than one way.

- The "Golden Rule" or absurdity exception, which is an exception to the plain meaning rule, allows judges to look beyond the ordinary meaning of the text to extratextual sources when the statute would be absurd if interpreted as written.

- The Scrivener's Error exception to the plain meaning rule permits judges to correct obvious clerical or typographical errors. It is a very narrow exception.

- The Constitutional Avoidance Doctrine allows a court to avoid the ordinary meaning of the text when that meaning would raise serious questions about the constitutionality of the statute.

Chapter 5

Canons Based on Intrinsic Sources: Grammar and Punctuation

Roadmap

- Realize the limited role that grammar and punctuation play in interpretation.
- Understand the basic grammar and punctuation rule.
- Learn the Doctrine of Last Antecedent.
- Explore the rules relating to "and" and "or," singular and plural words, and masculine and feminine words.

A. Introduction to This Chapter

We continue looking at intrinsic sources in this chapter. To do so, we move from the most important source, the words, to a relatively unimportant source, grammar and punctuation. You will likely be surprised to learn of the surprisingly small role that grammar and punctuation play in interpretation. Hence, this is a relatively short chapter. Because of the small role they play, this chapter might have appeared near the end of the text; however, because grammar and punctuation are intrinsic sources, they are included early with the other intrinsic sources.

B. The General Punctuation & Grammar Rule

In England, "until 1849 statutes were enrolled upon parchment and enacted without punctuation. No punctuation appearing upon the rolls of Parliament such as was found in the printed statutes simply expressed the understanding of the printer." *Taylor v. Inhabitants of Caribou*, 67 A. 2 (Me. 1907). Because the "printer" or clerk added punctuation after the statute was enacted, English judges refused to consider punctuation when interpreting a statute.

In contrast, in the United States, Congress passes
bills with the punctuation included; hence, "[t]here
is no reason why punctuation, which is intended
to and does assist in making clear and plain the
meaning of all things else in the English language,
should be rejected in the case of the interpretation
of [American] statutes." *Id.* at 2. American legislators are presumed to know and apply common rules
of grammar and punctuation (syntactic rules). Because the plain meaning rule
presumes that legislators use grammar and punctuation appropriately, the general rule provides that punctuation and grammar matter unless the plain meaning rule suggests that they should be ignored. 2A Jabez Gridley Sutherland
Statutes and Statutory Construction § 47.15 at 346 (7th ed. 2007 Norman Singer ed.) ("[A]n act should be read as punctuated unless there is some
reason to do otherwise....").

> The plain meaning rule presumes that grammar and punctuation are relevant, unless there is a reason to ignore them.

Sometimes, there is a reason for ignoring grammar entirely. For example,
in *U.S. National Bank of Oregon v. Independent Insurance Agents of America,
Inc.*, 508 U.S. 439 (1993), the Supreme Court ignored the placement of quotation marks to conclude that a specific section of a statute had not been repealed. In so doing, the Court said,

> A statute's plain meaning must be enforced, of course, and the
> meaning of a statute will typically heed the commands of its punctu-
> ation. But a purported plain-meaning analysis based only on punctuation
> is necessarily incomplete and runs the risk of distorting a statute's true
> meaning.... No more than isolated words or sentences are punctua-
> tion alone a reliable guide for discovery of a statute's meaning. Statu-
> tory construction is a holistic endeavor and, at a minimum, must
> account for a statute's full text, language[,] as well as punctuation,
> structure, and subject matter.

Id. at 455.

When grammar and punctuation are used correctly and consistently, a
reader's understanding of written material is enhanced. However, not everyone uses grammar and punctuation correctly or consistently, not even legislators. Indeed, some syntactic rules are optional. Let's look at just such an
example: the serial comma rule (also known as the Oxford or Harvard comma
rule). The serial comma rule directs that when a series of items are separated
by a comma, each item is separate from the others. This is the rule, but not every
English writer follows it. Indeed, while the Chicago Manual of Style insists on
its use, the Associated Press considers it superfluous.

Let's see why the serial comma is important. Serial comma adherents use a comma to separate each item in a list (yellow, blue, red, and white), while non-serial comma adherents use a comma to separate all but the final two items in a list (yellow, blue, red and white). Someone who uses a serial comma might interpret the second phrase to include only three types of items: (1) those that are yellow, (2) those that are blue, and (3) those that are red and white. Yet the writer may have intended four types of items: (1) those that are yellow, (2) those that are blue, (3) those that are red, and (4) those that are white. Without knowing whether the writer is a serial comma user, the reader cannot know which meaning the writer intended. But when the comma is included, ambiguity disappears. Thus, because the serial comma aids clarity, legal writers should always use serial commas when writing.

> The serial comma should be used to separate each item in a list of three or more items.

[handwritten margin note: Oxford comma aids in getting rid of ambiguity]

Used incorrectly or inconsistently, grammar and punctuation can easily confuse a reader. For example, one familiar and fun example is the following: "With gratitude to my parents, the Pope and Mother Teresa." Without the serial comma after the word "Pope," the sentence suggests that the writer's parents are the Pope and Mother Teresa, rather than additional recipients of the writer's gratitude. Thus, punctuation is a fallible standard of meaning and is used only as a last resort in construing doubtful statutes. "Punctuation is a minor, and not a controlling, element in interpretation, and courts will disregard the punctuation of a statute, or re-punctuate it, if need be, to give effect to what otherwise appears to be its purpose and true meaning." *United States v. Ron Pair Enter., Inc.*, 489 U.S. 235, 250 (1989) (O'Connor, J., concurring) (internal quotation marks omitted). Hence, punctuation and grammar matter, but only when viewed within their textual context.

C. Special Punctuation Rules

1. Commas: The General Rule

Commas are particularly troubling in the English language—their use is "exceedingly arbitrary and indefinite." *United States v. Palmer*, (3 Wheat.) 610, 638 (1818) (separate opinion of Johnson, J.). Commas are troubling, in part, because comma rules are not consistently followed, yet their placement can be critical to meaning. Lynne Truss famously pointed out: "[A] panda eats shoots and leaves" means something very different from "a panda eats, shoots, and leaves." LYNNE TRUSS, EATS, SHOOTS & LEAVES THE ZERO TOLERANCE APPROACH TO

PUNCTUATION (2003). The two sentences vary by only two commas. But their meanings are entirely different. The phrase "the panda eats shoots and leaves" tells us what the panda has for dinner. The phrase "the panda eats, shoots, and leaves" tells us in what order the panda had his dinner, shot his companions, and left the party. Note that the second sentence again illustrates the importance of the serial comma rule that we saw above: when a comma separates a series of items, each item is distinct from the others.

In statutes, comma placement can be critical. For example, in *Peterson v. Midwest Security Insurance Co.*, 636 N.W.2d 727 (Wis. 2001), a recreatonal immunity statute provided immunity to owners of "real property and buildings, structures and improvements thereon, and waters of the state." *Id.* at 728. The plaintiff had fallen from a tree stand the defendant owned. The defendant, who did not own the land beneath the tree stand, argued that he was immune from the suit based on the recreational immunity statute. The plaintiff responded that the statute protected only owners of structures who also owned the real property on which the structure was located; thus the defendant was not immune from suit. The parties argument centered on the absence of a serial comma between the words "real property" and "buildings" in the statute; a comma should have been used if the legislature intendd to protect three, rather than two, categories of property.

Despite the absence of this comma (and the presence of the word "thereon"), the majority found the language to be clear and broadly interpreted the statute to provide immunity to (1) owners of real property, (2) owners of buildings, structures, and improvements on *any* real property, and (3) owners of the waters of the state. *Id.* at 578 & n.7. In ignoring the punctuation, the majority stated, "We decline to give the absence of a comma such interpretive significance." *Id.* at 575.

Noting that the drafter had regularly used a serial comma in other parts of the statute, the dissent questioned "whether the legislature's choice of punctuation in a statute could be dismissed so easily." *Id.* at 586 (Bradley, J., dissenting). The dissent observed that the missing comma and the word "thereon" allowed for four possible interpretations: Frist, the statute could be read as the majority had suggested. *Id.* at 588. Second, the statute could be read to provide immunity to (1) owners of real property along with the buildings, structures, and improvements *on that* real property, and (2) the waters of the state. *Id.* Third, the statute could be read to provide immunity to (1) owners of real property, (2) owners of buildings, structures, and improvements *on that* real property, and (3) owners of the waters of the state. *Id.* Fourth, and most consistently with the serial comma rule, the statute could be read to provide immunity to (1) owners of real property and buildings, (2) owners of structures, and improvements *on that* real property or buildings, and (3) owners of waters of the state. *Id.* (Note that the legislature could have avoided the ambiguity simply by inserting numbers before each category or by using semi-colons to separate each category.) Finding the language ambiguous, the dissent turned to the purpose of the statutue—encouraging property owners to allow *outdoor* recreational activities. In light of this purpose, the dissent concluded that the majority's interpretation—that owners of *any* building or structure were protected—was simply too broad even if that interpretation made sense in this case. *Id.* at 592.

2. Commas: *Reddendo Singula Singulis* & the Doctrine of Last Antecedent

Reddendo singula singulis means "rendering each to his own." This canon is appropriate when a complex sentence has multiple subjects and either multiple verbs or objects that are incorrectly placed. "Under the canon *reddendo singula singulis,* where a sentence contains several antecedents and several consequents they are to be read distributively. In other words, the words are to be applied to the subjects that seem most properly related by context and applicability." *In re Macke Intern. Trade, Inc.,* 370 B.R. 236, 251–52 (9th Cir. 2007) (internal quotation marks omitted).

By "rendering," or associating, each object or verb to its appropriate subject, the sentence is correctly understood. To illustrate, assume that a will provides, "I devise and bequeath my real property and personal property to State University." The term "devise" is more appropriate for real property, while the term "bequeath" is more appropriate for personal property. The sentence would have been clearer if written as follows: "I devise my real property and bequeath my personal property to State University." Notice that this second sentence is much longer, even while being clearer and more accurate. *Reddendo singula singulis* allows a reader to interpret the first sentence as if it were written like the second. In other words, the canon allows readers to ignore grammar and interpret the language as intended. To illustrate again, a contract might say "for money or other good consideration paid or given." *Reddendo singula singulis* tells us that the phrase really means "for money paid or other good consideration given."

The *Doctrine (or Rule) of Last Antecedent,* is a subset of *reddendo singular singulis.* Jabez Sutherland created the doctrine of last antecedent in 1891, when he wrote his famous treatise on interpreting contracts and statutes. He created the doctrine to help interpreters derive the meaning of contract clauses that contained multiple obligations or conditions. To understand the doctrine, you must first understand what an antecedent is. In grammar parlance, an "antecedent" is a word, phrase, or clause that is replaced by a pronoun or other substitute later (sometimes earlier) in the same or in a subsequent sentence. For example, in the sentence "*The professor asked the students whether they liked him*," the phrase "the students" is the antecedent of "they," and the "professor" is the antecedent of "him." Pronouns are generally understood to replace their closest antecedent. Thus, in the following sentence, "The professor asked the student whether he liked the reading," the pronoun "he" could be ambiguous because "he" could refer either to "the student" or "the professor." Most readers will assume that "he" refers to the last antecedent in the sentence: "the student." If the writer did not intend that meaning, the writer should repeat the noun "professor" rather than use the pronoun.

The doctrine of last antecedent builds on this assumption. Assume that rather than using a pronoun to replace an antecedent, the writer included a list of items with a modifying phrase. The doctrine states that when a qualifying word or phrase is used with a group of obligations or conditions, the qualifying words are presumed to modify only the condition or obligation that immediately precedes it (the "last antecedent"). For example, Article Two of the Federal Constitution provides, "No person except a natural born Citizen, or a Citizen of the United States, at the time of the Adoption of this Constitution, shall be eligible to the Office of President...." The phrase "at the time of the Adoption of this Constitution" is the modifying phrase. Pursuant to the doctrine, this qualifier modifies only the phrase "a Citizen of the United States." If the doctrine were otherwise—so that the phrase was understood to modify both "a natural born Citizen" and "a Citizen of the United States"—then the U.S. would have run out of presidential candidates long ago.

The doctrine further states that if a comma separates a modifying phrase from a list of prior antecedents, then the modifying phrase modifies each of the prior antecedents. Conversely, if there is no comma, then the modifying phrase modifies only the final antecedent. Thus, if a statute applied to "dentists, nurses, and doctors in a hospital," pursuant to the doctrine of last antecedent, the limiting phrase "in a hospital" would modify only "doctors" and not "dentists [and] nurses," unless a contrary legislative intent were found. In contrast, if the statute applied to "dentists, nurses, and doctors, in a hospital," the limiting phrase "in a hospital" would modify all of the professionals because a comma separates "in a hospital" from all

> The doctrine of last antecedent states that if a modifying phrase is separated by a comma from a list of prior items, then the modifying phrase modifies each item, not just the last item in the list.

three antecedents. Notice how one, simple comma can significantly affect meaning under this doctrine.

Importantly, this doctrine is not absolute (which is why the term "doctrine" is used here, rather than "rule"); it is meant to be an aid to interpretation, especially as it conflicts with general comma rules. *Lessee v. Irvine*, 3 U.S. (3 Dall.) 425, 444 (1799). The choice to put a comma between the qualifying phrase and the preceding list of antecedents is grammatically optional. *United States v. Bass*, 404 U.S. 336, 340 n.6. (1971). For this reason, judges will ignore the doctrine when applying it would result in an absurd result or would make no sense because, for example, the legislature has been unclear. Two cases illustrate what happens when a legislature is unclear about comma placement: *In Re Forfeiture of 1982 Ford Bronco*, 673 P.2d 1310 (N.M. 1983), and *State v. One 1990 Chevrolet Pickup*, 857 P.2d 44 (N.M. Ct. App. 1993). In both cases, the issue before the court was whether the owners of the vehicles had used their cars to transport drugs for the purpose of selling them. In the *Ford Bronco* case, the car owner argued that the sale had already taken place prior to the arrest so the transportation of the drugs could not have been for the purpose of selling them. In the *Chevrolet* case, the owner argued that the drugs were for personal use, not for later sale.

In the *Ford Bronco* case, the court interpreted a forfeiture statute that provided:

> [A]ll conveyances, including aircraft, vehicles or vessels, which are used, or intended for use, <u>to transport,</u> <u>or in any manner to facilitate the transportation</u> *for the purpose of sale of [drugs]....*

Ford Bronco, 673 P.2d at 1312 (quoting N.M. STAT. 30-31-34(D) (N.M. 1978)) (emphasis added). The issue was whether the phrase "for the purpose of sale" only modified the phrase "or in any manner to facilitate the transportation" or whether it also modified the phrase "to transport." Notice that (1) a comma separates these two phrases ("or in any manner to facilitate the transportation" and "to transport"), (2) the relevant language appears with the second phrase, and (3) there is no comma in the second phrase between "or in any manner to facilitate the transportation" and "for the purpose of sale." Applying the doctrine of last antecedent, the court found the absence of a comma between the phrases "or in any manner to facilitate the transportation" and "for the purpose of sale" to be fatal to the car owner's claim. *Id.* Transporting drugs alone without intending to sell the drugs satisfied the statute. In other words, the language "for the purpose of sale" applied only to the language following the comma after "to transport."

Unhappy with the result in the *Ford Bronco* case, the legislature amended the statute by deleting three commas: one between the words "used" and "or," one between the words "use" and "to," and one between the words "transport" and "or." The amended version provided:

> [A]ll conveyances, including aircraft, vehicles or vessels, which are used_ or intended for use "to transport" or in any manner to facilitate the transportation *for the purpose of sale of [drugs]*. . . .

Chevrolet Pickup, 857 P.2d at 46 (quoting N.M. STAT. 30-31-34(D) (1981)) (emphasis added). Underlines have been added to the excerpt so that you can see where the commas were removed. The issue before the court in the new case was the same as in the preceding case: What did the phrase "for the purpose of sale" modify? In this case, the choice was whether "for the purpose of sale" modified the phrase "are used or intended for use" or the phrase "in any manner to facilitate the transportation." *Id.* The City argued that the relevant language still modified only the latter phrase ("in any manner to facilitate the transportation") and that the removal of the commas was irrelevant because the legislature did not amend the statute in the way that the *Ford Bronco* case had recommended. *Id.* Remember that the *Ford Bronco* case held that the absence of a comma between "in any manner to facilitate the transportation" and "for the purpose of sale" made the qualifying phrase ("for the purpose of sale") apply only to the last antecedent following the comma ("in any manner to facilitate the transportation").

The *Chevrolet* court rejected the City's argument. Applying "a less technical version of the 'last antecedent rule,'" the court held that "for the purpose of sale" modified all three clauses connected by the term "or": (1) "conveyances . . . which are used . . . to transport [drugs]," (2) "conveyances . . . which are . . . intended for use to transport . . . [drugs]," and (3) "conveyances . . . which are used . . . in any manner to facilitate the transportation of [drugs]." *Id.* at 648. The court then held that the forfeiture statute applied only when a car owner possessed drugs and planned to sell them. Having drugs for personal use did not qualify.

While the court said it applied "a less technical version" of the doctrine, the reality is that the court simply ignored the doctrine. Assuming the legislature wanted to criminalize the actions of those persons trying to sell drugs, the statute was poorly written initially. And the legislature's subsequent decision to remove all commas did not fix this error. If the legislature wanted the forfeiture statute to apply only when a defendant intended to sell drugs, the legislature should have written the statute as directed by the *Ford Bronco* court and add one comma. Instead the legislature removed all the commas it could find. Likely, the *Chevrolet* court recognized that the legislature simply did not understand the doctrine of last antecedent and its relationship to commas.

The court, thus, interpreted the statute to further the legislative intent to change the holding in the *Ford Bronco* case.

Here is another, well-known example. To make the issue a little clearer, the actual statute has been modified. Assume that a statute provided "that alcohol shall not be sold between eleven at night and six in the morning, nor on Sunday *except if the licensee is a hotel.*" The relevant phrase in this statute is in italics. According to the doctrine of last antecedent, the phrase "except if the licensee is a hotel" should only qualify the phrase "on Sunday" because there is no comma between "Sunday" and "except." The highlighted phrase should not be understood to qualify the phrase "between eleven at night and six in the morning" at all. Thus, pursuant to the doctrine of last antecedent, hotels can sell alcohol on Sundays, but not between 11:00 PM and 6:00 AM. This mock statute is similar to the statute at issue in *Commonwealth v. Kelly,* 58 N.E. 691 (Mass. 1900). In that case, the court followed the doctrine of last antecedent and held that the statute did not allow the defendants, presumably hotel owners, to sell alcohol after eleven. In addition to the doctrine of last antecedent, the court found the title of the Act, "An act to prohibit the sale of spirituous and intoxicating liquors between the hours of eleven at night and six in the morning" and the purpose of the Act further supported this interpretation. *Id.*

What if a drafter would prefer to have the qualifying phrase apply to all the preceding antecedents? As noted above, all a drafter would have to do to have a phrase modify all the preceding nouns is add a comma between the modifier and the last antecedent. "Evidence that a qualifying phrase is supposed to apply to all antecedents instead of only to the immediately preceding one may be found in the fact that it is separated from the antecedents by a comma." 2A JABEZ GRIDLEY SUTHERLAND STATUTES AND STATUTORY CONSTRUCTION § 47.33 at 491-92 (7th ed. 2007 Norman Singer ed.). Thus, if the Massachusetts's statute had provided "that alcohol shall not be sold between eleven at night and six in the morning, nor on Sunday, *except if the licensee is a hotel,*" then the qualifying phrase "except if the licensee is a hotel" would modify both the phrase "between eleven at night and six in the morning" and the phrase "on Sunday." A hotel could sell alcohol all the time, with no exceptions. Every other establishment would not be able to sell alcohol either on Sundays or on weekdays between 11:00 PM and 6:00 AM. The addition of one simple comma between the words "Sunday" and "except" would completely change the interpretation.

As textualism has gained currency and the linguistic canons have gained favor, this doctrine has become more of a hard-and-fast rule than a rule of thumb. In 2003, Justice Scalia brought the doctrine to the forefront of judicial attention. In *Barnhart v. Thomas,* 540 U.S. 20 (2003), a social security claimant

appealed the denial of her application for disability insurance benefits and supplemental security income on the ground that the administrative law judge
should have taken into account that opportunities to perform her previous
work no longer existed in significant numbers within the national economy. The
statute provided:

> An individual shall be determined to be under a disability only if his
> physical or mental impairment or impairments are of such severity
> that he is *not only unable to do his previous work* but cannot, consid-
> ering his age, education, and work experience, engage in *any other
> kind of substantial gainful work which exists in the national economy.* ...

42 U.S.C. § 423(d)(2)(A) (2006) (emphasis added). Writing for the majority,
Justice Scalia applied the doctrine of last antecedent to hold that the clause
"which exists in the national economy" modified only the phrase "any other kind
of substantial gainful work." Justice Scalia acknowledged that "this rule is not
an absolute and can assuredly be overcome by other indicia of meaning," but
that "construing a statute in accord with the rule is quite sensible as a matter
of grammar." *Barnhart*, 540 U.S. at 26. More interestingly, he provided the
following, humorous example:

> Consider, for example, the case of parents who, before leaving their
> teenage son alone in the house for the weekend, warn him, "You will
> be punished if you throw a party or engage in any other activity that
> damages the house." If the son nevertheless throws a party and is
> caught, he should hardly be able to avoid punishment by arguing that
> the house was not damaged. The parents proscribed (1) a party, and
> (2) any other activity that damages the house. As far as appears from
> what they said, their reasons for prohibiting the home-alone party
> may have had nothing to do with damage to the house-for instance,
> the risk that underage drinking or sexual activity would occur. And even
> if their only concern was to prevent damage, it does not follow from
> the fact that the same interest underlay both the specific and the gen-
> eral prohibition that proof of impairment of that interest is required
> for both. The parents, foreseeing that assessment of whether an activity
> had in fact "damaged" the house could be disputed by their son, might
> have wished to preclude all argument by specifying and categorically
> prohibiting the one activity—hosting a party—that was most likely
> to cause damage and most likely to occur.

Id. at 27–28. Importantly, *Barnhart* represents the first time a Justice of the Supreme Court chose to explain the doctrine's application in some detail, rather than simply apply or not apply it. But has Justice Scalia automated application of the doctrine too much? Admittedly, he is likely correct in his interpretation of the teenager admonishment above; however, consider the following example:

> [A] law firm partner instructs her associate to review a client's file?"for emails or documents written by the CEO." Although [the sentence is] ambiguous, an astute associate would not apply the Rule, but would read the modifying clause, ?"written by the CEO," as modifying both the first and last antecedent and search for both emails written by the CEO and documents written by the CEO.

Jeremy L. Ross, *A Rule of Last Resort: A History of the Doctrine of the Last Antecedent in the United State Supreme Court*, 39 Sw. L Rev. 325 (2010). In *Jama v. Immigration & Customs Enforcement*, 543 U.S. 335 (2005), Justices Scalia and Souter debated whether the doctrine should apply to a statute that contained a number of itemized subsections when only the final subsection included the language at issue. Because each subsection ended with a period and the qualifying language was contained only in the final subsection, Justice Scalia, writing for the majority, applied the doctrine of last antecedent to limit the qualifier to apply only to the final subsection. *Id.* at 344. Justice Souter disagreed with the majority's decision to apply the doctrine, finding instead that other indicia of legislative intent militated in favor of applying the modifying clause to each subsection. *Id.* at 355–57 (Souter, J., dissenting).

Thus, as with all the canons but even more so with this canon, the doctrine of last antecedent must be used, not robotically, but with common sense and an understanding of context. Indeed, one might say that to call it a "rule" as many judges do is, at best, "oxymoronic." Ross, *supra*, at 336.

D. Special Grammar Rules

We turn now from punctuation rules to the general grammar rule and its exceptions. Keep in mind that the same two general rules apply: (1) grammar matters, unless the plain meaning rule suggests that it should be ignored, and (2) courts presume that legislatures use grammar accurately and consistently. For example, in *Robinson v. City of Lansing*, 782 N.W.2d 171 (2010), grammar was dispositive. In that case, the plaintiff tripped on a sidewalk, fracturing her wrist and requiring surgery. Both parties agreed that the portion of the sidewalk where she tripped was less than two inches above the depressed portion. The Michigan legislature had codified a common law rule, known as the two-inch rule, which relieved municipalities of liability when the difference in a sidewalk was less than two inches. The statute provided:

> (1) Except as otherwise provided by this section, a municipal corporation has no duty to repair or maintain, and is not liable for injuries arising from, a portion of *a county highway* outside of the improved portion of the highway designed for vehicular travel, including a sidewalk, trailway, crosswalk, or other installation....
> (2) A discontinuity defect of less than 2 inches creates a rebuttable inference that the municipal corporation maintained the sidewalk, trailway, crosswalk, or other installation outside of the improved portion of *the highway* designed for vehicular travel in reasonable repair....

Id. at 178 (quoting Mich. Comp Laws § 691.1402a) (emphasis added). The plaintiff sued, claiming that the City had failed to maintain the sidewalk in reasonable repair. In response, the City raised the two-inch rule as an affirmative defense. The issue for the court was whether subsection 2 of the statute — which created a rebuttable inference that a discontinuity defect of less than two inches in a sidewalk meant that the municipality maintained the sidewalk in reasonable repair — applied to sidewalks adjacent to state highways or only to sidewalks adjacent to county highways. The court focused on the definite article "the" preceding the word "highway" in subsection 2 to conclude that the highways referred to in subsection 2 were "county highways," which were first identified in subsection 1 and were not highways "in general." *Id.* at 179-80. Had the legislature used the indefinite article "a," the result may well have been different.

Thus, courts generally presume that legislatures use grammar appropriately, and grammar can be outcome determinative. Let's explore some specific grammar issues that you may face; some of these cases follow this general rule while others specifically do not.

1. The Meaning of "And" & "Or"

Two simple words that are typically used to connect items and phrases in sentences can be critical. These words are "and" and "or." Generally, they mean different things. The word "or" means *either.* In contrast, the word "and" means *all.* But sometimes the word "and" is used to mean *either* and the word "or" is used to mean *all*. For example, consider the phrase: "Would you like cream *or* sugar?" Surely, you could choose both cream and sugar, or you could choose neither cream or sugar. In the last sentence, the writer used the word "or" to mean none, one, the other, or both. Similarly, sometimes the word "and" is used to mean either: consider the phrase, "She was forced to choose between getting gas *and* making it to class on time." In this sentence, "and" does not mean both; it means one or the other; either she would have time to get gas and be late for class or she could chose not to get gas and arrive at class on time. When drafting, it can be difficult to know whether to use "and" or "or." To counteract this conundrum, many legal drafters have resorted to using the imprecise wording "and/or;" a practice that should be discouraged as imprecise and lazy.

When legislators draft statutes, they generally do not use "and/or." Instead, they use the conjunctive "and" when two or more requirements must be fulfilled to comply with a statute. Where failure to comply with any one requirement would be fatal, the disjunctive "or" is generally used. 1A Jabez Gridley Sutherland Statutes and Statutory Construction (7th ed. 2009 Norman Singer ed.). Ordinarily, "and" and "or" are not interchangeable in statutes. But because the use of these two terms baffles legislators as much as other legal writers, judges will construe the word "and" to mean "or" whenever such a conversion is mandated to effectuate the obvious intention of the legislature. Often, just as in both examples above, textual or other context can help determine which meaning was intended.

In some cases, however, discerning whether "and" truly means "and" can be difficult. In *Comptroller of Treasury v. Fairchild Industries, Inc.*, 493 A.2d 341, 343–44 (Md. 1985), the court rejected the state's argument that "and" meant "or." In that case, a taxpayer incurred a net operating loss that it was legally entitled to "carry back" to a prior year. In essence, the taxpayer would get a refund on taxes it had already paid because it incurred a loss in a subsequent year. The issue was whether the taxpayer was also entitled to receive the interest on the money paid that was then refunded. *Id.* at 342. A state tax statute required that interest be paid on income tax refunds except where the tax, as originally paid, was due to "a mistake or error on the part of the taxpayer *and* not attributable to the State...." *Id.* at 343. The state argued that the word "and" in this statute really meant "or." In other words, the state argued that the conditions in the statute were disjunctive: so long as an error was not the state's fault, the state did not have to pay the taxpayer interest on the refund regardless of whether the taxpayer made the error. *Id.* Rejecting that argument, the court said that there was nothing in the statute or legislative history to suggest that "and" meant anything other than what it normally means in a conjunctive sense. *Id.* Thus, unless the taxpayer made an error *and* that error was the state's fault, the taxpayer was entitled to interest. In this case, the taxpayer had not made an error.

In summary, generally "and" and "or" are understood as grammar intended; however, occasionally, they are not.

2. Singular & Plural

Unlike the canon above, the canons relating to number usage do not follow the general grammar rule; just the opposite is true. For ease of drafting, statutes are typically written in the singular. But for statutory interpretation, a legislature's use of the singular is assumed to include the plural, and the legislature's use of the plural is assumed to include the singular. The *United States Code* provides, "In determining the meaning of any act or resolution of Congress, unless the context otherwise indicates, words importing the singular include and apply to several persons, parties, or things; words importing the plural include the singular...." 1 U.S.C.

> A legislature's use of the singular includes the plural and the legislature's use of the plural includes the singular.

§ 1 (2012). Many states have similar statutes, for example, Minnesota and Pennsylvania. MINN. STAT. § 645.08(2) (2012); 1 PA. CONS. STAT. §§ 1921–28 (2012).

In *Homebuilders Association v. Scottsdale*, 925 P.2d 1359 (Ariz. Ct. App. 1996), the court articulated the reason why courts ignore grammar in this instance. "The historical purpose of construing plural and singular nouns and verbs interchangeably is to avoid requiring the legislature to use such expressions as 'person or persons,' 'he, she, or they,' and 'himself or themselves.' Under this principle, the plural has often been held to apply to the singular in a statute, absent evidence of contrary legislative intent." *Id.* at 1366. In that case, the court interpreted the words "council men" to include the singular "council man." The statute at issue had provided that the number of signatures required to place a referendum petition on the ballot would be determined based on the percentage of those voting at the city election at which "the mayor or council *men* were chosen last." *Id.* at 1364 (quoting ARIZ. REV. STAT. § 19-142(a)) (emphasis added). After finding the statute ambiguous, the court applied this canon and held that the signature requirement should be calculated as a percentage of those voting at the last city election, even if only one council man was elected. *Id.* at 1368.

As with the other canons of statutory construction, a judge will ignore this canon when the court finds a contrary legislative intent. For example, in *Van Horn v. William Blanchard Co.*, 438 A.2d 552 (N.J. 1981), the court rejected the interpretation that would have resulted from application of this canon. In that case, the court analyzed New Jersey's Comparative Negligence Act and held that the singular "person" did not include the plural "persons." *Id.* at 554. Despite the existence of a statutory directive urging that "any word importing the singular number ... shall be understood to include and apply to several persons or parties as well as to one person or party," the majority rejected the plaintiff's argument that the word "person" should include the plural "persons." *Id.* at 554–55. The context, according to the court, illustrated that the legislature had intended the singular to be used in this specific situation; thus, the directive was inapposite. Perhaps the court accurately discerned the legislative intent, perhaps not; in direct response to this case, the New Jersey legislature promptly amended the statute to reflect the interpretation the plaintiff advocated and the majority rejected, that person and persons were both covered. N.J. STAT. ANN. § 2A:15-5.3 (West 2012).

3. Words with Masculine, Feminine, & Neuter Meaning

The third grammar canon relates to masculine, feminine, and neuter words; it too defies typical grammar rules. Until the 1980s or so, statutes were generally written using the masculine gender because the masculine pronoun was used as a "generic" pronoun reference. Legislators did not intend to refer only to men when using the masculine pronoun; rather, this grammatical practice was just accepted as a language norm of the time. Thus, for statutory interpretation purposes, the masculine pronoun is generally interpreted to include the feminine and the neuter. For example, 1 U.S.C. § 2 (2012), provides, "words importing the masculine gender include the feminine as well." Most states have similar provisions. "Words used in the masculine gender may include the feminine and the neuter." OR. REV. STAT. 174.110(2) (2012).

> A legislature's use of the masculine gender includes the feminine and neuter.

A simple application of the canon can be seen in *Commonwealth. v. Henninger*, 25 Pa. 3d 625 (Pa. Ct. Com. Pl. 1981). In that case, the court applied the gender canon when it held that females can commit statutory rape. The statute provided, "A person who is 18 years of age or older commits statutory rape, a felony of the second degree, when *he* engages in sexual intercourse with another person not his spouse who is less than 14 years of age." *Id.* at 626 (citing 18 PA. CONS. STAT. § 3122) (emphasis added). The female defendant argued that the gender-based language "he" demonstrated an "intent on the part of the legislators to protect only women." *Id.* Citing the gender canon, the court rejected the defendant's argument. *Id.*

Notice that the statutes above only allow for the masculine to include the feminine and neuter, but not the feminine to include the masculine and neuter. Remember that the canon exists because the masculine pronoun was thought to be gender-neutral. Should the canon be used interchangeably such that the feminine pronoun should be understood to include the masculine? Perhaps, but in *In Re Compensation of Williams*, the court refused to interpret the word "woman" to include men. 635 P.2d 384, 386 (Or. Ct. App. 1981), *aff'd,* 653 P.2d 970 (Or. 1982). The statute at issue in that case provided that an unmarried woman was entitled to compensation when the man with whom the woman was cohabitating was accidentally injured. *Id.* at 385 n.1 (citing OR. REV. STAT. § 174.110(2)). In the case, it was a woman who was injured and a man who sought compensation. The court reasoned that the word "woman" in the statute did not include men because "woman" was not a word used "in the *masculine* gender." *Id.* at 386. Because Oregon's gender directive (quoted above) allowed masculine words to be interpreted to include the feminine, but not feminine words to be interpreted to include the masculine, the court held that the canon was inapplicable. *Id.* However, note that reading a gender limitation into a statute might raise a constitutional question regarding whether the statute violates equal protection. To avoid the constitutional question that would be raised (See Chapter 13), a court might apply the canon despite the gender specific nature of the statute.

4. Mandatory & Discretionary

While the preceding canons did not follow grammar usage, this last canon does. One issue that may arise when a court interprets a statute is whether the action at issue is required or allowed, in other words, are the statutory requirements mandatory or discretionary. To resolve this question, courts will most commonly examine the form of the verb used in a statute. For example, a court will look to see whether something may, shall, must, or should be done. The legislature's verb choice is the most important consideration in determining whether a statute is mandatory. Ordinarily, "may" is considered discretionary, "shall" is considered mandatory, "must" is considered mandatory when a condition precedent is present, and "should" is considered discretionary. *Daniel v. United Nat'l Bank*, 505 S.E.2d 711 (W. Va. 1998).

When the legislature uses "shall" or "must," judges generally interpret those words as excluding judicial or executive discretion to take into account equity or policy. *Escondido Mut. Water Co. v. LaJolla Indians*, 466 U.S. 765, 772 (1984) ("The mandatory nature of the language chosen by Congress [shall] appears to require that the Commission include the Secretary's conditions in the license even if it disagrees with them."). Sometimes, though, "shall" can mean *may*:

Ordinarily, the use of the word 'shall' in a statute carries with it the presumption that it is used in the imperative rather than in the directory sense. But this is not a conclusive presumption. Both the character and context of the legislation are controlling.... The mandatory sense to the word 'shall' should not be given, if by so doing the door to miscarriages of justice should be opened.

Jersey City v. State Bd. of Tax Appeals, 43 A.2d 799, 803-04 (N.J. Sup. Ct. 1945) (refusing to interpret "shall" in a statute to be mandatory); *Cobb Cnty. v. Robertson*, 724 S.E.2d 478, 479 (Ga. App. 2012) ("Even though the word 'shall' is generally construed as mandatory, it need not always be construed in that fashion"), *cert. denied* (Sept. 10, 2012).

Conversely, "may" sometimes means *shall* or *must*:

The word "may" generally denotes a discretionary provision while the use of the word "shall" suggests that the provision is mandatory. However, when the context indicates otherwise, "may" can have the effect of "must" or "shall".

Fink v. City of Detroit, 333 N.W.2d 376, 379 (Mich. Ct. App. 1983) (holding that "may" was mandatory) (internal citations omitted).

One way to determine whether a statute is mandatory or discretionary is to see if the statute provides a penalty for the failure to comply with its terms. If it does, the terms are likely mandatory; if not, the terms are likely discretionary. *Christian Disposal, Inc. v. Village of Eolia*, 895 S.W.2d 632, 634 (Mo. Ct. App. 1995) ("Although 'shall' when used in a statute will usually be interpreted to command the doing of what is specified, the term is 'frequently used indiscriminately and courts have not hesitated to hold that legislative intent will prevail over common meaning.'"). When the meaning cannot be ascertained from the text alone, judges may look to other sources to discern the legislative intent.

E. Mastering This Topic

Return to the hypothetical ordinance provided in Chapter 1 on page 9. Assuming you think the term "motor vehicles" is ambiguous as applied to the various hypotheticals and especially the ambulance hypothetical, does the grammar or punctuation of the statute help resolve the ambiguity? Section 2 of the Ordinance provides:

(2) No cars, motorcycles, or other motor vehicles may enter or remain in Pioneer Park, except as provided in section 3 hereof.

You might be tempted to turn to the doctrine of last antecedent for the language "may enter or remain in Pioneer Park," for a comma does not separate it from the words "cars" and "motorcycles." Thus, you might incorrectly conclude that the phrase does not apply to these items. You would be incorrect because the phrase "may enter or remain in Pioneer Park" is not a modifying phrase needing one or more antecedents. Rather it is the predicate (or verb portion) of the sentence. The doctrine does not apply to verb phrases.

But wait, there is a modifying clause, can you identify it? The phrase "except as provided in section 3 hereof" modifies the items preceding it. There is a comma between the final item "other motor vehicles" and the modifier "except as provided in section 3 hereof." The doctrine of last antecedent tells us that the modifier would apply to all of the antecedents, cars, motorcycles, and other motor vehicles. Here is the exception:

> (3) Motor vehicles may be used by authorized public groups:
>   a. in maintaining Pioneer Park, and
>   b. in placing barricades for parades, concerts, or other entertainment in Pioneer Park.

None of the exceptions apply in the case of the ambulance, so the doctrine of last antecedent may or may not have helped you resolve the ambiguity.

Is there any other relevant grammar or punctuation issues? You might have noticed that the plural form of vehicle was used. You now know that the plural includes the singular, so it is irrelevant that only one ambulance was used. Likely, you knew this intuitively, but the grammar canon helps you confirm your intuition.

Ultimately, the grammar and punctuation in this statute provide little aid to interpretation, which is often true. As mentioned at the start of this chapter, grammar and punctuation play a very small role in interpretation. Thus, grammar and punctuation matter, but they matter substantially less than the words of the statute because grammar and punctuation are not used consistently or even correctly by English writers and legislators. In the next chapter, we move to a more important player in this area, the linguistic canons.

Checkpoints

- The general grammar and punctuation rule provides that both grammar and punctuation matter unless clear legislative intent suggests that they should be ignored.

- In statutes, comma placement can be critical. Commas are troubling, in part, because comma rules are not consistently followed. Yet, their placement can be critical to meaning.

- The Doctrine of the Last Antecedent directs that words and phrases modify only the immediately preceding noun or noun phrase in a list of items. All a drafter need do to have a phrase modify all the preceding nouns is add a comma between the modifier and the last antecedent.

- Generally, the word "and" has a conjunctive meaning, while the word "or" has a disjunctive meaning. However, when context dictates, courts will interchange these two words.

- For ease of drafting, statutes are typically written in the singular. But for statutory interpretation, the legislature's use of the singular is assumed to include the plural, and the legislature's use of the plural is assumed to include the singular.

- Also for ease of drafting, the masculine pronoun is generally interpreted to include the feminine or neuter. The feminine pronoun may be interpreted to include the male or neuter.

Chapter 6

Canons Based on Intrinsic Sources: The Linguistic Canons

Roadmap

- Discover that the linguistic canons are simply rules reflecting commonly understood agreements about word and grammar usage.

- Learn *in pari materia*: both the whole act and whole code aspects.

- Learn the linguistic cannons including the presumption of consistent usage and meaningful variation, the rule against surplusage, *noscitur a sociis*, *ejusdem generis*, and *expressio unius est exclusio alterius*.

A. Introduction to This Chapter

In this chapter, we continue our exploration of the text and turn to another intrinsic source. Here, you will learn that one of the first sources judges turn to after finding ambiguity or absurdity is the linguistic canons. These canons reflect commonly understood rules about the use of language. Because many of the canons have Latin names, they seem erudite. In reality, these canons reflect the common rules native to all English speakers and are, for the most part, quite simple, despite their scary names.

B. The Linguistic Canons: Our Latin Friends

The linguistic canons, or rules of thumb, help judges draw inferences from the words of a statute. These canons are not hard and fast rules, but rather guides or presumptions to which judges turn to further help them discern the legislative intent from the words used, or if textualists, to determine the public meaning of the words used. The linguistic canons simply reflect shared assumptions about the way English speakers and writers use language and grammar. *State v. Peters*, 263 Wis. 2d 475, 491 (2003) (Abrahamson, C.J., concurring) ("The canon [*ejusdem generis*] is an 'intrinsic aid' that is germane to a textualist approach to statutory interpretation; that is, it is both compatible with and necessary to the plain meaning rule....").

These canons were the bedrock of early Anglo-American statutory interpretation, and many early treatises were organized around these canons. Although the canons fell out of favor with the federal courts when purposivism edged out textualism as the preferred statutory interpretation approach, the linguistic canons remained important to state court judges. Indeed, many states have codified these canons. For example, both Minnesota and Pennsylvania have statutory construction acts that codify some of these various canons. MINN. STAT. ANN. §645 (West 2012); 1 PA. CONS. STAT. ANN. §§1921–28 (West 2012). Today, the linguistic canons have enjoyed a comeback with the reemergence of textualism.

Most commonly, the linguistic canons are applied either to help identify ordinary meaning or after the plain meaning rule has failed to resolve ambiguity. In particular, the textualists like these canons because, like dictionaries, these canons appear to be a neutral source of meaning. Moreover, textualists believe that turning to the linguistic canons early in the process will help further the drafting process. If courts apply the canons predictably and if legislators know how courts will apply the canons, then legislators can more easily enact text that will be interpreted as intended. The linguistic canons serve a communication function, if you will, ones that aid predictability.

These canons presume common understandings regarding how people write. Some of the canons are merely weak presumptions that act as tie-breakers (e.g., *noscitur a sociis*). Others are stronger presumptions that regularly inform meaning (e.g., *in pari materia*). While rigid application of these canons can make interpretation somewhat mechanical and simplistic, judges love them anyway.

These canons should be used cautiously for many reasons. First, and most importantly, using the linguistic canons makes sense only when both the drafter and the interpreter are aware of them, understand them, and correctly use them. If a drafter is unaware of a particular canon and did not use it while drafting, then it makes little sense to apply that canon to that drafter's final product. In truth, legislatures rarely consciously think about these canons while drafting; thus, it makes little sense to apply them religiously.

Second, the canons are presumptions based on how *ordinary* English writers use language. The canons may be unsuitable in legal drafting because *legal* writers are trained to write differently than ordinary English writers. Legal writing is replete with redundancy and wordiness. Legal writers are less concerned with repeating themselves than with covering all their bases (think of "cease and desist" and "will and testament"). For example, legal writers learn to include a comprehensive list of items with a general catch-all phrase to ensure that no circumstance is omitted or overlooked. Yet, one of the linguistic canons—the rule against surplusage—directs that every word in a list should have independent meaning. Here, the writers' legal training and the linguistic canon directly conflict; legal writers expect that their drafting may have overlap; indeed, legal drafters prefer such overlap to inadvertent omission.

Third, the canons presume that the legislature carefully considered every word in the statute and included each word for a reason. Hence, the presumption is that the linguistic canons should apply because the legislature chose its words carefully. The reality: Legislatures are far more concerned with the big picture than with the small details. Moreover, legislation is the result of compromise. Fighting over one word could halt the enactment process entirely. Thus, legislators cannot be concerned with the exact wording of a statute, or their job would never be done. Rather, each legislator must choose his or her battles.

Fourth, the linguistic canons mask subjectivity. The canons are appealing, in part, because, like dictionaries, they appear to offer a neutral way of resolving the meaning of language. In other words, these canons provide the appearance of neutrality for decision-making. They "do not, on their face at least, express any policy preference, but simply purport to be helpful ways of divining the nature and limits of what the drafters of the legislation were trying to achieve." David L. Shapiro, *Continuity and Change in Statutory Interpretation*, 67 N.Y.U. L. Rev. 921, 927 (1992).

But this apparent objectivity simply masks subjectivity. The linguistic canons, like every method of interpretation, are merely rebuttable presumptions. As such, they can be manipulated to produce a desired result. Liberal justices use the canons to further liberal agendas, while conservative justices use the canons to further conservative agendas. "[T]he canons [do not have] an independent, constraining effect on the Justices' decisionsmaking—in particular, they are not functioning as a set of overarching 'neutral principles' in the hands of either liberal or conservative Justices." James J. Brudney & Corey Ditsler, *Canons of Construction and the Elusive Search for Neutral Reasoning*, 58 Vand. L. Rev. 1, 55-56 (2005). In 1949, Professor Karl Llewellyn tried to show that for every canon of construction (the "thrust") there is an equal, but opposing canon (the "parry"). Karl N. Llewellyn, *Remarks on the Theory of Appellate Decision and the Rules of Cannon about How Statutes are to be Construed*, 3 Vand. L. Rev. 395, 401 (1949). His point was to debunk the myth that application of the canons was an unbiased method of interpretation; judges can easily use the canons to mask the real reason for deciding a case in a particular way.

Perhaps Llewellyn's critique was overstated. The linguistic canons merely set forth *presumptions* about statutory meaning. The very nature of a presumption is that it can always be overcome by other evidence; presumptions are rebuttable. This ability to be rebutted allows judges to use discretion when applying the canons, which, of course makes their application somewhat unpredictable. Llewellyn's "parrys" identify the circumstances when the "thrusts," or presumptions, should fail.

There is another subjectivity issue. Often, more than one canon may apply. When that happens, which canon controls? There is no hierarchy within the linguistic canons; thus, selecting which canon to argue may simply depend on which better leads you to your client's preferred outcome. While there is no hierarchy, the choice of one canon can be outcome determinative. Often, the canon that furthers the interpreter's choice of meaning is the one selected. One famous example involving multiple, conflicting canons is the case of *Babbitt v. Sweet Home Chapter of Communities*, 515 U.S. 687 (1995). In that case, the majority and dissenting justices used many of the linguistic canons, including *in pari materia*; *noscitur a sociis*; *ejusdem generis*; *expressio unius*; the rule against surplusage; and the presumption of consistent usage. The majority and dissent focused on different canons to reach their desired outcome.

The issue in the case was whether the Secretary of the Interior could promulgate a regulation making it unlawful for anyone to significantly modify the habitat of an endangered species. *Id.* at 690 (citing 16 U.S.C. § 1532(9)(a)(1)). The Endangered Species Act of 1973 prohibited anyone from "tak[ing]" any endangered species. The Act further defined "take" as "to harass, *harm*, pursue, hunt, shoot, wound, kill, trap, capture, or collect, or to attempt to engage in any such conduct." *Id.* at 691 (citing 16 U.S.C. § 1532(19)) (emphasis added). The Secretary interpreted the word "harm" to include "significant habitat modification or degradation where it actually kills or injures wildlife...." *Id.* (citing 50 C.F.R. § 17.3 (1994)). The majority found the Secretary's interpretation reasonable using *in pari materia* (which allows a court to look at the statute in its entirety) and the rule against surplusage (which suggests that every word in a statute must have independent meaning). *Id.* at 701–02.

In contrast, the dissent focused on the other words in the statute surrounding the word "harm" (*noscitur a sociis*) to conclude that Congress intended the word "harm" to mean "affirmative conduct intentionally directed against a particular animal or animals." *Id.* at 720–21 (Scalia, J., dissenting). The dissent concluded that, because the Secretary's definition included non-affirmative conduct, such as the logging targeted in the case, the definition was unreasonable. *Id.* What is interesting about this case is that both the majority and dissent specifically rejected the other side's argument that the identified canon was controlling. For example, the majority criticized the dissent for "denying [the word "harm" of any] independent meaning." *Id.* at 688. The dissent accused the majority of ignoring the realities of legal drafting. *Id.* at 721 (Scalia, J., dissenting).

For all these reasons, the linguistic canons should be used with common sense and a realization that lawyers often draft differently than the canons presume. The canons are, for the most part, presumptions, gap-fillers, and tie-breakers. When there is better evidence of legislative intent, the canons should take a back seat. Also, because the canons counter each other, it is important to remember that, as a litigant, you will win your case based on the underlying equities, not based on a canon. Like the theories in Chapter 2, the linguistic canons simply give you the language to *help* the judge rule in your client's favor once the judge has made up his or her mind. In other words, it is still up to you to make the judge *want* to rule in your client's favor.

Below are the contemporary linguistic canons. While other canons may have been used in the past, they are less common today and have not been included for that reason.

C. The Contemporary Linguistic Canons: Explained

1. *In Pari Materia*

The most popular and least controversially used linguistic canon is *in pari materia*. Unlike the linguistic canons we will cover next, *in pari materia* is not a canon about how words are used, but because it has a Latin name, it is generally included with the other linguistic canons. *In pari materia* is a canon that identifies the statutory material that judges may legitimately look at to discern meaning or fill gaps. *See, e.g., Fla. Dep't of Highway Safety & Motor Vehicles v. Hernandez*, 74 So. 3d 1070, 1076 (Fla. 2011) (noting that a statute that allowed the state to suspend the driver's license of any person who refused to submit to a "lawful" breathalyzer test must be read *in pari materia* with a different statute that defined the parameters of a lawful breath-alcohol test).

This canon answers the question of which parts of a bill, statute, or code are relevant to meaning. As such, the canon works in tandem with the other linguistic canons. So, for example, a judge might very well apply the canon of consistent usage (that identical words should have identical meanings) to interpret a word that appears in more than one section of a bill, even though only the one section of the bill is applicable to the facts before the court. Such was the case in *Mohasco Corp. v. Silver*, 447 U.S. 807 (1980). In that case, the Supreme Court held that Congress intended the word "filed" to have the same meaning in subsections (c) and (e) of section 706 of the Civil Rights Act of 1964; subsection (e) was the only subsection at issue in the case. *Id.* at 809. As you can see from this example, *in pari materia* is the canon that allowed the Court to look for meaning in language beyond the narrow language being interpreted. Be aware that many judges (and academics) incorrectly equate *in pari materia* with the presumption of consistent usage. It is true, they work in harmony, but they are different. One identifies the material to be considered (*in pari materia*); the other explains what to do with that material (presumption of consistent usage).

"*In pari materia*" in Latin means "part of the same material." This canon has two aspects—the whole act aspect and the whole code aspect. First, the *whole act* aspect directs that a section of a legislative act should not be interpreted in isolation. Rather, the entire act is relevant. Second, the *whole code* (or related acts) aspect directs that new statutes should be interpreted harmoniously with existing statutes concerning the same subject. *In pari materia* promotes coherence. Both aspects of *in pari materia* together attempt to ensure internal consistency across acts, statutes, related statutes, and even the code as a whole. Let's look at each aspect in turn, starting with the less controversial aspect: the whole act aspect.

a. The Whole Act Aspect of In Pari Materia

When a bill is enacted, the entire act is not simply placed in serum (in order) in the code; rather, sections of the act are codified (placed into the code) where appropriate. The *whole act rule* presumes that although the sections of the act are not codified together, the act's sections should be interpreted to work harmoniously. For example, sections of the Patriot Act can be found throughout the *United States Code.* Those sections that penalize activities were placed in the penal section of the code, while those sections that relate to library record retention were placed in another section of the code. Yet, the Patriot Act was enacted as one bill. Hence, all of the Patriot Act's provisions should be interpreted together. If the word "terrorist" is used in more than one section of the Act, then "terrorist" should have the same meaning throughout the Act (pursuant to the presumption of consistent usage), unless the legislature clearly indicated a different intent.

The whole act aspect of *in pari materia* is based on the idea that there was a single drafter for the bill, whether that drafter was an individual legislator or a committee. Yet, the single-drafter assumption does not reflect the political reality. Legislation comes about from the compromises of many legislators from different political parties, different constituencies, and with different agendas. Even the president has a role. To suggest that one drafter (whether it be a unified group or an individual) wrote the bill with internal consistency simply ignores the reality of the legislation process. "'No man should see how laws or sausages are made.'" *Cmty. Nutrition Inst. v. Block*, 749 F.2d 50, 51 (D.C. Cir. 1984) (quoting Otto Van Bismarck).

The court in *Rhyne v. K-Mart Corp.*, 594 S.E.2d 1, 20 (N.C. 1994), turned to the whole act aspect of *in pari materia*. In that case, the court had to determine whether the words "a defendant" in a punitive damages statute meant each defendant or each verdict; the statute limited punitive damages to $250,000:

> Punitive damages awarded against *a defendant* shall not exceed... [$250,000]. If a trier of fact returns *a verdict* for punitive damages in excess of the maximum amount specified under this subsection, the trial court shall reduce *the award* and enter judgment for [the maximum amount].

Id. at 7 (quoting N.C. GEN. STAT. § 1D-25(b)) (emphasis added).

The defendant's employees had allegedly roughly handled two dumpster-divers. Both dumpster-divers sued and were awarded punitive damages of $11.5 million each, in addition to compensatory damages. *Id.* at 6. K-Mart argued that the ordinary meaning of the statute, which referred to "*a* defendant," allowed only one, $250,000 award rather than two separate awards. The court disagreed. The court stated, "[W]e construe statutes *in pari materia*, giving effect, if possible, to every provision." *Id.* at 20. In the same section of the act being interpreted, the legislature also referred to "*a verdict*" and to "*the* award." Because verdicts and awards apply to each plaintiff rather than to each defendant, the court held that the limit applied to each plaintiff's *verdict* or *award*, not to the defendant's damages. *Id.* The dumpster-divers both received the $250,000 award. Another way the court could have reached this result would have been to interpret "defendant" in its plural sense, for generally words written in the singular have both their singular and their plural meaning. (See Chapter 5.)

b. *The Whole Code Aspect of* In Pari Materia

In *Rhyne*, the court also looked at another statute within the same chapter of the code. This aspect of *in pari materia* is known as the *whole code aspect*. In *Rhyne*, one code section in particular was relevant; that code section identified the aggravating factors for a court to consider when awarding punitive damages. *Id.* (citing N.C. GEN. STAT. § 1D-15(a)). Because aggravating factors are, under common law, applied to each plaintiff's cause of action and not to each defendant's damages, the court's interpretation was consistent with this code section as well. Thus, in *Rhyne*, the court looked at other words in the same section of the act at issue (whole act aspect), as well as other words in another statute in another chapter in the code (whole code aspect), to discern the meaning of the language at issue.

The whole code aspect of *in pari materia* directs that new statutes should be interpreted harmoniously with existing statutes *concerning the same subject*. This aspect of *in pari materia* presumes that the legislature was aware of all existing statutes when it enacted the one in question; thus, the new statute should be interpreted harmoniously with all existing statutes. Thus, if a statute criminalizes certain behavior, that statute should be consistent with other statutes criminalizing the same or similar behavior. Practically speaking, it is highly unlikely that the legislature was aware of every statute, yet the presumption persists.

One challenge with this aspect of the canon is defining what statutes concern the same or similar subject matter. Do rape statutes defining sexual intercourse concern the same subject as incest statutes defining sexual intercourse? While many of us would think they did, the Massachusetts Supreme Court disagreed. In *Commonwealth v. Smith*, 728 N.E.2d 272, 278–79 (Mass. 2000), the court held that the definition of sexual intercourse used in a rape statute did not apply to an incest statute because the statutes did not concern sufficiently similar subject matters and were located in separate chapters in the code.

In contrast, in *Rhyne*, the court, without explanation, believed that the punitive damages statute concerned the same subject matter as the aggravating factors statute because both statutes were located in the same chapter of the code. But location within the same code chapter probably should not be enough for a court to find two statutes to be *in pari materia*. "The mere fact that the statutes appear in the same chapter [does not show the statutes relate to a common subject matter.] The Legislature may choose to employ a term differently in two different statutes. In each statute, the term should be construed to effectuate the purposes of that particular statute." *Id.* at 280 (Ireland, J., dissenting). Thus, a court should look to see whether the two statutes share similar purposes such that the legislature was likely aware of the existing statute when it drafted the newer statute and, thus, intended harmony.

2. The Presumption of Consistent Usage and Meaningful Variation

After *in pari materia*, the next most commonly used and least controversial linguistic canon is *the presumption of consistent usage and meaningful varia-*

tion (also known as the identical words presumption). This canon presumes that when the legislature uses the same word in different parts of the same act, the legislature intended those words to have the same meaning (consistent usage). And, contrariwise, if the legislature uses a word in one part of the act, then changes to a different word in the same act, the legislature intended to change the meaning (meaningful variation). The purpose of this canon is, like the purpose of *in pari materia*, to promote internal consistency; lawyers are taught that a change in word usage signifies new meaning. In English class, variety of word usage is commended. However, monotony in statutory drafting is a good thing. The Michigan Supreme Court turned to this canon in *Robinson v. City of Lansing*, 782 N.W.2d 171 (Mich. 2010). In that case, the court stated, "unless the Legislature indicates otherwise, when it repeatedly uses the same phrase in a statute, that phrase should be given the same meaning throughout the statute." *Id.* at 182.

Like all the linguistic canons, this canon can be rebutted with evidence that the same or a different meaning was intended. For example, in *Jensen v. Elgin, Joliet & Eastern Railway Co.*, 182 N.E.2d 211 (Ill. 1962), the court held that the canon was not applicable to the word "children" in Section 9 of the Federal Employers' Liability Act. That Act allowed lawsuits to survive the death of an employee-plaintiff for the benefit "of the surviving ... *children* of such employee...." *Id.* at 213 (quoting 45 U.S.C. § 59) (emphasis added). In that case, an employee had been injured while at work but later died of unrelated causes during the pendency of his personal injury lawsuit. His daughter, also his administratrix, was substituted to maintain the case. An appellate court dismissed the case after holding that "children" in Section 9 meant "minor dependent children." The court reached this holding because it believed that the Supreme Court had, in two earlier cases, interpreted the word "children" in another section (Section 1) of the Act to mean dependent children. *Id.* at 385 (citing *Jensen*, 175 N.E.2d at 564). For the appellate court, the fact that Congress used the same word in both sections meant that the word should have the same meaning. But the appellate court misunderstood the Supreme Court's holdings. The Supreme Court had held that Section 1 of the Act did not apply to children who were no longer dependent because Section 1 of the Act was the wrongful death section of the statute; wrongful death statutes permit only *dependent* family members to bring an action for their own losses. Thus, contrary to the lower court's understanding, the Supreme Court had not actually interpreted "children" to mean dependent children in Section 1 of the Act. Rather, the legal basis for recovery compelled the result.

On appeal, the Illinois Supreme Court correctly understood the Supreme Court's holding. As the Illinois Supreme Court pointed out, the two sections of the Act, Sections 1 and 9, actually allowed recovery for different things. Section 9 allowed the injured employee's estate to continue the action for *injuries the employee sustained*. Any recovery would go to the surviving spouse or children as heirs. In contrast, Section 1 allowed the dependents of the injured employee to bring suit to recover *for their own loss* in no longer having their parent to care for them. Because only dependent children would have any injury under this latter section, "children" was necessarily limited to dependent children. In other words, the nature of the recovery gave the word "children" a different meaning in the two different sections of the Act. Recognizing that the appellate court was wrong to conclude that "children" in the wrongful death section of the Act had been given anything other than its ordinary meaning (all children), the Illinois Supreme Court reversed. *Id.* at 213.

This case also illustrates the whole act aspect of *in pari materia*: The appellate court looked at "children" in Section 1 of the Act to help understand the meaning of "children" in Section 9 of the Act, albeit the court did so wrongly.

3. The Rule against Surplusage (or Redundancy)

The next four canons are more controversial and interrelated: the rule against surplusage, *noscitur a sociis*, *ejusdem generis*, and *expressio unius*. These canons often conflict with one another and, like the other canons, do not always reflect the reality of legal drafting. Let's take a closer look at each, starting with the rule against surplusage (which is the least reliable canon).

According to the *rule against surplusage*, the proper interpretation of a statute is the one in which every word has meaning; nothing is redundant or meaningless. There are two separate aspects to this canon: (1) every word must have independent meaning; and (2) two different words cannot have the same meaning. If different words had the same meaning, then the second word would be surplusage, meaning surplus. Note that this canon compliments the identical words presumption in that both canons require different words in a statute to mean different things.

Courts often refer to the rule against surplusage. For example, in *Feld v. Robert & Charles Beauty Salon*, 459 N.W.2d 279 (Mich. 1990), the court applied the canon to hold that a workers' compensation claimant could not bring her attorney with her to a medical exam the defendant requested. The statute specifically allowed the claimant to bring "a physician provided and paid for by himself or herself," but was silent concerning the claimant's right to have an attorney, or anyone else for that matter, present. *Id.* at 280 (quoting MICH. COMP. LAWS § 418.385). Holding that the quoted language would be surplusage if anyone other than physicians were permitted to attend, the court concluded that the legislature intended only physicians to be able to accompany the claimant. *Id.* at 284. The dissent disagreed, finding the language ambiguous despite the canon. *Id.* at 286–87 (Cavanaugh, J., dissenting).

The rule against surplusage presumes three things: (1) that the statute was drafted with care, (2) that each word was the result of thoughtful deliberation, and (3) that if the legislature had found extra words, it would have removed them during the deliberation process. In other words, the canon presumes that the legislature would not include surplus language to communicate its meaning. But these presumptions are flawed. Statutes are not always carefully drafted. Legal drafters often intend to include redundant language to cover any unforeseen gaps or they simply fail to identify the redundancy timely. Legislators are not likely to waste time or energy arguing to remove redundancy when there are more important issues to address. Thus, the presumptions simply do not match political reality. "[A] statute that is the product of compromise may contain redundant language as a by-product of the strains of the negotiating process." Richard A. Posner, *Statutory Interpretation — In the Classroom and the Courtroom*, 50 U. Chi. L. Rev. 800, 812 (1983). For these reasons, not all judges are persuaded by this canon. "Redundancy is common in statutes; we do not subscribe to the view that every enacted word must carry independent force." *Mayer v. Spanel Int'l Ltd.*, 51 F.3d 670, 674 (7th Cir. 1995).

Like many of the other linguistic canons, this canon is a tie-breaking presumption and yields to contrary legislative intent. Thus, courts can reject words "as surplusage" when they are "inadvertently inserted or if repugnant to the rest of the statute...." *Chickasaw Nation v. United States*, 534 U.S. 84, 94 (2001) (quoting K. Llewellyn, The Common Law Tradition 525 (1960)). In *Chickasaw Nation*, the Supreme Court held that the rule against surplusage did not apply when the rule produced an interpretation that conflicted with the intent of Congress. *Id.* The canon was particularly inappropriate in the Court's view because the surplus words were simply a numerical cross-reference in a parenthetical. *Id.* Such minor surplusage should not overcome the ordinary meaning of the rest of the statute.

4. *Noscitur a Sociis*

Most words have multiple meanings; the next two canons — *noscitur a sociis* and *ejusdem generis* — are fancy, Latin terms for a common sense notion: that words can best be understood in their textual context. *Noscitur a sociis* literally means "it is known from its associates." This canon is based on the simple presumption that when a word has more than one meaning, the appropriate meaning should be gleaned from the words surrounding the word being interpreted, in other words, from the textual context. 2A JABEZ GRIDLEY SUTHERLAND STATUTES AND STATUTORY CONSTRUCTION § 47.16, at 352 (Norman Singer ed. 7th ed. 2007). In practice, we use this canon all the time when we communicate. For example, Justice Scalia has famously said: "If you tell me, 'I took the boat out on the bay,' I understand 'bay' to mean one thing; if you tell me, 'I put the saddle on the bay,' I understand it to mean something else." ANTONIN SCALIA, A MATTER OF INTERPRETATION: FEDERAL COURTS AND THE LAW 26 (1997). And as one of my students suggested, if you tell me that "Fido bays at the moon," I might understand "bay" to mean a third thing altogether. Similarly, "answer" might mean a legal document that responds to a complaint or it might mean a response to a question. *Noscitur a sociis* helps identify which meaning was intended. Without *noscitur a sociis*, we would need a new word for each situation identified above. The English language is wordy enough already!

While *noscitur a sociis* has force when any word is being interpreted (as we saw with "bay" above), it is most often used by courts to interpret lists of words. When applying *noscitur a sociis*, courts try to find the common trait, or unifier, in the shared list of items. Thus, in the following list: "yellow, blue, red, chartreuse, and white," all items are colors; color is the unifier. Even if a reader did not know what chartreuse was, the reader would likely surmise that it was a color.

Courts use *noscitur a sociis* regularly to narrow lists that legislators draft. Legislators as legal drafters are trained to include every possibility. Thus, in *People v. Vasquez*, 631 N.W.2d 711 (Mich. 2001), the court applied *noscitur a sociis* to determine whether a defendant who lied to a police officer about his age "obstruct[ed], resist[ed], oppose[d], assault[ed], beat, or wound[ed]" that officer. *Id.* at 714 (quoting MICH. COMP. LAWS § 750.479). Applying *noscitur a sociis*, the majority concluded that the words shared the common trait of threatened or actual *physical* interference. *Id.* at 716. Because lying was not *physical* interference, the majority concluded that the defendant had not violated the statute when he lied to the police about his age. *Id.*

The dissent disagreed for two reasons. First, the dissent thought the term "obstruct" was clear, obstructing an officer includes lying to the officer. Because it was inappropriate to turn to the linguistic canon absent ambiguity, the dissent said that the majority unnecessarily narrowed the term "obstruct" by resorting to *noscitur a sociis*. *Id.* at 731 (Corrigan, C.J., dissenting). Second, the dissent argued that even assuming the canon was appropriate, the majority incorrectly identified the unifier. The dissent suggested that the unifier was simply *interference*, not *physical* interference. *Id.* And lying was interference. Thus, the dissent would have reversed the dismissal of the indictment.

This case nicely illustrates one problem with this canon—how similar must items in a list be? At times, *noscitur a sociis* and the rule against surplusage may conflict. *Noscitur a sociis* directs that words share meaning, while the rule against surplusage directs that each word should have independent meaning. Arguably, the majority in the last case violated the rule against surplusage by interpreting the terms in the statute so similarly they lost independent meaning. What, under the majority's interpretation, is the difference between "obstruct" and "resist" if physical interference is required? The dissent's interpretation preserved the distinction better than the majority's interpretation.

There is a second problem with this canon. Some judges have said that when a word has only one "fixed, commonly understood meaning," *noscitur a sociis* is not appropriate. One might ask whether a word can ever have one fixed, commonly understood meaning. For example, does the word "pig" mean the same thing to everyone? Not surprisingly, judges disagreed in *G.C. Timmis & Co. v. Guardian Alarm Co.*, 662 N.W.2d 710 (Mich. 2003). In that case, the majority and dissent argued about whether *noscitur a sociis* would be appropriate to apply to the list "Duck, Goose, Pig, Swan, Heron." *Id.* at 723 (Young, J., dissenting). The dissent thought not; a pig is what it is: a swine. If *noscitur a sociis* were applied, the court would have to interpret "pig" to be some type of waterfowl. *Id.* at 723. But the majority thought that the word "pig" could have multiple meanings (including someone who eats too much); thus, *noscitur a sociis* would help identify which of the many possible meanings was intended, the animal meaning. *Id.* at 718 n.12. In reality, both are right. A reader of the language above would intuitively interpret the word "pig" to mean a pink animal that oinks. If the list instead said, "cop, fuzz, pig," a different meaning would likely suggest itself. English speakers intuitively understand which meaning was intended because of *noscitur a sociis*. In *G.C. Timmis & Co.*, like *Vasquez*, the difference between the dissent and the majority is the degree of similarity *noscitur a sociis* demands when there is a list of items. In other words, can "pig" be included with a list of waterfowl and not be interpreted to be a kind of waterfowl? Of course it can. The majority was correct only because there is almost no word that has only one commonly, fixed meaning.

Thus, *noscitur a sociis* is not problem-free; yet, the basic notion that textual context aids interpretation is not arguable. Any language in which words have multiple meanings, like English, requires such a rule. For this reason, *noscitur a sociis* should apply regardless of ambiguity. Indeed, it is likely that judges intuitively apply the canon whether they say they are applying it or not. Yet the rhetoric continues. For example, in *Stryker Corp. v. Director, Division of Taxation*, 773 A.2d 674, 684 (N.J. 2001), the court refused to apply the canon because the text was clear.

5. *Ejusdem Generis*

Ejusdem generis is a subset, or type of, *noscitur a sociis*. "Whereas *ejusdem generis* tells us how to find items outside the list expressed in the statute, *noscitur a sociis* tells us how the list gives meaning to the items within it." *Stebbens v. Wells*, No. Civ.A. NC95-0324, 2001 WL 1255079 (R.I. Super. Ct. Oct. 12, 2001). *Ejusdem generis* literally means "of the same kind, class, or nature." The canon directs that when general words are near specific words, the general words should be limited to include only things similar in nature to the specific words. 2A JABEZ GRIDLEY SUTHERLAND STATUTES AND STATUTORY CONSTRUCTION§ 47.17 at 359-60 (Norman Singer 7th ed. 2007). *Ejusdem generis* is similar to *noscitur a sociis* in that it is used most commonly when there is a list of items in a statute (e.g., lemons, limes, grapefruits, and others); however, unlike *noscitur a sociis*, *ejusdem generis* should primarily be used when the statute ends with a general term, or a catch-all phrase, such as "and others."

You should be aware that judges often confuse these two canons. For example, in *Babbitt v. Sweet Home Chapter Communities*, 515 U.S. 687 (1995), the statute at issue, the Endangered Species Act, included a list of ways that someone could "take" an endangered species: "harass, harm, pursue, hunt, shoot, wound, kill, trap, capture, collect, … or to attempt to engage in any such conduct." *Id.* at 691 (quoting 16 U.S.C. § 1532(19)). The word being interpreted was "harm," not the catch-all "such conduct." For this reason, *noscitur a sociis* was the correct canon, as Justice Scalia pointed out in his dissent. *Id.* at 720 (Scalia, J., dissenting). In a legal opinion discussing the proposed regulation, the Solicitor of the Fish and Wildlife Service incorrectly identified the appropriate canon as *ejusdem generis*, which would have been correct if the term being interpreted was "such conduct." *Id.* (quoting 46 Fed. Reg. 29490, 29491 (1981)).

The confusion is understandable. Both canons share the same principle — when there are several items in a list that share a common attribute, the other item (*noscitur a sociis*) or the catch-all (*ejusdem generis*) should be interpreted as possessing that same attribute. *Ejusdem generis* should be applied only when there is a general term, or catch-all. "The *ejusdem generis* rule is generally applied to general and specific words clearly associated in the same sentence in a pattern such as '[specific], [specific], or [general]' or '[general], including [specific] and [specific].'" *State v. Van Woerden*, 967 P.2d 14, 18 (Wash. Ct.

App. 1998) (internal citations and quotation marks omitted) (alterations in original). In contrast, *noscitur a sociis* is applied when there is no catch-all or an item in the list is being interpreted.

Notice that when used to interpret a general catch-all phrase, *ejusdem generis* adds by implication the phrase "everything else of the same type as those in the list." *Cleveland v. United States,* 329 U.S. 14 (1945). Thus, in the last example, "lemons, limes, grapefruits, and others," most readers would assume that "others" would likely include other citrus fruits like oranges but would not include vegetables such as broccoli. Note how the canon actually restricts the general catch-all from an extremely broad phrase ("others"), which is capable of including almost anything, to a relatively narrow phrase ("citrus fruit"). The canon presumes that if the legislative body had intended the general words to be used in an unrestricted sense, the specific words would have not have been included.

Of course, there are numerous difficulties with this canon, including determining (1) what the commonality between the listed items is, and (2) how narrowly to focus the class. In other words, in the list above ("lemons, limes, grapefruits, and others"), is the commonality "fruit," "citrus fruit," or "sour citrus fruit"? Moreover, application of *ejusdem generis* can lead to an interpretation at odds with the ordinary meaning of words. For example, in *Commonwealth v. Plowman*, 86 S.W.3d 47 (Ky. 2002), the majority interpreted the word "building" in an arson statute to include bulldozers, an interpretation surely at odds with the ordinary meaning of "building." The majority reached this result because the statute defined the word "building" as "any dwelling, hotel, … automobile, truck, watercraft, aircraft … or other structure or vehicle…." *Id.* at 49 (quoting KAN. STAT. ANN. § 513.010). Applying *ejusdem generis* to the general catch-all "other structure or vehicle," the majority concluded that a bulldozer was a vehicle; hence, the defendant committed arson. The dissent claimed to "subscrib[e] to the less-than-radical notion that a bulldozer is not a 'building.'" *Id.* at 50 (Keller, J., dissenting). Actually, the dissent disagreed with the majority's holding that a bulldozer was a "vehicle."

Likewise, in *McKinney v. Robbins*, 892 S.W.2d 502 (Ark. 1995), the majority refused to interpret the phrase "domesticated animals" to include kittens, again a meaning not readily apparent from the words alone. In that case, the defendant had shot and killed the plaintiff's dog. A state statute permitted an individual to kill a dog when that dog killed the individual's "domesticated animal[]." *Id.* at 597 (citing ARK. CODE ANN. § 20-19-102(b)(2)). At trial, the defendant moved for summary judgment on the theory that he was justified in shooting the dog under the statute because the dog had killed his kittens a few days earlier. *Id.* The trial court granted summary judgment; the plaintiff appealed. The Arkansas Supreme Court reversed and remanded for trial. The statute specifically defined "domesticated animals" as "include[ing], but [] not limited to, sheep, goats, cattle, swine, and poultry." *Id.* at 598 (citing ARK. CODE ANN. § 20-19-102(a)(1)). In this case, the general term preceded the specific listed items. For *ejusdem generis* purposes, placement is irrelevant. Concluding that the term "domesticated animals" was ambiguous, the court applied *ejusdem generis* to this general term and found that the specific terms following it—sheep, goats, cattle, swine, and poultry—all shared the commonality of livestock. Thus, the general phrase "domesticated animals" did not include pets. *Id.* at 599.

Like the other linguistic canons, this canon does not reflect the reality of legal drafting: Legislatures use catch-alls not to limit lists but to broaden lists; if the legislature wished the list to stay narrow, then the legislature could simply leave the list alone. By adding catch-alls, legislatures do not intend to narrow lists, but rather include a catch-all because they cannot identify, in advance, everything they would want included within the list. Thus, legislatures would likely prefer that general catch-alls and general terms be interpreted broadly, not narrowly, to cover all possible, but similar, contingencies.

Ejusdem generis, like all the linguistic canons of construction, is not an ironclad rule, but rather is a guide to meaning. When the list of things is not sufficiently similar, *ejusdem generis* should not apply. Moreover, some judges refuse to apply the canon absent ambiguity. One absurd case illustrating this point is *People v. Fields*, 105 Cal. App. 3d 341 (1980). In that case, a statute prohibited "the knowing destruction or concealment of any book, paper, record, instrument in writing, or *other matter or thing* ... about to be produced in evidence upon any trial, inquiry, or investigation...." *Id.* at 343 (quoting CAL. PENAL CODE § 135). The defendant flushed marijuana down the toilet while in the county jail. The court refused to apply *ejusdem generis* to limit the general catch-all phrase "*other matter or thing*" to written items because, according to the court, the language was not ambiguous (hence the canon was unnecessary) and included "an unending variety of physical objects." *Id.* at 344. The court was simply wrong in this instance; while "other matter or thing" may not be ambiguous, the phrase is certainly vague, overly broad, and unclear without being narrowed by *ejusdem generis*. Moreover, the rule of lenity (see Chapter 13) should have limited the statute to its written items.

If *ejusdem generis* is only applied when ambiguity is found, the canon should never be appropriate. Judges who refuse to apply the linguistic canons in the absence of ambiguity are simply wrong. This can be seen in the Supreme Court's recent split over the applicability of this canon in *Ali v. Federal Bureau of Prisons*, 552 U.S. 214 (2008). In that case, the petitioner had been a federal prisoner at one federal penitentiary and was moved to another penitentiary. During the move, some of his personal belonging disappeared. He sued. While the Federal Government is generally immune from suit absent a clear statement to the contrary (see Chapter 13), in the Federal Tort Claims Act (the "FTCA") Congress had waived immunity for claims arising out of torts committed by federal employees. However, the FTCA specifically exempted "any claim arising in respect of ... the detention of any goods, merchandise, or other property by any officer of customs or excise or *any other law enforcement officer.*" *Id.* at 216 (quoting 28 U.S.C. §2680(c)) (emphasis added). The issue for the Court was whether "any other law enforcement officer" included all law enforcement officers or just law enforcement officers acting in a customs or excise capacity. *Id.*

Rejecting petitioner's *ejusdem generis* and *noscitur a sociis* arguments, the majority held that the word "any" was clear on its face and meant exactly that: "Congress' use of 'any' to modify 'other law enforcement officer' is most naturally read to mean law enforcement officers of whatever kind." *Id.* at 220. The majority refused to apply the canons to "clear" text. The dissent disagreed and relied heavily on these two linguistic canons. Justice Breyer explained that the issue for the Court was "not the *meaning* of the words," but was instead "the statute's *scope.*" *Id.* at 243 (Breyer, J., dissenting). And *ejusdem generis* and *noscitur a sociis* were essential to that inquiry:

> The word "any" is of no help because all speakers (including writers and legislators) who use general words such as "all," "any," "never," and "none" normally rely upon context to indicate the limits of time and place within which they intend those words to do their linguistic work. And with the possible exception of the assertion of a universal truth, say by a mathematician, scientist, philosopher, or theologian, such limits almost always exist. When I call out to my wife, "There isn't any butter," I do not mean, "There isn't any butter in town." The context makes clear to her that I am talking about the contents of our refrigerator.
>
> That is to say, it is context, not a dictionary, that sets the boundaries of time, place, and circumstance within which words such as "any" will apply. Context, of course, includes the words immediately surrounding the phrase in question. And canons such as *ejusdem generis* and *noscitur a sociis* offer help in evaluating the significance of those surrounding words.

Id. Justice Breyer was correct: English speakers use context to narrow meaning. The word "any" standing alone is broad and ambiguous. Thus, *ejusdem generis* would help identify whether Congress intended to waive immunity for all law enforcement officers. In fact, that is exactly the purpose of this canon, to narrow an otherwise overly broad catch-all. Additionally, given that a clear statement from Congress is needed to waive immunity, the Court should have erred on finding limited immunity in this case.

6. *Expressio Unius Est Exclusio Alterius*

The next canon, *expressio unius*, is a rule of negative implication: it literally means "the inclusion of one thing means the exclusion of the other." Young children use *expressio unius* all the time. For a simple example, let's assume that a mother tells her child not to "hit or push" any of the other children. When that child then kicks another child on the playground and gets in trouble, the child argues, "But you didn't tell me I couldn't *kick* anyone!" Parents learn early to try to anticipate every contingency in their communications. Courts presume that legislatures do the same.

Expressio unius is implicated when a statute has a gap. The existence of the gap permits two very different inferences: either the legislature intended to omit the circumstance or the legislature never considered the circumstance. *Expressio unius* presumes the former: that when the legislature includes some circumstances explicitly, then the legislature intentionally omitted other similar circumstances that would logically have been included. In other words, the canon presumes that the legislature considered and rejected every related possibility. It further presumes that if the legislature had intended to cover every circumstance, then the legislature would have included a general catch-all. If we return to a modified version of our hypothetical statute from the last section "lemons, limes, and grapefruits," *expressio unius* would tell us that oranges, which are not specifically included, are specifically omitted because (1) they are not included separately, although they are sufficiently similar to the other items; and (2) there is no general catch-all. While the presumption is that the legislature intentionally left out those things omitted, the reality is that the legislature likely never considered the omitted circumstance at all.

In *Dickens v. Puryear*, 276 S.E.2d 325 (N.C. 1981), the court used *expressio unius* to determine the appropriate statute of limitations in a tort case. The primary issue before the court was whether the defendant committed assault or intentional infliction of emotion distress when he threatened to kill the plaintiff if the plaintiff did not leave the state. The court held that this threat of future harm was a claim for intentional infliction of emotional distress, not for assault. *Id.* at 336. The relevant statute provided that a one year statute of limitations applied to actions involving "libel, slander, assault, battery, or false imprisonment." *Id.* at 330 n.8. The plaintiff had filed suit more than one year after the threat. Applying *expressio unius*, the court reasoned that because intentional infliction of emotional distress was not listed with the other torts in the statute, it was not subject to the one year limitation. *Id.* Hence, another statute of limitations applied instead.

This canon, like so many others, presumes something about legislative drafting that simply does not reflect reality. It presumes that the legislature actually considered all the possible options and included those options it wanted. Nonsense! "[*Expressio unius*] is increasingly considered unreliable, for it stands on the faulty premise that all possible alternative or supplemental provisions were necessarily considered and rejected by the legislative draftsmen." *Nat'l Petroleum Refiners Ass'n v. FTC*, 482 F.2d 672, 676 (D.C. Cir. 1973). In reality, legislatures omit things for a variety of reasons, some intentional, some not. Despite its limitations, some courts still consider and rely on this canon. Hence, as a practitioner, you need to be aware that it exists.

In conclusion, the linguistic canons provide common sense rules for understanding how English speakers and writers use words. As such, these canons are merely presumptions and should yield when there is either evidence that the drafter did not follow the canons or evidence that the drafter did not intend for a particular canon to apply to a specific situation. Because these canons help us understand how English writers ordinarily use words, the canons may not accurately reflect how legal writers use words and should be used with some caution. Finally, it is simply illogical, as some judges argue, to apply the canons only after ambiguity or absurdity is found. The point of the canons is to help a reader understand the ordinary meaning of the words used; hence, the canons should be used in the search for ordinary meaning. Despite the limitations of using these canons, they have come back into vogue with the renewed emphasis on the text.

Next, we move to the final intrinsic source to be covered: the other components in the bill. Surprisingly, these components play a less-central role in interpretation than the intrinsic sources we have covered so far.

D. Mastering This Topic

Return to the hypothetical ordinance provided in Chapter 1 on page 9. Assuming you think the term "motor vehicles" is ambiguous as applied to the various hypotheticals and especially the ambulance hypothetical, do the linguistic canons help resolve the ambiguity? The ordinance (in non-marked up form) provides:

An Ordinance

To Prohibit Motor Vehicles in Pioneer Park

Be it enacted by the Council of the City of Pioneer assembled,

(1) The short title of this ordinance shall be the Pioneer Park Safety Ordinance.

(2) No cars, motorcycles, or other motor vehicles may enter or remain in Pioneer Park, except as provided in section 3 hereof.

(3) Motor vehicles may be used by authorized public groups:

    a. in maintaining Pioneer Park, and

    b. in placing barricades for parades, concerts, or other entertainment in Pioneer Park.

(4) Anyone violating this ordinance shall be subject to a $1,000 fine, provided no injuries occurred. If any injury occurred, the fine shall be doubled.

Let's look at each of the linguistic canons in turn starting with *in pari materia*. Remember that this canon identifies the statutory material that is relevant to the interpretive process. Here, the whole act aspect lets us know that we should look at the ordinance as a whole (in the bill form), so the whole ordinance is included above. We don't have other related ordinances from this city's code, so the whole code aspect is inapplicable to our problem. But as a prosecutor, you might have looked to see if there were special ordinances related to ambulances, for example, or motor vehicles that might provide insight.

Turning to the presumption of consistent usage and meaningful variation, you should note that the phrase "motor vehicles" is used twice, consistently. Thus, because the council did not alter the phrase at all, you can assume that the phrase was meant to have the same meaning in sections 2 and 3. This canon does not resolve the ambiguity in the statute, however.

Does the rule against surplusage help resolve the ambiguity? This canon directs that all words and phrases must have independent meaning. In other words, "motor vehicles" does not mean "vehicles." Also, "motor vehicles" must mean more than just cars and motorcycles. But the canon does not seem to resolve the ambiguity in the statute as it applies to ambulances.

How about *nosciture a sociis* or *ejusdem generis*; do either of these canons resolve the ambiguity? First, you must determine which canon is appropriate. Because the language being interpreted is the catchall, "other motor vehicles," you know that *ejusdem generis* is the appropriate canon, not *nosciture a sociis*. Next, you need to identify the attribute the items share so that you can interpret the catchall to be of the same type as the items listed. Cars and motorcycles are vehicles that people drive to get places. They have motors and they carry people. Does an ambulance share these attributes? Yes, hence, your application of *ejusdem generis* should suggest that the council would have intended that an ambulance be included within the general catchall, and, thus, the ambulance driver should be cited. While this may not be the outcome you would prefer, the canon does provide guidance.

Finally, let's turn to *expressio unius est exclusio alterius*, is this canon appropriate? After all, ambulances were not specifically included in the listed items; therefore, can't one argue that the legislature intended to omit them (or allow them to be driven in the park)? Unfortunately, no, the ambulance driver cannot make this argument for the simple reason that the legislature included a general catchall, which shows that the council did not intend to identify in the ordinance every possible type of vehicle that was prohibited from driving in park. The canon should not apply to section 2.

But the canon would apply to section 3. Section 3 specifically identifies two excepted vehicles that can be driven in the park and does not include a catchall. Ambulances are not included within this list. Therefore, *expressio unius* would confirm that ambulances are not excepted for the council showed that it knows how to exclude certain vehicles, it chose not to exclude ambulances, and it chose not to include a general catchall to broaden the exclusions. Again, this may not be the outcome you would prefer, but the canon does provide guidance.

In summary, after applying the linguistic canons, you should conclude that while many of them do not help resolve the ambiguity, two are applicable: *ejusdem generis* and *expressio unius*. Applying these two canons, you should conclude that the ambulance driver must be cited. Helpfully, both canons point to the same result. Perhaps you are satisfied with this result, and if you are a textualist, you may well be. If the council wants to exclude ambulances, then it should say so (and include helicopters, airplanes, statutes of vehicles, etc.). But if you are dissatisfied with this result and are a textualist, there is one final intrinsic source that may provide help in resolving the ambiguity: the components. We turn to this topic next.

Checkpoints

- The linguistic canons simply reflect shared assumptions about the way English speakers and writers use language and grammar. These canons are rules of thumb that help judges draw inferences from the words of the statute.

- The linguistic canons should be used with common sense and a realization that lawyers draft differently than the canons presume. When there is better evidence of legislative intent, the canons should take a back seat.

- *In pari materia* directs judges to look at an entire act and related statutes to determine meaning. The canon helps ensure internal consistency across acts, statutes, related statutes, and even the code as a whole.

- The presumption of consistent usage and meaningful variation presumes that when the legislature uses the same word in different parts of the same act, the legislature intended those words to have the same meaning (consistent usage). And, contrariwise, if the legislature uses a word in one part of the act, then changes to a different word in the same act, the legislature intended to change the meaning (meaningful variation).

- According to the rule against surplusage, the proper interpretation of a statute is the one in which every word has meaning; nothing is redundant or meaningless.

- *Noscitur a sociis*, meaning "it is known from its associates," directs that when a word has more than one meaning, the appropriate meaning should be gleaned from the textual context, meaning the other words in the statute.

- *Ejusdem generis*, meaning "of the same kind, class, or nature," directs that when general words are near specific words, the general words should be limited to include only things similar in nature to the specific words. This canon is a subset of *noscitur a sociis*.

- *Expressio unius* presumes that when the legislature includes some circumstances explicitly, then the legislature intentionally omitted other similar circumstances that would logically have been included.

Chapter 7

Canons Based on Intrinsic Sources: The Components

Roadmap
- Understand the codification process.
- Identify the components of a bill, including headings, titles, enacting clauses, preambles, purviews, effective date provisions, and provisos.
- Learn the role that a bill's various components have on interpretation.

A. Introduction to This Chapter

In this chapter, we survey our final, and surprisingly least relevant, intrinsic source: the remaining components of a bill or act. Using a bill that was pending before Congress when this text was originally written, this chapter will identify the various bill components and explore the canons surrounding their relevance to the interpretation of the ensuing statute. The House bill and the Senate's companion bill are reproduced in full in Appendices D and E. For ease of reference, however, each section in this chapter includes the relevant component from the sample bill or another bill so that you can see actual bill language.

B. Codification

To understand the role components play in interpretation, you must first understand what codification is. To begin, some history: In early American history, acts were not codified. Rather, they were simply placed in books sequentially. RONALD B. BROWN & SHARON J. BROWN, THE SEARCH FOR LEGISLATIVE INTENT 150 (2002). If you will remember, during these days there were far fewer statutes; hence, codification was less necessary. Eventually, smart entrepreneurs figured out that codifying statutes—placing statutes with similar subject matters together—would be profitable. *Id.* These entrepreneurs were right. Today, all federal and state acts are codified.

The codification process is simple. When Congress passes a bill, it becomes an enrolled bill and is presented to the president for approval. If the president signs (or fails to effectively veto the bill), it becomes an act. The act is delivered to the Archivist of the United States; duplicates of the act are published chronologically in official pamphlets called "slip laws," which the Government Printing Office publishes. Ultimately, slip laws are officially bound, also chronologically bound, into "session laws" and placed into the *Statutes at Large*. Acts may be only one page long or hundreds of pages in length. They may cover just one topic or a variety of topics.

As you might imagine, researching the *Statutes at Large* would be time consuming and frustrating because the acts are arranged chronologically, not topically. Moreover, laws are regularly amended and repealed; thus, extensive cross-referencing would be essential. For this reason, most acts are rearranged and published in a topical code. This process, inserting sections of an act into a code, is called *codification*. The official code for federal statutes is the the *United States Code* ("Code") which is divided into fifty different "titles" based on subject matter. Title 18, for example, contains many of the federal criminal statutes. Title 26 contains the tax statutes. The Code is much simpler to search than the *Statutes at Large*. But you cannot search the code for a named act, such as the Patriot Act. Sections of the Patriot Act are scattered throughout the code. Rather, you would find the Patriot Act in the *Statutes at Large*.

The Office of the Law Revision Counsel of the U.S. House of Representatives ("LRC") maintains the Code. LRC determines which acts in the *Statutes at Large* should be codified. It also determines whether a new statute amends or repeals any existing statutes and whether any existing statutes have lapsed.

Because the legislature originally had nothing to do with the placement of a statute in a particular section of the code, placement was considered irrelevant to meaning. Even when the states and federal government began officially codifying statutes, the legislature continued to have no role in this process; hence, where a statute was located in a code continued to be irrelevant to meaning. Today, however, the legislature may specifically indicate where sections or parts of an act should be placed in the code. When the legislature identifies placement, placement may affect meaning. For example, in *Commonwealth v. Smith*, 728 N.E.2d 272 (Mass. 2000), the court found the placement of a statute within a particular chapter of that state's code to be determinative. In that case, the defendant had sexually molested his daughter for many years, but had never had sexual intercourse with her. He was charged with violating the incest statute: "Persons with the degrees of consanguinity within which marriages are prohibited or declared by law to be incestuous ... who ... have *sexual intercourse*, shall be punished...." *Id.* at 275 n.2 (citing MASS. GEN. LAWS ch. 272, § 17) (emphasis added). In an earlier case, the court had interpreted the words "sexual intercourse" in a rape statute to mean male penetration of the female "sex organ." *Id.* at 275-76 (citing *Commonwealth v. Gallant*, 369 N.E.2d 707 (1977)). The issue for the *Smith* court was whether this same definition applied to the phrase "sexual intercourse" in the incest statute. The majority held that it did not because the incest statute was located in one penal code chapter, which was entitled "crimes against chastity, morality, decency, and good order," rather than in another penal code chapter, which was entitled "crimes against persons" and included the rape statutes. *Id.* at 275. Hence, the statutes were not *in pari materia* according to this court solely because they were located in different chapters of the code.

The dissent did not believe that simply because statutes are in the same chapter of a code, they are *in pari materia. Id.* at 279-280 (Ireland, J., dissenting). As the dissent noted, the drug-rape statute (another statute) was no more *in pari materia* to the incest statute than the rape statutes, even though the drug-rape statute was in the same chapter as the incest statute. *Id.* at 280 (Ireland, J., dissenting). Hence, placement within the code, which was determinative to the majority, was irrelevant to the dissent.

One reason that placement should not affect meaning is that codification is not perfect. Many statutes cover more than one subject. For example, tax evasion is a felony. But the relevant statute criminalizing tax evasion is found in the tax chapter of the Code, not the criminal chapter. It cannot be placed in both, yet arguably it relates to both subjects.

Regardless of the relevancy of placement in the Code, relying solely on the Code and ignoring the *Statutes at Large* can create some issues. First, codification is imperfect. For the most part, the code is accurate; but occasionally, there have been transpositions or other errors. While the Code is *prima facie* evidence of the laws, the text of the *Statutes at Large* is "legal evidence" of the laws as enacted. *Stephan v. United States*, 319 U.S. 423, 426 (1943). Thus, on the rare occasion when there is conflict, the Statutes at Large control. "[T]he very meaning of 'prima facie' is that the Code cannot prevail over the Statutes at Large when the two are inconsistent." *Id.* For example, 12 U.S.C. § 92 was omitted from the Code for decades. Despite that fact, Congress amended § 92 in 1982. In *U.S. National Bank of Oregon v. Independent Insurance Agents of America, Inc.*, 508 U.S. 439 (1993), the parties disputed whether § 92 had remained valid law. Despite omission from the Code, the Supreme Court held that the section was still valid law because the *Statutes at Large* so dictated. *Id.* at 440.

A second reason that placement should not affect meaning is that not every section (or component) of an act is codified. Acts have a variety of components. Some components are required, such as enacting clauses and titles; many are optional, such as findings clauses and short titles. Generally, only those components that follow the enacting clause, which we will talk about later, are codified. The enacting clause itself is not codified, only the language following it. Moreover, "[w]hile the enacting clause is required for the act to become law, it does not itself become law, nor is that required to be the case." *State v. Phillips*, 560 S.E.2d 852, 856 (N.C. Ct. App. 2002). Long titles and preambles, which precede the enacting clause, are not codified. Similarly, provisions for the effective date of amendments to existing laws may not be codified. When not codified, these titles, preambles, and effective date provisions can only be found by referring to the *Statutes at Large*.

Does codification affect the role the components have on meaning? Surprisingly, no. "[Oddly], some of the language that is not [codified] can affect interpretation, while some of the language that *is* [codified] is not normally relevant to interpretation. And, even when it is relevant, it is given little weight." LINDA D. JELLUM & DAVID C. HRICIK, MODERN STATUTORY INTERPRETATION: PROBLEMS, THEORIES, AND LAWYERING STRATEGIES 197 (2d ed. 2009). Let's explore this dichotomy more closely.

C. The Components and Their Canons

1. Heading

In the box on the next page, you will find a copy of the beginning, or heading, of the sample bill (it was not passed, so technically, it is not an act. In this section, we are careful to use "act" to refer to an enacted bill). You can find the entire bill in Appendix D. This heading identifies the Congress responsible for enacting the bill (the 110th), the session in which the bill was debated (first), the bill designation (H.R. 916), the primary sponsor (Representative Scott of Georgia) and other sponsors of the bill, what happened to the bill, and when it happened (the bill was referred to the Committee on the Judiciary on February 8, then sent to the Committee of the Whole on May 14, 2007). A sponsor signs a bill before introducing it; a bill number is assigned when the bill is introduced.

Component: Bill Heading

> Union Calendar No. 88
>
> 110TH CONGRESS
>
> 1ST SESSION   H. R. 916
>
> [Report No. 110–148]
>
> To provide for loan repayment for prosecutors and public
> defenders.
>
> ———————
>
> **IN THE HOUSE OF REPRESENTATIVES**
>
> **FEBRUARY 8, 2007**
>
> Mr. SCOTT of Georgia (for himself, Mr. GORDON of Tennessee,
> Mr. LEWIS of Georgia, Mr. PAYNE....) introduced the following
> bill; which was referred to the Committee on the Judiciary
>
> **MAY 14, 2007**
>
> Additional sponsors: Mr. LINCOLN DAVIS of Tennessee, Mr.
> COOPER, Mr. CHANDLER, Mr. UDALL of Colorado....
>
> **MAY 14, 2007**
>
> Reported with an amendment, committed to the Committee of
> the Whole
>
> House on the State of the Union, and ordered to be printed
>
> ———————
>
> A BILL

None of the information in this heading is codified, but some of it can be useful for further research. For the most part, none of this information is relevant to interpretation. Following the heading are the components relevant to interpretation, beginning with titles: long titles, short titles, and section titles.

2. Titles

There are three types of titles in an act: (1) long titles, (2) short titles, and (3) section titles. The canon for using any of the three in interpretation is identical and simple: titles are not controlling. But the rationale for each differs somewhat. In a bill, a long title precedes the other two, so we will start there.

a. Long Titles & Enacting Clauses

Every act has a long title. Look in the box below. The long title immediately follows the words "A Bill." Generally, all long titles begin with the words "to" or "relating to"; they then identify the purpose of the bill and where the bill will fit within existing law. Is it a new section? Does it amend, repeal, or replace an existing section? One purpose of the long title is to answer these questions. Another purpose of the long title is to provide the reader, including legislators, with a convenient way to determine what a pending bill is about without having to read the whole bill. Titles are required at both the federal and state level to prevent a legislator from including extraneous provisions in a bill while attempting to avoid legislative or public notice.

Component: Long Title & Enacting Clause

> **A BILL**
>
> To provide for loan repayment for prosecutors and public defenders.
>
> *Be it enacted by the Senate and House of Representatives of the United States of America in Congress assembled,*

The long title of this bill is "To provide for loan repayment for prosecutors and public defenders." This long title is actually very short! A more illustrative long title, which has been severely edited, looks like the one in the box below.

> A BILL … To amend Chapter 12 of Title 16 of the Official Code of Georgia Annotated, relating to offenses against health and morals, … to provide for definitions; to require that a female give her informed consent prior to an abortion; to require that certain information be provided to or made available to a female prior to an abortion; to require a written acknowledgment of receipt of such information; to provide for the preparation and availability of certain information; to provide for procedures in a medical emergency; to provide for reporting; … and for other purposes.

To understand the limited role that long titles have in statutory interpretation, we must turn to our English heritage. In England, the clerks in parliament historically added long titles to bills; thus, the early English rule prohibited judges from looking to the long title for interpretative assistance. For the most part in England, that rule still holds today.

In contrast, in the United States, the legislature writes its own long titles; therefore, a different rule developed. Here, "[t]he title of an act cannot control its words, but may furnish some aid in showing what was in the mind of the legislature." *Church of the Holy Trinity v. United States,* 143 U.S. 457, 462 (1892). In other words, a judge may look at a long title to resolve ambiguity or correct drafting errors. In *Holy Trinity,* the Supreme Court did just that. In that case, Holy Trinity Church hired a pastor from England. However, a federal statute prohibited employers from importing any foreigner "to perform labor or service of any kind...." *Id.* at 463. Finding the word "labor" in the statute at issue to be ambiguous—it could mean manual labor or all forms of labor—the Court looked to the long title of the statute to resolve the ambiguity. The long title was "[a]n act to prohibit the importation and migration of foreigners and aliens under contract or agreement to perform labor in the United States...." *Id.* at 458. From the legislative history and this title, the Court concluded that Congress had intended the Act to "reach[] only to the work of the manual laborer, as distinguished from that of the professional man." *Id.*

If a legislature writes the long title, why would such a title be less controlling than the words of the statute? One reason might be that long titles are not codified because they precede the enacting clause. But this reason alone is not sufficient because short titles, which follow the enacting clause and are codified, similarly do not carry as much weight as the text. Hence, codification alone cannot be the answer. More likely, the reluctance to give weight to titles stems from our English heritage, where titles were not considered in interpretation.

Following the long title is the enacting or resolving clause. Enacting clauses are used for bills, both at the federal and state levels, while resolving clauses are used for joint resolutions. In other countries, they are omitted. In the United States, enacting clauses are required, and their language is prescribed. 1 U.S.C. §§ 101, 102 (2012). Indeed, in Texas, a "bill" without an enacting clause cannot be amended by adding an enacting clause, nor may "such a bill" be referred to committee under that state's house and senate rules. Texas legislators must get it right the first time.

For a federal bill, the required language for an enacting clause is "*Be it enacted by the Senate and House of Representatives of the United States of America in Congress assembled....*" 1 U.S.C. § 101 (2012). Notice that the enacting clause on the preceding page, in the box above right, has this magic language. For a joint resolution, the language differs slightly: "*Resolved by the Senate and House of Representatives of the United States of America in Congress assembled....*"

1 U.S.C. § 102 (2012). Everything following the enacting clause is codified; everything preceding the clause is not. 1 U.S.C. § 103 (2012). Thus, everything we have looked at up to this point would not be put into the Code. There are no interpretation issues surrounding enacting clauses because the language is required and never varies.

b. Short Titles

For some bills, a short title may also be included, even if the long title is not all that long. The short title is located in a separate section of the statute, usually the first section. The short title typically is written as follows: "This act may be cited as the _____ Act of _____." The short title of our sample bill is the "John R. Justice Prosecutors and Defenders Incentive Act of 2007."

Component: Short Title

> **SECTION 1. SHORT TITLE.**
>
> This Act may be cited as the "John R. Justice Prosecutors and Defenders Incentive Act of 2007".

In this case, the short title is almost as long as the long title! So why would a legislature include one? Legislatures include short titles for a variety of reasons. One obvious reason is that, when a title is truly long, a short title eases reference. However, short titles are used for other reasons as well. Short titles are often used to persuade either legislators or the public to support the bill. For example, consider the following two acts and their short titles: "The No Child Left Behind Act" and "The Patriot Act." A legislator would be hard-pressed to vote against children and patriotism! Additionally, the short title can be used, as in this case, to honor someone involved in either the bill process or the subject. In this case, John R. Justice was the Solicitor (the highest state prosecutor) of South Carolina; the bill's title was chosen to honor his public service work.

Unlike the long title, the short title follows the enacting clause, and thus, is codified. As such, it may play a stronger role in interpretation for some judges, particularly textualists. But the canon remains the same: "the name given to an act by way of designation or description … cannot change the plain import of its words." *Caminetti v. United States*, 242 U.S. 470, 490 (1917). In *Caminetti*, the defendants were convicted of violating the "White Slave Traffic Act" for bringing their mistresses across state lines. The statute prohibited the transportation of any woman for the purpose of prostitution, debauchery, or "*any*

One Hundred Eleventh Congress
of the
United States of America

AT THE SECOND SESSION

Begun and held at the City of Washington on Tuesday,
the fifth day of January, two thousand and ten

An Act

To modernize the air traffic control system, improve the safety, re-liability, and availability of transportation by air in the United States, provide for modernization of the air traffic control system, reauthorize the Federal Aviation Administration, and for other purposes.

Be it enacted by the Senate and House of Representatives of
the United States of America in Congress assembled,

SHORT TITLE

SECTION 1. This Act may be cited as the "   Act of   ".

other immoral purpose." Id. at 485. The Court found the text of the catchall clear; any immoral purpose included bringing women across state lines to be mistresses. Thus, the majority refused to consider the defendants' argument that Congress intended the Act to reach only commercial trafficking of women (or prostitution). *Id.* at 485. The dissent disagreed. Finding that the short title of the Act "[gave] more than a title; it [made] distinctive the purpose of the statute," the dissent argued that the short title should be used to narrow the expansive meaning of the text in this case. *Id.* at 497 (McKenna, J., dissenting).

Interestingly, sometimes during the drafting process, errors can occur. In 2010, Congress enacted and President Obama signed into law the "The ___ Act of ____." See the text box above and note the short title. The error has not been corrected!

c. Section & Code Titles

Almost all bills have section titles or headings to aid the reader in determining the content of a particular section of a bill. A section title is merely a short-hand reference to the general subject matter in the section. Earlier, you might have noticed that a section title preceded the short title of the John R. Jones Prosecutor and Defenders Incentive Act. The section title reads: *Section 1: Short Title.* If not, go back and find this section title; while it is not hugely helpful to the reader, it does provide some focus. Section titles can provide guidance. But generally, section titles do no more than indicate the content of the section in a general manner, especially when text is complicated and prolific. It would be impossible for the legislature to attempt to capture everything contained within the section with one short section title. Thus, section titles were never meant to take the place of the detailed provisions of the text; hence, they offer little to courts interpreting statutory language.

The canon for section titles is identical to that of the other titles: the section title cannot limit the ordinary meaning of the text. For interpretative purposes, section titles are relevant when the text is ambiguous or absurd. In other words, section titles "are but tools available for the resolution of a doubt. But they cannot undo or limit that which the text makes plain." *Brotherhood of R.R. Trainmen v. Balt & O.R. Co.*, 331 U.S. 519, 529 (1947).

Sometimes, legislatures do not even write the section titles; instead, a publisher of a code may add them. Such was the case in *Michigan Avenue National Bank v. County of Cook*, 191 Ill. 2d 493 (2000). In that case, the plaintiff relied on a caption that was not in the official version of the statute, but rather was added by West Publishing in its publication of the statute. Not surprisingly, the court rejected the argument that the caption should carry any interpretative weight. *Id.* at 506.

In addition to section titles, there are also code titles for various sections of the code. For example, the code title of 17 U.S.C. is "Copyright." The laws related to copyright are generally found within this section of the code. Code titles are irrelevant to meaning. The Office of the Law Revision Council prepares and publishes the United States Code. State law is similar. For example, in *State v. Bussey*, 463 So. 2d 1141 (Fla. 1985), the court found that a statute penalizing the sale of drugs was a criminal statute despite being located in the "Fraudulent Practices" section of the code. The court reasoned, "The arrangement and classification of laws for purposes of codification in the Florida Statutes is an administrative function of the Joint Legislative Management Committee of the Florida Legislature. The classification of a law or a part of a law in a particular title or chapter of Florida Statutes is not determinative on the issue of legislative intent...." *Id.* at 1143 (internal citation omitted).

3. Preambles, Purpose Clauses, and Legislative Findings

After either the short title, if there is one, or the enacting/resolving clause if there is no short title there may be a section called legislative findings or purpose. These clauses are generally called *preambles* when they precede the enacting clause and *findings, purpose, or policy clauses* (or some combination) when they follow the enacting clause. Findings clauses and purpose clauses differ somewhat from each other. Findings clauses identify the legislative facts that lead the legislature to act, while purpose clauses identify the purpose for the act. While findings and purpose clauses can be separate sections of a bill, or one can be included and the other not included, the common practice is to include both clauses together in one section.

While preambles, legislative findings, and purpose clauses are not required, they can be informative. The sample bill has a simple purpose clause, which is in the box below. While the language of the clause would suggest it applies only to one section of the bill (it says "[t]he purpose of this section"), there is really only one relevant section in the bill; thus, the purpose clause applies to all the important provisions in the bill.

Component: Purpose Clause

> "SEC. 3111. GRANT AUTHORIZATION.
>
> "(a) PURPOSE. — The purpose of this section is to encourage qualified individuals to enter and continue employment as prosecutors and public defenders.

Commonly, findings and purpose clauses are much longer and more detailed. A highly edited sample findings and purpose clause from The Rehabilitation Act appears in the box on the following page. Notice that this example clause contains findings, purposes, and policy.

In England, judges gave preambles great weight because preambles were considered the best source for determining the statutory purpose. You might remember that purpose played an important and early role in interpretation when society was less technologically advanced, and carbon paper (let alone Xerox machines!) was not available.

In contrast, the United States' rule is more modest; generally, the preamble and findings and purpose clauses cannot control clear, enacted text. In other words, the canon for preambles and findings and purpose clauses is identical to the titles' canon. But, like titles, preambles and findings and purpose clauses can help resolve ambiguity, if a judge is willing to consider them. Whether a judge is willing to consider such clauses depends largely on that judge's approach to interpretation. Because preambles precede enacting clauses, some judges, particularly textualist judges, refuse to consider them at all. Unlike preambles, however, findings and purpose clauses follow the enacting clause. As such, textualist

Component: Finding & Purpose Clause

Sec. 2. Findings; Purpose; Policy

(a) **Findings**

Congress finds that— ...

(3) disability is a natural part of the human experience and in no way diminishes the right of individuals to—

(A) live independently;

(B) enjoy self-determination;

(C) make choices;

(D) contribute to society;

(E) pursue meaningful careers; and

(F) enjoy full inclusion and integration in the economic, political, social, cultural, and educational mainstream of American society; ...

(b) **Purpose**

The purposes of this Act are— ...

(2) to ensure that the Federal Government plays a leadership role in promoting the employment of individuals with disabilities....

(c) **Policy**

It is the policy of the United States that all programs, projects, and activities receiving assistance under this Act shall be carried out in a manner consistent with the principles of—

(1) respect for individual dignity ...

judges are much more willing to consider findings and purpose clauses once the judges have found the statute to be ambiguous. For example, in *PRB Enterprises, Inc. v. South Brunswick Planning Bd.*, 518 A.2d 1099, 1101 (N.J. 1987), the court stated that a purpose clause that followed an enacting clause was substantive, unlike a preamble. Therefore, it could be relevant to meaning. But few judges see the enacting clause as such a rigid dividing line.

Increasingly, Congress is placing its findings and purposes within the enacted part of a bill to increase the likelihood that a judge will use the findings or purpose to interpret it. Findings and purpose clauses can play an important role in interpretation. For example, in *Sutton v. United Air Lines, Inc.*, 527 U.S. 471 (1999), the Supreme Court turned to the findings provision to limit the reach of the Americans with Disabilities Act (the "ADA"). In the case, two severely myopic sisters sued United Airlines when it denied their application to become commercial pilots. Claiming that they were not disabled under the ADA because the sisters' vision could be corrected, United Airlines sought dismissal. The term "disability" was not defined in the statute. Thus, the Court turned to the findings clause. The findings clause provided that "some 43,000,000 Americans have one or more physical or mental disabilities, and this number is increasing as the population as a whole is growing older." *Id.* at 484 (citing U.S.C. § 12101(a)(1)). According to the Court, "The findings enacted as part of the ADA require the conclusion that Congress did not intend to bring under the statute's protection all those whose *uncorrected* conditions amount to disabilities." *Id.* In other words, if correctable conditions were included, that number would have been much larger. Hence, Congress must have intended to include only uncorrectable disabilities within the statute's protection.

A state case that highlighted the role of a findings clause is *Commonwealth v. Besch*, 674 A.2d 655 (Pa. 1996). In that case, the defendants sold marijuana and cocaine to each other. The State of Pennsylvania charged the defendants with violating its Corrupt Organizations Statute (the State equivalent of the Federal Racketeering and Organized Crime Act). The issue for the court was whether the state could prosecute a wholly illegitimate drug conspiracy under the Act. The language at issue in the statute was "enterprise," which the statute defined as any "legal entity." *Id.* at 658 (quoting 18 PA. CONN. STAT. § 911(h)(3)). The court did not find this definition dispositive, so it turned to the findings clause, which stated that the Act was designed to prevent "organized crime [from] infiltrate[ing] and corrupt[ing] *legitimate businesses....*" *Id.* at 659 (quoting § 18 PA. CONN. STAT. § 911(a)) (emphasis added). Because the statute was aimed at protecting legitimate businesses from money laundering, the defendants did not violate the Act. In essence, the court concluded that the defendants were too guilty to be guilty! It took the state legislature only two months to legislatively overturn this decision.

4. The Purview: The Substantive Provisions

After the introductory clauses identified above, the substantive provisions begin. By law, each section of a bill must be separately numbered. 1 U.S.C. § 104 (2012). The sample bill began numbering with the short title. Additionally, "as nearly as may be" each section must contain only a single proposition of enactment. *Id.*

Order of provisions is important. Generally, the substantive provisions follow a particular organization: definitions first, principal operative provisions second, enforcement provisions third, and severability provisions last. Intermingled within these provisions are many other provisions, including effective date provisions, savings provisions, and provisos. When this expected order is not followed, ambiguity may result. For example, in *Bank One v. Midwest Bank & Trust Co.*, 516 U.S. 264 (1996), the Supreme Court had to determine whether it had jurisdiction under the Expedited Funds Availability Act to hear a case one bank brought against another. The Act was poorly drafted because the section authorizing interbank litigation, an enforcement provision, was placed in the wrong section of the Act. As Justice Stevens noted, "When Congress creates a cause of action, the provisions describing the new substantive rights and liabilities typically precede the provisions describing enforcement procedures; [this statute] does not conform to that pattern." *Id.* at 276 (Stevens, J., concurring).

Let's look at these sections in more detail.

a. Definitions

Not every bill includes a definitions section; but if the bill does have one, then the definitions should precede the substantive provisions. Only definitions that are applicable to the bill as a whole are included within the definitions section. Definitions used only in one particular section of a bill are usually placed within that specific section. The sample bill has a definition section contained within section 3. (See below.) Because this bill only has three sections, this definition section likely applies to all of the relevant provisions of the bill. But it would have been clearer had Congress placed the definition section in its own separate section. As drafted, section 3 of the bill is unwieldy. In a different, longer act, misplacement might create interpretation issues: Does the definition apply to all sections of the bill or just the section in which it is located?

Component: Definitions Section

"SEC. 3111. GRANT AUTHORIZATION....

"(b) DEFINITIONS. — In this section:

"(1) PROSECUTOR. — The term 'prosecutor' means a full-time employee of a State or local agency who —

"(A) is continually licensed to practice law; and

"(B) prosecutes criminal or juvenile delinquency cases (or both) at the State or local level, including an employee who supervises, educates, or trains other persons prosecuting such cases....

For statutory interpretation, definitions are critical and controlling. Often, the interpretation of a statute depends on the words in the statute. If the legislature has defined those words, then that definition trumps all other interpretations, *even if the legislature's definition makes no sense.* And sometimes, a legislature's definitions make no sense. In *Commonwealth v. Plowman*, 86 S.W.3d 47 (Ky. 2002), the court had to decide whether a defendant who set fire to a bulldozer "start[ed] a fire ... with intent to destroy or damage a building." *Id.* at 49 (quoting KY. REV. STAT. ANN § 513.030). While one would normally not understand the word "building" to include bulldozers, in this case, the legislature had specifically defined "building" as follows: " 'Building' in addition to its ordinary meaning, specifically includes any ... automobile, truck, watercraft, aircraft, ... or other ... vehicle...." *Id.* (quoting KY. REV. STAT. ANN. § 513.010). Because of the definition, the issue for the court was whether a bulldozer was a "vehicle." The court decided that the bulldozer was a vehicle, thus, holding that a bulldozer was a building. This odd result occurred entirely because of the definitions within the statute at issue.

One famous, but fictional, criminal case showing the importance of definitions is *Regina v. Ojibway*, 8 Crim. L.Q. (Can.) 137 (Sup. Ct. 1965) (Blue, J.). In that case, the defendant was riding his pony in a public park. He was using a pillow filled with down as a saddle. After the pony broke its leg, the defendant shot it. He was then charged with having violated the Small Birds Act, which stated: "Anyone maiming, injuring or killing small birds is guilty of an offence and subject to a fine not in excess of two hundred dollars." The trial court dismissed the charges, finding that the defendant had killed a horse and not a small bird. On appeal, the court disagreed, stating:

> In light of the definition section my course is quite clear. Section 1 defines "bird" as "a two legged animal covered with feathers." There can be no doubt that this case is covered by this section.... We are not interested in whether the animal in question is a bird or not in fact, but whether it is one in law.... Different things may take on the same meaning for different purposes. For the purpose of the Small Birds Act, all two-legged, feather-covered animals are birds. This, of course, does not imply that only two-legged animals qualify, for the legislative intent is to make two legs merely the minimum requirement. The statute therefore contemplated multi-legged animals with feathers as well.... Therefore, a horse with feathers on its back must be deemed for the purposes of this Act to be a bird, and *a fortiori*, a pony with feathers on its back is a small bird.

Id.

Including definitions for every word might seem to be the perfect answer to avoiding ambiguity. If the legislature simply defined every word it used, ambiguity would disappear. However, it is not possible, nor even desirable, for the legislature to define every word used in a bill, for a number of reasons. First, bills would become unwieldy to say the least! Also, defining words can be challenging. Legislatures may not know in advance every circumstance they would want covered. Finally, where would drafters draw the line? Should they define common words like "the"? Less common words like "any"? Only very uncommon words? For all these reasons, legislators should only define those words and phrases (1) that have a unique, technical meaning (e.g., "summary judgment"), (2) that they wish to have a meaning broader, narrower, or different from the ordinary or dictionary definition (e.g., "discrimination"), or (3) that have been created to refer to a complex or wordy idea in a simpler way (e.g., "Department" for "Department of Health and Human Services").

b. Principal Operating Provisions & Enforcement Provisions

Following the definitions section are the principal operative provisions. There are two types of provisions within this category: (1) *substantive provisions*, which provide the rights, duties, powers, and privileges being created, and (2) *administrative provisions*, which address the creation, organization, powers, and procedures of the governmental organization that will enforce or adjudicate the law. If the law was drafted well, substantive provisions with general applicability will precede provisions with specific applicability, and general rules will precede any exceptions to those rules. The substantive provisions, along with the administrative and enforcement provisions, are the essence of the bill. Indeed, it is likely that the language that is being interpreted comes from one of these sections. For the most part, there are no unique canons that apply to these sections. Rather, the canons throughout this text help resolve the meaning of text in these subsections.

Component: Administrative Provision

"SEC. 3111. GRANT AUTHORIZATION.

"(c) PROGRAM AUTHORIZED. — The Attorney General shall ... establish a program by which the Department of Justice shall assume the obligation to repay a student loan ...
(d), for any borrower who —
 "(1) is employed as a prosecutor or public defender; and
 "(2) is not in default on a loan for which the borrower seeks forgiveness.

As explained above, the administrative provisions identify how the law will be implemented. In these provisions, the legislature will create or identify the governmental organization or organizations that will be responsible for administering and enforcing the law. Moreover, these provisions should identify how the government will administer and enforce the law. In the sample bill, the Department of Justice would be in charge of administering the bill should it pass. An excerpt is in the box above.

The final substantive provisions of an act are enforcement provisions. Generally, the purpose for enacting a bill is to affect conduct. The legislature can best affect conduct by enacting a rule then prescribing a punishment for noncompliance or a reward for compliance with that rule. The rule is the substantive provision, while the consequence (reward or punishment) is the enforcement provision. The more common enforcement provisions include (1) establishing a criminal penalty, a civil penalty, or an administrative penalty; and (2) allowing suit for injunctive relief or civil liability. In the text box below is the penalty for anyone receiving funds under the John R. Justice Prosecutors and Defenders Incentive Act. Essentially, the bill allows the federal government to recover funds owed to it by any legal means.

Component: Enforcement Provision

> "SEC. 3111. GRANT AUTHORIZATION.
>
> "(d) TERMS OF LOAN REPAYMENT. —
>
> "(1) BORROWER AGREEMENT. —
>
> "(C) if the borrower is required to repay an amount to the Attorney General under subparagraph (B) and fails to repay such amount, a sum equal to that amount shall be recoverable by the Federal Government from the employee (or such employee's estate, if applicable) by such methods as are provided by law for the recovery of amounts owed to the Federal Government.

c. Severability & Inseverability Provisions

Provisions may be included in a bill to address issues relating to the severability of various sections of the act. Severability and inseverability (also known as non-severability) provisions address the validity of the bill should any section of it be found invalid. Severability provisions allow for the remaining sections of the bill to remain valid, while inseverability provisions require that the bill as a whole be held invalid if any one section is invalid. Inseverability provisions come in two types: "general" and "specific." *General inseverability provisions* provide that *none* of the provisions of a bill are severable; in contrast, *specific inseverability provisions* provide that *specific* provisions of a bill are not severable from one another. Early statutes had neither severability nor inseverability provisions; however, in response to judicial interpretations of acts not having these provisions, severability clauses began to appear in statutes in the early 1900s. Inseverability provisions are a more modern, less utilized creature.

i. Severability Provisions

Severability provisions raise many issues including constitutional issues, relevance issues, and effectiveness issues. Constitutional issues arise when a court strikes one part of an act, but not another. By altering the law as written, one could argue that the court has effectively rewritten the act in violation of the Constitution. Under the Constitution, it is the legislature's job to write laws. By striking some sections of the act and not others, the court effectively redrafts the law. Would the legislature have wished the act to become law if it were not to become law in its entirety? Possibly not. Thus, when the judiciary alters the law as written, separation of powers concerns arise.

Effectiveness and relevance issues arise because, despite the clear text of these clauses, their ordinary meaning does not control. The *doctrine of severability* is simply stated: statutes are presumed severable. The Supreme Court has said repeatedly that severability provisions are merely presumptions about what the legislature intended. In other words, Congress's clearly expressed intent in such a clause is merely a rebuttable presumption that can be overcome "by strong evidence that Congress intended otherwise." *Alaska Airlines, Inc. v. Brock*, 480 U.S. 678, 686 (1987).

That presumption is overcome in two situations. First, the presumption fails if the statute, without its unconstitutional provisions, cannot function. Illustrative of this situation is *Warren v. Mayor & Aldermen of Charlestown*, 68 Mass. (2 Gray) 84 (1854). In that case, the Massachusetts Supreme Court held that a state statute that would have annexed Charlestown to Boston violated the Constitution because the statute would deny the citizens of Charlestown effective federal representation. *Id.* at 99. The court then invalidated the statute as a whole, concluding that "various provisions of the act ... are so connected with each other" that the legislature could not have intended the remaining, constitutional statutory remnants to remain in force. *Id.* at 100.

Second, the severability presumption fails if Congress "intended otherwise," meaning that Congress would have preferred no legislation at all to the enacted legislation without its unconstitutional provisions. Surprisingly, Congress's inclusion of a severability clause does not resolve the question. Rather, a severability clause merely preserves the general severability presumption just outlined. Why? Commonly and much like boilerplate language in contracts, legislatures include severability provisions with little thought about their true impact, partly because their true impact can be unknowable. Rather than carefully consider whether some provisions in a bill should survive if others do not, legislatures, without thought, simply include a severability clause directing that all provisions remain valid regardless of what the act might actually look like after litigation has excised some provisions. Thus, the doctrine that severability provisions are presumptions makes sense; if the legislature does not think about what it is doing, then courts should not rubber-stamp the decision to include such a provision.

In situations where there is evidence that Congress actually thought about this issue and wanted the legislation to be severable or inseverable that intent should control. For example, the Bipartisan Campaign Finance Reform Act (the "McCain-Feingold Act") resulted from a legislative bargain: Members of Congress agreed that in exchange for a ban on soft-money contributions, then-existing hard-money contribution limits would be increased. Without this compromise, the Act would have failed. But the compromise raised a potential conflict: If a court found the soft-money ban to be unconstitutional, should the increase in allowable hard-money contributions remain in effect?

To anticipate this issue, Congress specifically included a severability provision. Pub. L. No. 107-155, § 401 (2012). But it did not do so without considering the issue thoroughly. After two Republican senators attempted to include an *inseverability* provision, the bill's sponsors and the Democratic leadership effectively inserted a severability provision. Michael D. Shumsky, *Severability, Inseverability, and the Rule of Law*, 41 Harv. J. on Legis. 227, 229–30 (2004). The debate over whether to have the provision was long and arduous. Given that Congress actually considered and fought over the severability provision in the McCain-Feingold Act, that unambiguously expressed intent of Congress should control. Parenthetically, in *Citizens United v. FEC*, 558 U.S. 310 (2010), the Supreme Court held that the First Amendment of the Federal Constitution prohibits the government from restricting independent political expenditures by corporations and unions.

Regardless of their validity, severability provisions are actually unnecessary because courts uniformly construe statutes as severable regardless of whether there is a severability provision in them. Indeed, some states even provide as much by statute. For example, Texas has a statute that says all statutes are severable unless the statute specifically indicates that it is not. Tex. Gov't Code Ann. §§ 311.032

& 312.013 (West 2012). Thus, if the Texas legislature wishes for an entire act or specific sections of an act to be held invalid, the legislature must so provide.

Virginia's history with severability provisions is interesting. In that state, the legislature changed the presumption by statute in 1986. Before 1986, courts presumed that statutes were not severable. In 1986, the legislature changed that presumption. "The provisions of all statutes are severable unless (i) the statute specifically provides that its provisions are not severable, or (ii) it is apparent that two or more statutes or provisions must operate in accord with one another." VA. CODE. ANN § 1-17.1 (2012). Now, all statutes, not just those enacted after 1986, without severability provisions are presumed to be severable in Virginia. *Elliott v. Virginia*, 593 S.E.2d 263, 267 (Va. 2004). You should identify the presumption in your own state.

ii. Inseverability Clauses

In contrast to the commonness and, thus, thoughtlessness of including severability provisions, inseverability provisions are included much less frequently. Arguably, they demonstrate more clearly a legislature's intent. "A non-severability [provision] is almost unheard of and constitutes a legislative finding that every section [of an act] is so important to the single subject that no part of the act can be removed without destruction of the legislative purpose." *Farrior v. Sodexho, U.S.A.*, 953 F. Supp. 1301, 1302 (N.D. Ala. 1997).

Inseverability clauses are different from severability clauses for another reason as well. If an inseverability clause is included in a bill, its very presence likely represents proof that the bill was a compromise of competing interests:

> When Congress includes an inseverability clause in constitutionally questionable legislation, it does so in order to insulate a key legislative deal from judicial interference. Such clauses are iron-clad guarantees—clear statements by Congress that it would not have enacted one part of a statute without the others. Legislation containing an inseverability clause can thus be conceived of as a contract among competing political interests containing a structural enforcement mechanism designed to alleviate the concerns of those legislators who were willing to vote for ... a particular statutory scheme only if credibly assured that certain limiting provisions would be secure in the enacted legislation.

Shumsky, *Severability, Inseverability, and the Rule of Law, supra* at 267–68.

Congress rarely uses inseverability provisions; thus, the Supreme Court has not yet addressed their validity. *Id.* at 243–44. Because there is no guidance from the Supreme Court, lower courts have tended to treat inseverability clauses in the same way that the Court has treated severability clauses; "a non-severability clause cannot ultimately bind a court, it establishes [only] a presumption of non-severability." *Biszko v. RIHT Fin. Corp.*, 758 F.2d 769, 773 (1st Cir. 1985). Thus, again, "[d]espite the unambiguous command of … inseverability clauses … [they] create only a rebuttable presumption that guides—but does not control—a reviewing court's severability determination." Shumsky, *Severability, Inseverability, and the Rule of Law, supra* at 230. So, for example, in *Stiens v. Fire & Police Pension Ass'n*, 684 P.2d 180, 184 (Colo. 1984), the court held that the legislature intended the benefit provisions of a pension act to be severable from the Act's unconstitutional funding provisions, despite the existence of an inseverability provision.

If a severability or inseverability provision is included in a bill, it generally is placed at the end of the act. The John R. Justice Prosecutor and Defenders Incentive Act contains neither a severability nor inseverability provision. Instead, two sample provisions are provided in the box below.

Component: Severability & Inseverability Clauses

SEC. 10A. SEVERABILITY.

If any provision of this Act or its application to any person or circumstance is held invalid, the invalidity does not affect other provisions or applications of this act that can be given effect without the invalid provision or application, and to this end the provisions of this Act are declared to be severable.

SEC. 10B. INSEVERABILITY.

Section 1 of this Act, prohibiting the sale of alcohol without a license, and Section 2 of this Act, imposing a tax on the sale of alcohol, are not severable, and neither section would have been enacted without the other. If either provision is held invalid, both provisions are invalid.

---

d. Effective Date & Saving Provisions

Often, a bill expressly provides a starting date, known as the *effective date*. If it does not, a federal statute is effective on the date the president signs the bill or on the date that Congress overrides any veto. Because of this default rule, many federal bills, like the John R. Justice Prosecutor and Defenders Incentive Act, contain no effective date provision. But if the bill is to be effective on a date other than the signing date, Congress must provide that effective date in the bill.

States take a variety of approaches to this issue. Most commonly, a state's constitution or statute will provide a default date for any statute not containing an effective date provision. For example, in Alaska, a bill takes effect at 12:01 a.m. on the ninetieth day after the governor signed it, unless the legislature specifies a different date. ALASKA CONST. ART. II, § 18; ALASKA STAT. § 01.10.070 (Michie 2009). The Texas Constitution states that a bill becomes effective ninety-one days from the date of the legislature's final adjournment. TEXAS CONST. art III, § 39.

Generally, effective date provisions raise few interpretation issues. But what if Alaska's legislature enacted a bill with an effective date provision, then forwarded the bill to the governor for signature after the effective date identified in the statute? Remember that bills are not enacted until after the executive signs it. What would the effective date of the act be: the date provided in the statute, the day after the governor signed the bill, or the default—ninety days after the governor's signature? And to add another wrinkle, what if the appropriate effective date was a state holiday? These were the facts in *Fowler v. State*, 70 P.3d 1106 (Alaska 2003). The legislature passed a bill that expanded the definition for felony drunk driving. *Id.* at 1107. While the prior law had designated drunk driving as a felony if the defendant had two prior convictions within the preceding five years, the new law upped the time frame to ten years. *Id.* In other words, the new law increased the "look-back" provision from five to ten years.

Although the legislature included an effective date of July 1, 2001, the legislature delayed sending the bill to the Governor until June 20. The Governor did not sign the bill until July 3. On July 4, the defendant committed the offense of driving while intoxicated. He had had two prior convictions within the preceding ten years, but not within the preceding five. *Id.* If the bill was in effect on July 4, the defendant committed a felony; if not, the defendant committed a misdemeanor. The defendant convincingly argued that the bill could not be effective on July 1, because it had not yet been signed. That left three possible effective dates: July 4—the date after the Governor signed the bill (but a holiday)—July 5—the next business day after the Governor signed the bill—and October 1—the default rule of ninety days after the Governor's signature. The court held that the existence of the effective date provision showed that the legislature did not intend for the default rule to apply, but rather wanted the statute to become effective as soon as possible. *Id.* at 1109. Thus, in this case, waiting until the default date "would not achieve the legislature's purpose." *Id.* Rejecting the holiday extension argument, the court held that the statute became effective at 12:01 a.m. on July 4, the day after the Governor signed the bill. *Id.* The defendant lost his arguments. Additionally, the court rejected the defendant's rule of lenity argument (the rule of lenity is a canon of construction that directs courts to adopt the less penal of two possible interpretations of a penal statute, see Chapter 13), finding the effective date statute not to be a penal statute. *Id.* at 1110.

Related to effective date provisions are *saving provisions.* Such provisions "save," or exempt, behavior or legal relationships that existed before or on the effective date of a new law. The sample bill does not have a savings provision. Another example has been provided in the box below. These provisions are commonly used when a penal statute is amended or repealed. For example, when many states raised the drinking age in the 1980s from eighteen to twenty-one, those individuals who were between eighteen and twenty on the date the law became effective were "grandfathered" into the statute, meaning they could legally continue to drink alcohol despite being underage.

Component: Savings Provision

SECTION 9. SAVING PROVISION

(a) The change in law made by this Act applies only to an offense committed on or after the effective date of this Act. For purposes of this section, an offense is committed before the effective date of this Act if any element of the offense occurs before that date.

(b) An offense committed before the effective date of this Act is covered by the law in effect when the offense was committed, and the former law is continued in effect for that purpose.

---

e. Sunset Provisions

A sunset provision terminates or repeals all or portions of an act after a specific date, unless further legislative action is taken to extend the act. Most laws do not have sunset provisions; in such cases, the law goes on indefinitely. The John R. Justice Prosecutor and Defenders Incentive Act does not have such a provision.

A famous act that includes such a sunset provision is the Patriot Act. Under the sunset provision in that Act, many of the surveillance sections were set to expire in December of 2005. Congress has temporarily extended these sections repeatedly. *See, e.g.*, Economic Growth and Tax Relief Reconciliation Act of 2001 Pub. L. No. 107-16, 115 Stat. 38 (2001).

f. Exceptions & Provisos

Exceptions, also known as *provisos*, are provisions or clauses that limit the effect of a statutory provision. In other words, provisos create an exception or limit a general rule. They typically begin with the words "except for," "provided however," and "provided that." Hence, they are also called provisos. One famous proviso, the Wilmot Proviso, was introduced by Representative David Wilmot in the House of Representatives in 1846 as a rider to a $2 million appropriations bill, which President Polk had introduced to facilitate negotiations with Mexico over the settlement of the Mexican-American War. The proposed language read:

> Provided, That, as an express and fundamental condition to the acquisition of any territory from the Republic of Mexico by the United States by virtue of any treaty which may be negotiated between them, and to the use by the Executive of the money herein appropriated, neither slavery nor involuntary servitude shall ever exist in any part of said territory except for crime, whereof the party shall first be duly convicted.

Louise Weinberg, *Dred Scott and the Crisis of 1860*, 82 CHI.-KENT L. REV. 97, 99 (2007) (quoting CHAPLAIN W. MORRISON, DEMOCRATIC POLITICS AND SECTIONALISM: THE WILMOT PROVISO CONTROVERSY 18 (1967)). Wilmot's purpose in submitting the proviso was to prevent slavery from being introduced into any territory the United States acquired from Mexico. While the House approved the bill with the proviso included, Congress adjourned before the Senate could vote on it; thus, the bill and its proviso failed. Yet, some commentators have suggested that this proviso may have been a cause of the Civil War.

Because provisos exempt something from an act's reach or qualify something within the statute, provisos are narrowly construed. Narrow interpretation makes sense because the statute provides the general rule while the proviso limits that general rule or provides an exception to it. Thus, any limit or exception should be confined to its express and clear terms. Otherwise, the proviso's exception would swallow the substantive rule.

The proviso canon is somewhat similar to *expressio unius* in that both are rules of negative implication. However, application of the proviso canon leads to a result that is opposite that of the application of *expressio unius*. With *expressio unius*, that which is omitted in the statute is *omitted* in the statute's application; in contrast, with exceptions and provisos, that which is omitted in the exception or proviso is *included* in statute's application. Those claiming a benefit under a proviso have the burden of proving that they come within the proviso's terms. *Gay & Lesbian Law Students Ass'n v. Bd. of Tr.*, 673 A.2d 484, 474 (Conn. 1996).

This chapter, components, was our last on intrinsic sources. It might have surprised you that components, for the most part, are less relevant to interpretation than are the linguistic canons and other intrinsic sources; however, England's influence in this area continues to have an impact. Next, we turn to the first of our extrinsic sources, those sources related to timing.

D. Mastering This Topic

Return to the hypothetical ordinance provided in Chapter 1 on page 9. Remember our question: "An ambulance entered Pioneer Park to pick up and take to the hospital a man who has just suffered a heart attack. Did the ambulance driver violate the Pioneer Park Safety Ordinance (PPSO)?" Assuming first that you have concluded that the statute is ambiguous as you would need to do for textualism, how might the components of the ordinance help you resolve the ambiguity?

First, let's look at the titles. The long title of the ordinance is "To Prohibit Motor Vehicles in Pioneer Park." This long title offers no interpretive help. In contrast, the short title of the ordinance is located in section 1: "the Pioneer Park Safety Ordinance." This short title suggests that the purpose of the ordinance is to protect the safety of those using the park. Because allowing an occasional ambulance into the park to assist those needing medical care would not jeopardize the safety of the individuals using the park and, indeed, might increase their safety because they would get access to medical care more quickly if injured, the short title suggests that ambulances should not be included within the ordinance's ban.

Let's turn to findings, purpose, or policy clauses. There are none in this ordinance, so these clauses can offer no interpretive guidance. Consider, however, how it might have helped your interpretation had the council included the legislative facts that led to the ordinance's enactment. The legislative history noted that, "The ordinance will address the recent concerns created by a spat of accidents in Pioneer Park. In two of these accidents, a car struck a pedestrian and another struck a bicyclist on park roads. In the third, a motorcyclist drove off road and hit a pedestrian." Had these legislative findings been included in the ordinance, you might conclude that the purpose of the ordinance is to further safety and exclude the ambulance from the ordinance's reach. Note that a strict textualist would need to have the findings included within the ordinance, not the legislative history, and that all textualists would first need to find the language ambiguous to consider the findings, while the other theorists would not.

Next, let's turn to the purview and consider whether any of these components aid interpretation. There are no definitions, though it would have been helpful had the council defined "motor vehicle." There are two provisos, one in section 2 — "except as provided in section 3 hereof" — and one in section 4, the enforcement provision, — "provided no injuries occurred." Remember that provisos are narrowly construed. The proviso in section 2 identifies the few excepted motor vehicles that can drive in the park. Ambulances are not included and are not like the vehicles excepted (*noscitur a sociis*); thus, if this proviso is narrowly interpreted, ambulances should be prohibited from driving within the park. Yet, the enforcement proviso suggests again that the purpose of the ordinance is to further safety; no one was injured when the ambulance drove in the park; indeed, someone's safety was enhanced.

Finally, while they do not assist in interpretation in this situation, note that the ordinance does not contain the following provisions: severability and inseverability provisions and savings or sunset provisions. It does have an effective date provision.

Checkpoints

- Acts are rearranged and published in a topical code. This process, inserting sections of the act into the code, is called codification.

- Bills have a variety of components; some components are required while others are optional. Some components are relevant to meaning, others are not.

- The heading comes first. It identifies the sponsor of the bill, the bill number, and the activity taken on the bill.

- All bills have long titles, which precede the enacting clause and, thus, are not codified. Some bills also have short titles, which follow the enacting clause and are codified. The canon for both is the same: titles cannot control clear text.

- Similarly, preambles, findings, and purpose clauses cannot control clear text.

- When the legislature defines a word or phrase in a statute, that definition is controlling.

- Many interpretative issues arise in the substantive portion of the bill, which contains the operative provisions, the enforcement sections, and other relevant sections.

- Severability provisions allow for the remaining sections of an act to remain valid, while inseverability provisions require that an act as a whole be held invalid if any one section is invalid. By default, courts construe sections of a act as severable, even when the legislature includes an inseverability provision.

- Acts are presumed severable. That presumption is overcome in two situations. First, the presumption fails if the act, without its unconstitutional provisions, cannot function. Second, the severability presumption fails if Congress would have preferred no legislation at all to the enacted legislation without its unconstitutional provisions. Inseverability clauses do not necessarily rebut this presumption.

- Exceptions and provisos, which are provisions that exclude something from a statute's reach or qualify something within a statute, are narrowly construed.

Chapter 8

Canons Based on Extrinsic Sources & Legislative Process: Timing

---

Roadmap

- Learn how courts resolve issues involving statutes that conflict: specific statutes trump general statutes and later enacted statutes trump earlier enacted statutes.

- Learn what repeal by implication is and that it is disfavored.

- Understand when statutes can have retroactive effect and what that means.

- Discover that legislatures often borrow statutory language from other states and jurisdictions or use model or uniform acts.

A. Introduction to This Chapter

In this chapter, we turn from the intrinsic sources to the first of the extrinsic sources: conflicting statutes, implied repeals, retroactivity, and borrowed statutes. We cover these extrinsic sources first because their use is less controversial than those sources in the next chapter, which relate to legislative history. This chapter covers topics related to the timing of the legislative process. The canons based on the timing of the legislative process are presumptions based on how a legislature normally or ideally operates. The canons presume that the legislature intended to act "normally," unless there is evidence that it intended to act otherwise. For example, if two statutes both address an issue, the statute that was enacted last controls unless there is evidence that Congress would have wanted the earlier statute to control. Similarly, if one state copies another state's statute, the copying, or borrowing, state also presumptively borrows the judicial interpretations of that statute from the lending state *up to the date of enactment*. But again, if the borrowing legislature is clear that it did not intend to adopt the judicial interpretations of the other state, then the ju-

dicial interpretations do not accompany the borrowed statute. The topics covered in this chapter share one concept: timing. Let's start with conflicting
statutes: What happens when multiple statutes address the same issue?

B. Extrinsic Sources

Before we begin this discussion, a brief reminder might be in order; extrinsic sources are those sources outside of the official act, but within the legislative process that created the act. In other words, these are sources intimately
related to the enactment process, such as legislative history, purpose, administrative regulations, and the like; but they are separate from the text.

C. Conflicting Statutes

Sometimes, two sections of one statute or, more commonly, two different statutes conflict. For example, assume that statute A provides that all
criminal defendants are entitled to parole, while statute B provides that only
non-violent criminal defendants are entitled to parole. These hypothetical
statutes conflict. When a judge is faced with two conflicting statutes or sections of a statute, the judge will first see if the conflict between the two can
be reconciled, because the judge will assume that the legislature, when it
passed the second statute, did not intend to interfere with or abrogate any
existing statutes relating to the same topic. This policy of reconciling first
is based on the assumptions that the legislature (1) was aware of all relevant statutes when it enacted the new one, (2) would have expressly repealed
or amended an existing statute had it wanted the new statute to replace the
existing one, and (3) failed to repeal the existing statute because the legislature intended for both statutes to exist in harmony. These assumptions
fail to reflect reality: A legislature cannot possibly know every law that exists when it enacts legislation. And even if the legislature was aware of a
conflicting, existing statute, the conflict between the existing statute and
the new statute may not have been apparent when the second statute was
enacted. At times, conflicts only appear after a statute has been applied to
a particular set of facts. Finally, as we have seen, it is difficult to pass legislation. There are many reasons why the legislature might have chosen not
to amend or repeal a conflicting, existing statute. Yet, despite the reality,
the assumptions remain.

When conflict cannot be reconciled, judges apply three canons to reconcile the conflict: (1) specific statutory language controls general statutory language, (2) later enacted statutes control earlier enacted statutes, unless the earlier statute is more specific, and (3) repeal by implication is disfavored. Stated simply,

> [i]f statutes appear to conflict, they must be construed, if possible, to give effect to each. If the conflict is irreconcilable, the later enacted statute governs. However, an earlier enacted specific, special, or local statute prevails over a later enacted general statute unless the context of the later enacted statute indicates otherwise.

UNIF. STATUTE & RULE CONSTR. ACT, § 10a (1995). Let's explore each of these canons in more detail, starting with specific and general statutes. If two statutes so conflict that, despite a judge's best attempts to reconcile them, they are irreconcilable, what should a judge do? How does a judge know which statute was meant to be repealed, wholly or partially, and which was meant to apply? These next sections resolve these questions.

1. Specific Statutes Trump General Statutes

The first canon seems simple: a specific statute governs a general statute. This canon has special force when Congress has enacted a comprehensive statutory scheme, deliberately targeting specific problems with specific solutions. The general-specific canon is often applied to statutes in which a specific prohibition or permission contradicts a general permission or prohibition. To eliminate the contradiction, the specific provision is construed as an exception to the general one, because "the presumption is that the legislature intended the specific provision to be an exception to the general [provision]." RONALD B. BROWN & SHARON J. BROWN, STATUTORY INTERPRETATION: THE SEARCH FOR LEGISLATIVE INTENT 90–91 (2002). But the canon applies equally as well to statutes in which a general authorization and a more limited, specific authorization can exist side-by-side. "There the canon avoids not contradiction but the superfluity of a specific provision that is swallowed by the general one, 'violat[ing] the cardinal rule that, if possible, effect shall be given to every clause and part of a statute.'" *RadLAX Gateway Hotel, LLC v. Amalgamated Bank*, 132 S. Ct. 2065, 2070–71 (2012). The general-specific canon is not absolute; however, it is merely a strong indication of statutory meaning that textual indications pointing in the other direction can overcome.

When two statutes conflict, courts ask first whether one of the two statutes is more specific than the other. What is the difference between a general and specific statute? General statutes apply universally, while specific statutes apply only in certain situations. Thus, a statute regulating domesticated animals would be general while, one regulating swine would be specific. But determining whether a statute is general or specific can be more difficult than it might seem. The case of *Williams v. Kentucky*, 829 S.W.2d 942 (Ky. Ct. App. 1992), illustrates how judges struggle with this determination. In that case, a state statute directed the trial judge to consider whether a criminal defendant was entitled to community service as an alternative to prison *in every case. Id.* at 944 (citing KY. REV. STAT. ANN. § 500.095) (the "community service statute"). This statute was mandatory in that it required a judge to consider community service for every criminal case. A second statute prohibited defendants who used a gun from being eligible for "probation ... or conditional discharge" at all. *Id.* (citing KY. REV. STAT. ANN. § 533.060(1)) (the "gun statute"). This statute was also mandatory, for it prevented a judge from considering probation for any defendant who used a gun during the commission of a crime. The two statutes conflicted; it was unclear whether the judge should have considered community service for a defendant who used a gun in the commission of a crime. To resolve the conflict, the court tried to determine whether one statute was more specific than the other statute.

The court concluded that both statutes were specific; thus, the general-specific canon was inapposite. *Id.* at 945. This conclusion seems wrong. The community service statute is more general; it applies to all criminal defendants. The gun statute is more specific; it applies only to defendants who used a gun. The court could simply have determined that the gun statute, being the more specific statute, applied to the defendant's situation; thus, no parole. To resolve the conflict, however, the court turned to a second canon: the last-in-time (or later enacted) canon, which we will study in more detail in a moment.

In another case, the Florida Supreme Court addressed the same question — when is a statute specific and when is it general. *Palm Beach Cty. Canvassing Bd. v. Harris*, 772 So. 2d 1220 (Fla. 2000). This case was one of the many cases that addressed the 2000 election battle between then presidential contenders, Republican George W. Bush and Democrat Vice-President Albert Gore, Jr. The election in Florida was extremely close. An automatic recount was triggered and was conducted. *Id.* at 1226 (citing FLA. STAT. ANN. § 102.141(4) (2000)). After the recount, the vote was still extremely close, so the Florida Democratic Executive Committee requested that sample manual recounts of a percentage of the vote be conducted in certain counties. The manual recounts narrowed George Bush's lead. *Id.* Based on these recounts, several of the county canvassing boards determined that the sample manual recounts showed potential error, which could affect the outcome of the election. *Id.* Based on this determination, several canvassing boards voted to conduct countywide manual recounts pursuant to Florida's election law. *Id.* (citing FLA. STAT. ANN. § 102.166(5)(c) (2000)).

The problem was that Florida law required that all county returns be certified by 5 p.m. on the seventh day after an election; the recounts simply could not be done within that time frame. So, one canvassing board sought an advisory opinion from the Division of Elections as to whether this deadline applied. *Id.* The Division of Elections concluded that the deadline was firm. *Id.* Relying upon this advisory opinion, the Florida Secretary of State, Republican Katherine Harris (the "Secretary"), said that she would ignore returns from the manual recounts received after the deadline. The canvassing boards sued seeking a declaratory judgment and injunctive relief that the Secretary should count all late returns.

The trial court held that the deadline was mandatory, but that the Secretary could consider, in her discretion, amended returns that came in after the deadline. *Id.* at 1227. The amended returns were filed. But the Secretary, exercising her discretion, refused to consider them. *Id.* As a result of her refusal to consider the returns, the Florida Democratic Party and Al Gore, in a separate action, filed a motion seeking to compel the Secretary to accept the amended returns. *Id.* The trial court denied that motion. Both cases were consolidated for appeal to Florida's Supreme Court.

There were many issues before the court. The relevant one here was whether the Secretary was required to consider the returns when the returns were received after the seven day deadline set forth in sections 102.111 and 102.112 of Florida's election law. *Id.* at 1228. Florida law provided that "any candidate whose name appeared on the ballot ... or any political party whose candidates' names appeared on the ballot may file a written request with the county canvassing board for a manual recount" accompanied by the "reason that the manual recount is being requested." *Id.* at 1231–31 (quoting FLA. STAT. ANN. § 102.166(4)(a) & (b)). This statute further provided that the written request had to be made prior to the time the Canvassing Board certified the returns or within seventy-two hours after the election, whichever occurred later. *Id.* The recount would likely take some time, but the statute did not identify a time frame within which the recount had to be completed. Thus, the recount provision conflicted with Florida law sections 102.111 and 102.112, which required the boards to submit returns to the Elections Canvassing Commission by 5:00 p.m. of the seventh day following the election or face a penalty. *Id.* at 1233. What penalty had to be imposed was unclear because 102.111 and 102.112

conflicted: 102.111 *required* the Division of Elections to ignore late returns, while 102.112 *allowed* the Division of Elections to ignore late returns, but required it to impose a fine. *Id.* at 1234. In other words, 102.111 was mandatory, while 102.112 was permissive regarding whether the Division of Elections could ignore the late returns.

To resolve the conflict, the court turned first to the general-specific canon. *Id.* at 1234. Finding that 102.111 (the mandatory statute) was the more general statute, the court held that 102.112 (the permissive statute) controlled the issue of whether the returns could be considered when filed after the deadline because it was more specific:

> First, it is well-settled that where two statutory provisions are in conflict, the specific statute controls the general statute. In the present case, whereas section 102.111 in its title and text addresses the general makeup and duties of the Elections Canvassing Commission, the statute only tangentially addresses the penalty for returns filed after the statutory date, noting that such returns "shall" be ignored by the Department. Section 102.112, on the other hand, directly addresses in its title and text both the "deadline" for submitting returns and the "penalties" for submitting returns after a certain date; the statute expressly states that such returns "may" be ignored and that dilatory Board members "shall" be fined. Based on the precision of the title and text, section 102.112 constitutes a specific penalty statute that defines both the deadline for filing returns and the penalties for filing returns thereafter and section 102.111 constitutes a non-specific statute in this regard. The specific statute controls the non-specific statute.

Id. at 1234. Because the permissive statute was specific, the court held that it controlled in this conflict. Ultimately, the United States Supreme Court stopped the recount altogether. *Bush v. Gore*, 531 U.S. 98 (2000) (holding that the Florida Supreme Court's method for recounting ballots was unconstitutional and that no alternative method could be established within the time limits established by the statute). Had the Supreme Court not stepped in, then the specific-general canon may have decided the 2000 election!

Thus, when two statutes conflict and cannot be reconciled, the starting point for the court should be to determine whether one of the two statutes is more specific. While determining whether one statute is more specific can be challenging, generally, where one statute has a broader application, it is the more general statute. When the general-specific inquiry fails, however, courts apply a second canon: the last-in-time, or later enacted, canon.

2. Later Enacted Statutes Trump Earlier Enacted Statutes

If both statutes are specific or general, then judges apply a different tie-breaking canon: The newer statute (or provision) generally trumps the older one (the last-in-time canon). The more recently enacted statute is viewed as the clearest and most recent expression of legislative intent. This last-in-time canon respects the power of each legislature: Legislatures have the power to enact laws only while in office. One legislature cannot bind the ability of a future legislature to enact statutes; thus, subsequent legislatures can always amend, repeal, modify, or leave alone a statute. Hence, the latter enacted statute controls to the extent of any inconsistency between it and an existing statute, unless the legislature intended otherwise. Often these two canons — specific versus general and last-in-time — are examined serially in judicial opinions.

For example, in the first case in the last section, *Williams v. Kentucky*, 829 S.W.2d 942 (Ky. Ct. App. 1992), the court had to reconcile two, apparently inconsistent (and specific) statutes. One statute, the "community service statute," directed the trial judge to consider whether a criminal defendant was entitled to community service as an alternative to prison *in every case*. *Id.* at 944 (citing KY. REV. STAT. ANN. § 500.095). A second statute, the "gun statute," prohibited judges from considering "probation . . . or conditional discharge" for defendants who used a gun during the commission of their crime. *Id.* (citing KY. REV. STAT. ANN. § 533.060(1)).

Remember that the majority concluded that both statutes were specific. *Id.* at 945. Prior to reaching that result, however, the majority first considered whether the community service statute should trump the gun statute because the community service statute was enacted later. Concluding that if the community service statute were controlling, it would "make a nullity of the [gun statute]," the court rejected the result the last-in-time canon suggested. *Id.* at 945. In contrast, the dissent concluded that, because the mandatory statute was enacted later than the gun statute, the mandatory statute should have controlled. *Id.* at 947 (Huddleston, J., concurring in part and dissenting in part).

Ultimately, in *Williams*, none of the timing canons helped the majority resolve the issue. First, the majority could not reconcile the statutes; second, the majority rejected the last-in-time canon; and third, the majority rejected the general versus specific canon. The majority had to turn to the linguistic canon *in pari materia* to resolve the issue; the court looked at other, related statutes that the parties did "not otherwise present[] or argue[] in [the] appeal." *Id.* at 945. Looking at the comprehensive scheme presented by all the statutes, the majority concluded that the gun statute applied; thus, the court held that the trial court correctly refused to consider community service. *Id.* at 946.

Notably, the majority applied these two canons in the wrong order. A court should look first to whether one statute is more specific than the other, and only when that canon fails should the court turn to the last-in-time canon. This order better allows courts to give effect to both statutes, rather than find that one trumps the other. The majority in *Williams* did not approach the canons in the correct order. But in *Palm Beach County Canvassing Board*, the court approached this inquiry properly. In that case, the court addressed the timing of the statutes only after addressing their specificity. According to the court, "the provision in section 102.111 stating that the Department 'shall' ignore returns was enacted in 1951.... On the other hand, the penalty provision in section 102.112 stating that the Department "may" ignore returns was enacted in 1989.... The more recently enacted provision may be viewed as the clearest and most recent expression of legislative intent." *Palm Beach Cty. Canvassing Bd.*, 772 So. 2d at 1234.

Sometimes, neither of these two canons resolves the conflict. Then the issue is whether one statute or provision impliedly repealed the other.

3. Repeal by Implication Is Disfavored

New statutes should be interpreted harmoniously with existing statutes whenever possible. But, sometimes, harmony is simply not possible. When two statutes cannot be reconciled, one way to address the conflict is to conclude that the later statute repealed the earlier statute either explicitly or implicitly. Judges presume that a legislature would not go through the legislative process without intending to change existing law in some way. Thus, every new act should change the status quo, by adding to, modifying, or repealing existing law. But while modification is to be expected, outright repeal is not. Normally, when a legislature wants to repeal a statute or a section of a statute, it does so expressly. Thus, in the absence of an express repeal, it is likely the legislature did not intend any repeal at all. When a legislature intends to repeal a statute, it should say so clearly; repeals should not be implied. Thus, courts apply a canon of negative presumption: repeals—full or partial—by implication are disfavored. This canon rests on the potentially flawed presumption that the legislature was aware of the conflicting with the existing statute and specifically opted not to repeal it. Hence, this presumption yields when there is evidence that the legislature intended for the second statute to repeal the first. For example, if the new statute comprehensively covers the entire subject matter of the existing statute and is complete in itself, then the legislature likely intended the new statute to supersede any existing statutes on the subject. Also, if the new statute is completely incompatible with an existing statute, repeal may be appropriate.

In statutory interpretation cases, this issue arises when a judge finds (1) a statute conflicts with an existing statute, (2) the conflict is irreconcilable, and (3) the legislature did not explain how the conflict should be resolved. If there are two reasonable interpretations, the judge should choose the interpretation that does not repeal the existing statute or any part of it. If there is irreconcilability, then the second statute is only repealed to the extent of the irreconcilability; if any part of the earlier statute can exist in harmony with the later statute, that part of the earlier statute is not repealed.

Sometimes, Congress repeals an existing statute with a later statute and then later repeals the later statute. In the past, courts had held that when this happened, the earlier statute was revived, or become effective, again. But Congress and many state legislatures have abolished this old common law canon. 1 U.S.C. § 108 (2012). Hence, today, an express or implied repeal of one statute does not revive an earlier statute. The original statute remains repealed.

Also, just because a statute is no longer necessary does not mean it is automatically repealed. For example, state sodomy laws were not repealed as society's mores changed. Rather, state legislatures would have to repeal any existing statutes. For this reason, sodomy laws remain on the books in many states, although they are unconstitutional under *Lawrence v. Texas*, 539 U.S. 558 (2003).

One of the more well-known cases addressing implied repeal is *Morton v. Mancari*, 417 U.S. 535 (1974). This case involved the irreconcilability of two statutes: the Indian Reorganization Act of 1934 ("IRA") and the Equal Employment Opportunity Act of 1972 ("EEO"). The earlier Act, the IRA, provided that "qualified Indians shall hereafter have the preference to appointment to vacancies in [the Bureau of Indian Affairs ("BIA")]." *Id.* at 538 (citing 25 U.S.C. § 472). But the EEO, which was enacted subsequently, specifically provided, "[a]ll personnel actions affecting employees of applicants for employment ... [with] the Federal Government ... shall be made free from any discrimination based on race color, religion, sex, or national origin." *Id.* at 540 (citing 42 U.S.C. § 2000e-16(a)). The EEO did not expressly repeal the IRA. Plaintiffs, who were non-Indian, BIA employees, challenged the agency's hiring preference adopted under the IRA. *Id.* at 535. Although the district court held that the EEO impliedly repealed the IRA, the Supreme Court disagreed. Citing the implied repeal canon, the Court said, "[i]n the absence of some affirmative showing of an intention to repeal, the only permissible justification for a repeal by implication is when the earlier and later statutes are irreconcilable. Clearly, this is not the case here." *Id.* at 550 (citing *Georgia v. Penn. R.R.*

Co., 324 U.S. 439, 456–57 (1945)). Somewhat disingenuously, the Court concluded that a specific provision aimed at furthering Native American self-government could exist harmoniously with a general rule prohibiting employment discrimination based on race. *Id.* In essence, the BIA preference became an implied exception to the EEO; generally, employers cannot discriminate on the basis of race, except when the employer is the BIA and the race is Native American. In this case, the Court heralded the canon disfavoring repeal by implication to reach this result; additionally, the Court turned to the canon that directs that specific statutes, like the IRA, trump general statutes, like the EEO.

There is a related aspect to this implied repeal canon: The presumption against repeal is especially strong when the second bill is an appropriations (or budget) bill. The presumption is stronger because appropriations bills have a limited and specific purpose: providing funds for authorized programs. These types of bills are supposed to be purely fiscal in nature and not make substantive changes to the law; hence, courts consider it highly unlikely that a legislature would repeal existing law through an appropriations bill. But, as with all canons, this presumption can be overcome with specific evidence that the legislature did intend to repeal the existing law impliedly through the later appropriations bill.

The quintessential case rejecting such an argument is *Tennessee Valley Authority v. Hill*, 437 U.S. 153 (1978). *Tennessee Valley* is well-known in the environmental arena because the Court permanently enjoined construction of the Tellico Dam, which was virtually complete, to protect the snail darter, a very small and non-descript species of fish. Construction on the dam started in 1967. In 1973, Congress passed the Endangered Species Act, which authorized the Secretary of the Interior (the "secretary") to declare animal species "endangered" and to identify any "critical habitat" of that species. *Id.* at 159–60 (citing 16 U.S.C. § 1531 *et seq.* (1976)). The secretary was further authorized to take "such action necessary to insure that *actions* authorized, funded, or carried out by [the federal government] do not jeopardize the continued existence of [an] endangered species ... or result in the destruction or modification of habitat of such species...." *Id.* at 160 (quoting 16 U.S.C. § 1536 (1976)) (emphasis added). The issue in the case was whether the word "actions" in the Act included almost completed projects.

In late 1975, the secretary identified the snail darter as endangered and declared that the area that the Tellico Dam would affect was the snail darter's "critical habitat." The secretary then directed the Tennessee Valley Authority, which was building the dam, to stop construction. *Id.* at 161–62. Litigation ensued. While the litigation was pending and despite the secretary's order, Congress continued to appropriate funds for the dam's completion: "The [House Committee on Appropriations] directs that the project ... should be completed as promptly as possible...." *Id.* at 164 (citing H.R. REP. NO. 94-319, at 76 (1975)).

Meanwhile, the litigation was winding its way through the courts. Because the dam was so close to completion, the district court refused to stop the dam construction, despite agreeing with the Secretary that completion of the dam would completely destroy the fish's habitat. *Id.* at 165-66. But the Sixth Circuit and a majority of the Supreme Court disagreed. Both held that the language of the Endangered Species Act permitted no exceptions, even for projects near completion. *Id.* at 169.

As for the fact that Congress had continued to provide appropriations for the Tellico Dam, the Supreme Court majority cited *Morton v. Mancari*, 417 U.S. 535 (1974), for the cardinal rule that repeals by implication are disfavored. *Tennessee Valley*, 437 U.S. at 189. The majority further explained that "the [canon] applie[d] with even *greater* force when the claimed repeal rests solely on an Appropriations Act." *Id.* The majority identified the rationale behind this canon as follows: When voting to approve appropriations bills, legislators should be able to assume that the funds earmarked in the bill will be devoted to projects that are lawful. Without such an assurance, every appropriations measure might alter substantive legislation, repealing by implication any prior statute that conflicted with the expenditure. Thus, members of Congress would need to exhaustively review every appropriation in excruciating detail before voting on it. *Id.* Moreover, a House Rule specifically prohibited appropriations bills from "changing existing law...." *Id.* at 191 (citing House Rule XXI(2)). Hence, the Supreme Court ordered construction on the dam to halt.

Justice Powell dissented. Powell believed that the word "actions" in the Endangered Species Act did not apply to projects that were completed or substantially so, for such an interpretation would be absurd and not what Congress likely intended. *Id.* at 196 (Powell, J., dissenting). Rather, he believed that the language in the statute applied only to *prospective* actions. As for the appropriations bill argument, Powell agreed that appropriations acts are not entitled to significant weight, but in this case the bills and the statements made during their enactment simply confirmed the original congressional intent: that the dam be completed. *Id.* at 210 (Powell, J., dissenting). Interestingly, Powell concluded his dissenting opinion with a statement that Congress would likely soon rectify the majority's error. Powell was correct. In 1980, after prolonged fighting, Congress added a rider to another appropriations bill that authorized the Tennessee Valley Authority to continue construction on the dam despite the Endangered Species Act. Energy and Water Development Appropriation Act of

1980, Pub. L. No 96-69, tit. IV, 93 Stat. 437, 449 (1979). Thus, Congress expressly limited the Endangered Species Act as it applied to the Tellico Dam in an appropriations act.

In summary, when two statutes conflict and the conflict cannot be reconciled, courts ask first whether one statute is specific and the other general. If that distinction does not resolve the dispute, courts look next to whether one statute was enacted later than the other because the last in time should control. Finally, if neither of these tie-breakers resolves the issue, the court will determine whether one statute expressly or impliedly repealed the other statute. Generally, implied repeals are disfavored, especially when the later, conflicting statute is an appropriations act.

D. Retroactive Statutes

Another time-related issue is retroactivity. In addition to addressing conflicts among statutes, judges must also determine whether a particular statute was meant to apply to past behavior. Legislatures have the power to amend statutes and to decide that the amended statute applies to events occurring before the statute's effective date. But for a variety of reasons—most notably that statutes that apply retroactively may violate due process—legislatures normally enact statutes with prospective effect, meaning that the statute will apply only to future conduct. Rarely do legislatures enact statutes with retroactive as well as prospective effect, meaning that the statute will apply to both past and future conduct.

But retroactivity provisions can serve legitimate purposes. For example, such provisions allow a legislature to respond to emergencies, to correct mistakes, to prevent circumvention of a new statute in the interval immediately preceding its passage, and to give comprehensive effect to a new law. The requirement that a legislature clearly state its intention to make a statute retroactive helps ensure that the legislature actually thought about this issue and concluded that the benefits of retroactivity outweighed the potential for disruption or unfairness.

The applicable canon thus states that statutes are applied prospectively rather than retroactively absent a retroactivity provision or clear legislative intent to the contrary. In other words, prospective application is the default. *Landgraff v. USI Film Products*, 511 U.S. 244, 286 (1994) (Scalia, J., concurring) ("[A] legislative enactment affecting substantive rights does not apply retroactively absent [a] *clear statement* to the contrary.") The basis for prospective application being the default is that "[e]lementary considerations of fairness dictate that individuals should have an opportunity to know what the law is and to conform their conduct accordingly; settled expectations should not be lightly disrupted." *Id.* at 265. The *Ex Post Facto Clause* of the U.S. Constitution flatly prohibits retroactive application of *penal* legislation; thus, retroactivity issues should arise only in civil actions. We will explore the retroactive effect of penal statutes in more detail in Chapter 13; this section is limited to the application of this canon in civil cases.

Let's look at the canon at work. In *Landgraff*, an employee sued her former employer for a co-worker's sexual harassment and retaliation. *Id.* at 248. At the time she sued, Title VII did not authorize any recovery of damages even though the plaintiff had been injured. *Id.* at 250. While the action was pending, however, the Civil Rights Act of 1991 was enacted, which created a right to recover compensatory and punitive damages for violations of Title VII and provided for jury trial when such damages were claimed. *Id.* at 249. Plaintiff argued that the Act applied retroactively to her case. Applying the canon, the Court disagreed and held that the Act did not apply to cases pending on appeal when it was enacted. *Id.* at 286.

Retroactive statutes are not impermissible in all cases. Before deciding whether a statute is *impermissibly* retroactive, a court must ask first whether the effect of a statute is retroactive. A statute has retroactive effect when the statute defines the legal significance of actions or events that occurred prior to the statute's enactment. The Maryland Court of Appeals applied this test in *State Ethics Commission v. Evans*, 855 A.2d 364 (Md. 2004). Before the facts giving rise to the case occurred, the defendant had been convicted of nine counts of wire and mail fraud. Thirteen months later and in direct response to the defendant's actions, the Maryland legislature amended its government code to permit the State Ethics Commission (the "commission") to revoke the registration of any lobbyist who had been convicted of bribery or similar crimes. *Id.* at 365–66. After serving his prison sentence, the defendant registered as a lobbyist. Relying on the amendment, the commission revoked his registration. *Id.*

The majority and dissent disagreed as to whether the revocation of the defendant's registration based on a criminal conviction that had occurred prior to the effective date of the statute constituted a retroactive or prospective application of the law. Further, they disagreed over the appropriate test for determining whether a statute was retroactive. The dissent offered a two-factor test for retroactivity: (1) whether the commission's action impaired a vested right, or (2) whether it changed the legal significance of a completed transaction. *Id.* at 374 (Cathell, J., dissenting). The dissent said that, in this case, the commission's action did neither; hence, the statute had only prospective effect. *Id.*

In response to the dissent's analysis, the majority stated that it was "hard-pressed to understand" how a statute that, for the first time, permitted the commission to revoke a lobbyist's registration solely on the basis that the lobbyist had been convicted of certain criminal offenses did not change the legal significance of a conviction that occurred prior to the effective date of the statute. *Id.* at 373. In any event, the majority disagreed with the dissent's vested-rights prong of the test because that prong conflated retroactivity with *constitutionally impermissible* retroactivity. *Id.* at 374. The majority described the test as whether the statute " 'purports to determine the legal significance of acts or events that [] occurred prior to the statute's effective date....' " *Id.* (quoting *St. Comm'n on Human Rel. v. Amecom Div.*, 360 A.2d 1, 3 (Md. 1976)).

Simply because a statute is retroactive does not make it *impermissibly* retroactive. Retroactive statutes are allowable in certain situations. A statute may apply retroactively when (1) there is clear evidence that the legislature intended retroactive effect, and (2) no vested right is impaired. *Id.* The first caveat is a statutory interpretation caveat, while the latter caveat is a constitutional one. *Id.* Looking only at the first caveat, the majority in *Evans* found that, even though the statute had been amended specifically in response to the defendant's actions, that fact alone did not rebut the presumption against retroactivity. *Id.* A clearer statement from the legislature was needed. The majority never reached the constitutional issue of whether this statute impaired a vested right. *Id.*

As noted, evidence that the legislature intended retroactive effect can rebut this presumption of future effect, but such evidence is not found easily. For example, in *McClung v. Employment Development Department*, 99 P.3d 1015 (Cal. 2004), the Supreme Court of California rejected an argument that a statutory amendment was retroactive despite language in the amendment that the amendment was meant to clarify a prior statute. *Id.* at 1021. The facts of the case are largely irrelevant, but the procedural history is central. In an earlier case, *Carrisales v. Department of Corrections*, 988 P.2d 1083 (1999), the court had interpreted a California statute prohibiting employment discrimination to impose liability on employers, but not on nonsupervisory employees. The state legislature did not agree with *Carrisales'* holding. Thus, following the *Carrisales'* decision, the state legislature amended the statute to impose personal liability on nonsupervisory employees who committed harassment. Importantly, the legislature added language to the amendment that said it was "declaratory of existing law." *McClung*, 99 P.3d at 1017 (citing CAL. GOV'T CODE § 12940(j)(2)). The issue for the court was whether the amendment should have retroactive effect (1) when the amendment stated that it simply declared existing law, but

(2) when the amendment conflicted with an existing judicial interpretation of that statute.

The court noted that if the amendment merely stated existing law, then the issue of retroactivity would not be presented because a statute that merely clarifies existing law and does not change existing law would have no retroactive effect even if applied to circumstances predating its enactment. *Id.* at 1019. In other words, liability would have attached at the time the act became law; the later amendment would not have changed liability. In contrast, when an amendment changes the law, then issues related to retroactivity do arise. In *McClung*, the court then asked two questions: First, did the amendment merely clarify the law or change it? And second, if the amendment changed the law, did that change apply retroactively? *Id.*

Holding that *Carrisales* stated the law because the judiciary is charged with interpreting statutes, the court held that the later amendment changed rather than clarified the law because the amendment conflicted with *Carrisales*'s holding. *Id.* at 1021. As a side point, the plaintiff had argued that because *Carrisales* postdated the actions in the lawsuit in question, even the court's interpretation should pose retroactivity issues. But the court disagreed and explained that judicial interpretations may always apply retroactively because "a judicial construction of a statute is an authoritative statement of what the statute meant before as well as after the decision of the case giving rise to that construction." *Id.* In other words, courts interpret statutes as of the enactment date forward; hence, there is no retroactivity issue when courts interpret statutes.

The court then turned to the question of whether the amendment could apply retroactively. The court noted that prospective application is the presumption, but this presumption can be overcome with a showing that the legislature intended otherwise. *Id.* Finding nothing in the statute or legislative history to overcome the presumption, the court held that the amendment was prospective only. *Id.* The court rejected plaintiff's argument that subsection 12940(j)(2) showed such an intent because that subsection predated *Carrisales* and was inserted in reference to another change to the statute. *Id.* at 1022. The dissent disagreed with the second step of the majority's analysis and argued that subsection 12940(j)(2) showed clear legislative intent for retroactive effect. *Id.* at 1024 (Moreno, J., concurring and dissenting).

In summary, courts presume that statutes apply prospectively. For civil statutes, the presumption can be rebutted with clear evidence that the legislature intended the statute to apply retroactively if retroactive application will not impair a vested right. And, a statute has retroactive effect when that statute defines the legal significance of acts or events that occurred prior to the statute's enactment. In contrast, criminal statutes never apply retroactively without violating the *ex post facto* clause. Chapter 13 addresses this issue in detail, for the prohibition against penal statutes applying retroactively is constitutionally based.

E. Statutes from Other Jurisdictions

The next two subsections address two issues that cross jurisdictions. What relevance should judicial interpretations from other jurisdictions, whether state or federal, have on the interpretation of a statute? For common law decisions, the judicial interpretations of other jurisdictions are merely persuasive, never more than that. But when statutory interpretation is involved, judicial interpretations are important in two situations: when a state borrows a statute from another jurisdiction and when a state enacts a uniform or model act.

1. Modeled & Borrowed Statutes

A legislature may model one statute after an existing statute; modeling happens intra-jurisdictionally. For example, the Age Discrimination in Employment Act ("ADEA") was modeled after three acts: the National Labor Relations Act, the Fair Labor Standards Act ("FLSA"), and Title VII of the Civil Rights Act. When Congress models, courts will look to the modeling statute and its settled judicial interpretations for guidance on interpreting the modeled statute. Thus, in *Lorrillard v. Pons*, 434 U.S. 575 (1978), the Supreme Court looked at FLSA to determine whether ADEA provided a right to jury trials because ADEA specifically provided that it be interpreted in accordance with the "powers, remedies, and *procedures*" of FLSA. *Id.* at 579 n.5 (quoting 29 U.S.C. §626(b)). Because FLSA provided such a right, the Court held that ADEA did as well. *Id.* at 579.

Similarly, states routinely borrow statutes, in whole or in part, from other jurisdictions: borrowing occurs inter-jurisdictionally. States borrow because it is simpler than creating a statute anew. When a state legislature borrows a statute from another jurisdiction—whether state or federal—courts assume that the borrowing legislature took not only the statutory language, but also any settled judicial opinions interpreting that statute from the highest court in the patterning jurisdiction at the time of the adoption. *Zerbe v. State*, 583 P.2d 845, 846 (Alaska 1978) (refusing to adopt the judicial opinion of a lower court). This canon is based on the presumptions that the borrowing legislature (1) was aware of the judicial interpretations in the patterning jurisdiction, and (2) intended those interpretations to guide its own judiciary. But after the borrowing occurs, subsequent judicial opinions in the patterning jurisdiction are simply informative; the borrowing state's judiciary remains free to reject the later interpretations.

For example, in *Van Horn v. William Blanchard Co.*, 438 A.2d 552 (N.J. 1981), the plaintiff sued two defendants, a general contractor and a subcontractor, after he fell at his workplace. *Id.* at 553. The jury found that the plaintiff was 50% at fault, the general contractor was 30% at fault, and the subcontractor was 20% at fault. The state's comparative negligence statute barred recovery when a plaintiff's negligence was "greater than the negligence of *the person* against whom recovery is sought." *Id.* at 554 (quoting N.J. STAT. ANN. 2A:15-5.1) (emphasis added). In this case, because the plaintiff's negligence was greater than the *individual* negligence of either of the joint tortfeasors, the trial court entered judgment for the defendants. The plaintiff argued that the court should have taken an aggregate, rather than an individual, approach to the determination: if the plaintiff's negligence was less than the defendants' *combined* negligence, the plaintiff should be able to recover. *Id.* at 553–54.

The New Jersey Supreme Court disagreed. In doing so, the court noted that the New Jersey statute was borrowed "nearly verbatim" from Wisconsin; therefore, it applied the borrowing presumption. The court reasoned that when the New Jersey legislature borrowed the statutory language from Wisconsin, it also borrowed the settled jurisprudence. Because the court believed that Wisconsin applied the individual approach, this court had to as well. *Id.* at 555–56.

The dissent did not dispute the majority's description of the general borrowing presumption. Instead, the dissent pointed out that it was unclear whether Wisconsin was the sole patterning state; the legislative history was unclear on this issue. *Id.* at 559 (Handler, J., dissenting). Thus, "[t]he decisions of the Wisconsin Courts do not constitute persuasive evidence of the intent of the New Jersey Legislature on this facet of the Act." *Id.* at 563. He noted that other possible patterning jurisdictions applied the aggregate approach. Because there was no clear patterning state, the dissent reasoned that the court's hands were not bound, and it could decide which approach the New Jersey legislature intended. Perhaps the dissent was right; a mere year later, the New Jersey Legislature amended the statute to require the aggregate approach. N.J. STAT. ANN. § 2A:15-5.3 (West 2012). You might also note that the majority ignored the canon that the plural can include the singular. (See Chapter 5.)

2. Model and Uniform Acts

Uniform and model acts are similar to borrowed acts, but these acts are borrowed from another source altogether. The National Conference of Commissioners on Uniform State Laws, the American Law Institute, and other in-

stitutional drafters develop model and uniform acts. Both types of acts are created to address multijurisdictional issues, such as interstate commerce or child
custody. Some familiar examples of these acts include the Uniform Commercial Code, the Model Business Corporation Act, the Uniform Child Custody
Jurisdiction and Enforcement Act, and the Model Penal Code. Interestingly,
Nevada appears to have adopted the most model and uniform acts with the
least number of changes. American Law Sources On-Line, *Uniform Law and
Model Acts*, AMERICAN LAW SOURCES, http://www.lawsource.com/also/usa.cgi?usm.
(last visited July 15, 2012). In addition to the web, model and uniform acts
can be found in the Uniform Laws Annotated, which is a set of books that includes the laws and annotations showing where the laws have been adopted, interpreted, and cited.

The principal difference between model and uniform acts is the importance
of uniform adoption and interpretation. For *uniform acts*, uniformity is essential. *Pileri Indus., Inc. v. Consolidated Indus., Inc.*, 740 So. 2d 1108, 1114
(Ala. Civ. App. 1999) (Crawley, J., dissenting). The Commissioners draft a
uniform act in two situations: (1) when they anticipate enactment in a large
number of jurisdictions, and (2) when they have uniformity among the various jurisdictions as a principal objective. NATIONAL CONFERENCE OF COM-
MISSIONERS ON UNIFORM STATE LAWS, STATEMENT OF POLICY ESTABLISHING
CRITERIA AND PROCEDURES FOR DESIGNATION AND CONSIDERATION OF ACTS
(2001). Thus, the Commissioners encourage state legislatures to adopt a uniform act in its entirety with as few changes as possible. The Commissioners'
principal goal when drafting a uniform act is to obtain immediate uniformity,
not uniqueness, among the states on a particular legal subject. This goal affects
interpretation in that the judicial interpretations from other states are always
strongly persuasive, regardless of when they occur.

> While opinions by courts of sister states construing a uniform act
> are not binding upon this court, we are mindful that the objective of
> uniformity cannot be achieved by ignoring utterances of other juris-
> dictions.... This does not mean that this court will blindly follow de-
> cisions of other states interpreting uniform acts but, this court will
> seriously consider the constructions given to comparable statutes in other
> jurisdictions and will espouse them to maintain conformity when they
> are in harmony with the spirit of the statute and do not antagonize
> public policy of this state.

Holiday Inns, Inc. v. Olsen, 692 S.W.2d 850, 853 (Tenn. 1985). In *Holiday
Inns*, the court agreed with other states that had interpreted the term "busi-

ness earnings" in the Uniform Division of Income for Tax Purposes Act. The court thereby rejected the state tax department's interpretation of the statute. When courts conform their interpretations of uniform acts to those of other states, courts help ensure that the construction of such acts remains standard and uniform. *Blitz v. Beth Isaac Adas Israel Congregation*, 720 A.2d 912, 918 (Md. 1998) (interpreting the word "disbursements" in the Uniform Arbitration Act to include attorney's fees, in part, because other states had done so even though the text of the Act suggested that attorney's fees should not be included).

In contrast, uniformity is less central for model acts. The Commissioners choose to draft a model act in two situations: (1) when uniformity is desirable but not primary, and (2) when the purposes of an act can be substantially achieved even though the act is not adopted in its entirety by every state. NATIONAL CONFERENCE OF COMMISSIONERS ON UNIFORM STATE LAWS, STATEMENT OF POLICY ESTABLISHING CRITERIA AND PROCEDURES FOR DESIGNATION AND CONSIDERATION OF ACTS (2001). A model act may develop new or unusual approaches to particular legal problems; the effectiveness of these approaches will likely become clearer with time. Model acts are intended as guidelines that states may adapt to best address their unique circumstances. Hence, uniformity of interpretation and application, which is so important for uniform acts, is less critical for model acts. While uniformity is less critical, it is still a guiding principle when the model act has been widely adopted. "When the words of a statute are materially the same and where the reasoning of another court interpreting the statute is sound, we do not sacrifice sovereign independence, nor undermine the unique character of Wyoming law, by relying upon the precedent of a foreign jurisdiction." *Brown v. Arp & Hammond Hardware Co.*, 141 P.3d 673, 680 (Wyo. 2006) (internal quotation marks omitted).

Sometimes a uniform act is adopted in fewer states than was originally expected. When this happens, the Commissioners may either formally or informally relegate such an act to *model-act* status; the Uniform Construction Lien Act was one such act. Such a change illustrates simply that the act was less popular than originally expected. Importantly, state legislatures are not always clear that they are adopting a model or uniform act. Hence, it may be necessary to check the legislative history to determine whether it was intended to be such an act.

The canons in this chapter all relate to the timing of legislative enactments. Courts make certain assumptions about how legislatures would expect legislation to be interpreted based on the legislative process. Hence, later statutes generally control earlier ones, specific statues generally control general ones, implied repeals are generally disfavored, and jurisdictions often borrow statutes and the judicial opinions that interpreted the patterning statute up to the point of the adoption. In the next chapter, we explore other canons related to the legislative process—those canons related to context.

F. Mastering This Topic

Return to the hypothetical ordinance provided in Chapter 1 on page 9. Remember our question: "An ambulance entered Pioneer Park to pick up and take to the hospital a man who has just suffered a heart attack. Did the ambulance driver violate the Pioneer Park Safety Ordinance (PPSO)?" The hypothetical did not provide an issue relating to conflicting statutes, nor any of the other issues in this chapter; however, let's assume that another ordinance provided as follows:

An Ordinance

To Exempt Emergency Vehicles from Traffic Regulations

Be it enacted by the Council of the City of Pioneer assembled,

(1) As used in this section the term "emergency vehicle" means any vehicle used for emergency purposes by:
 (a) The Pioneer City Police;
 (b) A rescue squad;
 (c) An emergency management agency if it is a publicly owned vehicle;
 (d) The Pioneer City Fire Department; and
 (e) An ambulance service or medical first-response provider licensed by the Pioneer Board of Emergency Medical Services, for any vehicle used to respond to emergencies or to transport a patient with a critical medical condition.
(2) Traffic regulations set forth in the Pioneer Revised Ordinances do not apply to emergency vehicles in the following circumstances:
 (a) When responding to emergency calls; or
 (b) To police vehicles when in pursuit of an actual or suspected violator of the law; or
 (c) To ambulances when transporting a patient to medical care facilities; and
 (d) The driver thereof.
(3) No portion of this subsection shall be construed to relieve the driver of the duty to operate the vehicle with due regard for the safety of all persons using public property.
(4) The driver of an emergency vehicle, when responding to an emergency call, or of a police vehicle in pursuit of an actual or suspected violator

of the law, or of an ambulance transporting a patient to a medical care facility and giving the warning, upon approaching any red light or stop signal or any stop sign shall slow down as necessary for safety to traffic, but may proceed past such red or stop light or stop sign with due regard for the safety of persons using the street or highway.

(5) The driver of an emergency vehicle, when responding to an emergency call, or of a police vehicle in pursuit of an actual or suspected violator of the law, or of an ambulance transporting a patient to a medical care facility and giving warning required by subsection (5) of this section, may drive on the left side of any highway or in the opposite direction of a one-way street provided the normal lanes of traffic are blocked and he does so with due regard for the safety of all persons using the street or highway.

(6) The driver of an emergency or public safety vehicle may stop or park his vehicle upon any street or highway, provided that, during the time the vehicle is parked at the scene of an emergency, at least one warning light is in operation at all times.

Effective: July 15, 1980.

The first question you should ask is whether this second hypothetical ordinance ("the traffic regulation exception") applies at all. While the traffic regulation exception explicitly applies to emergency vehicles including ambulances, it exempts such vehicles only from "traffic regulations." Is the PPSO (the other ordinance) a traffic regulation? Using the skills you've learned to date, determine whether the PPSO is a traffic regulation. You should be able to do this step on your own.

Assuming that you conclude that the PPSO is a traffic regulation (or that the traffic regulation exception would apply in this situation regardless), you now have two ordinances that conflict. The traffic regulation exception exempts ambulances from traffic regulations, although it makes clear that "No portion of this subsection shall be construed to relieve the driver of the duty to operate the vehicle with due regard for the safety of all persons using public property." The PPSO prohibits all motor vehicles from entering and driving in Pioneer Park. Can you reconcile these two ordinances? Perhaps: you might say that the PPSO applies in all cases in which there is *no* emergency and that the traffic regulation exception applies when there are emergencies. Such an analysis would make the traffic regulation exception an implied exception to the PPSO.

Perhaps, instead, you conclude that the conflict cannot be so easily reconciled. In that case, you must apply the rules relating to conflicting statutes: specific controls general and later controls earlier. Which ordinance is more specific? The traffic regulation exception is specific to emergency vehicles, while the PPSO applies to all motor vehicles (with identified exceptions). One might argue then that the more specific traffic regulation ordinance controls over the PPSO; thus, the driver should not be cited. However, arguably the PPSO is the specific ordinance, while the traffic regulation exception is the general ordinance: The PPSO is specific as to location—it applies only to Pioneer Park— while the traffic regulation exception applies to all locations. Lastly, both ordinances might be specific: The PPSO is specific as to location—it applies only to Pioneer Park—while the traffic regulation exception is specific as to vehicles—it applies only to emergency vehicles. Here, you see the difficulty with trying to determine whether one statute is specific and another general. You might, thus, conclude that this canon does not resolve the conflict

Moving onto the second canon—that the later enacted ordinance controls the earlier—you would conclude that the PPSO has an effective date of August 15, 1998, while the traffic regulation exception has an effective date of July 15, 1980. Because the PPSO was enacted after the traffic regulation exception, the PPSO should control; thus, the driver should be cited.

Does such a result mean that the Pioneer Council impliedly repealed all or a portion of the traffic regulation ordinance? You will remember that implied repeals are disfavored, and here there is no clear evidence of legislative intent suggesting that the Council thought about the existing ordinance at all, let alone intended to repeal any portion of it. Thus, you should conclude that the PPO did not implicitly repeal the traffic regulation exception.

Ultimately, you probably see that these canons are not terribly helpful in resolving this issue. If you were inclined to cite the driver, you have an argument to do so: the PPSO, as the later enacted statute, controls. If you were inclined not to cite the driver, you have an argument to do so: the traffic regulation exception is more specific to ambulances. Subjectivity continues.

Checkpoints

- Reminder: extrinsic sources are those sources outside of the enacted act but within the legislative process that created the act.

- When two statutes or sections of a statute conflict, a judge will first see if the conflict between the two can be reconciled, meaning that the statutes can be harmonized.

- Where two statutes are in conflict and the conflict cannot be reconciled, a specific statute controls a general statute. If neither statute is specific, then the later enacted statute controls the earlier enacted statute. These canons can both be overcome with evidence that the legislature did not intend for the conflict to be resolved as the canons direct.

- If conflict remains, then a judge will check to see if one statute repealed, in whole or in part, the other. But repeals by implication are disfavored. When a legislature wishes to repeal an existing statute, the legislature should be clear.

- Statutes are applied prospectively rather than retroactively absent a retroactivity provision or clear legislative intent to the contrary.

- When a state legislature borrows a statute from another jurisdiction—whether state or federal—courts assume that the borrowing legislature took not only the statutory language, but also any settled judicial opinions interpreting that statute from the highest court in the patterning jurisdiction at the time of the adoption as well.

- When a state legislature enacts a *uniform act*, uniformity is essential. Thus, the interpretations of other jurisdictions are always persuasive, regardless of when they occur. When a state legislature enacts a *model act*, uniformity is less important, unless the model act is widely adopted.

Chapter 9

Canons Based on Extrinsic Sources & Legislative Process: Enactment Context

---

Roadmap

- Learn to use what occurred *prior to* and *during* the enactment process.
- Understand what legislative history is, where to find it, how to use it, and how to criticize its use.
- Understand how to find purpose and discover its relevance to interpretation.

A. Introduction to This Chapter

We continue with our examination of extrinsic sources and turn to enactment context. Legislative intent and purpose can often be found by understanding what motivated the legislature to act, by knowing what information the legislature considered when it acted, and by knowing what was said during the enactment process. This chapter will explore the canons related to using legislative history and *unexpressed* purpose to discern meaning.

B. Using What Occurred Prior to and During Enactment

1. Context

Knowing why a legislature chose to act may help a judge interpret a statute. *Contextualism* is the process of using context to determine why a legislature acted to better understand what a statute means. There are different types of context, including social and historical events (social or historical context), the legal and political climate (legal or political context), economic or market factors (economic context), and even textual and linguistic patterns (textual context). We already looked at textual and linguistic context in preceding chapters (See Chapters 4–6).

In this chapter, we move to other sources of context. A judge's interpretative theory determines which, if any, of these other contexts are relevant to that judge. (See Chapter 2.) For example, textualists will look at textual, legal, and linguistic context to understand the way that a particular legislature may have used words and phrases. In contrast, purposivists will look at social, historical, legal, economic, and political context; any one of which may help them identify the statutory purpose. These types of context can help reveal the purpose of the act by showing how events of the time might have impacted a legislature's choices. For example, consider how the contexts of the following statutes may be germane to meaning:

- *Social and historical context*—the Patriot Act, which was enacted in response to the terrorist attacks of 9-11,
- *Political context*—the McCain-Feingold Act, which was enacted in response to perceived, illegal political spending,
- *Legal context*—consider the act approving appropriations to continue building the Tellico Dam, which was enacted during the pendency of *Tennessee Valley Authority v. Hill*, 437 U.S. 153 (1978),
- *Economic context*—statutes enacted during the New Deal were enacted in response to the Great Depression

Intentionalists will look at social, historical, legal, political, economic, and political context, which may help them identify the specific legislative intent. But most relevant to intentionalists is the enactment process itself. As we have seen, a statute is often the result of political compromise; contextualism allows intentionalist judges to interpret the statute so as to promote that compromise, thereby furthering legislative intent. *Mohasco Corp. v. Silver*, 447 U.S. 807, 819–20 (1980).

For some judges, context can trump ordinary meaning. For example, a federal statute prohibited bringing into the United States "*any* false, forged, or counterfeit coin or bar." *United States v. Falvey*, 676 F.2d 871, 872 (1st Cir. 1982) (quoting 18 U.S.C. §§ 485, 486) (emphasis added). The three defendants owned counterfeit Krugerrands, which are coins from South Africa and which are not in circulation in the United States. The ordinary meaning of the statute was clear: The defendants were guilty because they brought counterfeit coins into the United States. However, the court did not find the defendants guilty because earlier drafts of the bill and its legislative history demonstrated that "the only foreign coins covered by the [statute were] those 'current ... or in actual use and circulation as money within the United States.'" *Id.* at 873 (quoting the lower court opinion). Thus, the history of the statute's enactment trumped ordinary meaning in this case.

Historical, legal, economic, and social context can be found in many places, such as newspapers that were current at the time. Most commonly, as the First Circuit did in *Falvey*, judges turn to the legislative history of the bill at issue, including draft versions of the bill. Judges vary in their willingness to consider legislative history, and even in their willingness to consider all forms of legislative history; some forms of legislative history are believed to be more trustworthy than other forms. Also, some forms of legislative history are more relevant than other forms; let's explore these issues in more detail.

2. Legislative History

Legislative history can be defined as the written record of deliberations surrounding and preceding a bill's enactment. Legislative history includes all the documentation that was generated during the enactment process, including committee reports and hearing transcripts, floor debates, recorded votes, conference committee reports, presidential signing statements, veto messages, and more. Most legislative history is generated at the chokeholds, or vetogates, within the legislative process. (See Chapter 3 for a discussion of vetogates.)

Perhaps more than any other area in statutory interpretation jurisprudence, the use of legislative history to discern meaning is highly controversial. As a litigant, you need to be aware of what legislative history is relevant, how relevant it is, how to find it, how to use it, and how to criticize its use. This next section will explore the relevance of legislative history to interpretation.

a. The Legislative History Hierarchy

As mentioned above, legislative history includes everything developed during the legislative process, including committee reports, floor debates, conference committee reports, executive signing and veto statements, override memos, hearing transcripts, and even statements from sponsors. A search through all of the available documentation for the gold nugget of meaning can be burdensome, expensive, and time-consuming. Because not all legislative history has the same relevance, a savvy litigant should focus the search, especially when time and cost constraints matter. Some types of legislative history are more relevant than other types; in other words, there is a legislative history hierarchy, and smart litigants know where to focus their search.

At the top of that hierarchy is the conference committee report. This report is, perhaps, "the most persuasive evidence of congressional intent, next to the statute itself." *United States v. Salim*, 287 F. Supp. 2d 250, 340 (S.D.N.Y. 2003). You may remember from Chapter 3 that commonly the House and Senate pass different versions of a bill and that the conference committee—an ad hoc committee of select senators and representatives—meets, discusses the differences in the bill, resolves those differences, recommends action, and writes a report analyzing its work. This report is considered very good evidence of what the legislature wanted as a whole because it is the only report members from both chambers generate. It truly identifies the compromises that lead to the bill's passage. But even a conference committee report may not trump clear text. In *In the Matter of Sinclair*, 870 F.2d 1340 (7th Cir. 1989), the plaintiffs pointed to a conference committee report that contradicted the plain language of the statute. Writing for the majority, Judge Easterbrook, a textualist judge, refused to consider the report because the language of the statute was so clear. *Id.* at 1344.

Next on the hierarchy are committee reports. Committee reports are also considered to be reliable evidence of meaning because the committee primarily responsible for drafting, amending, considering, and reporting the bill to the full chamber generates them. Committee reports are written by the committee or committees (or its staff) that had jurisdiction over the bill. Generally, a committee report summarizes the bill and identifies the committee's recommendations and actions. Theoretically, all members of the committee read the report (or at least a summary of it) and vote based on the content of the report. The report follows the bill to the floor of the House or Senate, where it is expected that all members of the chamber will read the report. For these reasons, judges often rely on committee reports. For example, the Court in *Church of the Holy Trinity v. United States*, 143 U.S. 457 (1892), relied on a committee report to understand which of two meanings the legislature intended for the word "labor" (manual labor or all labor). *Id.* at 464.

If you would like to see what a simple report looks like, you will find a section of the Senate Report for the sample bill we explored in Chapter 3 (actually it is for the Senate's companion bill) in Appendix F. You may recall that the sample bill established a loan forgiveness program for lawyers who become public defenders and prosecutors. The Senate Report identifies a further concern of at least two members of the Senate: the high cost of law school.

There is another form of legislative history that should be distinguished from committee reports called "committee prints." Committee prints are documents created for a congressional committee about topics related to that committee's legislative or investigatory responsibilities. Studies by committee staff members or experts on the subject matter of a proposed bill, committee rules, and summaries of the legislative history of earlier failed legislation are examples. Committee prints are drafted for the committee's internal use and are not always available publically. RONALD BENTON BROWN & SHARON JACOBS BROWN, STATUTORY INTERPRETATION: THE SEARCH FOR LEGISLATIVE INTENT 133 (2002). Arguably, because committee prints vary significantly in content, are not always forwarded to the full chambers, and may not reflect the intent of the legislature, they should play less of a role in interpretation. *Id. at* 133–34.

Another potentially relevant source of legislative history is earlier drafts, or versions, of the bill and rejected amendments to it. The enactment process frequently involves numerous drafts as the language is refined with time. It can be instructive to see what the committee, subcommittee, or full chamber changed. Thus, earlier versions and rejected amendments might help explain what a legislature intended when it adopted the language it enacted. To illustrate, the dissent in *NLRB v. Catholic Bishop,* 440 U.S. 490, 515 (1979) (Brennan, J., dissenting), found rejected amendments informative.

It is less clear whether bills that were never enacted are relevant at all. If a prior legislature rejected those bills, they should have no relevance whatsoever. But if a legislature rejects a bill and instead adopts a compromise bill, the rejected bill might help a judge discern legislative intent. BROWN, STATUTORY INTERPRETATION, *supra,* at 137–38. Moreover, for some judges, the rejected bill might be evidence that the legislature acquiesced in, or agreed with, an earlier judicial interpretation of an act (see Chapter 10).

Some argue that the most relevant statements are the drafter's commentary because that commentary is prepared before the bill is subject to legislative manipulation by either those in favor or those opposed to the bill's passage. For example, the comments on the Uniform Commercial Code (UCC) that were prepared jointly by the National Conference of Commissioners on Uniform State Laws, the American Bar Association, and the American Law Institute are generally found to be very relevant to that Act's meaning. These drafters are considered experts in the area; they had tremendous knowledge of the bill and its purpose. Given that they are academics and practicing attorneys, their comments were deliberate and thoughtful, rather than political. Additionally, the legislature that voted to enact the UCC likely considered the comments and intended that the UCC be interpreted as the comments recommended. Had the legislature wanted a different interpretation, the legislature would likely have changed the language of the bill, which the legislature was free to do. Thus, in certain circumstances, drafters' commentary can aid interpretation. For example, Justice Rehnquist in his dissent in *United Steelworkers v. Weber,* 443 U.S. 193 (1979), referred to statements from both the Senate and House sponsors to argue that Title VII of the Civil Rights Act was color-blind. *Id.* at 231–44 (Rehnquist, J., dissenting).

Others, however, argue that statements from a drafter or sponsor (the legislator proposing the bill to Congress) are not relevant to meaning because the
critical intent is not that of the individual or individuals; it is that of the legislature that enacted the bill. Additionally, staff members or lobbyists may draft
bills, whose intent would be irrelevant. Regardless of these criticisms, some
judges will still consider drafter and sponsor statements. "[N]o one can gainsay
the overwhelming judicial support for the proposition that explanations by sponsors of legislation during floor discussion are entitled to weight when they cast
light on the construction properly to be placed upon statutory language." *Over-
seas Educ. Ass'n, Inc., v. Fed. Labor Relations Auth.*, 876 F.2d 960, 967 n.41 (D.C.
Cir. 1989) (citing more than ten cases relying on sponsor statements). In contrast, lobbyist materials are usually not considered relevant to interpretation.

Statements, remarks, and debates that take place in either the Committee
of the Whole or on the floor of either chamber are low on the legislative hierarchy. There are a few problems with relying on these types of colloquy. One
problem is that they reflect only one legislator's intent, not the intent of the legislature as a whole. Because each legislator may have a unique reason for voting for a particular bill, one person's intent shows little. "The floor statements
of individual legislators are larded with remarks which reflect a political ('sales
talk') rather than a legislative purpose." *In re Virtual Network Serv. Corp.*, 98 B.R.
343, 349 (Bankr. N.D. Ill. 1989).

A second problem is that in the past remarks can be added to the debate record
without ever having been spoken on the floor for other legislators to hear. For
example, in *Harrisburg v. Franklin*, 806 F. Supp. 1181 (M.D. Pa. 1992), the court
refused to consider a legislator's written statements, which were made after the bill
was passed and were "*never actually spoken on the floor of the legislature.*" *Id.* at 1184.
Importantly, a relatively recent rule has required that these statements be clearly
marked in the extension of remarks section of the legislative history; thus, this concern has lessened, but it should be kept in mind for statutes enacted less recently.

Another potential problem is that legislators do not always attend or hear all
debates; sometimes, speeches are made to empty chambers for political or other
reasons. And even if they are heard, some people question whether the remarks
were influential. There is simply no way to know. If not influential, should they
matter? Would not this rule set up a requirement that legislators respond to all
floor comments with which they disagree? Would such a rule be efficient?

Next on the hierarchy are floor debate comments made by those opposed
to the legislation. These carry even less weight than statements from those in
agreement. "[S]peeches by opponents of legislation are entitled to relatively
little weight in determining the meaning of the Act in question." *United States
v. Pabon-Cruz*, 391 F.3d 86, 101 (2d Cir. 2004).

For all these reasons, floor debate statements, both pro and con, are generally not considered as reliable as the other forms of legislative history. Despite these concerns, judges still rely on these statements when interpreting statutes. Most famously in *United Steelworkers v. Weber*, 443 U.S. 193 (1979), the majority and dissent both relied on different parts of the floor debates to prove that their interpretation of the word "discriminate" in Title VII of the Civil Rights Act was accurate.

Finally, we reach the tail end of the hierarchy: executive signing statements and veto messages. Signing statements are actually *subsequent* history for they generally follow the bill's enactment (presidents typically sign the bill and then issue a signing statement). Moreover, neither is *legislative* history in the sense that neither comes from the legislature, but instead both come from the executive. But they are similar enough to the other forms of legislative history to be included here. As noted in Chapter 3, signing statements may indicate how an executive intends to implement a law. The relevance (if any) these statements should have on interpretation is unclear. Those advocating for their use argue that signing statements illustrate the executive's position in negotiating with the legislature. Supporters further argue that, because the executive has a constitutional role to play in enactment, the statements are germane to meaning. Those opposed to the use of these statements argue that the legislature, and only the legislature, has the constitutional power to enact law. Only the enacting legislature's intent is relevant; the executive's understanding or misunderstanding is irrelevant. Further, those opposed to the use of these statements fear that the executive has an incentive to alter meaning when writing signing statements, a fear which recent presidents have proved to be founded. Thus, opponents argue that signing statements should be irrelevant, even though the executive has to sign the bill before it becomes law. The majority took this approach in *Hamdan v. Rumsfeld*, 548 U.S. 557 (2006), when it gave no weight to President Bush's memorandum regarding his understanding of the Detainee Treatment Act of 2005.

Regardless of whether they play any role in interpretation, increasingly presidents include such statements. For example, former President George W. Bush regularly used signing statements to limit the reach of some laws. In July 2006, a task force of the American Bar Association challenged his use of the statements in this way as "contrary to the rule of law and our constitutional system of separation of powers." American Bar Association, *Blue-Ribbon Task Force Finds President Bush's Signing Statement Undermine Separation of Powers*, July 24, 2006 Press release. President Obama has also issued signing statements regularly to indicate his disagreement with portions of a bill.

b. Finding Legislative History

Now that you know what to look for, you may ask: Where do I look? This section explores text-based resources. Because online research has become so common, in Appendix C, you will find a detailed summary of where to find federal legislative history online, which Denise Gibson, a research librarian at Mercer University School of Law, compiled.

Before beginning your research, you should know the following pieces of information: (1) the public law citation (*e.g.*, Pub. L. No. 106-23) or the *Statutes at Large* citation (*e.g.*, 121 Stat. 3), and (2) the bill number and the Congress that enacted the law (*e.g.*, H.R. 3162 from the 107th Congress). If you look at the sample bill included in Appendix D, you should see that the bill number is H.R. 916 and that the Congress is the 110th. The companion bill included in Appendix E is bill number S. 442 also from the 110th Congress. Neither bill has a public law citation or Statutes at Large citation because neither was enacted, although President Obama signed an identical bill into law as part of the Higher Education Opportunities Act (Pub. L. No. 110-315, section 952).

If you know only the popular name of the statute (*e.g.*, No Child Left Behind Act), you may check *Shepard's Acts* and *Cases by Popular Names* or the Popular Names Table included with the *United States Code*, *United States Code Annotated*, or the *United States Code Service* to find the public law and Statutes at Large citation. To find numbers for bills enacted since 1904, check in the United States Statutes at Large. To locate bill numbers for laws passed prior to 1904, check Eugene Nabors, Legislative Reference Checklist: The Key to Legislative Histories from 1789 to 1903 (1982).

Armed with the information above, you may start your research. One starting point for researching legislative history is to begin with compiled legislative histories. A compiled legislative history is a resource that has already researched and collected the relevant legislative documents for a particular act. Because it is very time-consuming (and thus costly) to exhaustively research the legislative history of a particular bill, it can be helpful to rely on history that has already been compiled. Here are some compilations to consider:

- Nancy P. Johnson, Sources of Compiled Legislative Histories: A Bibliography of Government Documents, Periodical Articles, and Books (Rothman ed., 1979 & Supps.). This publication identifies government and commercial sources that contain either the text of or citations to legislative history documents.

- Bernard D. Reams Federal Legislative Histories: An Annotated Bibliography and Index to Officially Published Sources (Greenwood Press 1994). This publication includes histories published by Congressional committee staff, the Congressional Research Service, or executive agencies. It includes legislative histories for laws passed between 1796 (4th Congress, 1st Session) and 1990 (101st Congress, 2d Session). Although the scope of this text is narrower than Nancy Johnson's work, it does have some histories that she does not cover.

The *United States Code Congressional and Administrative News* ("U.S.C.C.A.N." published by Thomson Reuters) also contains selected House and Senate reports (for most laws, either a House or a Senate report is reprinted), presidential proclamations and executive orders, information on the status of pending legislation, and the full text of the Public Laws signed during the reporting period. Each bound volume has a "contents" page, which lists the following: (1) the identities of the president and cabinet members, (2) the identity of senators and representatives, and (3) congressional committees. The final volume has a series of tables that help researchers find Public Laws (1) by bill number, (2) by reference to the affected section of the *United States Code* and the *United States Code Annotated*, and (3) by popular name. One table identifies the "legislative history" of Public Laws by bill number. Other tables identify administrative regulations, proclamations, executive orders, and major bills that are pending with a record of House and Senate action to date. U.S.C.C.A.N. is an excellent place to begin your research. While the CCH Index would be useful for historical information on bills (back to 1937), the Library of Congress's online resource might be a better place to start for more recent bills: http://thomas.loc.gov/home/thomas.php. Of note: U.S.C.C.A.N. began in 1941 as the *U.S. Code Congressional Service*.

The *Congressional Record* is the official source for House and Senate debates. There are four separately paginated sections to *The Congressional Record*: the Proceedings of the Senate, the Proceedings of the House, the Extension of Remarks section, and the Daily Digest. *The Congressional Record*'s page numbers begin with a letter that represents each of these four sections: H for the House, S for the Senate, E for the Extension of Remarks section, and D for the Daily Digest. The Daily Digest is issued each day while Congress is in session. The bound *Congressional Record* is the final, permanent edition. These sections contain summaries of committee meetings, lists of witnesses from committee hearings, legislative action taken on bills, and the Senate and the House debates.

An index to *The Congressional Record* is published every two weeks; the index contains two sections. One section indexes the proceedings by subject and by speaker; the other section indexes the history of bills and resolutions by number. The indexes help researchers trace the progress of legislation through Congress and locate Senate and House debates on legislation.

Additionally, the *CIS Annual*, which the Congressional Information Services publishes, covers laws from 1970 to the present. This publication is a comprehensive index to legislative history documents. *CIS Annual* abstracts and indexes most congressional information, including House and Senate reports, hearings, and committee prints, with additional citations to *The Congressional Record*. *CIS Annual* is published monthly and cumulated annually into the following parts: a subject index, abstracts, and legislative histories. From 1970 to 1983, the *CIS Annual* abstracts contained a condensed "Legislative History" section in the back of each volume, which lists congressional documents by public law number. From 1984 to the present, the *CIS Annual* has separate Legislative History volumes.

The indexes reference *CIS Annual*'s abstracts; while the abstracts contain complete bibliographic information and a summary of the publications. Legislative documents can be located either by bill number, by Public Law number, by report number, by subject, by title, by author, or by witness name.

CIS Annual has multi-year cumulative indexes for the following time periods: 1970–74, 1975–78, 1979–82, 1983–86, 1987–1990, and 1991–1994. Beginning in 1984, an annual Legislative Histories volume was added. Note that the year of the index does not necessarily correspond to the year of the publication that you are trying to locate. Items in each annual cumulative index include titles that CIS was able to acquire and index during that year.

There is also the *CCH Congressional Index*, a loose-leaf service that tracks legislation during a particular session of Congress. There is one volume for the House and another for the Senate. It is updated weekly when Congress is in session. This index is a good source for finding the current status of bills. Bills are indexed by bill number, author, and subject. Researchers are referred to committee reports, hearings, and voting records. Publication of this resource began with the 75th Congress in 1937.

Also, the *U.S. Congressional Serial Set*, commonly referred to as the Serial Set, contains House and Senate Documents and House and Senate Reports organized by session of Congress. The publication began in 1817 with the 15th Congress. Documents generated before 1817 may be found in the *American State Papers*. In general, the Serial Set includes the following: committee reports related to bills and other matters, presidential communications to Congress, treaty materials, certain executive department publications, and certain nongovernmental publications.

The General Accounting Office's Reports may also be informative. The U.S. General Accounting Office (the "GAO") is an administrative agency within the legislative branch of the government that conducts audits, surveys, investigations, and evaluations of federal agencies and programs. The GAO's findings and recommendations are made public in written form, as written reports to Congress, or in oral form, as testimony to congressional committees. Although GAO reports are not official *legislative* history because they come from the executive, they may be relevant, especially, when the GAO contributes to the drafting or review of a bill pending before Congress. For presidential signing statements and veto messages, you should consult the *Weekly Compilation of Presidential Documents*. This compilation is current from 1965 to date.

While agencies do not enact statutes, at some point, you may need to research the history of the enactment of an agency regulation. To do so, you will need to check the *Federal Register* and the *Code of Federal Regulations*. The Office of the Federal Register, National Archives and Records Administration, publishes *The Federal Register*, which is a daily publication containing newly promulgated regulations, proposed rules, and notices from federal administrative agencies. The notices of proposed regulations often contained detailed information regarding the goal of the agency in developing the regulation, public comments responding to drafts, and other relevant information. *The Federal Register* also contains executive orders and other presidential documents. The *Code of Federal Regulations* (the "C.F.R.") is the codification of the regulations enacted by federal agencies. Like the *United States Code*, the C.F.R. is divided by subject into fifty titles. Each volume of the C.F.R. is updated once each calendar year and is issued on a quarterly basis. It contains no history, only the text of the regulation.

While federal statutes often have extensive legislative history, state statutes often do not. Additionally, the availability of state legislative history is more sporadic. Some states maintain these records (like New York), while others do not (like Georgia). You will need to check your specific state for more information.

c. Using Legislative History

Assuming that you have found legislative history for your statute, what do you do with it? Typically, judges use legislative history for one of two reasons: (1) to shed light on the specific intent of the enacting legislature, or (2) to identify statutory purpose. This section will focus on the first reason, finding specific intent; we will look at the second reason later in this chapter. Generally, when judges use legislative history to find specific intent, they are looking to discover whether the legislature had a specific idea about the precise issue before the court.

If the text of your statute is clear, you face a threshold issue: whether a judge will look at legislative history at all. Generally, textualist judges will not look at legislative history, assuming they are willing to consider this source at all, when the text is neither ambiguous nor absurd. But other judges are willing to use legislative history to confirm the ordinary meaning of a clear statute. And some, but not many, are willing to use legislative history to defeat the ordinary meaning of a statute.

For example, in the following two bankruptcy cases, the judges took different approaches to using legislative history in the face of clear text. In one case, the court refused to look at legislative history at all. *In the Matter of Sinclair*, 870 F.2d 1340 (7th Cir. 1989). In *Sinclair*, the debtors had filed a bankruptcy action under Chapter 11. Subsequently, Congress enacted Chapter 12, specifically for small farmers like the debtors. The debtors moved to convert their Chapter 11 proceeding to a Chapter 12 proceeding, which was a more favorable proceeding for debtors. Chapter 12 provided, "The amendments made by subtitle B of title II *shall not apply* with respect to cases commenced under title 11 of the *United States Code* before the effective date of this Act." *Sinclair*, 870 F.2d at 1341 (quoting Pub. L. No. 99-54) (emphasis added). Despite this clear text, a Conference Committee report suggested that conversion was possible:

> It is not intended that there be routine conversion of Chapter 11 ... cases, pending at the time of enactment, to Chapter 12. Instead, it is expected that courts will exercise their sound discretion in each case, in allowing conversions only where it is equitable to do so.
>
> Chief among the factors the court should consider is whether there is a substantial likelihood of successful reorganization under Chapter 12.

Id. The bankruptcy judge denied the debtors' motion to convert, and the Seventh Circuit affirmed, basing its decision on the clarity of the statute's text. Because the court found the statute clear, the court refused to consider the conference committee report at all. In so doing, the court indicated that legislative history should be used only to clarify unclear text because of the constitutional allocation of powers. "Legislative history helps us learn what Congress meant by what it said, but it is not a source of legal rules competing with those found in the U.S. Code." *Id.* at 1344. It will likely not surprise you that the author of *Sinclair* was Judge Easterbrook, a strong advocate of textualism.

In contrast, in the second case, the court found the text clear, but still looked at the legislative history to see if it offered additional insight. *In Re Idalski*, 123 B.R. 222 (Bankr. E.D. Mich. 1991). In *Idalski*, the court found the text of another bankruptcy statute clear, but the court still looked to see if the legislative history suggested that a different meaning was intended. In this case, a debtor had voluntarily paid money into an ERISA retirement account while she was employed. At the time she had invested, the ERISA plan prohibited any voluntary or involuntary alienation of the plan benefits to creditors. In other words, creditors could not attach the ERISA plan funds for any reason. The money in the account was subsequently returned to her after she left her employment and filed for bankruptcy. The bankruptcy trustee sought to add the money refunded to the debtor to the bankruptcy estate to distribute to the debtor's creditors. The debtor claimed the money was exempt (meaning she could keep it) under the statute. *Id.* at 223.

The relevant statute provided, "A restriction on the transfer of a beneficial interest of the debtor in a trust that is enforceable under applicable *nonbankruptcy law* is enforceable in a case under this title." *Id.* (quoting 11 U.S.C. § 541(c)(2)) (emphasis added). The issue for the court was whether an ERISA plan was created under a nonbankruptcy law. The court held that it was. The court based its decision on the ordinary meaning of the text; ERISA laws are not bankruptcy laws. *Id.* at 225. Despite the clarity of the text, the court turned to the legislative history of the bankruptcy statute. Despite looking at the legislative history, the court found it to be unhelpful because it was unclear. Thus, the court adopted the ordinary meaning. In looking at the legislative history, the *Idalski* court disagreed with the *Sinclair* court that legislative history was only relevant when text was ambiguous. Rather, the court said, "the [plain meaning] rule should be applied [only] where the statutory construction urged by a party is so inherently improbable that it defies common sense." *Id.* at 228. In all other cases, a court should "consider evidence that may substantiate a statutory construction which a party claims most accurately reflects the legislative intent[.]" *Id.* at 227. The judge in *Idalski* believed that legislative history was almost always relevant.

Interestingly, both bankruptcy judges discussed the Supreme Court's use of legislative history over the years. The judge in *Sinclair* claimed the Court had been consistent; the judge in *Idalski* claimed the Court had not been consistent. The *Idalski* judge is correct; as the Court's membership and preferred statutory approach have changed over time, the willingness of the members' of the Court to consider legislative history has also changed. Thus, depending on the judge's approach, legislative history may be used to try to confirm the meaning of clear text, to explain the meaning of ambiguous or absurd text, or to defeat the meaning of clear text. While many judges are willing to review legislative history when faced with ambiguous or absurd text today, few judges are willing to review legislative history to confirm clear text. And even fewer judges are willing to review legislative history to defeat plain text, although this use may have occurred in the past. Let's explore that history now as we discuss ways that you can critique your opponent's use of legislative history.

d. Criticizing Your Opponent's Use of Legislative History

i. Understanding the Supreme Court's Use of Legislative History

In early England, judges refused to consider the legislative history of a statute for any reason. But the United States rejected this rule relatively early in its jurisprudential history. In 1892, in *Church of the Holy Trinity v. United States*, 143 U.S. 457 (1892), the Court began expressly to look to legislative history. In that case, the Supreme Court had to decide whether a statute that prohibited the importation of foreigners to perform "labor or service of any kind" applied to ministers. Despite the relative clarity of the text (rectoring is labor), the Court reviewed the legislative history of the bill and concluded that the enacting legislature had intended to stem the influx of cheap, manual labor from China. Because the purpose of the bill was to stem cheap Chinese labor, "labor" meant manual labor only. *Id.* at 464. Following *Holy Trinity's* approach, courts began regularly to turn to legislative history to discern legislative intent.

Over time, the Court's willingness to consider legislative history has waxed and waned. As the preferred statutory interpretation approach has changed, the use of legislative history has changed accordingly. When purposivism was popular, so was the Court's use of legislative history. At that time, the Court did not need a reason to look at legislative history, such as ambiguity or absurdity. Legislative history was considered regardless of the clarity of the text. "When aid to the construction of the meaning of words, as used in the statute, is available, there certainly can be no 'rule of law' which forbids its use, however clear the words may appear on 'superficial examination.'" *United States v. Am. Trucking Ass'ns, Inc.*, 310 U.S. 534, 543-44, 560 (1940) (footnotes omitted).

Similarly, when members of the Court preferred intentionalism, legislative history became central to their analyses, so much so that, in some cases, judges discussed the legislative history of a statute before addressing the text. For example, in *Chevron U.S.A. Inc. v. Natural Resources Defense Council, Inc.*, 467 U.S. 837 (1984), the Court first reviewed the legislative history of the relevant act to determine whether Congress had a specific intent regarding the language at issue. Only after reviewing the legislative history (and coming up with no answers) did the Court discuss the text of the statute.

All that changed, however, after Justice Scalia joined the Court (in 1986) and refocused the statutory interpretation discourse (something he had started while on the D.C. Circuit Court). As a result of his efforts, text reemerged as primary to the inquiry. In refocusing the inquiry, Justice Scalia directly assaulted the other Justices' use of legislative history. For example, in *Koons Buick Pontiac GMC, Inc. v. Nigh*, 543 U.S. 50 (2004), Justice Scalia said:

Needless to say, I also disagree with the Court's reliance on things that the sponsors and floor managers of the 1995 amendment failed to say. I have often criticized the Court's use of legislative history because it lends itself to a kind of ventriloquism. The Congressional Record or committee reports are used to make words appear to come from Congress's mouth which were spoken or written by others (individual Members of Congress, congressional aides, or even enterprising lobbyists).

Id. at 73 (Scalia, J., dissenting). While a few judges, such as Justices Scalia and Thomas, are unwilling to consider legislative history at all, most judges generally allow lawyers *some* opportunity to "prove" the correctness of their interpretation with evidence from the legislative history. For example, the remaining members of the Rehnquist Court did not agree that legislative history should always be out-of-bounds. In *Wisconsin Public Intervenor v. Mortier*, 501 U.S. 597 (1991), they rejected Justice Scalia's position on legislative history. "Our precedents demonstrate that the Court's practice of utilizing legislative history reaches well into its past. We suspect that the practice will likewise reach well into the future." *Id.* at 610 n.4 (internal citation omitted). Under the Roberts Court, most of the Justices continue to rely on legislative history; however, their use may be more cautious.

There can be no doubt that Justice Scalia's criticisms have had an effect on the use of legislative history in judicial interpretation. Judges are far less likely to rely significantly on legislative history today than in the past. And for some judges, litigants must first show that the statute as written is absurd or ambiguous before suggesting that the legislative history is relevant. But not all members of the judiciary have embraced textualism.

ii. The Criticisms of Using Legislative History

Why are Justices Scalia, Thomas, and Judge Easterbrook so critical of those using legislative history? They offer many criticisms of the practice, including the following: (1) constitutionality issues, (2) reliability concerns, and (3) accessibility and cost considerations.

First, they argue that reliance on legislative history is unconstitutional. State and federal constitutions provide a process for enactment: passage by both chambers in identical form (bicameral passage) and presentment to the executive for approval or veto (presentment). Legislative history does not follow this constitutional process; only the text of the statute does. Hence, legislative history is not law and should not even be consulted.

Moreover, they reason that the Constitution delegates law-making power to the legislature as a whole, not to committees or individual legislators. For this reason, statements made in committee reports and floor debates, which are only the statements of individual legislators, should not be cited as evidence of the whole legislature's intent. Complicating the issue further is the fact that staff members or lobbyists and not legislators regularly draft committee reports and other legislative documents. Justice Scalia once said:

> As anyone familiar with modern-day drafting of congressional committee reports is well aware, the [language was] ... inserted, at best by a committee staff member on his or her own initiative, and at worst by a committee staff member at the suggestion of a lawyer-lobbyist; and the purpose of [that language] was not primarily to inform Members of Congress about what the bill meant, ... but rather to influence judicial construction.

Blanchard v. Bergeron, 489 U.S. 87, 98–99 (1989). Thus, they believe that intent of staffers and lobbyists regarding the meaning of a law is simply irrelevant and, arguably, unconstitutional.

Finally, they note that due process requires that citizens have notice of the law. If judges cannot understand what a statute means without perusing the legislative history, how can an ordinary citizen, who is unlikely to have access to such history, expect to know what a statute means? Thus, they argue that it is unfair to base an interpretation on information that is not readily accessible to the public. Moreover, they point out that the use of legislative history unfairly favors political insiders and those with money to pay lawyers to search the legislative materials, for ordinary citizens can rarely afford such legal work. For all these reasons, constitutional considerations are implicated whenever legislative history plays any role in statutory interpretation.

A second criticism they make regarding the use of legislative history is that it may be unreliable. Legislators simply do not read every report or attend every debate; thus, comments made within those documents and during those hearings may not reflect the understanding of every legislator. For example, in *Amalgamated Transit Union Local 1309 v. Laidlaw Transit Services, Inc.*, 435 F.3d 1140 (9th Cir. 2006), the court relied on a Senate report to discern the purpose of the Class Action Fairness Act. However, that particular report was not submitted until after the House and Senate had voted on the bill and the President had signed it into law. *Id.* at 1096 (Bybee, J., dissenting) (order denying en banc rehearing). The report could have had no influence whatsoever on the legislators' decisions, yet it influenced the court's interpretation. This result makes no sense.

Similarly, in *Hamdan v. Rumsfeld*, 548 U.S. 557 (2006), Senators Jon Kyl and Lindsey Graham filed an amicus brief in which they offered a colloquy from *The Congressional Record* as evidence that Congress was aware that the Detainee Treatment Act would strip the Supreme Court of jurisdiction to hear cases the Guantanamo detainees filed. The Justice Department relied on this legislative history to argue that its interpretation of the Act was the correct one. Yet, the majority rejected this particular colloquy because it was inserted into *The Congressional Record* after the Senate debate. Id. at 734 n.10. In other words, members of Congress never considered the comments or had an opportunity to disagree with them. The majority did consider floor debates and other legislative history that was a part of the enactment process, but not these after-the-fact insertions into the record.

As you might imagine, Justice Scalia was not happy with the majority's willingness to consider any of the legislative history:

> The Court immediately goes on to discount numerous floor statements by the [act's] sponsors that flatly contradict its view, because "those statements appear to have been inserted into the Congressional Record after the Senate debate." Of course this observation, even if true, makes no difference unless one indulges the fantasy that Senate floor speeches are attended (like the Philippics of Demosthenes) by throngs of eager listeners, instead of being delivered (like Demosthenes' practice sessions on the beach) alone into a vast emptiness. Whether the floor statements are spoken where no Senator hears, or written where no Senator reads, they represent at most the views of a single Senator.

Id. at 664–65.

Justice Scalia believes that all floor debate comments are valueless, whether made during the legislative process or inserted into the record after-the-fact. His position seems odd. If comments are made when other legislators cannot object or disagree with them, those comments should not be relevant to meaning. It should be immaterial that even when legislators read and hear comments, they may choose not to disagree with what is said or written for various reasons. At least the legislators had the opportunity to attend the hearings, to consider the information, and to speak against the comments if they wished. Hence, there is a difference between comments inserted into the record after enactment and those that occurred during enactment.

These critics raise another criticism of the use of legislative history. They note that it is often voluminous and includes contradictory statements. When contradictory legislative history exists, which history counts? This issue was apparent in *United Steelworkers v. Weber*, 443 U.S. 193 (1979). In that case, the Justices used different aspects of the legislative history to support their interpretation that Title VII did or did not allow affirmative action programs. *Weber* illustrates a problem with using legislative history; litigants tend to rely on the history that supports their interpretation while ignoring or minimizing the history that contradicts that interpretation. In *Weber*, the Justices can be faulted for doing the same.

The facts of the case are straightforward. In 1974, Kaiser, the defendant's employer, and the United Steelworkers of America, a labor union, agreed that Kaiser would create a new training program in response to the employer's historical discrimination of African-American workers. According to the collective bargaining agreement, Kaiser would admit one African-American into the program for every African-American that applied until the percentage of African-American workers in the program was equal to the percentage of African-American workers in the local work force. Weber was a Caucasian employee who sued when he was not selected for a place in the program, while other African-American workers with less seniority were chosen instead.

The issue for the Court, as framed by the majority, was whether Title VII of the Civil Rights Act forbade Kaiser from adopting this *voluntary* affirmative action program to remedy past discrimination against African-American workers. *Id.* at 200. Title VII prohibited employers from "*discriminat[ing]* against any individual ... because of such individual's race." *Id.* at n.2 & 3 (quoting 42 U.S.C. §§ 2000e-2(a) & (d)). The majority held that Kaiser's program was permitted precisely because it was a *voluntary* program aimed at correcting past discrimination. *Id.* at 208.

In reaching this holding, the majority agreed that the word "discriminate" was not ambiguous, but suggested that a literal construction of the text would be misplaced. *Id.* at 200 (citing *Holy Trinity Church v. United States*, 143 U.S. 457, 459 (1892)). Title VII must "be read against the background of the legislative history ... and the historical context from which the Act arose." *Id.* Reasoning that the purpose of this section was to remedy "the plight of the Negro in our economy," the majority held that Title VII's prohibition did not apply when an employer *voluntarily* enacted an affirmative action program to remedy past discrimination and forestall future litigation. *Id.* at 201, 208. Note that the majority used legislative history to find the general purpose of the statute, not the specific intent of the legislature.

To find this general purpose, the majority looked to various parts of the legislative history. First, the majority cited the Senate floor debate comments of Senator Humphrey, who worked tirelessly to move the bill through the Senate. During the floor debates, Senator Humphrey said, "The rate of Negro unemployment has gone up consistently as compared with white unemployment for the past 15 years. This is a social malaise and a social situation which we should not tolerate. That is one of the principal reasons why the bill should pass." *Id.* at 202 (quoting 110 CONG. REC. 7220 (1964) (remarks of Sen. Humphrey)).

During the debates, Senator Humphrey had specifically indicated that without well-paying jobs past discrimination could not be corrected. "'The crux of the problem (was) to open employment opportunities of Negroes in occupations which have been traditionally closed to them.'" *Id.* at 203 (quoting 110 CONG. REC. 6548 (1964) (remarks of Sen. Humphrey)). Additionally, the majority noted that the House Report accompanying the bill when it was sent to the Senate stated that the bill would "*create an atmosphere conducive to voluntary or local resolution of other forms of discrimination.*" *Id.* at 203 (quoting H.R. REP. No. 914, at 18 (1963)). The majority suggested that Congress was concerned about the plight of African-American workers and wanted to remedy that "mischief."

In response to one of the dissent's primary arguments, the majority suggested that another section of the Act (section 703(j)) was specifically included to protect employers from being *required to* implement affirmative action programs, not to stop them from *choosing to* implement such programs. The majority suggested that Congress could easily have included language in section 703(j) that would not "permit" employers to remedy past discrimination. Because Congress chose not to do so, voluntary programs were permissible. *Id.* at 206–07.

According to the majority's understanding of this legislative history, Congress wanted a law that would not only prevent discrimination in the future but would allow past discrimination to be voluntarily remedied. This history suggested to the majority that the purpose of Title VII was to help African-American workers secure jobs by increasing employment opportunities. Because the statute was enacted to help African-American workers, it would be ironic, the majority believed, were it to become the legal impediment to voluntary attempts to correct past discrimination. *Id.* at 202.

The dissent disagreed with the majority's characterization and selection of the legislative history. According to the dissent, the text and legislative history were abundantly clear: Congress intended to limit all forms of discrimination, not just prohibit discrimination against African-American workers. *Id.* at 228–29 (Rehnquist, J., dissenting).

Unlike the majority, which looked for the general purpose of the statute, the dissent looked for and found specific legislative intent. To so do, the dissent detailed the passage of Title VII of the Civil Rights Act in excruciating detail. The Civil Rights Act was originally introduced in the House, where it was immediately sent to the Judiciary Committee. *Id.* at 231. The Judiciary Committee amended the bill by adding Title VII and later reported the Act to the House floor with both majority and minority committee reports accompanying it. *Id.* The majority report "advanced a line of attack which was reiterated

throughout the debates in both the House and Senate and which ultimately
led to passage of § 703(j)." *Id.* The minority concern was that employers would
be forced to address past discrimination under the language of the amendment because "discriminate" was not defined. The minority report included
hypotheticals, including one in which an employer was forced to hire non-
Caucasians to racially balance its workforce. *Id.* Note that the legislature specifically discussed the language at issue in this case: "discriminate."

In response to the concerns raised in the minority report, the sponsor of
the bill and chair of the Judiciary Committee, Representative Celler, said that
the "Bill would prevent employers from discriminating against or *in favor of* workers." *Id.* at 233 (quoting 110 Cong. Rec. 1518 (1964)). The battle-lines were drawn,
but ultimately the bill with the amendment was passed in the House by a vote
of 290 to 130. The bill was the sent to the Senate where the longest debate in
that body's history took place. *Id.* at 234. The Senate voted to address the bill
directly and not forward it to any of the committees, which was highly unusual.

During the ensuing debate, many senators remained concerned that employers would be expected to correct past discrimination by requiring quotas
despite the colloquy from the House. Senator Humphrey, a strong proponent
of the bill, repeatedly assured those who were concerned that "not only does
Title VII not require use of racial quotas, *it does not permit their use.*" *Id.* at
238 (Rehnquist, J., dissenting). But the senators were not as easily persuaded
as the representatives had been, and the debate continued.

While the debate in the Senate raged, a bipartisan coalition drafted an
amendment, which included a new subsection — section 703(j) — to allay the
racial-quota concern. That subsection provided, " 'Nothing contained in (Title
VII) shall be interpreted to require any employer ... to grant preferential treatment to any individual or to any group because of the race ... of such individual
or group on account of' a racial imbalance in the employer's work force." *Id.*
at 244 (quoting 42 U.S.C. § 2000e-2(j)). Remember that the majority had suggested that this language prohibited only *required* affirmative action programs,
not *voluntary* affirmative action programs. *Id.* at 206–07. The dissent was in-
credulous:

> Not once during the 83 days of debate in the Senate did a speaker,
> proponent or opponent, suggest that the bill would allow employers
> *voluntarily* to prefer racial minorities over white persons. In light of
> Title VII's flat prohibition on discrimination "against any individual ...
> because of such individual's race," § 703(a), 42 U.S.C. § 2000e-2(a),
> such a contention would have been, in any event, too preposterous

to warrant response. Indeed, speakers on both sides of the issue, as the legislative history makes clear, recognized that Title VII would tolerate no voluntary racial preference, whether in favor of blacks or whites. The complaint consistently voiced by the opponents was that Title VII, particularly the word "discrimination," would be interpreted by federal agencies such as the [Equal Employment Opportunity Commission] to require the correction of racial imbalance through the granting of preferential treatment to minorities. Verbal assurances that Title VII would not require — indeed, would not permit — preferential treatment of blacks having failed, supporters of H.R. 7152 responded by proposing an amendment carefully worded to meet, and put to rest, the opposition's charge. Indeed, unlike §§ 703(a) and (d), which are by their terms directed at entities — e. g., employers, labor unions — whose actions are restricted by Title VII's prohibitions, the language of § 703(j) is specifically directed at entities — federal agencies and courts — charged with the responsibility of interpreting Title VII's provisions.

Id. at 244–46 (Rehnquist, J., dissenting). Finally, the dissent concluded, "In light of the background and purpose of § 703(j), the irony of invoking the section to justify the result in this case is obvious." *Id.* at 246. The legislative history was overwhelmingly clear to the dissent: Title VII was meant to be racially blind. Because affirmative action programs, whether voluntary or involuntary, discriminate against Caucasian workers, such programs were prohibited under the Act. Who was right?

Critics of the *Weber* holding note that Justice Rehnquist's dissent more faithfully explored and characterized the legislative history. The enacting Congress likely did intend a race-blind act. Thus, the majority can be criticized for missing (or perhaps ignoring) the specific intent of the enacting legislature. But Justice Rehnquist is not without fault. His opinion failed to take into account critical facts in the case. Title VII was enacted in 1964. More than ten years later, the workforce at the Kaiser plant where Weber worked was still 98.2% Caucasian even though the local workforce was 39% African-American — "fishy numbers ten years after Title VII had prohibited race discrimination...." WILLIAM ESKRIDGE, JR. ET AL., CASES AND MATERIALS ON LEGISLATION: STATUTES AND THE CREATION OF PUBLIC POLICY 218 (3d ed. 2001). Likely, the enacting Congress anticipated that employment decisions after the Act's passage would not be based on race. But what if they were? The legislative history could not address the issue of what to do about employers that refused to abide by Title VII after its passage; yet, those were precisely the facts in the

Weber case. "This [omission] undermines Justice Rehnquist's specific intent argument: It is not clear that Congress considered affirmative action in the context of Weber's case." *Id.* The majority's purposivist approach better addresses these facts. Perhaps the most accurate approach was that of Justice Blackmun who, in concurrence, considered both factors. While he shared many of Justice Rehnquist's concerns about the specific intent of the enacting legislature, he ultimately sided with the majority's general purpose argument because circumstances had changed since Title VII had been passed:

> The bargain struck in 1964 with the passage of Title VII guaranteed equal opportunity for white and black alike, but where Title VII provides no remedy for blacks, it should not be construed to foreclose private affirmative action from supplying relief. It seems unfair for respondent Weber to argue, as he does, that the asserted scarcity of black craftsmen in Louisiana, the product of historic discrimination, makes Kaiser's training program illegal because it ostensibly absolves Kaiser of all Title VII liability. Absent compelling evidence of legislative intent, I would not interpret Title VII itself as a means of "locking in" the effects of segregation for which Title VII provides no remedy.

Weber, 443 U.S, at 214–15 (Blackmun, J., concurring).

Those who criticize the use of legislative history point to cases like *Weber* to demonstrate that legislative history is malleable; it can be manipulated to support any result a judge or litigator wants. Judge Harold Leventhal has said quite famously, "the trick is to look over the heads of the crowd and pick out your friends." ANTONIN SCALIA, A MATTER OF INTERPRETATION: FEDERAL COURTS AND THE LAW 36 (1997). Some critics have even suggested that legislators may insert language into legislative history for the sole purpose of influencing later judicial interpretations; the facts of *Hamdan* lend some weight to this argument. Thus, for these reasons, critics argue that the reliability of legislative history can be problematic.

The third criticism of legislative history is that it is not equally accessible and available to all. Legislative history is often voluminous, obscure, hard to find, and poorly indexed, especially at the state level. It can be expensive and time-consuming to examine. Lawyers are trained to search exhaustively for the "smoking gun." Doing so in this context may cost a client a lot of money. Moreover, some clients cannot afford to pay for the search, putting them at a disadvantage.

All of these concerns are valid and are ones that you or your opponent should be aware of and be able to articulate. But rather than prohibit the use of legislative history entirely, these concerns merely show that legislative history should be relegated to a non-leading role in interpretation. Legislative history is certainly not law, but legislative history can offer insight into what some or all of the legislators may have been thinking when the act, which did go through the constitutional process, was enacted. Thus, legislative history offers context for the enactment process of a particular act. A skilled litigant will know where to find legislative history, how to use it, and how to criticize an opponent's use of it.

iii. The "Dog Does Not Bark" Canon: When Congress Is Silent

What if the legislative history is silent on a particular issue? Ordinarily, "[s]ilence in the legislative history about a particular provision ... is not a good guide to statutory interpretation and certainly is not more persuasive than the words of a statute." *Am. Online, Inc. v. United States*, 64 Fed. Cl. 571, 578 (2005). However, silence can sometimes be illuminating. Suppose, for example, that a statute on its face makes a radical and controversial change in the law — one that you would expect Congress would have discussed and debated. Yet, the legislative history is silent; Congress did not mention the change at all. Under these circumstances, wouldn't silence speak volumes? Generally, the answer is no; occasionally, the answer is yes.

To illustrate, in *Harrison v. PPG Industries, Inc.*, 446 U.S. 578 (1980), the issue for the Supreme Court was whether the general catch-all term "any other final action" in the Clean Air Act meant *any* final agency action or just acts similar in nature to the specific actions preceding the general catch-all. *Id.* at 587, 592. In other words, did the other surrounding, listed actions narrow the general catch-all, as *ejusdem generis* would suggest? A broad interpretation would dramatically shift responsibility for reviewing the Environmental Protection Agency's actions under this Act from the district courts to the courts of appeals. *Id.* at 585. For this reason, the Fifth Circuit found it unlikely that Congress would have intended such a major jurisdictional shift without expressly addressing this change during the enactment process. For the court, "[t]he 'most revealing' aspect of the legislative history of [the subsection at issue] ... was the complete absence of any discussion of such a 'massive shift' in jurisdiction." *Id.* at 585 (citing *PPG Indus., Inc. v. Harrison*, 587 F.2d 237 (5th Cir. 1979)).

On appeal, the Supreme Court rejected this "silence speaks volumes" argument. "In ascertaining the meaning of a statute, a court cannot, in the manner of Sherlock Holmes, pursue the theory of the dog that did not bark." *Id.* at 592. The Court was referring to A. CONAN DOYLE, SILVER BLAZE, IN THE COMPLETE SHERLOCK HOLMES (1927), in which the following exchange took place:

> "Is there any point to which you would wish to draw my attention?" asked the Scotland Yard Detective.

To which Holmes responded, "To the curious incident of the dog in the night-time."
Detective: "The dog did nothing in the night-time."
"That was the curious incident," replied Sherlock Holmes.

Id. at 335.

Despite the language in this last case, the-dog-did-not-bark argument can, at times, sway some judges; hence, it should not be ignored. For example, in *Chisom v. Roemer*, 501 U.S. 380 (1991), the majority found this argument persuasive. In that case, the Supreme Court had to determine whether section two of the Voting Rights Act, which protected individuals' rights to elect "*representatives*," applied to the election of state judges. *Id.* at 384. The petitioners, African-American voters, alleged that Louisiana's method of electing two Justices to the Louisiana State Supreme Court at-large from the New Orleans area impermissibly diluted the minority vote; the state responded that the Act did not apply to the election of state judges because judges were not representatives. *Id.* at 385, 390.

The legislative history was telling precisely because it was not telling! Congress had amended section two of this Act in 1982. Prior to the amendment, there was no question that judges were covered. *Id.* at 392. With the amendment Congress had responded to a prior judicial interpretation of the statute that had required proof of intent to discriminate. Congress had eliminated this judicially imposed intent requirement. *Id. at* 393. The majority concluded that had Congress intended, by using the word "representatives," to exclude vote dilution claims involving judges, "Congress would have made it explicit in the statute, or at least some of the Members would have identified or mentioned it at some point in the unusually extensive legislative history of the 1982 amendment." *Id.* at 396. Thus, because no legislator had ever suggested that judges would no longer be covered, Congress must have meant to maintain the status quo in this regard despite its choice of the term "representatives." Thus, silence spoke volumes.

Justice Scalia, in dissent, chastised the majority's dog-does-not-bark analysis:

Finding nothing in the legislative history affirming that judges were excluded from the coverage of § 2, the Court gives the phrase "to elect representatives" the quite extraordinary meaning that covers the election of judges.

As method, this is just backwards, and however much we may be attracted by the result it produces in a particular case, we should in every case resist it. Our job begins with a text that Congress has passed and the President has signed. We are to read the words of that text as any ordinary Member of Congress would have read them … and apply the meaning so determined. In my view, that reading reveals that § 2 extends to vote dilution claims for the elections of representatives only, and judges are not representatives…. Apart from the questionable wisdom of assuming that dogs will bark when something important is happening, we have forcefully and explicitly rejected the Conan Doyle approach to statutory construction in the past.

Id. at 405, 406 (Scalia, J., dissenting) (internal citations omitted).

The dog-did-not-bark theory was also raised in *Mississippi Poultry Ass'n, Inc. v. Madigan*, 992 F.2d 1359 (5th Cir. 1993) *aff'd on reh'g*, 31 F.3d 293 (5th Cir. 1994) (en banc). At issue in *Mississippi Poultry* were the 1985 amendments to section 466(d) of the Poultry Products Inspection Act ("PPIA"). *Id.* at 1360 n.1 (citing 21 U.S.C. §§ 451–70 (1988)). Section 466(d) specifically required that all imported poultry products "shall … be subject to *the same* … standards applied to products produced in the United States…." *Id.* at 1361 n.6 (quoting 21 U.S.C. § 466(d) (1988)). Congress had given the Secretary of Agriculture (the "secretary") the power to interpret this statute. The secretary promulgated a regulation interpreting this statute to require that "[t]he foreign inspection system must maintain a program to assure that the requirements referred to in this section [are] *at least equal to* those applicable to the Federal system in the United States…." 52 Fed. Reg. 15963 (May 1, 1987) (emphasis added). The secretary's interpretation that "same" meant "at least equal to" was challenged.

On appeal, the majority reviewed the dictionary and the statute as a whole and found the language clear; the term "the same" in the statute meant identical and did not mean equivalent, as the agency had concluded. The majority then refused to explore other sources of meaning, such as legislative history. *Id.* at 1363.

In contrast, the dissent found the language unclear and found the silence in the legislative history to be telling. Prior to 1985, the statute had required that poultry standards in other countries be "substantially equivalent" to the United States' standards for import; by regulation, the secretary had interpreted this language to require standards "at least equal to" those in the United States. *Id.* at 1378 (Reavley, C.J., dissenting) (citing 9 C.F.R. § 381.196(a)(2)(iv) (1984)). In 1985, the Senate Agriculture Committee drafted amending language for the PPIA, including "at least equal to" language. The committee approved the bill and sent it to the full Senate for vote. *Id.* at 1378 (citing S. REP. NO 99-145, 516, 99th Cong., at 339–40 (1st Sess. 1985)). But during the floor debate, Senator Helms, the chair of the Senate Agriculture Committee, offered a "purely technical" amendment, substituting the words "the same as" for the words "at least equal to" to "'clarif[y] the provision to reflect the original intent of the provision as adopted by committee in markup.'" *Id.* at 1378 (quoting 131 CONG. REC. 33358 (Nov. 22, 1985)). The Senate adopted the new language without debate, discussion, comment, or recorded vote. *Id.* Notably, Senator Helms was from North Carolina, a huge chicken producing state.

The dissent found the lack of congressional debate regarding Senator Helm's floor amendment compelling. While Senator Helms had suggested that the amendment was minor, the amendment had major trade implications. If the language "the same as" meant identical, then the amendment imposed a complete trade barrier; no foreign country's poultry could enter the United States because its inspection system could never be identical to the U.S. system. Thus, the change would completely close trade with other countries. The dissent found it inconceivable that Congress would enact a statute with such major trade implications without talking about "why a barrier was justified, what it was supposed to accomplish, or how its effectiveness would be monitored." *Id.* In this case, for the dissent, the lack of legislative history was telling. Perhaps the dissent was right, for immediately after the decision, Congress amended the statute thereby overturning the holding and eliminating the trade barrier. Pub. L. No. 103-465 (as amended at 21 U.S.C. § 466 (d) (1) (1994)). Despite the reality that Congress is unlikely to make a radical shift in law or policy without some discussion, the presumption remains that legislative silence during enactment is not relevant to meaning. If the legislature did not mean what it wrote, then the legislature, not the court, should fix the error, as it did here.

We have now surveyed the various types of legislative history, learned how to find legislative history, examined the Supreme Court's use of legislative history over time, explored the many criticisms of using legislative history, and explored the relevance of silence during the enactment process. We turn now to another way to use legislative history: to identify unexpressed statutory purpose.

3. Finding and Using Purpose

While statutory interpretation may center on the language in the text, language is more than simply finding ordinary meaning from dictionary definitions. Some argue that statutes consist of a body and soul: "[T]he letter of the law is the body of the law, and the sense and reason of the law is the soul of the law." William N. Eskridge, Jr., *All About Words: Early Understandings of the "Judicial Power" in Statutory Interpretation, 1776–1806*, 101 COLUM. L. REV. 990, 1001 (quoting *Eyston v. Studd*, 75 Eng. Rep. 688, 695–700). In other words:

Legislation has an aim; it seeks to obviate some mischief, to supply an inadequacy.... That aim ... is not drawn, like nitrogen, out of
the air; it is evinced in the language of the statute, as read in the light
of other external manifestations of purpose.

Felix Frankfurter, *Some Reflections on the Reading of Statutes*, 47 Colum. L.
Rev. 527, 538–39 (1947). We turn now to the soul of the law: purpose. Below,
you will learn first how to find it, then how to use it.

a. Finding Purpose

In Chapter 7, we examined preambles, findings, and purpose clauses. When
Congress includes one of these, finding purpose is easier. Whether purpose
can be used if it is located in one of these clauses was explored in Chapter 7.
But many statutes, particularly older statutes, do not have preambles, ex-
planatory findings, or other indicia of purpose. And because of the political
nature of the legislative process, even when bills contain these clauses, the
clauses may be incomplete or unhelpful. When statutes have no such clause
or incomplete clauses, one area from which you can derive purpose is from
the remainder of the act. Discerning a statute's purpose from text alone can be
challenging, but it is the first place to start.

There is, of course, no more persuasive evidence of the purpose of a
statute than the words by which the legislature undertook to give expression to its wishes. Often these words are sufficient in and of themselves to determine the purpose of the legislation.

United States v. Am. Trucking Ass'ns, Inc., 310 U.S. 534, 543 (1940).
In 1584, the quintessential purpose case was decided in England, *Heydon's
Case*, 76 Eng. Rep. 637 (Ex. 1584). The facts were few: King Henry VIII adopted
a statute that specified which property interests would be invalidated if used
to avoid the King's ability to seize property. In the case, the property owner
used copyhold interests (an ancient form of landownership), which were not
expressly identified in the statute. The court thus had to decide whether to expand the statute to include these types of property interests—even though
they were not explicitly included within the text—and give the King more
property, or whether to limit the statute to its words, even though this interest had likely been omitted inadvertently. To decide whether these interests
should be included, the court identified a four-step process: *first*, identify the
law as it existed prior to a statute's enactment; *second*, identify the "mischief"
that the legislature wished to remedy by enacting the statute; *third*, identify
the remedy the legislature devised to correct that mischief; *finally*, interpret

the statute to further that remedy and minimize that mischief. This four-step process is known as the *Mischief Rule*. Applying this four-step process in *Heydon's Case*, the court extended the statute to include the omitted property interest because this interpretation would correct the "mischief," people evading royal property confiscations. *Id.* at 638.

How does one identify the mischief and remedy? Professors Henry Hart and Albert Sachs simplified the rule in *Heydon's Case* as follows:

> In interpreting a statute a court should:
> (1) Decide what purpose ought to be attributed to the statute...; and then
> (2) Interpret the words ... to carry out the purpose as best it can, making sure, however, that it does not give the words ...
> (a) a meaning they will not bear....

WILLIAM N. ESKRIDGE, JR. & PHILIP P. FRICKEY, INTRODUCTION TO HENRY M. HART, JR. & ALBERT M. SACKS, THE LEGAL PROCESS (1994) 1374 (William N. Eskridge, Jr. & Philip P. Frickey, eds., 1994).

In our modern era, judges often turn to legislative history to identify purpose, especially when the text is unhelpful. Knowing why a bill was enacted can explain the purpose behind the legislation. The seminal case in this area, *Church of the Holy Trinity v. United States*, 143 U.S. 457 (1892), was one of the first cases in which American judges used legislative history to discern purpose. In that case, Holy Trinity Church had paid a rector to come over from England to serve as the church's pastor. A federal statute prohibited the church from importing "any alien ... into the United States ... to perform *labor or service of any kind.*" *Id.* at 458 (emphasis added). The Supreme Court conceded that "the act of the corporation [was] within the letter of this section, for the relation of rector to his church is one of service, and implies labor on the one side with compensation on the other." *Id.* But the Court rejected this interpretation. Stating the infamous phrase, "[i]t is a familiar rule, that a thing may be within the letter of the statute and yet not within the statute, because not within its spirit, nor within the intention of its makers," the Court turned to the legislative history of the statute. *Id.* at 459. According to the Court, the legislative history, specifically the committee reports and floor debates, was clear that the mischief Congress had tried to stem was the influx of "cheap, unskilled labor ... not brain toilers." *Id.* at 464. Hence, the statute was inapplicable to the rector because including rectors would not further the statutory purpose. Thus, in this case, the Court looked to legislative history to discover the statute's purpose. As a side note, the rector did not stay in the United States for long. Shortly after this decision, he left New York claiming that it was an "immoral place to be."

Thus, when a statute does not include a purpose clause or the clause is unhelpful, purpose may be found in the text of the statute, in its legislative history, or even in the social and historical context surrounding a bill's enactment. Once you identify purpose, how do you use it?

b. Using Purpose

Judges use purpose in many ways. Judges may use purpose to confirm ordinary meaning, to resolve ambiguity, or to provide guidance in the case of absurdity. In addition, some judges may use purpose to trump ordinary meaning. For example, in *Holy Trinity*, the Court stated first that the language at issue was not ambiguous and included rectoring (although that concession is debatable) and then used purpose, which it found in the legislative history, to trump the ordinary meaning. Similarly, in a more modern case, the Ninth Circuit used purpose to hold that "less" actually meant "more." In *Amalgamated Transit Union Local 1309 v. Laidlaw Transit Services, Inc.*, 435 F.3d 1140 (9th Cir. 2006), the court rejected the ordinary meaning of the text of the Class Action Fairness Act. That Act provided that "a court of appeals may accept an appeal ... denying a motion to remand a class action to the State court from which it was removed if application is made to the court of appeals *not less than 7 days* after entry of the order." *Id.* at 1142 (quoting 28 U.S.C. § 1543(c)(1)) (emphasis added). The ordinary meaning of the text of the statute imposed a seven day waiting period but contained no upper time limit for appealing. The Ninth Circuit found this ordinary meaning "illogical" but not necessarily absurd. *Id.* The court then turned to the legislative history of the Act (specifically a senate committee report) to discern the purpose of the Act and concluded that Congress had intended the Act to impose a *time limit* for appealing rather than a waiting period to appeal. *Id.* at 1146. A textualist court could have reached this same result using the scrivener's error doctrine.

One member of the Ninth Circuit, Judge Bybee, was so upset with the majority's decision that he *sua sponte* called for an en banc rehearing, which was denied. *Amalgamated Transit Union Local 1309 v. Laidlaw Transit Servs., Inc.*, 448 F.3d 1092 (9th Cir. 2006). Judge Bybee then dissented from the order denying the rehearing, which is also very unusual. *Id.* at 1094 (Bybee, J., dissenting). In his dissent, Judge Bybee chastised the majority for rejecting the ordinary meaning of the statute when the text was so clear. According to Judge Bybee, none of the reasons for avoiding the plain meaning canon applied. The statute was not absurd or ambiguous, there was no scrivener's error, and there was no constitutional question. (See Chapter 4.) Hence, if there was an error, then

Congress, not the courts, should correct it. *Id.* at 1096–98. Judge Bybee was particularly concerned that the majority relied on a Senate committee report that "was not submitted until eighteen days after the Senate had passed the bill, eleven days after the House had passed the bill, and ten days after the President signed the bill into law." *Id.* at 1096. In Judge Bybee's opinion, the majority relied on legislative history that no member of Congress or the President considered to interpret the statute to mean the exact opposite of what the statute actually said. *Id.*

Was Judge Bybee correct? Could Congress truly have meant to enact a statute identifying an appeal timeline that created a waiting period rather than a time limit? And, assuming not, who should fix the error? Consider the implications of waiting for Congress to fix its mistake. Textualists would say the legislature must correct its own errors, while purpovists and intentionalists would say the courts should do so when a mistake is so clear.

The debate between the majority and dissent in this case illustrates nicely the impact that a judge's theory of interpretation can have on meaning. In this case, the majority was willing to look beyond clear text to purpose, as found in the legislative history, to interpret the statute as Congress likely intended but certainly did not state. In contrast, the dissent was unwilling to look beyond the clear text because no exceptions applied, even though it was likely that Congress never intended the statute to mean what it actually said. The majority's decision to "rewrite" the statute is unusual, especially today.

> To let general words draw nourishment from their purpose is one thing. To draw on some unexpressed spirit outside the bounds of the normal meaning of words is quite another.

Addison v. HollyHill Fruit Prods., Inc., 322 U.S. 607, 617 (1944).

Using purpose to trump clear text is not common. Purpose is more commonly used when a statute is unclear, absurd, or when purpose confirms the ordinary meaning of the text. For example, in *Church of Scientology v. United States*, 612 F.2d 417 (9th Cir. 1979), the Ninth Circuit reviewed the legislative history of a statute to confirm the text's ordinary meaning. The Church of Scientology had requested certain documents from the Department of Drug Enforcement Administration ("DEA") under the Freedom of Information Act ("FOIA"). FOIA generally requires disclosure of all government records subject to limited exceptions. The exception at issue in the case exempted from disclosure "all investigatory records compiled for law enforcement purposes … [if] the production of such records would … disclose the identity of a *confidential source* … [or if the records were] furnished only by the *confidential source....*" *Id.* at 419 n.2 (quoting 5 U.S.C. § 552(b)(7)(D)) (emphasis added). The issue for the court was whether the term "confidential source" included non-human sources, such as law enforcement offices.

Starting with the text, the majority found it clear: "'[C]onfidential source' includes foreign state and local law enforcement agencies....*" Id.* at 420. Even though the majority found the text clear, the majority turned to the legislative history to look for the specific legislative intent and statutory purpose regarding the statutory exception. Finding no evidence of specific intent, the majority searched for purpose. Reviewing the conference committee report, the President's veto statement, and floor debates surrounding the override, the majority concluded that the legislature did not use the term "confidential source" to mean only human sources. *Id.* at 424–25. Rather, this history showed that the purpose of the exception was to ensure that law enforcement would be able to gather information. Hence, the majority concluded that a broad interpretation of the language in the exception was appropriate in the case based both on the purpose and the text. *Id.* at 426.

The dissent disagreed with the majority's interpretation of the legislative history. Agreeing that the text was clear, the dissent also perused the legislative history for evidence of specific intent. Unlike the majority, the dissent found specific legislative intent: Congress intended to cover only human "confidential sources." *Id.* at 430 (Wallace, J., dissenting). Further, the dissent disagreed with the majority that the purpose of the exception was the appropriate purpose to consider. Rather, the dissent concluded that the purpose of FOIA as a whole, not FOIA's exception, was relevant. Because the basic policy of FOIA "is in favor of disclosure," the dissent argued that the act should be narrowly, not broadly, interpreted. *Id.* at 431. Thus, unlike the majority but like the *Holy Trinity* Court, the dissent would have allowed the legislative history and general purpose to trump the ordinary meaning. This case raises an interesting question: Sometimes the purpose of an exception in a statute conflicts with the statute's general purpose. When this occurs, which purpose should matter: the purpose of the statute as a whole or the statute's exception? Currently, there is not agreed answer to this question.

Sometimes a statute has more than one purpose. What should a court do when these purposes conflict? One case that addressed this issue is *Office Planning Group, Inc. v. Baraga-Houghton-Keweenaw Child Development Bd.*, 697 N.W.2d 871 (Mich. 2005). In that case, the majority and dissent disagreed on which purpose should control. The applicable act, the Head Start Act, required Head Start agencies to provide "reasonable public access to information...." *Id.* at 874 (quoting 42 U.S.C. 9839(a)). The issue for the court was whether the statute had an implied right for citizens to bring private lawsuit. An individual who had lost a bid to supply office equipment to a Head Start program sued to seek information about the other bids. The majority reasoned that the purpose of the Act was "to promote school readiness by providing services to low-income children and their families." *Id.* at 886. Because the Act did not contemplate any benefit to private corporations, the court refused to interpret the statute such that contractors who were denied information had a right to sue. *Id.* at 876.

The dissent disagreed and chastised the majority's reliance on just one of the Act's purposes: providing services to low-income children and their families. According to the dissent, the majority ignored Congress's other "goal of maintaining open accountability in the use of public funds," which was also expressed in the statute. *Id.* at 893 (Kelley, J., dissenting). Thus, because implying a private right of action would better further this second purpose and not adversely affect the other purpose, the dissent would have implied such a right. *Id.* at 894.

When multiple purposes of a statute conflict and are impossible to reconcile, which purpose should control? There is no easy answer to this question, but the dissent's approach to further more of the purposes seems preferable. By furthering as many purposes as possible, the dissent's approach does not elevate one purpose at the expense of others. Generally, a court will try first to find an interpretation that would further more of the purposes, but when the court cannot reconcile the purposes, the court should read an exception's purpose narrowly, much like a proviso. (See Chapter 7.) This approach mirrors the courts' approach to conflicting statutes: reconcile if at all possible.

What if two, related statutes have purposes that conflict? Which should control? Generally, courts try to reconcile both of the statutes' purposes, but when that is not possible, the purpose of the statute at issue controls. For example, in *Kentucky Off-Track Betting, Inc. v. McBurney*, 993 S.W.2d 946 (Ky. 1999), the defendant gambled $390,000 at the plaintiff's track. Although the defendant wrote various personal checks, he admitted to the plaintiff that he had insufficient funds to cover them. The plaintiff agreed not to cash the checks and instead accepted the defendant's promissory note. When the defendant failed to pay on the promissory note, the plaintiff sued and moved for summary judgment. The relevant statute provided: "*Every contract . . . for the consideration . . . of money . . . lost or bet in any . . . wager . . . is void.*" *Id.* at 947 (quoting KY. REV. STAT. ANN. § 372.010) (emphasis added). This statute had been enacted when gambling was illegal. In 1992, new statutes were enacted that permitted some forms of gambling (the 1992 amendments). The purposes of the 1992 amendments, to allow some forms of gambling, seemed to conflict with the purpose of the statute at issue, to prevent people from lending money for all forms of gambling.

The Kentucky Supreme Court held that the relevant statute was the earlier statute, not the 1992 amendments, and under that statute the debt was void and unenforceable; "every contract" included the promissory note. Discerning purpose solely from the text of the various statutes and the court's understanding of the social mores at the time of enactment, the majority reasoned that the purpose of the 1992 amendments was to legalize some forms of gambling. But simply because the state legislature intended to legalize some forms of gambling did not mean the legislature intended to legalize the lending of money for gambling. Hence, according to the majority, the debt was void under the earlier statute. *Id.* at 949.

In contrast, the dissent focused on the purpose of the earlier statute and on how the 1992 amendments affected that purpose. *Id.* at 950 (Johnston, J., dissenting). The dissent believed that the purpose of the earlier statute was to prevent *illegal* gambling by rendering the gambling contract void and unenforceable; if gamblers could not borrow money, they would not be able to gamble. *Id.* at 949. Until 1992, when the amendments were enacted, gambling was illegal; hence, the earlier statute was designed to prevent all forms of gambling. But, with the 1992 amendments, the legislature legalized some forms of gambling. Social perceptions of gambling had changed; thus, the dissent argued that the earlier statute should be read in conjunction with the 1992 amendments legalizing gambling. Doing so, the dissent found the earlier statute to be inapplicable because that statute's purpose was to curb money lent for *illegal* gambling not *legal* gambling. *Id.* In the end, the dissent harmonized the purposes of the various statutes, while the majority focused solely on the purpose of the statute in question. Interestingly, neither the majority nor dissent relied on any sources to find the purposes of these statutes beyond the statutes' texts. Again, the dissent in this case likely had the better approach because he reconciled the purposes of related statutes, while the majority essentially ignore the 1992 Amendments altogether.

In conclusion, as statutes have become more complex and detailed, purpose seems to have become less valuable to many judges than in years past. Perhaps the days in which purpose can overcome ordinary meaning have ended. But wholesale rejection of purpose is not appropriate either. Like legislative history, purpose has a role in interpretation, albeit only a supporting role.

In this chapter, we have explored the role in interpretation of the context that precedes and accompanies the enactment process. In the next chapter, we turn to the role in interpretation of the context following enactment.

C. Mastering This Topic

Return to the hypothetical ordinance provided in Chapter 1 on page 9. The first question that was asked was the following: "An ambulance entered Pioneer Park to pick up and take to the hospital a man who had just suffered a heart attack. Did the ambulance driver violate the Pioneer Park Safety Ordinance (PPSO)?" How should you, as prosecutor, attempt to answer that question using what you've learned in this chapter?

Let's start with the legislative history to see if we can find specific intent regarding whether the legislators intended to allow ambulances (or other emergency vehicles) in the park. We have three pieces of legislative history: the Public Park Committee Report (the equivalent of a Senate or House committee report), a summary of the floor debates (generally, the floor debates of the chambers are not summarized), and the Mayor's signing statement (the equivalent of a presidential signing statement). From our review of the legislative history hierarchy, we know that the committee report carries the most weight. Looking at that report, we see that there is no evidence of specific intent regarding ambulances or even emergency vehicles. (Note that the report does show specific intent regarding parade vehicles, but that is not the issue you are researching.) We turn next to the summary of the floor debates. Again, the summary provides no evidence that the council members had a specific intent about ambulances or emergency vehicles; however, if we had a question about water-skiing, we would have specific intent and, thus, guidance. Finally, we look at the Mayor's signing statement. It provides no evidence of a specific legislative intent (as a statement from the executive, query whether a signing statement ever could). Generally, signing statements carry little weight, which we will see in Chapter 11. Thus, in this case, the legislative history provides no evidence of specific intent on this issue.

Let's turn to purpose. The ordinance does not include a purpose or related clause, so we must search for unexpressed purpose. We begin with the text. Section 4 of the ordinance increases the fines for anyone violating the ordinance and causing injury while doing so: "If any injury occurred, the fine shall be doubled." This section suggests that one possible purpose for the ordinance was to improve safety for pedestrians and others while in the park. The purpose could suggest either that ambulances should be allowed in the park because ambulances help injured people receive treatment sooner, or that ambulances should not be allowed in the park because they can injur pedestrians and others as easily as cars and motorcycles. The text in the case is ambiguous regarding purpose.

Let's apply the mischief rule. First, we need to identify the law as it existed prior to the ordinance's enactment. Here, motor vehicles of all kinds were permitted to enter the park. Second, we need to identify the "mischief" that the council wished to remedy by enacting the ordinance. Here, the "mischief" that the council wanted to remedy, according to the committee report, was injuries caused by cars and motorcycles striking pedestrians and bicyclists. Moreover, the summary of the debate suggests that noise and pollution were also of concern. Finally, as noted above, the ordinance increases the penalty for anyone causing injury while violating the ordinance. Third, we need to identify the remedy the council devised to correct that mischief. Here, the remedy was to prohibit all motor vehicles from coming into the park with specific exceptions for maintenance and parade vehicles. Lastly, we need to interpret the statute to further that remedy and minimize that mischief. Here, the mischief rule would suggest that ambulances should not be permitted. They might strike pedestrians or bicyclists, and they are noisy and cause pollution. Thus, the unexpressed purpose of this ordinance, as found in the text and legislative history, suggests that ambulances should not be allowed to enter the park and that the driver should be cited.

Checkpoints

- Contextualism is the process of using the context to determine why the legislature acted or to determine what a statute means. Context includes a range of sources including social and historical events, legal and political climate, economic and market factors, and even textual and linguistic context.

- Legislative history is the written record of deliberations surrounding and preceding a bill's enactment. Judges vary in their willingness to consider legislative history.

- Typically, judges use legislative history for one of two reasons: (1) to shed light on the specific intent of the enacting legislature or (2) to identify the statutory purpose.

- Some judges refuse to consider legislative history in any case. The use of legislative history has been criticized for many reasons, including the following: (1) constitutionality concerns, (2) reliability issues, and (3) accessibility and cost considerations.

- Silence in the legislative history about a particular provision is generally not a good guide to meaning; however, sometimes, silence may have meaning pursuant to the "dog did not bark" canon.

- Judges may use purpose in many ways: to resolve ambiguity and absurdity, to confirm ordinary meaning, and to overcome ordinary meaning.

Chapter 10

Canons Based on Extrinsic Sources & Legislative Process: Post-Enactment Legislative Context

---

Roadmap

- Learn to use what occurred *after* the enactment process.
- Understand the role of super strong *stare decisis*.
- Understand the role of subsequent legislative action, including legislative acquiescence and reenactment.

A. Introduction to This Chapter

In this chapter, we continue with our examination of extrinsic sources and context. We move from an exploration of what happens during the legislative process to an examination of what occurs afterward. Subsequent events may shed light on what a statute means. This chapter will explore the canons related to subsequent actions of the legislature. In the next chapter, we will take a look at the subsequent actions of the executive, namely signing statements and interpretations by administrative agencies.

B. Using What Occurred Subsequent to Enactment

If using what occurred prior to and during enactment can be controversial, using what occurred after enactment is even more so. If the goal of interpretation is discerning the intent of the enacting legislature, regardless of whether that is accomplished by finding purpose or intent, then anything that happens after passage should be irrelevant. Instead, if discerning the common understanding of words when the text was originally adopted is the goal, subsequent events should similarly be irrelevant. Yet, complete irrelevancy is not the presumption. While some subsequent acts are generally considered irrelevant (*e.g.,* affidavits of legislators), some are relevant at times (*e.g.,* legislative acquiescence), others (*e.g.,* agency interpretations) are not only relevant, they may well be conclusive.

1. Subsequent Judicial Action: Super Strong *Stare Decisis*

Stare decisis is Latin, meaning to stand by things decided. It means that courts are reluctant to overturn prior judicial decisions absent a good reason to do so. *Stare decisis* furthers certainty in the law and faith in the judicial system. It also gives the appearance of objectivity; judges decide cases based on legal principles rather than based on political leanings and personal values.

There are two components to *stare decisis*. First, the decisions of higher courts bind lower courts within the same jurisdiction. Second, a court should not overturn its own precedents without good reason. *Stare decisis* is not absolute; when the existing judicial opinion is clearly wrong, courts will overturn it. The most famous example of this latter principle is the Supreme Court's decision in *Brown v. Board of Education*, 347 U.S. 483 (1954). In *Brown*, the Court overturned *Plessy v. Ferguson*, 163 U.S. 537 (1896), in which the Court had held that racial segregation in public accommodations was constitutional.

For cases involving statutes, the Supreme Court (and some lower courts) applies a heightened form of *stare decisis* known as super strong *stare decisis*. This concept simply means that judicial decisions interpreting statutes should be overruled even less easily than decisions refining the common law because Congress is the more appropriate body to correct erroneous interpretations of statutes. Under super strong *stare decisis*, even when a prior decision is inarguably wrong, the Justices are reluctant to overrule it.

A federal case illustrating super strong *stare decisis* is *Faragher v. Boca Raton*, 524 U.S. 775 (1998). In that case, a female lifeguard, who worked for the City of Boca Raton, was sexually harassed by her supervisors. She brought suit against the supervisors and the city under Title VII of the Civil Rights Act of 1964, which provided, "[i]t shall be an unlawful employment practice for an employer ... to fail or refuse to hire or to discharge any individual, or otherwise to discriminate against any individual with respect to his compensation, terms, conditions, or privileges of employment, because of such individual's race, color, religion, sex, or national origin." *Id.* at 786 (citing 42 U.S.C. § 2000e-2(a)(1)).

In an earlier case, the Court had held that sexual harassment so "severe or pervasive" so as to "'alter the conditions of [the victim's] employment and create an abusive working environment'" violated Title VII. *Id.* at 786 (quoting *Meritor Savings Bank, FSB v. Vinson*, 477 U.S. 57 (1986)). The issue for the Court in *Faragher* was whether the city should be liable for the actions of its employee-supervisor. The Court answered the question affirmatively. In its reasoning, the Court explained:

> We are bound to honor *Meritor* on this point not merely because of the high value placed on *stare decisis* in statutory interpretation, ... but for a further reason as well. With the amendments enacted by the Civil Rights Act of 1991, Congress both expanded the monetary relief available under Title VII to include compensatory and punitive damages and modified the statutory grounds of several of our decisions. The decision of Congress to leave *Meritor* intact is conspicuous. We thus have to assume that in expanding employers' potential liability under Title VII, Congress relied on our statements in *Meritor* about the limits of employer liability. To disregard those statements now (even if we were convinced of reasons for doing so) would be not only to disregard *stare decisis* in statutory interpretation, but to substitute our revised judgment about the proper allocation of the costs of harassment for Congress's considered decision on the subject.

Id. at 804 n.4 (internal citations omitted).

Heightened *stare decisis* may make sense in situations like *Faragher*, where Congress bases future legislative action on the Court's existing interpretation. But sometimes the Court's unwillingness to overturn a prior decision for this reason makes little sense. Most notably, in *Flood v. Kuhn*, 407 U.S. 258 (1972), the Court examined the issue of whether baseball should continue to be exempt from federal anti-trust laws. Curtis Flood had been the center fielder for the St. Louis Cardinals. He missed a fly ball in the 7th inning of the 1968 World Series with Detroit. His error cost his team the series. Not surprisingly, the following year St. Louis traded him, along with six other players, to the Philadelphia Phillies. Flood did not want to go to Philadelphia, for a variety of reasons. He wrote to the Commissioner of Baseball and asked the Commissioner to let other teams know of his availability. The Commissioner refused. Flood sued, claiming the Commissioner's action violated federal anti-trust laws. *Id.* at 265.

The issue for the Court was whether baseball was interstate trade or commerce. In two of its earlier cases, *Federal Baseball Club v. National League*, 259 U.S. 200 (1922) and *Toolson v. New York Yankees, Inc.*, 346 U.S. 356 (1953), the Court had held that baseball was not interstate trade or commerce, which is an element of the anti-trust law. In 1922, the Court may have been correct that baseball did not affect interstate commerce, but by 1972, it was clear that baseball did have such an effect. Yet, the majority in *Flood*, while acknowledging that these earlier cases had been wrongly decided, refused to overturn them. 407 U.S. at 279. The majority reasoned that because of the long-standing nature of the opinions, Congress should make any change. *Id.* at 283–84. The Court was concerned, in part, that baseball had developed during these fifty years under the assumption that it was exempt from the anti-trust laws. To change the rules now would be unfair because judicial interpretations of statutes apply retroactively while legislative actions usually apply only prospectively.

The dissent disagreed, arguing that the earlier cases were wrong and that it was time to overturn them. "This is a difficult case because we are torn between the principle of *stare decisis* and the knowledge that the decisions in *Federal Baseball Club* ... and *Toolson* ... are totally at odds with more recent and better reasoned cases." *Id.* at 290 (Marshall, J., dissenting). As Justice Marshall explained:

> We do not lightly overrule our prior constructions of federal statutes, but when our errors deny substantial federal rights, like the right to compete freely and effectively to the best of one's ability as guaranteed by the antitrust laws, we must admit our error and correct it. We have done so before and we should do so again here.

Id. at 292–93. In Justice Marshall's dissenting opinion, it was enough that the prior decisions were wrong and that the holdings deprived a litigant of a "substantial federal right[]." *Id.* at 292.

Who was right? Justice Marshall's standard for reversing Supreme Court precedent is perhaps too light, while the majority's unwillingness to reexamine and correct interpretations that are wrong and at odds with the rest of the Court's jurisprudence also seems wrong. In this case, Flood, an African-American, "was profoundly offended by the reserve clause, which resembled slavery in some ways and would result in his being forced move to a less tolerant community." William N. Eskridge, Jr. et al., Legislation and Statutory In-

TERPRETATION 278 (2000). Particularly given this background, the Court's refusal to change an interpretation that no longer made any sense seems unjustifiable. *Stare decisis* is important for many reasons noted above, but it should yield when time proves the earlier decisions to be wrong under modern standards. Given the realities of the legislative process, it can be extremely difficult for Congress to change precedent and fix its own mistakes; here, the Court was asking Congress to go one step further and correct the Court's mistake. Fixing its own mistakes should be the Court's job. For all these reasons, many academics urge that super strong *stare decisis* be relaxed so that opinions interpreting statutes can be afforded ordinary *stare decisis*.

Regardless, the rule remains that *stare decisis* plays a heightened role in statutory interpretation cases; indeed, cases can be wrong, but still be right, as *Flood* demonstrates. But *stare decisis* is not an absolute rule. Typically, the Supreme Court overrules at least one statutory interpretation case each term. *Id.* at 281.

2. Subsequent Legislative Action

a. "Subsequent Legislative History"

Sometimes, while enacting a new law, the legislature will comment on an existing statute. This *subsequent legislative history* should be irrelevant. Note the irony in the title: How can subsequent events ever be historical? While the legislature's comments might be relevant to the interpretation of the new act, those comments are generally not relevant to the interpretation of the existing act. "[S]ubsequent legislative history will rarely override a reasonable interpretation of a statute that can be gleaned from its language and legislative history prior to its enactment." *Consumer Prod. Safety Comm'n v. GTE Sylvania*, 447 U.S. 102, 117–18 n.13 (1980). Use of these comments for interpreting a statute is extremely controversial, but done, for the reasons identified by Justice Scalia below:

> The legislative history of a statute is the history of its consideration and enactment. "Subsequent legislative history"—which presumably means the *post*-enactment history of a statute's consideration and enactment—is a contradiction in terms. The phrase is used to smuggle into judicial consideration legislators' expressions *not* of what a bill currently under consideration means (which, the theory goes, reflects what their colleagues understood they were voting for), but of what a law *previously enacted* means. . . .

In my opinion, the views of a legislator concerning a statute already enacted are entitled to no more weight than the views of a judge concerning a statute not yet passed. In some situations, of course, the expression of a legislator relating to a previously enacted statute may bear upon the meaning of a provision in a bill under consideration — which provision, if passed, may in turn affect judicial interpretation of the previously enacted statute, since statutes *in pari materia* should be interpreted harmoniously. Such an expression would be useful, if at all, not because it was subsequent legislative history of the earlier statute, but because it was plain old legislative history of the later one.

Arguments based on subsequent legislative history, like arguments based on antecedent futurity, should not be taken seriously, not even in a footnote.

Sullivan v. Finkelstein, 496 U.S. 617, 631 (1990) (Scalia, J., concurring). In other words, comments made during the enactment of a new bill do not reflect what the enacting legislature intended or what the words meant when the existing statute was drafted. Thus, any such comments would show no more than what a latter legislature believed an earlier legislature thought. Any other balance would elevate the intent of the second legislature above that of the enacting legislature.

Occasionally, however, a court will find subsequent legislative history relevant. To illustrate, in *Montana Wilderness Ass'n v. U.S. Forest Service*, 655 F.2d 951 (9th Cir.), *cert. denied*, 455 U.S. 989 (1981), the court addressed the issue of whether a railroad had a right of access across federal lands. The parties disputed whether subsection 1323(a) of the Alaska National Interest Lands Conservation Act (the "Alaska Act") applied to the country as a whole or just to Alaska. *Id.* at 953. The Alaska Act required the Secretary of Agriculture to provide access to nonfederally-owned land "within the boundaries of the *National Forest System*" in certain situations. *Id.* (citing Pub. L. No. 96-487, § 1323(a), 94 Stat. 2371 (1980)) (emphasis added). The next subsection of the Act, subsection (b), was expressly limited to lands situated in the National Forest System *in Alaska. Id.* at 953–54 (citing Pub. L. No. 96-487, § 1323(b), 94 Stat. 2371 (1980)). There was no similar express limitation in the subsection at issue — subsection (a).

The issue for the court was whether "National Forest System" as used in subsection (a) meant only national forests in Alaska or all national forests within the United States. *Id.* at 954. Looking at the sections *in pari materia*, the court agreed that the two subsections seemed to apply just to Alaska because the limitation in the second subsection (b) could be read to limit the first subsection (a). *Id.* at 954–55. But the court did not stop its analysis after applying this linguistic canon. The court reviewed the Alaska Act's legislative history, which it found to be unilluminating. *Id.* So, the court turned to the legislative history of an act passed *three weeks later*, the Colorado Wilderness Act. *Id.* at 956. The conference committee report from this subsequent act showed that the members of the same Congress that had enacted the Alaska Act believed that subsection (a) applied nationwide. The court acknowledged that, generally, subsequent legislative history is not entitled to "great weight," but suggested that subsequent legislative history would be entitled to significant weight when it was clear that the subsequent conference committee (1) had carefully considered the issue, and (2) had relied on a specific interpretation of the first act when drafting the second act. *Id.* at 957. Thus, the court held that subsection (a) of the Alaska Act applied to lands nationwide despite the strong *in pari materia* argument that it did not.

Montana Wilderness represents the exception to the rule that subsequent legislative history is irrelevant to interpretation; when a legislature crafts a new law based on an interpretation of an existing law, then it may well make sense to give the prior law the subsequent meaning if only to harmonize both acts. Generally, however, subsequent legislative history is not relevant to the interpretation of a previously enacted statute. Were the rule different, legislators could use after-the-fact statements to manipulate the interpretation process relatively easily. Moreover, the enacting legislature's intent and purposes would take a back seat to those of the new legislature.

b. Testimony by and Affidavits from Legislators and Staff Members

Sometimes, during litigation, one party will introduce the testimony or affidavit of a legislator or staff member who was present when the statute was enacted. This "evidence" of intent is generally considered irrelevant to the meaning of the statute, even when the affidavit comes from the drafter of the bill. "[E]vidence of a ... draftsman of a statute is not a competent aid to a court in construing a statute." *S.D. Educ. Ass'n v. Barnett*, 582 N.W.2d 386, 400 (S.D. 1998) (Zinter, J., concurring in part and dissenting in part) (quoting *Cummings v. Mickelson*, 495 N.W.2d 493, 499 n. 7 (S.D. 1993)).

There are three reasons why such evidence is ignored. First, these affidavits indicate only one specific legislator's or, even worse, a lobbyist or staffer's understanding of the meaning and not the intent of the legislature as a whole. "Views of individuals involved with the legislative process as to intent [are of] no assistance ... [for] it is the intent of the legislative body that is sought, not the intent of the individual members who may have diverse reasons for or against a proposition...." *Am. Meat Inst. v. Barnett*, 64 F. Supp. 2d 906, 916 (D. S.D. 1999). Second, the affidavits are created to support one party's position in litigation after the legislative process has concluded. Memories may be inaccurate, incomplete, or intentionally wrong. Giving these statements weight could encourage gamesmanship. Finally, allowing such evidence of meaning would set legislators as rivals against one another and might give an individual legislator too much power to determine the meaning of a statute a body enacts. But when the affidavit is "provided as background as to the nature of the problem and why and how the Legislature sought to address it," these concerns disappear. *S.D. Educ. Ass'n*, 582 N.W.2d at 397 (Gilbert, J., concurring).

c. The Reenactment Canon

You will remember that codification refers to the insertion of sections of an act into the relevant section of the code, whether state or federal. Codification was covered in detail in Chapter 7. Recodification simply means to codify again. Reenactment means, essentially, the same thing.

Occasionally, legislatures recodify or reenact the whole or portions of a code. Legislatures recodify for many reasons, including to simplify and consolidate statutes, to eliminate defects in the original enactment, to remove inconsistencies and obsolete provisions, to expand titles to permit past or future growth, and to reorganize to make provisions easier to find. For example, Congress recodified the criminal code in 1948. When it did so, Congress changed some statutory language, but left other language intact. When a legislature recodifies a code, the presumption is that the recodification clarified the law, but did not make substantive changes, unless the new language unmistakably indicates the legislature's intent to make substantive changes. *Fourco Glass Co. v. Transmirra Products Corp.*, 353 U.S. 222, 227 (1957).

When the text is changed, new interpretations will likely follow. But when a statute is reenacted in identical or similar form (for example, when statutes are simply renumbered), there is a presumption that the legislature knew of any existing judicial or administrative interpretations of that statute and intended to continue those interpretations. *Lorillard v. Pons*, 434 U.S. 575, 580–81 (1978). Otherwise, the presumption continues, that the legislature would have amended the text. The reenactment canon is stated simply as follows: When Congress reenacts or recodifies a statute, which a court or an agency had previously interpreted, judges presume that Congress intended to continue that interpretation. This canon is similar to the super strong *stare decisis* canon discussed above. Yet, the reenactment canon is also broader because it applies not only to Supreme Court decisions but also to agency and lower court interpretations.

This presumption is bolstered when there is evidence that the reenacting Congress was aware of the specific interpretation. For example, Congress reenacted the Voting Rights Act on two separate occasions. Both times the legislative history was clear that Congress agreed with earlier interpretations of the Act. Thus, those interpretations would survive reenactment. "When a Congress that re-enacts a statute voices its approval of an administrative or other interpretation thereof, Congress is treated as having adopted that interpretation, and this Court is bound thereby." *United States v. Bd. of Comm'rs*, 435 U.S. 110, 134 (1978). This presumption can be overcome with evidence that the legislature was unaware of or did not intend the existing interpretation.

d. Subsequent Acts

Enactment of a subsequent act may affect the meaning of an existing act. *Franklin v. Gwinnett Cnty. Pub. Sch.*, 503 U.S. 60 (1992). For example, in *Franklin*, the Supreme Court had to decide whether, under Title IX's implied causes of action, a plaintiff could recover money damages in addition to injunctive relief.

The plaintiff in the case, a student at the public high school, was the subject of inappropriate and unwanted sexual advances by one of her teachers. *Id.* at 64. By the time the case was heard, both the student and teacher had left the school. Hence, injunctive relief would not have benefitted this student. As for the remedy, the legislative history was silent, which makes sense given that the cause of action was not express but was implied. The silence did not trouble the Court. "Since the Court ... concluded that this statute supported no express right of action, it is hardly surprising that Congress also said nothing about the applicable remedies for an implied right of action." *Id.* at 71.

Thus, the Court turned to another source to resolve the issue: subsequent legislative acts. In two related acts (the Rehabilitation Act Amendments of 1986 and The Rehabilitation Act of 1973), Congress broadly defined the express remedies available under those acts to include all forms of damages. *Id.* at 73. The majority and concurrence both found Congress's subsequent legislation to be "a validation of [its earlier] holding" and "an implicit acknowledgment that damages [were] available." *Id.* at 78 (Scalia, J., concurring). Thus, subsequent acts may provide insight into the contours of an existing act. The Court also used subsequent acts in *FDA v. Brown & Williamson Tobacco Corp.*, 529 U.S. 120 (2000), which is detailed in the next section; however, to understand the majority's opinion in that case, you must first understand legislative acquiescence.

e. Legislative Acquiescence

The most common legislative response to a judicial interpretation of a statute is silence. Some judges reason that a legislature's silence to an interpretation means acquiescence, or agreement, with that interpretation. One basis for finding silence to mean legislative acquiescence is the notion of super strong *stare decisis*. As you learned earlier in this chapter, super strong *stare decisis* refers to the heightened *stare decisis* effect given to Supreme Court opinions interpreting statutes. The Supreme Court presumes the correctness of its statutory precedents. Once it has authoritatively construed a federal statute, the Court believes that Congress is the more appropriate body to change the interpretation if there is any error. If Congress disagrees with the Court's interpretation, then Congress should change the interpretation. "When a court says to a legislature: 'You (or your predecessor) meant X,' it almost invites the legislature to answer: 'We did not.'" GUIDO CALABRESI, A COMMON LAW FOR THE AGE OF STATUTES 31–32 (1985). The fact that Congress did not change the interpretation suggests to the Court that Congress agreed with, or legislatively acquiesced in, the decision.

Legislative acquiescence is appropriate when the deciding court is the supreme court within a jurisdiction, rather than a lower court, because there is still a chance that the supreme court will correct the lower court's error. But, in fact, lower courts sometimes apply the canon anyway.

At times, the legislature probably does acquiesce to an interpretation by not acting in response. But more often, the political reality is that such silence means little. There are a multitude of reasons the legislature could have failed to amend the statute. The legislature could be unaware of the judicial opinion; the legislature might be unable to act in response to the interpretation; the legislature might have more pressing business; or the legislature might, indeed, agree with the decision.

Another criticism of legislative acquiescence is that when interpreting statutes, courts generally focus on finding the intent or purpose of the *enacting* legislature, not of a subsequent legislature. The legislature that silently approves the interpretation is most likely a different legislature than the legislature that enacted the statute. Silence from a subsequent legislature should have absolutely no relevance to the meaning the enacting legislature intended.

Finally, legislative acquiescence by-passes the constitutional process for enacting legislation; silence is neither passed bicamerally nor presented to the president. If silence is accepted as a legislative action, then Congress can effectively legislate in a way the Constitution does not contemplate. For this reason, textualists are particularly loathe to rest an interpretation on legislative acquiescence. At bottom, "legislative acquiescence [is] focused on the wrong legislature and it may be unreliable. On close analysis, it may even be unconstitutional [sic]. But, it is frequently invoked...." RONALD BENTON BROWN & SHARON JACOBS BROWN, STATUTORY INTERPRETATION: THE SEARCH FOR LEGISLATIVE INTENT 164 (2002).

Perhaps the best case for finding legislative acquiescence, if it should ever be found, is *Flood v. Kuhn*, 407 U.S. 258 (1972), which we studied earlier in this chapter. Remember in that case, the Supreme Court examined the issue of whether baseball was exempt from federal anti-trust laws. *Id.* at 265. The issue for the Court was whether baseball, specifically its reserve system, affected interstate commerce. The issue would have been simple to resolve were it not for two existing cases, *Federal Baseball Club v. National League*, 259 U.S. 200 (1922) and *Toolson v. New York Yankees, Inc.*, 346 U.S. 356 (1953), in which the Supreme Court had held that professional baseball did not affect interstate commerce. Shortly after these decisions, the Court had recognized that professional sports did impact interstate commerce and, thus, held that the anti-trust laws applied to other professional sports, such as wrestling and football. In doing so, the Court specifically expressed concern with its conflicting precedent and invited Congress to legislatively overrule *Federal Baseball Club* and *Toolson*. *Flood*, 407 U.S. at 273. In response, more than fifty bills were introduced in Congress; however, none of these bills were enacted. Of those bills that either the House or Senate passed, most would have expanded, rather than narrowed, the *Toolson* exception to apply to other professional sports. *Id.* at 281–82. Thus, Congress was not silent in response to *Federal Baseball Club* and *Toolson*; rather, it was simply unsuccessful at legislatively changing the outcome.

Because of this legislative response, the majority in *Flood* refused to overturn the Court's earlier holdings. *Id. at* 279. The majority was loathe to overturn the cases when "Congress, by its *positive inaction*, ... ha[d] clearly evinced a desire not to disapprove them legislatively." *Id.* at 283 (emphasis added). Despite recognizing the error of its earlier holdings, the majority refused to correct its mistake because Congress's "positive inaction" suggested acquiescence in the judicial decision. The majority suggested that *Flood* was not a case of legislative acquiescence; rather it was "something other than mere congressional silence and passivity." *Id.* Consider whether the majority's position is supportable: Congress had not acted, at least not successfully; hence, legislative acquiescence really did serve as the basis for the majority's holding.

The dissent was ready to correct the prior mistaken holdings. In response to the majority's legislative acquiescence argument, the dissent suggested that because the Court had, in prior decisions, treated other sports differently than baseball, Congress may not have been motivated to act. *Id.* at 290 (Marshall, J., dissenting). In any event, the dissent saw no reason to continue to uphold prior erroneous precedent when substantial rights were affected.

If *Flood* is a case in which legislative acquiescence could reasonably have been found because Congress indicated its awareness of the judicial holdings and tried but failed to act to expand those holdings, *Bocchino v. Nationwide Mutual. Fire Insurance, Co.*, 716 A.2d 883 (Conn. 1998), is a case in which legislative acquiescence should not have been found. In that case, the plaintiff sued his insurance company after his house burned to the ground. The insurance policy, pursuant to a state statute, had required the plaintiff to file his lawsuit within one year of the date of the loss. He did. But then, because of a computer error on the court's part, the suit was mistakenly dismissed. In response to the court's error, plaintiff re-filed within one year of the court's dismissal. But this refiling occurred more than one year from date of the loss. *Id.* at 884. A state failure-of-suit statute permitted a plaintiff to file a new action "[i]f any action, commenced within *the time limited by law*, has failed one or more times to be tried on its merits...." *Id.* at 883 n.2 (quoting CONN. GEN. STAT. § 52-592) (emphasis added).

The trial court dismissed the action as not being filed within the one year time limitation. The Connecticut Supreme Court affirmed, holding that the "time limited by law" exception did not apply to contractual limitations periods even when those provisions were required to be included in a contract because of a state law. Although the court acknowledged that the language in the failure-of-suit statute was ambiguous, the court reasoned that the ambiguity had been resolved by two of its prior decisions, *Chichester v. New Hampshire Fire Insurance Co.*, 74 Conn. 510 (1902), and *Vincent v. Mutual Reserve Fund Life Ass'n*, 74 Conn. 684 (1902). In these two prior opinions, the court had held that the failure-of-suit statute applied only to actions barred by a statute of limitations and not to actions limited contractually. The decisions in these cases were reaffirmed in *Monterio v. American Home Assurance Co.*, 177 Conn. 281 (1979). Because the legislature was silent in response to these opinions, the *Bocchino* majority assumed that legislature acquiesced in the holdings. Because the court determined that the time frame was contractual rather than required by law, the court affirmed the dismissal.

The decision is poorly reasoned. Unlike the *Flood* case, there was absolutely no proof that the legislature was aware of these old opinions. Moreover, the opinions addressed civil procedure issues, issues typically of more concern to the judiciary than to the legislature. Additionally, the prior holdings did not actually address the precise issue before the *Bocchino* court. In *Chichester*, the plaintiff's suit had been tried on the merits and failed; he was then precluded from bringing a second action. In *Monterio*, the plaintiff had commenced his action more than one year from the date he suffered the loss because his attorney was seriously ill. For these reasons, the dissent disagreed with the majority. The dissent argued that even if the opinions the majority cited actually were on point, the dissent would have overruled them. The language in the statute was clear: The filing time was in the statute because a state law required it to be; hence, the time to file "was limited by law." *Id.* at 891 (Berdon, J., dissenting). Given that the legislature was not likely aware of the prior opinions and that legislative acquiescence should be an exception in interpretation, not a rule, the dissent would have reversed.

If *Flood* presents one situation where Congress may have acquiesced, it is perhaps the only such case. Judges should find legislative acquiescence only rarely. It is, perhaps, legitimate to say that Congress acquiesced when it tried, but failed, more than fifty times to overturn a prior precedent. It is quite another thing to say that silence *in all cases* means that the legislature agreed with the opinion:

> It is perhaps too late now to deny that, legislatively speaking as in ordinary life, silence in some instances may give consent. But it would be going even farther beyond reason and common experience to maintain, as there are signs we may be by way of doing, that in legislation any more than in other affairs silence or nonaction always is acquiescence equivalent to action.

Cleveland v. United States, 329 U.S. 14, 22–24 (1946) (Rutledge, J., concurring). Silence can mean any number of things; judges should not presume silence always means agreement.

One final case in this area provides some additional insight as to what exactly is legislative silence and what role subsequent legislation may play. In *FDA v. Brown & Williamson Tobacco Corp.*, 529 U.S. 120 (2000), the Supreme Court considered whether the Food and Drug Administration (the "FDA") had authority to regulate tobacco under the Food, Drug, and Cosmetic Act as a "drug." For years, the FDA did not regulate tobacco and, in fact, claimed it lacked jurisdiction under the Act to do so, perhaps because the FDA knew that the tobacco companies had a strong influence in Congress and a sympathetic executive (Presidents Ronald Regan and George H. W. Bush).

During this time, Congress was not inactive. Some legislators attempted to amend the Act to give the FDA explicit authority to regulate tobacco, but their efforts proved unsuccessful. *Id.* at 147. Congress did, however, enact "six separate pieces of legislation" regulating the advertising of tobacco and requiring warning labels. *Id.* at 122. Congress also moved promptly to take away jurisdiction when the Federal Trade Commission (the "FTC") tried to regulate. *Id.* at 145. Thus, members of Congress were unsuccessful at expanding the FDA's jurisdiction in this area, but successful at limiting the FTC's jurisdiction and at enacting some oversight.

Then, President Bill Clinton was elected to office and the political climate changed, at least within the executive branch. As often happens when a new president takes office, the FDA reversed course, declaring tobacco to be a "drug" and cigarettes to be "combination products" that delivered nicotine to the body. The FDA then enacted regulations to control the sale and distribution of both cigarettes and tobacco. Not surprisingly, the tobacco companies quickly challenged the FDA's regulations.

The Court's majority rejected the FDA's attempt to regulate despite the ordinary meaning of the text: tobacco was a drug and cigarettes were combination products. The majority did so based on legislative acquiescence, although it denied that acquiescence was the basis for its decision. "We do not rely on Congress' failure to act — its consideration and rejection of bills that would have given the FDA this authority — in reaching this conclusion. Indeed this is not a case of simple inaction by Congress that purportedly represents its acquiescence in an agency's position." *Id.* at 155. Instead, the majority argued that Congress had not been silent. Against the backdrop of the FDA's repeated statements that it lacked jurisdiction to regulate, Congress had, over a period of thirty-five years, enacted various "tobacco-specific statutes" to "creat[e] a distinct regulatory scheme for cigarettes and smokeless tobacco." *Id.* Because Congress was not silent but legislated, albeit in another area, deference was inappropriate. In other words, the majority, like the majority in *Flood*, found "positive inaction."

The dissent disagreed, finding the language of the statute clear and determining that the FDA's inclusion of cigarettes as drugs supported the general purpose of the Act. In response to the majority's arguments, the dissent noted that the subsequent legislative activity was ambiguous at best. First, the failure of the legislature to enact legislation granting the FDA express authority to act proved only that Congress did not have enough votes to pass the bills. *Id.* at 183 (Breyer, J., dissenting). Second, that Congress moved quickly to take away jurisdiction from other agencies that tried to assert jurisdiction in this area might have shown, as the majority asserted, that Congress "resented agency assertions of jurisdiction in an area it had reserved for itself." *Id.* But if so, the dissent wondered, why then had Congress not immediately reacted when the

FDA changed course and asserted jurisdiction over tobacco? *Id.* If Congress were opposed to any agency assuming jurisdiction, then Congress should have acted immediately in response to the FDA's claim of authority. *Id.* Third, the dissent noted that the statutes that were enacted limited the authority of another agency, the FTC, not the FDA. The dissent questioned "[w]hy would one read the [labeling act's] pre-emption clause ... so broadly that it would bar a different agency from engaging in any other cigarette regulation at all?" *Id.* at 185. Thus, the dissent accused the majority of resting its opinion solely on legislative acquiescence, with which it disagreed.

This opinion is troubling for a number of reasons. First, the textualists on the bench signed onto a decision that ignored the ordinary meaning of clear text and did so by relying on legislative acquiescence, all while claiming not to do so. Similarly, the purposivists and intentionalists, in dissent, focused heavily, albeit not exclusively, on the text. This is one case in which the justices appear to have rejected their preferred theoretical approaches in favor of a preferred political outcome.

Second, this is not actually a case of legislative acquiescence to a prior judicial interpretation, even if you accept the reasons the majority stated. In this case, the Supreme Court had never determined whether the Act covered cigarettes and tobacco. Rather, the FDA did, saying first that cigarettes and tobacco were not covered and then later changing that interpretation when a new executive came into office. Thus, if Congress acquiesced in anything, then Congress acquiesced to the *FDA's* interpretation of a statute, not to a *court's* interpretation of a statute. It is not clear that the legislative acquiescence doctrine is appropriate when Congress acquiesces to an agency interpretation because this doctrine rests on concerns about *stare decisis* and separation of powers. *Stare decisis* has no application where there is no underlying judicial opinion to overturn. And the separation of powers issue relates not to the balance of power between the judiciary and legislature, but rather they relate to the balance of power between the executive and legislature. An agency should not be able to limit or expand a grant of authority from Congress, yet this opinion allowed that to occur. Moreover, an agency should not be able to bind Congress to a particular interpretation of an act: courts yes, but Congress no. (See Chapter 11.) Finally, if Congress and agencies are governed by the interpretations of a prior administration that later prove unwise in light of changing economic, technologic, and political realities, then executive flexibility may well be sacrificed. For all of these reasons, this case is very troubling.

In this chapter, we have discussed the role of subsequent legislative actions in interpretation. In the next chapter, we turn from the subsequent actions of the legislative branch and look at the subsequent actions of the executive branch, namely presidential signing statements and agency interpretations. Surprisingly, while subsequent legislative acts are generally irrelevant, subsequent executive acts are highly relevant to interpretation.

C. Mastering This Topic

Return to the hypothetical ordinance provided in Chapter 1 on page 9. The first question that was asked was the following: "An ambulance entered Pioneer Park to pick up and take to the hospital a man who has just suffered a heart attack. Did the ambulance driver violate the Pioneer Park Safety Ordinance (PPSO)?"

Is there anything is this chapter that could help you attempt to answer that question? Sadly, no. But that should not be surprising. In general, subsequent legislative acts, whether they be affidavits from legislators or silence from the legislature, are generally irrelevant to meaning. Thus, even if you had such information, it should play little, if any, role. For example, assume there was an earlier case in your jurisdiction that had held that firefighters were not exempt from the penalties in the PPSO. Assume further that, after this holding was issued, the council did not respond. Would the council's silence signal legislative acquiescence to the idea that emergency personnel were exempted from the PPSO's coverage? Certainly not. It is unlikely this council would have been aware of the decision, let alone had the time and or inclination to act on the interpretation. Unlike *Flood* and *Brown & Williamson*, there is simply no evidence of "positive inaction." Further, statements from the council members would not be relevant; the PPSO was not a recodified ordinance; there are no subsequently enacted ordinances to consider. Simply put, this chapter is mostly useless to you; however, it has helped you learn the weakness of your opponent's arguments should your opponent raise subsequent legislative action arguments.

Checkpoints

- Using subsequent events from the legislative or executive branches to discern meaning of a statute is highly controversial.
- Under super strong *stare decisis*, a heightened form of *stare decisis*, even when a judicial interpretation of a statute is wrong, judges are reluctant to overrule the decision.
- Generally, subsequent legislative history is not relevant to the interpretation of a previously enacted statute.

- Testimony by and affidavits from legislators and staff members are generally considered irrelevant to the meaning of a statute, even when the statement comes from the drafter of the bill.

- When Congress reenacts or recodifies a statute that a court or an agency had previously interpreted, judges presume that Congress intended to continue the interpretation.

- Subsequent acts may provide insight into the contours of an existing act.

- The most common legislative response to a judicial interpretation of a statute is silence. Silence can mean many things, including that the legislature agreed with the judicial interpretation. Legislative acquiescence is the doctrine that allows a court to presume the legislature's agreement with prior statutory interpretations.

- Legislative acquiescence rests on *stare decisis* and separation of powers concerns. It should be invoked rarely.

Chapter 11

Canons Based on Extrinsic Sources & The Executive Process: An Introduction to Agencies

---

Roadmap

- Appreciate what agencies are and what they do.
- Understand separation of powers.
- Learn the various ways that the legislature and executive exert control over agency authority.

A. Introduction to This Chapter

In Chapter 10, we covered post-enactment context: what happens both before and after enactment. You may have noticed that we covered both subsequent judicial action and subsequent legislative action but did not address subsequent executive action. We do so in these next two chapters. This chapter introduces agencies and explains how agencies fit into our constitutional structure, how agencies regulate, and how the legislature and executive control agencies and their personnel. In Chapter 12, we will talk about the role agencies play in statutory interpretation.

B. Agencies Defined

The Administrative Procedures Act (the APA), 5 U.S.C. § 551 *et. seq.* (2012), governs agencies and identifies their procedural law, which we call *adminis-*

Expressio Unius - Expression of one is the exclusion of another

252   11 · AN INTRODUCTION TO AGENCIES

trative law. You may wish to take a quick glance through the APA as we discuss this topic. "Agency" is defined as "each authority of the Government of the United States ... not includ[ing Congress, the courts, state governments, etc.]." 5 U.S.C. § 551(1). For purposes of the APA, the term "agency" includes all governmental authorities including administrations, commissions, corporations (*i.e.*, the Federal Deposit Insurance Corporation), boards, departments, divisions, and agencies.

There are a couple of things to note about the APA definition of an agency. First, it is very broad and, notably, does not define the term "authority." Second, the definition lists specific exclusions but does not exclude the president. Surprisingly, the issue of whether the president is considered an agency subject to the APA did not come before the Supreme Court until 1992, when the Court held that the president was not an agency. The Court rejected an *expressio unius* argument that the president should be considered an agency because the executive was not specifically excepted in the definition while Congress and the judiciary were. *Franklin v. Massachusetts*, 505 U.S. 788, 796 (1992). Despite the strong statutory interpretation argument, the Court held that the president was not an agency due to concerns regarding separation of powers.

There are two types of agencies: *independent agencies* and *executive agencies.* Independent agencies are less subject to the president's influence because they are headed by multimember groups from both political parties serving specific terms, and they can only be removed for cause. Examples of independent agencies include the Securities and Exchange Commission, the Federal Trade Commission, the Federal Election Commission, the Equal Employment Opportunity Commission, and the National Labor Relations Board.

Executive agencies, in contrast, are headed by individuals (generally called secretaries), who the president appoints, with the advice and consent of the Senate, and who serve at the discretion of the president. Examples include the Environmental Protection Agency, the Social Security Administration, and the Small Business Administration. The largest and most influential executive agencies are called *departments*; departments contain a host of sub-agencies. A few examples of departments include the Commerce Department, the Justice Department, the Department of Energy, the Department of Education, and the Department of Homeland Security. Sub-entities within the Department of the Interior include the Fish and Wildlife Service, the National Park Services, the Bureau of Indian Affairs, the Bureau of Reclamation, and the Bureau of Land Management. The heads of the departments are known collectively as the Cab-

inet. While presidents turned to the Cabinet for advice in the past, more recent presidents tend to turn to other entities.

C. Separation of Powers

Now that you know what agencies are, we need to talk about how agencies
fit into our constitutional structure. In Chapter 1, you learned that the powers of our government are split among three branches, such that no one branch
has too much power: Congress makes laws, the judiciary interprets laws, and
the executive executes the law. Where do agencies fit? In this section, we will
delve into the topic of separation of powers a little more deeply than we did
in Chapter 1 because of this doctrine's relationship to agency authority.

The Supreme Court has approached separation of powers issues in two different ways, one of which is more accepting of an overlap of powers, the other
of which is not. Legal scholars have identified these two approaches as *formalism* and *functionalism*. As we begin this discussion of separation of powers, be aware that these categories, as well as the Court's jurisprudence in this
area is imperfect. We will touch just the surface; for additional background on
the difference between formalism and functionalism, *see* M. Elizabeth Magill,
The Real Separation in Separation of Powers Law, 86 Va. L. Rev. 1127, 1132
(2000) (describing the formalist and functionalist approaches to separation of
powers). Let's begin with formalism.

1. Formalism

The *formalist* approach to separation of powers emphasizes the necessity of
maintaining three distinct branches of government, each with delegated powers: one branch legislates, one branch executes, and one branch adjudicates. These
powers are delegated in the vesting clauses of the U.S. Constitution. Article I
vests in Congress "[a]ll legislative Powers herein granted." U.S. Const. art. 1,
§ 1. Legislative power is the power "to promulgate generalized standards and
requirements of citizen behavior or to dispense benefits—to achieve, maintain,
or avoid particular social policy results." Martin H. Redish & Elizabeth J. Cisar,
*"If Angels Were to Govern": The Need for Pragmatic Formalism in Separation of
Powers Theory*, 41 Duke L.J. 449, 479 (1991). Congress therefore not only has
the power to create law, but also has the power to create procedural rules to ensure enforcement of those laws. Laws "alter[] the legal rights, duties, and relations of persons ... outside the Legislative Branch." *INS v. Chadha*, 462 U.S.

919, 952 (1983). Congress alters legal rights through enacting, amending, and repealing statutes.

Article II of the Constitution vests "[t]he executive Power ... in a President of the United States of America." U.S. CONST. art. II, § 1, cl. 1. Executive acts are those in which an executive official exercises judgment about how to apply law to a given situation. *Bowsher v. Synar*, 478 U.S. 714, 732-33 (1986). For the executive to execute the law there must be existing law to execute. In other words, while the legislature enacts laws, the executive enforces those laws.

Article III of the Constitution vests "[t]he judicial Power of the United States, ... in one supreme Court, and in such inferior Courts as the Congress may from time to time ordain and establish." U.S. CONST. art. III, § 1. Judicial power is the power to interpret laws and resolve legal disputes. "[T]o declare what the law is, or has been, is a judicial power, to declare what the law shall be is legislative." *Koshkonong v. Burton*, 104 U.S. 668, 678 (1881) (quoting *Ogden v. Blackledge*, 6 U.S. 272, 277 (1804)). In other words, while the legislature enacts laws, the judiciary interprets those laws. Thus, "the interpretation of the laws is the proper and peculiar province of the courts." THE FEDERALIST No. 78, at 523, 525 (Alexander Hamilton) (J. Cooke ed. 1961). The judiciary interprets laws by adjudicating cases and rendering dispositive judgments based on findings of law and fact; indeed, this is a court's primary power.

When confronting an issue raising separation of powers concerns, a formalist judge will use a two-step, rule-based approach. First, the judge will identify the power being exercised. Second, the judge will determine whether the appropriate branch is exercising that power in accordance with the Constitution. A formalist judge will therefore focus on the activity at issue by first categorizing it as legislative, executive, or judicial in nature. Next, a judge will analyze whether the appropriate branch is performing the activity. The chart

FORMALISM

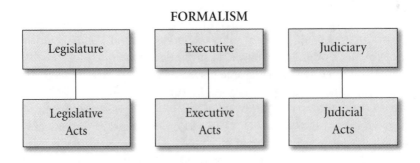

illustrates formalism in a very simplified way. Each branch may constitutionally perform any function that falls within its corresponding "Acts Box," but
may not constitutionally perform any function that falls within another branch's
"Acts Box."

Under formalism, a branch violates separation of powers if it attempts to
exercise a power that is not constitutionally delegated to it (or within its Acts
Box). Overlap is permitted only when constitutionally prescribed. So, for example, the president and Senate both play a role in appointing principal officers without violating separation of powers because the Constitution delegates
this power to both the executive and legislative branches. U.S. CONST. art. II
§ 2 cl. 2.

When the Supreme Court approaches a separation of powers issue under a
formalist approach, the Court regularly strikes down that exercise of power.
For example, in *Clinton v. New York*, 524 U.S. 417 (1998), the Court applied
a formalist approach to hold that the executive line-item veto was unconstitutional
because it enabled the executive to unilaterally amend and repeal legislation,
a power delegated to the legislature. *Id.* at 447–49. Similarly, the Court struck
down legislative veto provisions in *INS v. Chadha*, 462 U.S. 919 (1983). The
legislative veto allowed Congress to delegate lawmaking authority to the executive, but reserved, either to a single chamber or to a committee from a single chamber, the power to oversee and veto the executive's use of this delegated
authority. Because legislative veto provisions allowed one chamber of Congress to unilaterally amend legislation and thereby avoid constitutionally required
bicameral passage and presentment, the Court held that these provisions were
unconstitutional. *Id.* at 954–55.

Additionally, in *Youngstown Sheet & Tube Co. v. Sawyer*, 343 U.S. 579 (1952),
the Court held that President Truman's executive order seizing private steel
mills during the Korean War was unconstitutional because it altered private
property rights, a power reserved exclusively for Congress. *Id.* at 588–89. To
prevent a possible steel shutdown during the Korean War, President Truman
requested from Congress the authority to seize the mills. After Congress refused, the President, in the absence of any specific statutory or constitutional
authority, issued the order anyway. Therefore, the issue for the Court was
whether the President, absent any specific authority, had the *inherent* power
to issue the order under his constitutional authority to act as Commander-in-
Chief and to faithfully execute the laws. The Court held that the President did
not have this power. *Id.* at 582–87.

Under a formalist approach, the Court will generally reject any attempt by
one branch to usurp power from another branch. For example, in *Bowsher v.
Synar*, 478 U.S. 714 (1986), the Court held that Congress could not keep re-

moval power over an agency official working within the Government Accountability Office because the agency official exercised executive authority. *Id.* at 726-27. In *Stern v. Marshall*, 131 S. Ct. 2594 (2011), the Court held that a Bankruptcy Court—an Article I (executive) Court—lacked constitutional power under Article III to resolve a counterclaim based on state law. *Id.* at 2620. Similarly, in *Plaut v. Spendthrift Farm, Inc.*, 514 U.S. 211 (1995), the Court held that Congress could not retroactively require federal courts to re-open a judgment once it was final. *Id.* at 240. Finally, in *United States v. Klein*, 80 U.S. (13 Wall.) 128 (1871), the Court invalidated a statute that "prescribe[d] rules of decision" for a specific type of case. *Id.* at 146. According to the Court, by prescribing a rule of decision—or an outcome—in a pending case, "Congress[] inadvertently passed the limit which separate[d] the legislative from the judicial power." *Id.* at 147. Although Congress may amend the underlying substantive law to accomplish policy objectives, Congress may not dictate outcomes in particular cases. Because the power to decide cases by interpreting and applying existing law to a specific, factual situation is delegated to the judiciary, Congress violates separation of powers when it attempts to decide cases, reopen final cases, or interfere with a federal court's decision-making process.

Formalists are concerned about undue accretion of power to any one branch, no matter how small. The concentration of power in any one branch is viewed as unconstitutional regardless of whether that power is being misused. Formalists believe that accretion of power in and of itself is unacceptable because once power is acquired, it can be difficult to determine whether too much power has been ceded. Perhaps, more critically, once a branch acquires too much power, it would be too late to remedy the situation. Thus, formalists view separation of powers as a doctrine that is "prophylactic in nature ... designed to avoid a situation in which one might even debate whether an undue accretion of power has taken place." Redish & Cisar, *supra* at 476.

In sum, formalism is an approach that focuses on the separate, enumerated powers delegated to each branch in the vesting clauses of the Constitution. Overlap is not permitted for fear that one branch may accrete too much power. When the Court resolves a separation of powers issue using formalism, inevitably, the Court finds the exercise of power unconstitutional.

2. Functionalism

The Supreme Court Justices have never collectively embraced formalism. Rather, the Court has oscillated between formalism and functionalism throughout its history. Indeed, with a government adapted to the complexities of the twenty-first century, functionalism seems to be winning the war.

Functionalism's focus differs from that of formalism. While formalists focus on strict separation, functionalists focus on balancing the inevitable overlap of powers to preserve the core *functions* the Constitution assigns to each branch. To maintain a relatively balanced power distribution, a complete bar against any encroachment between the branches is unnecessary. Instead, functionalists focus on limiting encroachments into the core, constitutionally-appointed functions of each branch. For example, the executive's power of appointment is a core function. U.S. CONST. art. II, § 2, cl. 2. However, the appointment power is not absolute, as the power applies only to the appointment of *principal* not *inferior* executive officers and is subject to congressional approval. Similarly, the Constitution implicitly gives the executive the power to remove executive officers subject to conditions Congress imposes. It, therefore, is not absolute. Note, however, that although Congress has the authority to place limits on the executive's removal power, Congress does not have the authority to eliminate that power altogether. *Bowsher v. Synar*, 478 U.S. 714, 725–26 (1986); *Myers v. United States*, 272 U.S. 52, 126–27 (1926).

Like formalists, functionalists turn to the vesting clauses of the Constitution to define the most central, core functions of each branch: the legislature legislates, the judiciary adjudicates, and the executive executes the law. But unlike formalism, these core functions are not compartmentalized under functionalism. For example, the legislature's power to make law is a core function. The judiciary, however, also makes law, both by developing common law and by interpreting legislative-made law (statutes). Under formalism, this encroachment would be sufficient to trigger a separation of powers violation. In contrast, under functionalism, the judiciary's encroachment into a core function of the legislature does not. To trigger a separation of powers violation under functionalism, one branch would have to *unduly* encroach and aggrandize a core function of a separate branch.

Functionalists believe that overlap between the branches is practically necessary and even desirable. Functionalists emphasize the need to maintain pragmatic flexibility to respond to the needs of modern government. Indeed, the existence of the administrative system is an example of functionalism. As we will see in a moment, agencies, which are part of the executive branch, perform all of the functions separately delegated to each of the three branches in the Constitution. Yet, few today would suggest that agencies violate separation of powers. *But see* Peter B. McCutchen, *Mistakes, Precedent, and The Rise of the Administrative State: Toward a Constitutional Theory of the Second Best*, 80 CORNELL L. REV. 1, 11 (1994) (arguing that "[u]nder a pure formalist approach, most, if not all, of the administrative state is unconstitutional.").

While both formalism and functionalism share a common goal to ensure that no one branch acquires too much unilateral power, these approaches go about meeting this goal in different ways. Whereas formalists use a two-step, bright-line-rule approach to categorize acts as legislative, judicial, or executive, functionalists use a factors approach, balancing the competing power interests with the pragmatic need for innovation. Functionalists recognize the government's need for flexibility to create new power-sharing arrangements to address the evolving needs of the modern century. Functionalists do not want to "unduly restrict Congress's ability to take needed and innovative action...." *Commodity Futures Trading Comm'n v. Schor*, 478 U.S. 833, 851 (1986).

To foster flexibility, functionalists focus less on maintaining separateness of each branch, and instead favor independence of each branch, with oversight from other branches. This independence is achieved if each branch is able to perform its core functions while also being able to limit the accretion of power by the other branches. Justice Jackson's tripartite framework from his concurrence in *Youngstown Sheet & Tube Co. v. Sawyer*, 343 U.S. 579 (1952), is informative. Justice Jackson suggested that the Court review separation of powers issues differently, based upon the level of cooperation among the branches. Because the case involved President Truman's seizure of the steel mills, the framework specifically addressed executive power, but the analysis applies to all:

> First, "[w]hen the President acts pursuant to an express or implied authorization of Congress, his authority is at its maximum, for it includes all that he possesses in his own right plus all that Congress can delegate." Second, "[w]hen the President acts in absence of either a congressional grant or denial of authority, he can only rely upon his own independent powers, but there is a zone of twilight in which he and Congress may have concurrent authority, or in which its distribution is uncertain." In such a circumstance, Presidential authority can derive support from "congressional inertia, indifference or quiescence." Finally, "[w]hen the President takes measures incompatible with the expressed or implied will of Congress, his power is at its lowest ebb," and the Court can sustain his actions "only by disabling the Congress from acting upon the subject."

Id. at 635-38 (Jackson, J., concurring); *Medellín v. Texas*, 552 U.S. 491, 494 (2008). Simply put: when one branch unilaterally acts against the express or implied will of the other branches, the risk of tyranny is greatest.

While formalism was depicted above as a series of separate boxes with no overlap, functionalism might be pictured as a set of interlocking circles, as in the chart on the next page.

Functionalism

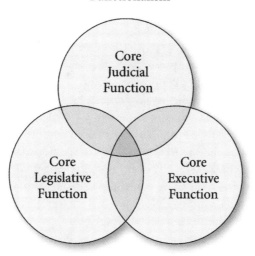

From this chart, it becomes clear that each branch possesses separate, constitutionally assigned, core functions. At the same time, each branch also has a penumbra of overlap that shades gradually into the core functions of the other two branches. So long as the branches steer relatively clear of the other branches' core functions, and so long as the branches do not enlarge the size of their own circle at the expense of another branch's circle, functionalist separation of powers is maintained.

Almost exclusively, when the Court approaches a separation of powers issue under a functionalist approach, the Court approves the exercise of that branch's power. For example, in *Commodity Futures Trading Commission v. Schor*, 478 U.S. 833 (1986), the Court held that Congress can delegate to the executive the power to adjudicate a "particularized area of law," specifically common law counterclaims. *Id.* at 852–57. According to the Court, the power arrangement "raise[ed] no question of the aggrandizement of congressional power at the expense of a coordinate branch." *Id.* at 856. In other words, separation of powers was not violated simply because Congress enabled the executive to encroach on a judicial function. The Court required a concurrent finding that Congress had correspondingly expanded, or aggrandized, the executive's power before finding a separation of powers violation. *Id.* at 856–57. To illustrate, under a formalist approach, the Court had earlier denied a broader judicial power grant to a non-Article III bankruptcy court. *N. Pipeline Constr. Co. v. Marathon Pipe Line Co.*, 458 U.S. 50, 57–58 (1982). But in *Schor*, the Court distinguished

Northern Pipeline by saying that "the [Act at issue] leaves far more of the 'essential attributes of judicial power' to Article III courts than did that portion of the Bankruptcy Act found unconstitutional in *Northern Pipeline*." *Schor*, 478 U.S. at 852. In short, the power transfer in *Schor* was not intrusive enough to raise concerns about aggrandizement.

Interestingly, the Court has approved Congress's delegation of limited legislative-like powers to the judiciary. In *Mistretta v. United States*, 488 U.S. 361 (1989), the Court upheld the constitutionality of the U.S. Sentencing Commission, even though three of the seven proposed commissioners were sitting federal judges. *Id.* at 368. The Court was unconcerned that members of the judiciary would be making law by drafting sentencing guidelines. The Court reasoned that drafting sentencing guidelines was similar to establishing court rules; therefore, "the Commission's functions ... [were] clearly attendant to a central element of the historically acknowledged mission of the Judicial Branch." *Id.* at 391. Hence, the intrusion was acceptable because it was minimal and already tolerated in other areas.

In summary, functionalists take a pragmatic view of separation of powers and seek to avoid the aggrandizement of a branch at the expense of another branch. Whereas formalists ask what kind of power is being wielded and whether the appropriate branch is wielding that power, functionalists ask whether one branch has encroached into the core functions of another branch and thereby aggrandized itself. To illustrate:

> [I]f the Supreme Court were to void a presidential pardon because it was given for improper motives, ... if the Court were to void a Senate impeachment proceeding because it had defects, ... [i]f the Court were to order the President to dismiss a Secretary of State who was facing criminal proceedings, the Court would violate the principal of separation of powers.

Aharon Barak, *Foreword: A Judge on Judging: The Role of a Supreme Court in a Democracy*, 116 HARV. L. REV. 16, 122 (2002). In all of these examples, the issue would not be whether the Court had the power to act. The Court likely has the power to require the executive and legislature to obey the Constitution. Rather, the issue would be whether, in doing so, the Court would impede the executive or legislature's ability to carry out their respective core functions and, in the process, aggrandize the Court's own role. At bottom, power given or taken by one branch must not "intru[de] on the authority and functions of [another] Branch." *Nixon v. Fitzgerald*, 457 U.S. 731, 754 (1982). Intrusions that impair another branch's ability to perform core functions are unconstitutional unless the "impact is justified by an overriding need to promote objectives within the constitutional authority of Congress." *Nixon v. Adm'r of Gen. Servs.*, 433 U.S. 425, 433 (1977).

Finally, it is important to know that, while the Founders were indeed concerned about the concentration of governmental power in any one of the three branches, they were primarily concerned with congressional self-aggrandizement. In keeping with this concern, the Court more closely scrutinizes legislation that expands Congress's authority rather than the authority of the other branches. The Court has been more accepting of judicial and executive aggrandizement. Indeed, at least one commentator has suggested that the Court uses formalism when Congress overreaches and uses functionalism when the judiciary or executive overreach. Ronald J. Krotoszynski, *On the Danger of Wearing Two Hats: Mistretta and Morrison Revisited*, 38 WM. & MARY L. REV. 417, 460 (1997).

3. The Delegation Doctrine

As we just saw, the U.S. Constitution anticipates a legislature, an executive, and a judiciary, and it defines each of their powers. Agencies are not mentioned. Likely, the Framers did not foresee the expansive role of agencies (and certainly not their proliferation) and, as a result, did not address them. How then are they constitutional?

Administrative agencies operate within the executive branch, either under the president of the United States or under the governor of a state. Although the executive is the branch that enforces the law, administrative agencies not only enforce law, but make law in areas that Congress or a state legislature delegates to them. Agencies enact rules, called *regulations*, which are similar to statutes Congress or a state legislature passes. Like statutes, these regulations make conduct illegal, or require people to act in specific ways. For example, the Federal Aviation Administration (FAA) has the power to enact a regulation that would require all airlines to inspect airplanes for fuselage cracks at least yearly. Airlines that fail to comply could be subject to a fine or other penalty, which the airline might adjudicate before the agency that penalized it.

If agencies are in the executive branch, how are they able to enact regulations that have the force and effect of law? The short answer to this question is that the Supreme Court long ago held that Congress has the ability (indeed, for decades that ability has been a necessity) to delegate such power to agencies pursuant to the Necessary and Proper Clause, U.S. CONST. art. I, § 8, so long as Congress provides intelligible principles, or standards, for agencies to use when exercising that power. *J.W. Hampton, Jr. & Co. v. United States*, 276 U.S. 394, 409 (1928); *Whitman v. Am. Trucking Ass'n, Inc.*, 531 U.S. 457, 474–76

(2001). Thus, before the FAA could enact the regulation identified above, Congress would first have to enact a statute delegating authority to the FAA to set safety standards for airlines and airplanes. Within this authorizing, or enabling, statute, Congress would delegate broad authority to the FAA to regulate air safety in general, but Congress would also provide standards, or intelligible principles, to guide the agency's actions. So long as Congress places some boundaries on agency authority, delegation is legitimate. If Congress sufficiently and explicitly constrains an agency's policy-making choices, then the agency is not making law; rather, the agency is refining congressionally made law. If, however, the delegation is too broad and ambiguous, then the delegation may be unconstitutional.

In the 1930s, the Supreme Court decided three cases in which it struck down statutes for violating this standard. You may remember that the 1930s represented a time of great turmoil for the United States. During this time, President Franklin Delano Roosevelt came into office promising to turn things around for the American people. Just five days after his election, Congress was called into session and enacted five major statutes after only forty hours of debate. This rate of speed was unprecedented, and the judiciary's reaction to the power grab was hostile, to say the least. Shortly thereafter, the federal judiciary found four major pieces of legislation unconstitutional and issued numerous injunctions.

With this background, the Supreme Court heard three delegation cases. In the first, *Panama Refining Co. v. Ryan*, 293 U.S. 388 (1935) (known as the "Hot Oil case"), the Court struck down a provision of the National Industrial Recovery Act ("NIRA") that allowed the president to prohibit the interstate transportation of oil in excess of that allowed by state law. *Id.* at 420–21. Under the NIRA, Congress wanted to prevent the evasion of strict state laws limiting the amount of oil that oil producers could sell. Striking down the statute, the Court held that Congress did not provide intelligible principles and stated: "As to the transportation of oil production in excess of state permission, the Congress has declared no policy, has established no standard, has laid down no rule. There is no requirement, no definition of circumstances and conditions in which the transportation is to be allowed or prohibited." *Id.* at 430.

In the second case, *A.L.A. Schechter Poultry Corp. v. United States*, 295 U.S. 495 (1935) (known as the "Sick Chicken case"), the Court struck down another provision in the NIRA that allowed the president to approve codes for "fair competition" that were established jointly with the chicken industry so long as the following conditions were met: (1) the code was written by a representative group of business, (2) the code did not promote monopolies, and (3) the code served goals identified in another section of the NIRA. *Id.* at 538–39.

The Court struck down the provision, stating that the President's authority was not sufficiently limited:

> [The provision] supplies no standards for any trade, industry or activity. It does not undertake to prescribe rules of conduct to be applied to particular states of fact determined by appropriate administrative procedure. Instead of prescribing rules of conduct, it authorizes the making of codes to prescribe them. For that legislative undertaking, section 3 sets up no standards, aside from [general aims]. In view of the scope of that broad declaration, and of the nature of the few restrictions that are imposed, the discretion of the President in approving or prescribing codes, and thus enacting laws for the government of trade and industry throughout the country, is virtually unfettered.

Id. at 541–42. Justice Cardozo, who dissented in the Hot Oil case, agreed and eloquently stated that "[t]his [was] delegation running riot." *Id.* at 553 (Cardozo, J., concurring). In this case, the Court was also concerned that the provision delegated legislative power to private entities (industry). *Id.* at 554.

The third case, *Carter v. Carter Coal Co.* 298 U.S. 238 (1936), presented the following issue for the Court: The statute in that case allowed certain mine owners and miners the authority to set maximum labor hours, which would be binding on other mine owners and miners. *Id.* at 279 (citing 15 U.S.C.A. § 801–827). The Court struck down the third party delegation and stated:

> The power conferred upon the majority is, in effect, the power to regulate the affairs of an unwilling minority. This is legislative delegation in its most obnoxious form; for it is not even delegation to an official or an official body, presumptively disinterested, but to private persons whose interests may be and often are adverse to the interests of others in the same business.

Id. at 311. While we will see that the delegation doctrine of today has no teeth, this third principle—that delegations to third parties is unconstitutional—remains vibrant.

As you might imagine, President Roosevelt was less than thrilled with the Court's attacks on his New Deal legislation. To influence future decision-making, he proposed adding an additional Justice to the Court for each Justice over the age of 70 (the "Court Packing Plan"). Although the plan was never adopted, the threat of adoption achieved the desired effect. For the next fifty years, the Court adopted a broader view of federal legislative power and never again struck down a statute on delegation grounds. For example, in *Whitman v. American Trucking Ass'n*, 531 U.S. 457 (2001), the Court reviewed the constitutionality of a section of the Clean Air Act that directed the EPA "to set primary ambient air quality standards 'the attainment and maintenance of which ... are requisite *to protect the public health.*'" *Id.* at 465 (quoting 42 U.S.C. § 7409(b)(1)) (emphasis added). The issue for the Court was whether the language "to protect the public health" sufficiently constrained the delegation; the Court held that it did. *Id.* at 472–73.

As can be seen from *Whitman*, the non-delegation principle is little more than a convenient rationale to give legitimacy to an institution that raises constitutional concerns while being essential to a functioning government. It is, perhaps, a fiction to say that agencies are enforcing congressionally made law. Indeed, some Justices of the Supreme Court have questioned whether Congress delegates *legislative* power or merely sets boundaries on nondelegated *executive* power. Justice Scalia, a formalist, identifies the delegated power as executive because to do otherwise would raise constitutional questions he would rather avoid. *Id.* at 472–76. Writing for the majority in *Whitman*, Justice Scalia framed the issue as "whether the statute ... delegated legislative power to the agency." *Id.* at 472. Noting that the Constitution "permits no delegation of those powers," Justice Scalia articulated his view that when agencies act pursuant to statutes containing intelligible principles, agencies are not exercising delegated legislative power, but are instead exercising nondelegated executive power. *Id.* at 472–73. A statute with no intelligible principles places no boundaries on the exercise of executive power; hence, such a statute would violate the Constitution. *Id.* at 472–74.

In contrast, Justice Stevens, a functionalist, suggested that the Court should "frankly acknowledge[]" that the power being delegated is legislative, but the intelligible principles in the statute adequately restrain it. He said, "I am persuaded that it would be both wiser and more faithful to what we have actually done in delegation cases to admit that agency rulemaking authority is 'legislative power.'" *Id.* at 488 (Stevens, J., concurring). As a functionalist, Stevens can accept the exercise of legislative power by the executive branch; as a formalist, Justice Scalia cannot.

Whether the legislature is delegating legislative power or constraining nondelegated executive power, there can be little doubt that agencies today have the power to enact regulations with the force and effect of law. The modern delegation doctrine today focuses the judicial inquiry on whether the legislature has provided sufficient standards (in the form of intelligible principles) to limit the scope of the agency's authority. And the answer to that question is almost always yes.

D. What Agencies Do

You know what agencies are, but you may wonder, what do they do? Agencies regulate private conduct, administer entitlement programs, collect taxes, deport aliens, issue permits, run the space program, manage the national parks, and so on. Simply put, agencies run the functions we think of as governmental, whether state or federal. Of more interest to us is *how* agencies do what they do. As we saw above, Congress delegates power to agencies. Agencies act in three ways: by adjudicating, by rulemaking, and by investigating. Agencies act like courts when they adjudicate, like legislatures when they make rules, and like the police when they investigate. Agency powers are spelled out in the APA. In this next section, we will explore the three ways that agencies act.

1. Adjudication

For an agency to have any power to act, Congress must enact a statute that creates the agency (if it does not already exist) and that identifies the agency's power and regulatory agenda. This statute is known as the *enabling*, or organic, statute. In its enabling statute, one power that Congress may authorize an agency to use is adjudicatory power. An agency's power to adjudicate is similar to that of a court in that the agency decides how a statute or regulation applies to a given set of facts. For example, the Social Security Administration might use adjudication to determine whether a person qualifies for disability benefits. Similarly, the Food and Drug Administration might use adjudication to determine whether a drug should be removed from the market. The final product of an agency's adjudication is called an *order*. 5 U.S.C. §551(6). The APA defines adjudication as the "agency process for the formulation of an order." 5 U.S.C. §551(7). This definition is so broad that any agency activity that is not rulemaking or investigating is adjudication (including the granting of a permit).

Under the APA, when an agency adjudicates, it does so either by holding a formal, trial-type hearing or by acting informally. You should keep in mind that Congress may, in the enabling statute, impose additional agency requirements than those the APA requires; however, this discussion will focus only on the APA requirements.

The APA identifies specific procedures that must be followed in formal adjudication. 5 U.S.C. §§554, 556. Formal administrative hearings resemble a civil trial with all the procedural accoutrements, including the right to notice, a hearing, a record, and a (mostly) neutral decision-maker. The primary differences between civil trials and formal administrative hearings are that (1) administrative hearings take place before an administrative law judge (ALJ) rather than a trial judge, and (2) the rules of evidence do not apply in administrative hearings. Similar to trial court decisions, agency adjudications are subject to judicial review.

ALJs generally preside over agency adjudications, although the person or persons in charge of the agency may choose to preside instead. 5 U.S.C. § 556(b). ALJs have the power to administer oaths, issue subpoenas, receive evidence, hold settlement conferences, dispose of procedural requests, take official notice of facts, and, most importantly, decide the case by either making an initial decision or by making a recommendation to the agency. 5 U.S.C. § 557(b). When the APA was first adopted, ALJs were known as Hearing Examiners and were expected only to assemble the record for the agency head; the term was changed to administrative law judges in 1978. The ALJ is an employee of the agency for which the ALJ performs functions similar to a trial judge. 5 U.S.C § 3105 (2012). To ensure that ALJs retain as much independence and neutrality as possible, agencies may not evaluate, discipline, reward, punish, or remove their ALJs; instead, the Merit Systems Protection Board makes these decisions, using a formal adjudication process. 5 U.S.C § 7521 (2012). Also, the APA prohibits the agency investigator and prosecutor from interacting with the ALJ about a pending case, unless the investigator is a witness. 5 U.S.C. § 554(d). For these reasons, and as a practical matter, ALJs view and conduct themselves as independent, neutral decision-makers.

To appeal an ALJ's initial decision — which includes findings of fact, conclusions of law, the basis for the findings, and the order — a party must appeal first to the agency itself. Unlike appeals in a court of law, appeals to the agency are made *de novo*: "the agency has all the powers which it would have in making the initial decision." 5 U.S.C. § 557(b). The process is similar, however, in that the parties submit written briefs and argue orally. If the agency rules against itself, there is no further appeal. If, however, the agency rules in favor of itself, the losing party may appeal to a court of law. The availability of judicial review is a very complex subject; one that is more appropriately covered in a text on administrative law.

While formal adjudication resembles civil adjudication, informal adjudication is altogether different. Often, no hearing is offered. Indeed, few procedures are required at all; under the APA, an agency need only promptly decide an issue and notify the affected party. 5 U.S.C. § 552. Informal adjudications can be as simple as an agency administrator approving an individual's application for a permit.

Although the APA requires little to no procedures for informal adjudication, the U.S. Constitution or the enabling statute may require additional procedures. In cases involving the deprivation of property or liberty rights, the Due Process Clause of the U.S. Constitution, U.S. CONST. amend. V, requires some form of a hearing; however, the required procedures vary in accordance with a balancing of competing interests: (1) the private interest being affected, (2) the risk of erroneous deprivation of this interest through the procedures being used, and (3) the administrative and fiscal burden of additional procedures (the government's interest). *Mathews v. Eldridge*, 424 U.S. 319, 335 (1976). Moreover, absent a really good reason, the government must offer some form of pre-deprivation hearing, although an abbreviated form is sufficient if the agency offers a post-deprivation hearing that comports with the *Mathews*'s requirements. *Cleveland Bd. of Educ. v. Loudermill*, 470 U.S. 532, 542 (1985). In sum, informal adjudication procedures are generally minimal, and the process is much faster in comparison to formal adjudication procedures. During either type of adjudication—formal or informal—an agency may interpret a statute. As we will see in the next chapter, the appropriate level of deference a court will give that interpretation appears to depend on whether the agency has acted formally or informally.

As you can imagine, agencies may prefer to act informally because the APA requires so few procedures for informal adjudication. Whether an agency must use formal instead of informal procedures is a question of statutory interpretation. Simply put, to determine whether an agency should have used formal adjudication procedures when it adjudicated a case, a court will look at the language of the enabling statute and the agency's interpretation of that language. The court will apply a deference standard known as the *Chevron* two-step (from *Chevron U.S.A., Inc. v. Natural Resources Defense Council, Inc.*, 467 U.S. 837 (1984)), which we will study in detail in the next chapter. In essence, a court would determine first whether Congress was clear as to which type of hearing was required, and if not, the court would determine second whether the agency's interpretation of the language was reasonable. *Dominion Energy v. Johnson*, 443 F.3d 12, 16 (1st Cir. 2006) (overruling an earlier case establishing a presumption in favor of formal adjudication); *Chemical Waste Mgmt. Inc. v. EPA*, 873 F.2d 1477, 1482 (D.C. Cir. 1989) (applying *Chevron*). In general, unless Congress included the magic language from APA § 554(a) in the enabling statute—"on the record after opportunity for an agency hearing"—an agency's decision to use informal adjudication procedures will be upheld.

2. Rulemaking

a. Legislative Rulemaking

In addition to or instead of authorizing adjudicatory power to an agency in the enabling statute, Congress may authorize an agency to use rulemaking powers to further its regulatory agenda. Agencies promulgate rules known as regulations. The APA defines a "rule" as "an agency statement of general ... applicability and future effect designed to implement, interpret, or prescribe law or policy." 5 U.S.C. § 551(4). Essentially, rules, like statutes, are laws that apply to large numbers of people once enacted, while adjudications apply ostensibly just to the parties and past conduct.

Like adjudication, there are two types of rulemaking under the APA: formal and informal. Additionally, in the enabling statute, Congress may require an agency to follow additional requirements to those the APA requires. This discussion will focus primarily on the APA requirements.

Oddly enough, formal rulemaking procedures are identical to formal adjudication procedures. Indeed, many of the same procedural rules apply to formal rulemaking and formal adjudication. 5 U.S.C. § 556 (applies to both formal adjudications and formal rulemakings). There is an administrative hearing with trial-like procedures. You will remember that formal administrative hearings resemble a civil trial with all the procedural accoutrements, including the right to notice, a hearing, a record, and a neutral decision-maker. Decisions are subject to judicial review. Hearings take place before an ALJ, and the rules of evidence do not apply. These procedures are the same whether the hearing is a rulemaking or an adjudication.

The primary difference between adjudication and rulemaking is the varying scope of applicability. At the end of a rulemaking process, the agency enacts a rule that broadly implements policy for many, while at the conclusion of an adjudication process, the agency enacts an order that narrowly applies to the parties. Because hearing processes are better suited to determine adjudicative rather than legislative facts, formal rulemaking is relatively rare at the federal level. It is, however, more common in the states; for example, Minnesota commonly uses formal rulemaking.

At the federal level, informal rulemaking (also known as "notice and comment rulemaking") is more common. Like its name suggests, notice and comment rulemaking requires an agency to publish notice of its proposed rule in the Federal Register (notice) and to solicit and respond to comments from the public and others about the proposed rule (comment). At the end of this notice and comment process, which can take years, the agency may enact a rule, also know at this point as a regulation. Although called informal rulemaking under the APA, notice and comment rulemaking is procedurally prescribed and requires the agency to follow time-consuming, detailed procedures to enact a regulation. Therefore, notice and comment rulemaking is informal in name only.

If these procedures were not arduous enough, Congress and the president may impose additional procedural requirements to those that the APA requires. For example, Executive Order 12866, which is discussed in detail below, requires agencies to conduct a cost-benefit analysis on all "significant" proposed rules. Exec. Order No. 12,866, 58 Fed. Reg. 51735 (1993). Additionally, the Regulatory Flexibility Act requires agencies to create a Regulatory Flexibility Analysis for any proposed rule that will significantly impact a substantial number of small businesses, organizations, or governments. 5 U.S.C. § 601 *et seq.* (2012). And the Unfunded Mandates Reform Act requires agencies to prepare a statement assessing the effect of any proposed regulation that will cause state, local, or tribal governments to incur more than $100 million annually. 2 U.S.C. § 1501 *et seq.* (2012). The number and variety of these additional procedures has led commentators to lament on the slowing-down, or "ossification," of the rulemaking process. Thus, Congress, the president, and even agencies can impose additional rulemaking procedures to those the APA requires. Importantly, however, in a landmark case, the Supreme Court held that courts cannot. *Vt. Yankee Nuclear Power Corp. v. Natural Res. Def. Council, Inc.*, 435 U.S. 519, 524 (1978).

Just as agencies prefer to avoid formal adjudication, they prefer to avoid formal rulemaking. The current test for whether an agency must use formal or informal rulemaking is summed up in *United States v. Florida East Coast Railway*, 410 U.S. 224 (1973). In that case, the Supreme Court held that the language "after hearing" in the Interstate Commerce Act was not the same as language required in section 553(c) of the APA to trigger a requirement of formal rulemaking: "on the record after opportunity for an agency hearing." *Id.* at 238. Thus, if Congress wants to require formal rulemaking (or formal adjudication), Congress must be explicit.

b. Non-Legislative Rulemaking

For rulemaking, agencies may also act in less formal ways than formal and informal rulemaking. For example, the APA exempts from the notice and comment requirements certain types of rules: (1) interpretative rules, (2) general statements of policy, and (3) rules of agency procedure and organization. 5 U.S.C. § 553(b)(3)(A). Interpretative rules and general statements of policy are called non-legislative rules, or publication rules. Peter L. Strauss, An In-

TRODUCTION TO ADMINISTRATIVE JUSTICE IN THE UNITED STATES, 222–24 (2d ed. 2002) (identifying non-legislative rules as "publication rules" because they must be published in the Federal Register or otherwise made available for public copying).

Because the process of notice and comment rulemaking has ossified agency rulemaking, and because non-legislative rulemaking is quicker, easier, and less final, many agencies opt to avoid notice and comment procedures altogether, at least when they can. Sometimes, their choice is legitimate, sometimes not. But, as we will see in Chapter 12, judicial deference to an agency's interpretation of a statute made during the rulemaking process depends, in large part, on the formality of the procedure the agency used to make that interpretation. Hence, an agency might choose legislative rulemaking instead of non-legislative rulemaking, even when the APA does not mandate legislative rulemaking.

While there are three kinds of non-legislative rules, two are relevant here: interpretative rules and policy statements. *Interpretative*, or *interpretive rules*, are self-describing; they are rules interpreting the agency's existing duties in a statute or regulation. The duty exists; the interpretive rule simply defines the parameters of that duty.

In contrast, *policy statements* are statements from an agency to prospectively advise the public and agency personnel on the way in which the agency plans to exercise discretionary power in the future. Agencies do not use policy statements to interpret existing duties (either from regulations or statutes). Rather, agencies use policy statements to announce new duties the agency plans to adopt by future adjudication or rulemaking. Note that there is no such thing as an "interpretive statement" or a "policy rule." Terminology is important.

Non-legislative rules arise in many ways. For example, after an agency enacts a regulation, questions may arise about how to interpret that regulation or the statute giving rise to the duty that the regulation further defines. Lower level administrators may seek guidance from senior level administrators about how to implement the new regulations. Questions may begin to arrive from the public. In response, agency administrators may develop a list of "frequently asked questions," marshal information in an agency manual, or provide the information in some other format. For example, the Corps of Engineers maintains Regulatory Guidance Letters, which are written guidance letters issued to field agencies to interpret or clarify existing regulatory policy. Similarly, the Internal Revenue Service maintains letter rulings, which are written statements issued to taxpayers that interpret tax laws. There are many different ways that an agency might issue a non-legislative rule. Because agencies do not go through a procedurally prescribed process when they enact these rules, such as notice and comment rulemaking, the rules are easily modifiable and non-binding.

Non-legislative rules play a legitimate and important role in agency decision-making. They help agencies apply law consistently across their many field offices by affording guidance to both the public and lower level agency personnel. Non-legislative rules ensure greater and faster public compliance than legislative rules alone, which may lack specificity and clarity. Finally, non-legislative rules also help agencies develop a flexible policy quickly and easily, while still giving the public some advance notice of the new policy. From an agency's perspective, non-legislative rules are "law" in a practical sense because they influence the conduct of administrative personnel and, thus, regulate their behavior. But legally, non-legislative rules are not truly "law" because they are not legally binding. If an agency wants the non-legislative rule to be legally binding on regulated entities, the agency must follow notice and comment or formal rulemaking procedures.

You need not fully understand the differences in the various processes described above, for this is not a text in administrative law. What should be clear, however, is that an agency can act with varying degrees of procedural formality. As we will see in Chapter 12, judicial deference to an agency interpretation of a statute increases as the formality of the decision-making process the agency used increases. Thus, while courts afford *some* deference to agency interpretations of statutes contained in non-legislative rules due to the agency's special knowledge and expertise in the area, the interpretation is not afforded as much judicial deference as interpretations made after notice and comment or formal rulemaking.

3. Investigation

Investigation is typically a function of the executive; thus, it should come as no surprise that Congress may grant agencies investigatory powers. As part of this power, agencies may determine whether a regulated entity is violating a regulation or statute. Additionally, some agencies have the power to compel regulated entities to turn over information that is in their possession. For example, the Federal Trade Commission may require corporations to submit information reports. Other agencies have the power to inspect buildings, worksites, and homes. For example, health inspectors visit restaurants to determine whether they are sanitary and clean. Child welfare workers visit homes to see if children are being abused and neglected. In general, agency personnel must interpret statutes and regulations in the course of their inspections and investigations.

E. Legislative & Executive Oversight

1. Legislative Oversight

Congress maintains power over agencies in ways other than through the delegation of authority. There are both formal and informal methods of legislative oversight. Formal methods of oversight include Congress's power to enact subsequent legislation and to fund agencies. With subsequent legislative action, Congress can narrow or revoke the authority it has given to an agency or require an agency to follow new procedures. For example, after a tremendous public outcry regarding the Food and Drug Administration's decision to ban saccharin, the only alternative sweetener at the time, Congress suspended regulatory action in this area and instituted a warning label to replace the proposed ban. 91 Stat. 1451 (1977). Similarly, in 1969, Congress required all agencies to consider the environmental impacts of major decisions with the National Environmental Policy Act, 42 U.S.C. §§ 4321-61 *et seq.* (2012). More recently, Congress enacted the Regulatory Flexibility Act of 1980, 5 U.S.C. §§ 601-12 *et seq.* (2012), which requires agencies to consider and minimize the economic effects of regulations on small businesses. And with the Unfunded Mandates Reform Act of 1995, 2 U.S.C. §§ 1501-71 *et seq.* (2012), Congress directed agencies to consider the impact of their regulations on state governmental agencies and adopt the least burdensome alternative that would further the agency's objectives or explain why another option was chosen. Thus, agency control is readily within Congress's grasp.

Additionally, Congress controls the purse. Agencies need funding to operate. Congressional approval of agency funding requires two things. First, the agency's enabling statute (or another statute) must provide authorization for legislative appropriations. Such authorizations may be limited by time or purpose, have a ceiling, or be unlimited. Second, each year Congress must approve the money agencies actually spent. To receive funding, agencies must submit annual budget requests to the Office of Management and Budget (OMB), which the president oversees. These budgets, after adjustments by OMB, are forwarded to the House and Senate appropriations committees, which hold hearings and allocate funding accordingly. Appropriation bills can impact regulatory policy and even statutory interpretation! For example, in *Tennessee Valley Authority v. Hill,* 437 U.S. 153 (1978), the Supreme Court Justices debated whether Congress's continued funding of the Tellico Dam project in Tennessee showed an intent to complete the dam, despite the discovery that completing the project would wipe out an endangered species.

Informal methods of legislative oversight include Congress's power to *investigate* agencies. Any congressional committee that has jurisdiction over an aspect of an agency's program may hold hearings and investigate the agency's implementation of its authority. Often, these hearings are publicized to mobilize public and political pressure. For example, in 2012, the House Judiciary Committee held hearings regarding the Bureau of Alcohol, Tobacco, Firearms and Explosives' Fast and Furious program, which was intended to track firearms that were transferred to higher-level drug traffickers in Mexican cartels, with the hope that tracking would lead to arrests and the dismantling of the cartels. The program was mostly unsuccessful. After a series of public hearings, Congress held Attorney General Eric Holder in criminal contempt for refusing to provide documents to the Committee. President Obama invoked executive privilege to prevent the disclosure.

Additionally, Congress has established other organizations to help oversee agencies, including the Congressional Research Service and the Governmental Accountability Office (previously known as the General Accounting Office (GAO)). While the GAO was originally created to oversee the use of agency budgeting and funding, its authority to oversee agency program implementation has been expanding, as we will see below.

2. Executive Oversight

a. Appointment & Removal

Another form of oversight is the executive's power to appoint and remove agency officers, such as the cabinet members. Although the executive has the power to appoint government officials, the power is not absolute. U.S. Const. art. II, §2 cl., 2. The Constitution gives the executive the power to appoint *principal* officers, subject to senate approval. Principal officers include all top level agency officials and many lower level officials, but the Court has never clearly defined the difference between a principal and inferior officer.

The executive does not have the power to appoint *inferior* officers. Congress can delegate that power. This issue was litigated in *Morrison v. Olson*, 487 U.S. 654 (1988), in which the Court held that Congress could give the judiciary the power to appoint an executive officer. At issue in that case was the Ethics in Government Act. 28 U.S.C. §§49, 591 *et seq.* (2012), which authorized a special division of the United States Court of Appeals for the District of Columbia to appoint independent counsel for the investigation and prosecution of high-ranking executive officials. *Morrison*, 487 U.S. at 661. The independent counsel would be performing executive functions. *Id.* at 691. Although the Act empowered the judiciary to appoint and oversee an officer who would be performing executive functions, the Court did not invalidate the Act. Instead, using a functionalist approach, the Court concluded that the independent counsel performed only limited investigative and prosecutorial work for a set period of time; hence, the officer was considered an inferior officer, not a principal officer. *Id.* at 671–72. Because the Constitution allows Congress to delegate the appointment of inferior officers to the judiciary, the appointment provision was constitutional. *Id.* at 673–74.

Similarly, the removal power is also constitutionally assigned to the executive, though the assignment is implicit. *Bowsher v. Synar*, 478 U.S. 714 (1986); *Myers v. United States*, 272 U.S. 52 (1926) (both holding that the president has the power to remove executive officials so as to control the operation of the executive branch). This power too is not absolute, as Congress can condition the executive's power to remove executive officers but cannot eliminate it altogether. *Morrison*, 487 U.S. at 686. Like the appointment power, the removal power was also at issue in *Morrison*. Under the Act, the Attorney General, a member of the executive branch, had the sole and unreviewable power to remove an independent counsel, but only for "good cause." *Id.* at 685. This removal provision presented two issues for the Court. The first was whether the good cause provision, taken by itself, impermissibly interfered with the president's exercise of a constitutionally appointed function. The second was whether, taken as a whole, the Act violated separation of powers by reducing the president's ability to control the prosecutorial powers of the independent counsel. *Id.* The Court rejected both issues. Recognizing that it had previously found statutes unconstitutional when Congress had reserved for itself the power to remove "executive" officers, the Court found no such problem here where Congress had given removal power to the executive even though the removal power was qualified. *Id.* at 686. The Court also noted that the president retained the power to supervise and control the independent counsel's power. *Id.* at 695. Thus, because the executive retained the ability to control, and ultimately to fire, any independent counsel, the president's removal power was not unduly burdened. *Id.* at 691.

b. *Signing Statements*

As mentioned in Chapter 3, when a president signs legislation that the president does not like but does not want to veto, the president may include a limiting *signing statement*. Because these statements often indicate how the executive intends to implement the law, they are another way that the executive oversees agencies. The question is whether signing statements have any effect beyond oversight. As we noted, these statements have become controversial, in part, because presidents have begun to use them to influence statutory interpretation.

President Reagan's administration persuaded West Publishing Company to include signing statements in the UNITED STATES CODE CONGRESSIONAL AND ADMINISTRATIVE NEWS, specifically to influence statutory interpretation. Courts, however, do not appear to have turned to signing statements in the manner that the administration wished. The Constitution specifically identifies the role that presidents have in enacting legislation — sign a bill into law or veto it. For example, the Constitution allows a president to note objections when vetoing a bill, but the Constitution does not require a president to announce the reasons for approving a bill. Moreover, if a president vetoes a bill, Congress, pursuant to a constitutionally prescribed procedure, is permitted to respond to the veto and raise objections in an attempt to override it. In contrast, there is no prescribed process for Congress to respond to presidential objections contained in signing statements. While this dichotomy does not require courts to ignore signing statements, it suggests that presidential signing statements that conflict with congressional intent should be discounted, at a minimum.

Relatedly, a president has constitutional authority to approve or veto a bill only in its entirety. Signing statements, however, often contain objections to specific statutory provisions, making them akin to line item vetoes. The president does not possess line item veto authority, and Congress cannot grant the president such authority. *Clinton v. City of N.Y.*, 524 U.S. 417, 447–49 (1998).

Whether for these or other reasons, the courts give little to no weight to signing statements. For example, in *DaCosta v. Nixon*, 55 F.R.D. 145, 146 (E.D.N.Y. 1972), the court rejected President Nixon's signing statement, which claimed that a provision in a statute did not "represent the policies of this Administration" and was "without binding force or effect." The court explained that a signing statement "denying efficacy to the legislation could have [n]either validity or effect." *Id.* And in *Hamdan v. Rumsfeld*, 548 U.S. 557 (2006), the majority completely ignored President Bush's signing statement when it held that the Detainee Treatment Act did not apply to pending habeas petitions of Guantanamo detainees. In a dissenting opinion (joined by Justice Alito), Justice Scalia criticized the majority for using legislative history while ignoring the President's signing statement. *Id.* at 666 (Scalia, J., dissenting) ("Of course in its discussion of legislative history the Court wholly ignores the President's signing statement, which explicitly set forth his understanding that the [statute] ousted jurisdiction over pending cases."). Lastly, in *United States v Stevens*, 559 U.S. 460 (2010), the Court noted that President Clinton's signing statement, which promised to limit prosecutions under an animal cruelty statute only to those cases of "wanton cruelty to animals designed to appeal to a prurient interest in sex," did not save an otherwise unconstitutionally overbroad statute. *Id.* As these cases show, signing statements generally have no relevance in court.

There are times, however, when a signing statement might provide limited judicial guidance. When a president has worked closely with Congress in developing legislation and when the enacted version of the bill addresses the president's veto concerns, then a court might consider an ensuing signing statement as evidence of the political compromises that were reached. In these situations, signing statements might help explain rather than negate congressional action. For example, former President Franklin Roosevelt issued a signing statement during World War II contesting the constitutionality of section 304 of the Urgent Deficiency Appropriations Act of 1943, ch. 218, 57 Stat. 431, 450 (1943). He indicated that he felt that he had no choice but to sign the bill "to avoid delaying our conduct of the war." *United States v. Lovett*, 328 U.S. 303, 313 (1946) (quoting H.R. Doc. No. 264, 78th Cong., 1st Sess). When the statute was challenged, the Court struck down the provision, citing the signing statement in its reasoning.

The growing use of signing statements to influence interpretation has attracted the attention of Congress. A few bills have been introduced to stop this practice. For example, Senator Arlen Specter introduced the Presidential Signing Statements Act of 2006, which would have prohibited courts from considering signing statements. Presidential Signing Statements Act of 2006, S. 3731, 109th Cong. §4 (2006) ("In determining the meaning of any Act of Congress, no State or Federal court shall rely on or defer to a presidential signing statement as a source of authority."). The bill died in committee. *See also* Congressional Lawmaking Authority Protection Act of 2007, H.R. 264, 110th Cong. §4 (2007) ("For purposes of construing or applying any Act enacted by the Congress, a governmental entity shall not take into consideration any statement made by the President contemporaneously with the President's signing of the bill or joint resolution that becomes such Act.").

Although signing statements are not generally relevant in court, such statements nonetheless greatly affect the actions of administering agencies. The president oversees agencies and sets administrative policy. While the executive's interpretation of a statute does not bind judges, it binds agency personnel. Moreover, as we will see in the next chapter, courts generally defer to agency interpretations of statutes that are made during rulemaking or other formal processes. To the effect that a signing statement impacts an agency's interpretation of a statute, that signing statement will impact interpretation, albeit indirectly. Thus, while signing statements may not have had the interpretive impact former Attorney General Meese would have liked, there is no question that they are having at least some impact.

c. Executive Orders

Presidents have issued executive orders since 1789. Although there is no constitutional provision or statute that explicitly permits the executive to issue an executive order, presidents assumed this power pursuant to their authority to "take Care that the Laws be faithfully executed." U.S. Const. art. II, § 3, cl. 5. Presidents generally use executive orders to guide federal agencies and officials in their execution of congressionally granted authority. However, presidents use executive orders in other ways as well. For example, presidents may use proclamations, a special type of executive order, for ceremonial or symbolic messages, such as when the president declares *National Take Your Child to Work Day*. Also, presidents issue National Security Directives, which concern national security or defense. Executive orders are printed in the Federal Register.

Many important policy and legal changes have occurred through executive orders. For example, President Lincoln emancipated slaves; President Truman integrated the armed forces; President Eisenhower desegregated schools; Presidents Kennedy and Johnson barred racial discrimination in federal housing, hiring, and contracting; President Reagan barred the use of federal funds for abortion advocacy (which President Clinton reversed); and President Clinton fought a war with Yugoslavia. All of these significant events occurred because of an executive order.

Executive orders are somewhat controversial because the Constitution gives Congress the power to make law, albeit with the executive's assistance. With executive orders, it might appear as if the executive is making law unilaterally. However, Congress often gives agencies considerable leeway in implementing and administering federal law and programs. In effect, this leeway leaves gaps to federal agencies and the president to fill. Simply put, when Congress fails to spell out the details of how a law should be executed, the door is left open for the president to provide those details, and executive orders are one way to do so.

If a president goes too far, deviates from "congressional intent," or exceeds the constitutional powers delegated to the executive, the executive order can be challenged in court. For example, when President Truman seized control of the nation's steel mills in an effort to settle labor disputes that arose after World War II, the Supreme Court held that the seizure was unconstitutional and exceeded presidential powers, as neither the Constitution nor any statute authorized the President to seize private businesses to settle labor disputes.

Youngstown Sheet & Tube Co. v. Sawyer, 343 U.S. 579 (1952). Notably, this outcome was unusual. Generally, the Court is fairly tolerant of executive orders and executive oversight.

i. Centralized Regulatory Review: Executive Order 12866

In 1980, President Reagan, who campaigned on a platform of deregulation, issued Executive Order 12291, which directed all executive agencies to perform a regulatory analysis assessing the costs and benefits of any "major" proposed regulations. Exec. Order No. 12,291, 3 C.F.R. § 127 (1982). One of Reagan's purposes for issuing this executive order was to limit unnecessary regulation. However, each president since Reagan has reissued this order, with slight changes. Former President Clinton issued Executive Order 12866, which mostly mirrored President Reagan's order; however, he changed the term "major rule" to "significant action." Next, former President George W. Bush adopted Clinton's order, but also issued two additional executive orders that slightly amended it; importantly, one of these orders added non-legislative rules to the order's coverage. Exec. Order No. 13422, 72 Fed. Reg. 2763 (2007). When President Obama took office, he repealed the two Bush orders, Exec. Order No.13497, 74 Fed. Reg. 6113 (2009), and amended Executive Order 12866 to allow agencies to consider not only monetary costs and benefits, but "human dignity" and "fairness" as well. Today, Executive Order 12866 is a fixture of executive agency rulemaking. While there is currently a bill pending in Congress to make regulatory analysis equally applicable to the independent agencies (Independent Agency Regulatory Analysis Act of 2012, S. 3468 (2012)), as this book goes to press in early 2013, the bill has not been enacted.

Executive Order 12866 provides guiding principles that executive agencies must follow when developing regulations that will have an economic effect of at least a one hundred million dollars. Pursuant to the Order, agencies may promulgate regulations only when the regulations are "required by law," "necessary to interpret the law," or "are made necessary by compelling public need, such as material failures of private markets to protect or improve the health and safety of the public, the environment, or the well-being of the American people." Exec. Order No. 12866 § 1(a), 58 Fed. Reg. 51735 (1993). Pursuant to Executive Order 12866, agencies must follow specific procedural steps when developing regulatory priorities, including the following: (1) identifying the problem the regulation was intended to address, including "the failures of private markets or public institutions that warrant new agency action;" (2) determining whether the problem could be addressed through modifications to existing regulations or laws; (3) assessing alternatives to regulation, such as economic incentives; (4) considering "the degree and nature of the risks posed by various substances or activities" within the agency's jurisdiction; (5) fashioning regulations "in the most cost-effective manner;" (6) assessing the costs and benefits, such that benefits justify the costs; (7) basing decisions "on the best reasonably obtainable scientific, technical, economic, and other information;" (8) recommending performance-based solutions rather than behavioral ones, when possible; (9) consulting with state, local, and tribal governments and assessing the impacts of regulations on these local governments; (10) avoiding duplications and inconsistencies among federal agencies; (11) minimizing the burdens; (12) considering the cumulative costs of regulation; and (13) writing all regulations in language that the general public can easily understand. Exec. Order No. 12866 §§ 1(b)(1)-(12), 58 Fed. Reg. 51735 (1993).

Most importantly, in deciding whether regulation is necessary, agencies must assess the costs and benefits of the regulatory alternatives, "including the alternative of not regulating." Exec. Order No. 12866 § 1(a), 58 Fed. Reg. 51735 (1993). "[U]nless [the] statute requires another regulatory approach," agencies must choose the regulatory path that maximizes net benefits. *Id.* Once an agency has completed this analysis, the agency submits the proposed regulation along with its analysis of that regulation to the Office of Information and Regulatory Affairs (OIRA), which is located within the Office of Management and Budget (OMB), is responsible for overseeing the Federal Government's regulatory, paperwork, and information resource management activities and which is located within the Office of Management and Budget (OMB). OMB is located within the executive office and is very closely aligned with the policies of the president. OIRA will review the proposed rule and analysis to ensure compliance with the executive order; in simple terms, OIRA acts as gatekeeper for the promulgation of all significant regulations.

Additionally, Executive Order 12866 imposes regulatory planning measures. All agencies, including independent agencies, must produce a semi-annual *regulatory agenda* of all regulations under development or review. Pursuant to another executive order, Executive Order 12291, the agencies provide their agenda in April and October of each year; a requirement that the Regulatory Flexibility Act has partially codified. 5 U.S.C. § 602(a). Each regulatory agenda should include a summary of the action to be taken, the agency's legal authority for acting, legal deadlines if any, and an agency contact. Exec. Order No. 12866 § 1, 58 Fed. Reg. 51735 (1993). An example of the 2012 Department of Health and Human Services regulatory agenda can be found at 77 Fed. Reg. 7946 (February 13, 2012), available at http://www.gpo.gov/fdsys/pkg/FR-2012-02-13/pdf/2012-1647.pdf.

In addition, pursuant to Executive Order 12866, all agencies must produce a *regulatory plan*, which identifies the most significant regulatory activities the agency has planned for the upcoming year. Exec. Order No. 12866 § 1(c), 58 Fed. Reg. 51735 (1993). While the regulatory *agenda* includes *all* proposed actions, the regulatory *plan* includes only the most important proposed actions. The agency must relate these plans to the president's priorities, determine anticipated costs and benefits, provide a summary of the legal basis for the action, and include a statement of why the action is needed. Regulatory plans are forwarded to OIRA on June 1st of every year. OIRA reviews the plans for consistency with the president's priorities, the requirements of Executive Order 12866, and the regulatory agendas of other agencies.

OIRA publishes the regulatory agendas and plans together in the Unified Agenda, which is available to the public online: http://reginfo.gov. Each edition of the Agenda includes the regulatory agendas from all federal entities that currently have regulations under development or review. In addition, the fall edition of the Agenda includes the agencies' regulatory plans. The Agenda is an integral part of the federal regulatory process. Its semiannual publication enables regulated entities, the public, companies, and other interested persons to understand and prepare for new rules that are planned or under development. The Agenda provides important information to agency heads, centralized reviewers, and the public at large, thereby serving the values of open government.

Finally, at the beginning of each planning period, the director of OMB convenes a meeting with the regulatory advisors and agency heads to coordinate regulatory priorities for the coming year. Exec. Order No. 12866 § 1(c)(1)(F)(2), 58 Fed. Reg. 51735 (1993).

While Executive Order 12866 is the most prominent analysis requirement to come from the executive office, it is not the only one. Over the years, presidents have required agencies to perform many different analyses. *See, e.g.,* Exec. Order No. 12630, 47 Fed. Reg. 30959 (1982) (requiring agencies to analyze the impact of proposed and final regulations on state and local governments); Exec. Order No. 13175, 65 Fed. Reg. 67249 (2000) (requiring agencies to analyze the impact of proposed and final regulations on tribal governments).

F. Mastering This Topic

Return to the hypothetical ordinance provided in Chapter 1 on page 9. The hypothetical includes the mayor's signing statement. You may have wondered how relevant executive signing statements are to interpretation. The discussion above should make clear that the proper role of signing statements in interpretation is far from settled, but that generally, signing statements are considered irrelevant in courts. Nevertheless, the signing statement may inform the relevant agency regarding the executive's preferences regarding enforcement. As prosecutor for the city, you work for the executive; thus, you may wish to consider the executive's preferences when choosing to bring an enforcement action. Does the mayor's statement give you any guidance regarding whether you should prosecute the ambulance driver? What about the other drivers in the hypothetical questions? The mayor seemed very concerned with pollution and noisy vehicles. An ambulance would not seem to fit within these concerns. Likely, you would choose not to prosecute in this situation, even though you know that this signing statement would have little impact in court.

Checkpoints

- The judiciary is not the only branch that must interpret statutes. Administrative agencies within the executive branch regularly interpret statutes as part of their job of enforcing those laws.

- Agencies are defined under the Administrative Procedures Act as any authority of the Government of the United States, excluding Congress, the courts, state governments, and others. The president is not an agency pursuant to common law.

- There are two types of agencies: independent agencies and executive agencies. Independent agencies are less subject to the president's influence because they are headed by multi-member, bi-partisan boards, serving terms.

- Agencies act in three ways: by adjudicating, by rulemaking, and by investigating. Some agency actions require more procedure than others. Judicial deference to an agency interpretation of a statute generally increases as the formality of the decision-making process the agency used increases.

- The *formalist* approach to separation of powers emphasizes the necessity of maintaining three distinct branches of government with delegated powers: one branch legislates, one branch executes, and one branch adjudicates.

- The *functionalist* approach to separation of powers accepts some overlap so long as no one branch appropriates or is given too much constitutionally assigned power from another branch.

- Congress has the authority to delegate power to agencies pursuant to the Necessary and Proper clause, U.S. Const. art. I, §8, so long as Congress provides intelligible principles or standards for agencies to use when exercising that power.

- Congress controls agencies using both formal and informal methods of legislative oversight. Formal methods of oversight include Congress's power to enact subsequent legislation and to fund agencies. Informal methods include Congress's power to investigate agencies.

- The executive controls agencies using the appointment and removal power, signing statements, and executive orders.

- Executive Order 12866 is the most prominent analysis requirement to come from the executive office and requires agencies to perform cost-benefit analysis on all proposed regulations that will have a significant impact on the economy.

Chapter 12

Canons Based on Extrinsic Sources & Executive Process: Deference to Agency Interpretation

---

Roadmap

- Learn the role that agencies play in interpretation.
- Understand the deference law pre- and post-*Chevron*.
- Learn *Chevron*'s two-step test, *Skidmore*'s power-to-persuade test, and *Auer*'s plainly wrong test.

A. Introduction to This Chapter

In the last chapter, you learned about agencies: what they are, what they do, and how the executive and legislature control them with oversight. When agencies act, they often interpret statutes. In this chapter, we address the level of deference courts give to agency interpretations of statutes. This topic is exploding, as the appropriate role agencies should play in this area is debated in legal and academic circles. Agencies are playing a more important and ever-expanding part. In sum, agencies play a leading role in statutory interpretation. Over the last forty years, the Supreme Court has struggled with the appropriate level of deference to give agency interpretations. The Court has vacillated from affording little to no deference, to affording high deference, and back again. This struggle reflects the Court's concern over ceding its interpretive power and respecting the appropriate roles of the executive, legislative, and judicial branches of government. Although members of the executive and legislative branches are generally accountable to the public, while members of the judiciary are not, it remains the duty of the judiciary to say what the law means.

Agencies are entrusted to implement complicated regulatory schemes. Congress delegates to agencies the power to regulate. With this delegation comes the power to make laws and adjudicate. Agencies have expertise that informs the choices they make in these areas. That expertise should not be ignored simply because the judiciary has the constitutional power to interpret laws. Moreover, to be able to respond to economic, technological, and political changes, agencies must maintain flexibility. Hence, some deference is appropriate. However, when agencies exceed the power delegated to them, deference is no longer appropriate.

The tension between respect for the judiciary's role and respect for the appropriate role of agencies permeates the jurisprudence in this area. To be an effective litigant, you must be aware of when and why agencies interpret statutes, know the level of deference judges will give to agency interpretations, and understand why agencies receive that level of deference. Because the appropriate level of deference has changed over time, the common-law history is extremely relevant here. We start, therefore, in the past.

B. The Interpretive Role Agencies Play

Article III of the Constitution grants the judiciary all "Judicial power." U.S. Const. art. III, § 1. According to *Marbury v. Madison*, "[i]t is emphatically the province and duty of the judicial department to say what the law is." 5 U.S. (1 Cranch) 137, 177 (1803). But the judiciary is not the only branch of government that must interpret statutes; administrative agencies must also interpret the statutes they administer and implement. Agencies regulate private conduct in many areas, including consumer protection, preservation of the environment, and individual health and welfare. They also administer entitlement programs such as welfare and Social Security. Finally, they collect taxes, regulate citizenship and immigration, handle national security, preserve and maintain national forests and parks, and regulate our nation's food and drug supply. In short, agencies control almost all aspects of modern society. In doing so, they regularly interpret statutes and regulations. Should agency interpretations of these laws control?

A formalist constitutional scholar might suggest that agencies should have no interpretive role, or, at the very least, not one that trumps the judicial role. Yet, this view is extreme. For many reasons, agency interpretation is necessary, making judicial deference appropriate. The modern administrative state is vastly complex. Agencies have expertise in their area of responsibility; consider the U.S. Department of Veterans' Affairs (VA), the Environmental Protection Agency (EPA), or the Food and Drug Administration (FDA). Each of these agencies has experts and specialists trained in the relevant field. Judges are generalists with expertise in law, not in the environment or food safety. Hence, it simply makes more sense for medical personnel within the VA to determine disability benefits for veterans, for scientists within the EPA to determine acceptable levels of pollutants in the air, and for nutritionists within the FDA to determine the composition of public school lunches.

Moreover, agencies may be more responsive to the electorate than the judiciary. National goals and policies change as society evolves. Administrators are accountable to the public via the Office of the President and therefore will be more likely to conform their policies to match populist expectations. Federal Judges, in contrast, are elected for life and are more insulated from political backlash. Thus, agencies should receive some deference when they interpret statutes within their area of expertise. Even *Marbury's* author, Chief Justice John Marshall, suggested that courts should respect an agency's "uniform construction" of "doubtful" statutes. *United States v. Vowell*, 9 U.S. (5 Cranch) 368, 371 (1810).

In this chapter, we will explore the level of deference a court will give to an agency interpretation of a statute or regulation. This is a politically important question because the power to say what the law means shifts to the executive branch when courts defer to agency interpretations. Linda D. Jellum, *The Impact of the Rise and Fall of* Chevron *on the Executive's Power to Make and Interpret Law*, 44 Loy. U. Chi. L.J. 141 (2012). Because of this shift in power, the appropriate level of deference has changed over time as the Justices have been more or less comfortable with deferring to the executive. The question is what level of deference judges should give to an agency when, in the process of developing a rule, the agency interprets a statute. As the Supreme Court has addressed this issue over the last seventy years, it has oscillated among three options: (1) complete deference, (2) limited deference, or (3) no deference. While the level of deference has changed, the rationale for affording deference has remained relatively consistent: agency expertise and intended congressional delegation. The next section will explore the Court's approach to deference prior to its landmark decision in *Chevron U.S.A., Inc. v. Natural Resources Defense Council, Inc.*, 467 U.S. 837 (1984).

C. Deference Pre-*Chevron*

Agencies interpret statutes in two distinct ways. First, they determine the legal standards that govern their authority. These types of questions are questions of law because the facts of individual cases are largely irrelevant. Second, agencies determine whether the law of a particular statute or regulation applies given the facts in a particular case. These types of questions are mixed questions of law and fact because they require the application of a law to a specific set of facts. This chapter focuses on the former types of questions: questions of law.

The appropriate standard applicable to mixed questions of law and fact is currently unclear. Some courts apply the test from *NLRB v. Hearst Publication, Inc.*, 322 U.S. 111 (1944): An agency's decision is to be accepted if it has "warrant in the record" and a reasonable basis in the law. *Id.* at 131. Other courts break the mixed question into its component parts of law and fact Courts review questions of fact under different standards pursuant to section 706(2) of the Administrative Procedure Act (APA). For agency findings of fact made during informal rulemaking and informal adjudication, the relevant standard is whether the agency's findings are arbitrary and capricious. 5 U.S.C. §706(2)(A). Under the arbitrary and capricious standard, a court determines whether the agency's findings were based on a consideration of irrelevant factors or whether the agency made a clear error of judgment. *Citizens to Preserve Overton Park, Inc. v. Volpe*, 401 U.S. 402, 416 (1971). For agency findings of fact made during formal rulemaking and formal adjudication, the standard is whether the agency's findings were supported by substantial evidence. 5 U.S.C. §706(2)(E). Under the substantial evidence standard, a court would determine whether the record contains "such evidence as a reasonable mind might accept as adequate to support a conclusion." *Consol. Edison Co. v. NLRB*, 305 U.S. 197, 229 (1938). While the two standards originally differed, today, they tend to converge, and the distinction is "largely semantic." *Ass'n. of Data Processing Serv. Org. v. Bd.of Governors*, 745 F.2d 677, 684 (D.C. Cir. 1984) (internal citation omitted) (internal quotation marks omitted). Because statutory interpretation generally involves questions of law, the rest of this chapter will focus on that issue.

In the 1940s and early 1950s, the Supreme Court primarily used two different deference standards: "no deference" (or a *de novo* standard) and "limited deference." While the deference world was never black and white, the standard the Court used seemed to depend on the type of interpretive issue presented. When an agency interpretation involved a question of law, the Court preferred a "no deference" standard. For example, in *Gray v. Powell*, 314 U.S. 402 (1941), the Court did not defer to the agency's determination that transferring coal from one entity to another without a transfer of title constituted coal that was "sold or otherwise disposed of" within the meaning of the Bituminous Coal Act of 1937. *Id.* at 414–17. Also, in *Hearst Publication*, the Court did not defer to the agency's determination that newsboys were "employees" under the National Labor Relations Act. 322 U.S. at 124–29. Similarly, in *O'Leary v. Brown-Pacific-Maxon, Inc.*, 340 U.S. 504 (1951), the Court determined *de novo* that the term "course of employment" in the Longshoremen's and Harbor Workers' Compensation Act did not include the common law understanding of that term. *Id.* at 506.

The Court did not apply the "no deference" standard when the agency interpretation involved a mixed question of law and fact. Instead, the Court used a "limited deference" standard. *See, e.g., Gray*, 314 U.S. at 410–13 (deferring to the agency's finding that the specific plaintiff was a coal producer); *O'Leary*, 340 U.S. at 507–08 (deferring to the agency's factual finding that a particular rescue occurred during the course of employment). The Court gave some deference to agency interpretations involving the application of law to fact because "Congress ... found it more efficient to delegate [these issues] to those whose experience in a particular field gave promise of a better informed, more equitable" resolution of the issues. *Gray*, 314 U.S. at 412. Deference was due because of agency expertise and express congressional delegation. *Hearst Publication*, 322 U.S. at 120. When the issue involved law application, the agency's expertise, and the likelihood that Congress intended to delegate these choices to the agency justified courts' decisions to give the agency's interpretations some level of deference. However, when the agency interpretation involved a pure question of law, the Court did not defer to the agency interpretation because judges were as competent, if not more so, than agencies to determine the intended meaning of ambiguous statutory language. Pursuant to this bifurcated deference approach, courts retained the primary responsibility for interpreting statutes. Courts generally reviewed questions of law *de novo*, giving the agency's interpretation no deference at all. Courts reviewed questions of law application more deferentially, giving the agency's interpretation some respect.

This bifurcated deference, or two-tracked, approach to the issue of judicial review of agency interpretations made sense because it was consistent with the judicial review approach in civil litigation. In civil cases, appellate judges determine questions of law *de novo* because appellate judges are experts at interpreting law; thus, no deference is due to trial courts' findings of law. But questions of fact and law application are reviewed under a more deferential standard. There is another reason that this breakdown made sense: leaving questions of law for judicial resolution was consistent with the APA, which provides that "the reviewing court shall decide all relevant questions of law, interpret constitutional and statutory provisions, and determine the meaning or applicability of the terms of an agency action." 5 U.S.C. § 706.

While courts deferred to agency interpretations involving law application, the level of deference was uncertain. In 1944, the Supreme Court decided two cases that addressed this issue. In the first case, _NLRB v. Hearst Publication_, 322 U.S. 111, the Court held that as long as an agency interpretation had a "warrant in the record and a reasonable basis in law," a court should not substitute its own interpretation for that of the agency entrusted with administering the statute. _Id._ at 130. In this case, the Court addressed the appropriate level of deference to give a National Labor Relations Board (the "Board") regulation, a legislative rule that applied

> Under _Hearst Publication's_ "reasonable-basis-in-the-law" test, an agency's interpretation is entitled to deference because agencies are experts in the field and Congress delegates authority to them to administer these programs.

the word "employee" in the National Labor Relations Act to newsboys. Because the Board had "familiarity with the circumstances and backgrounds of employment relationships in various industries," the Court held that determining the scope of the term "employees" "belongs to the usual administrative routine of the Board." _Id._ (internal citations omitted). Thus, the Court sustained the Board's interpretation under this "reasonable basis in the law" deference standard.

In the second case, _Skidmore v. Swift & Co._, 23 U.S. 134 (1944), the Court explained that agency interpretations should be given deference when they are persuasive, meaning they had "all those factors which give [the agency interpretation] power to persuade, if lacking power to control." _Id._ at 140. _Skidmore_ involved the appropriate level of deference for a court to give an _interpretive_ rule. The issue in this case was whether certain employees of Swift & Co. were entitled to overtime pay under the Fair Labor Standards Act of 1938 ("FLSA"). The employees were paid for the work they performed during the day, but were not paid overtime for their "in-active duty," or on-call time, during which

> Under _Skidmore's_ power-to-persuade test, an agency's interpretation is entitled to deference when (1) the agency interprets the language consistently over time, (2) the agency thoroughly considers the issue, and (3) the agency offers sound reasoning to support the interpretation.

they were required to remain on company premises even when not working. Without using notice and comment procedures, the Department of Labor issued an "interpretive bulletin," which indicated the Department's interpretation of FLSA on this issue. Both lower courts ignored the bulletin entirely and held that no overtime pay was warranted. The Supreme Court reversed and remanded, directing the Fifth Circuit to consider the bulletin.

In so doing, the Court made clear that the agency had "accumulated a considerable experience in the problems of ascertaining working time in employments involving periods of inactivity and knowledge of the customs prevailing in reference to their solution." *Id.* at 137–38. The Court noted that the agency's interpretation should not be ignored because the agency had expertise in this area. Further, the weight to give an agency's interpretation should depend on "all those factors which give it power-to-persuade, if lacking power to control." *Id.* at 140. According to the Court, the factors giving an agency's interpretation "power-to-persuade" include the following three factors: (1) the consistency in the agency's interpretation over time, (2) the thoroughness of the agency's consideration, and (3) the soundness of the agency's reasoning. *Id.* In other words, the more thoroughly considered and reasoned an agency interpretation is, the more a court should defer to that interpretation.

This "power-to-persuade" test is known as *Skidmore* deference. According to the Court, deference was appropriate because agencies are experts in their field and familiar with the industry customs surrounding certain issues. Hence, their expertise could inform a court's interpretation. Under this test, although agencies are akin to expert judicial advisors offering expertise in an area of judicial uncertainty, courts retain the majority of the interpretive power. Thus, a court reviewing an agency's interpretation would be free to use the traditional tools of interpretation, which are identified throughout the rest of this text. *Skidmore's* "power-to-persuade" test simply added an agency's interpretation as another factor for the court to consider in the statutory interpretive process.

While *Skidmore's* "power-to-persuade" test afforded agency interpretations some deference, the exact amount was unclear and indeterminate. Whereas some deference would be accorded, the amount of deference would vary depending on the circumstances surrounding the agency's interpretation in each case. In effect, agencies faced a balancing test. The more consistent, thorough, and considered their interpretations were, the more likely a court would defer to them. Agency interpretations that were persuasive received deference; those that were not persuasive received little to no deference. Under *Skidmore*, deference was earned, not automatic. But under *Skidmore*, certainty was lost.

Skidmore deference = power to persuade

D. *Chevron*

In 1984, after forty years of *Skidmore* deference, the Court instituted a new approach. In one of the most cited Supreme Court cases of all time, *Chevron U.S.A., Inc. v. National Resources Defense Council, Inc.*, 467 U.S. 837 (1984), the Court flipped the deference standard it had been using, in which agencies offered expertise, but courts were the final arbiters of what an ambiguous statute meant. *Chevron* addressed the level of deference appropriate for legislative—specifically notice and comment, rulemaking.

Chevron involved a question about the Clean Air Act. The provision of the Act at issue required plants to obtain a permit when the plant wished to modify or build a "stationary source[]" of pollution. *Id.* at 840. The term "stationary source" was not defined in the Act. *Id.* at 841. Thus, the Environmental Protection Agency ("EPA"), the agency in charge of implementing the Act, had to interpret the term. The EPA had issued two regulations interpreting "stationary source." The first regulation defined "stationary source" as the construction or installation of any new or modified equipment that emitted air pollutants. *Id.* at 840 n.2. But the following year, the EPA repealed that regulation and issued a new one that expanded the definition to encompass a plant-wide or "bubble concept" definition. *Id.* at 858. The bubble concept interpretation allowed a plant to offset increased air pollutant emissions at one part of its plant with reduced emissions at another part of the plant. So long as total emissions at the plant remained constant, no permit was required. *Id.* at 852. Not surprisingly, environmentalists sued. The issue for the Court was whether the EPA's interpretation of "stationary source" in the Clean Air Act was valid.

The Supreme Court upheld the agency's interpretation. *Id.* at 842. In so doing, the Court ignored *Skidmore's* power-to-persuade test and instead created a two-step deference framework, based in part on its holding in *Hearst Publications*. Pursuant to the first step, a court should determine "whether Congress has directly spoken to the precise question at issue." *Id.* In other words, is Congress's intent clear—however clarity may be discerned—or is there a gap or ambiguity to be resolved? According to the Court, clarity was to be determined by "employing traditional tools of statutory construction." *Id.* at 843 n.9. Under this first step, courts do not defer to agencies at all. Rather, "[t]he judiciary is the final authority on issues of statutory construction...." *Id.* at 843.

Assuming Congress's intent is not clear at step one, then, under step two, a court must accept any "permissible" or "reasonable" agency interpretation, even if the court believes a different policy choice would be better. *Id.* at 843. Deference to the agency under *Chevron*'s second step is much higher. Indeed, if a litigant challenges an agency interpretation and loses at step one, that litigant will likely lose the case. According to one empirical study that is now somewhat dated (1995–96), agencies prevail at step one 42% of the time and at step two 89% of the time. Orin S. Kerr, *Shedding Light on* Chevron: *An Empirical Study of the* Chevron *Doctrine in the U.S. Courts of Appeals*, 15 YALE J. REG. 1, 31 (1998). While some scholars have suggested that *Chevron*'s second step is simply arbitrary and capricious review, it is not.

While both standards are reasonableness standards, the material a court looks while applying the standards is very different. For arbitrary and capricious review, a court will look to see whether the agency's factual determinations and policy choices are reasonable given the record before the court. In contrast, for *Chevron*'s second step, a court will look to see if the agency's legal interpretations are reasonable given the wording of the statute, the legal history, and the purpose of the statute.

> *Chevron*'s two-step deference framework:
> • *Step one:* a court should determine "whether Congress has directly spoken to the precise question at issue."
> • *Step two:* if Congress has not spoken, then a court must accept any "permissible," or "reasonable," agency interpretation.

why deference?

The Court offered three reasons to justify its decision to increase the level of deference given agency interpretations. First, the Court continued *Skidmore*'s rationale that agency personnel are experts in their field while judges are not. *Chevron*, 467 U.S. at 865. Congress entrusts agencies to implement law in a particular area because of this expertise. For example, scientists and analysts working for the Food and Drug Administration (FDA) are more knowledgeable about food safety and drug effectiveness than are judges. Because agencies are specialists in their field, they are in a better position to implement effective public policy. Courts are more limited in both knowledge and reasoning methods. While agencies can develop policy using a wide array of methods, courts are limited to the adversarial process. Hence, deferring to these experts makes sense.

1) Expertise

Second, Congress simply cannot legislate every detail in a comprehensive regulatory scheme. Gaps and ambiguities are inevitable; an agency must fill and resolve these gaps and ambiguities. In *Chevron*, the Court presumed that by leaving these gaps and ambiguities, Congress impliedly delegated the authority to the agency to resolve them. *Id.* at 843–44. Finally, administrative officials, unlike federal judges, have a political constituency to which they are accountable. "[F]ederal judges—who have no constituency—have a duty to respect legitimate policy choices made by those who do." *Id.* at 866. Thus, in

2) Efficiency

creating its two-step deference framework, the Court provided three reasons: agency expertise, implied congressional delegation, and democratic theory. Deference, which had been earned by agencies through reasoned decision-making under *Skidmore*, became essentially an all-or-nothing grant of power from Congress under *Chevron*. Either Congress was clear when it drafted the statute and the judiciary should not defer to the agency at all, or Congress was ambiguous or silent and the judiciary should defer completely to an agency's reasonable interpretation.

Shortly after the case was decided, however, debate arose regarding the nature of the inquiry at the first step. The debate centered around two questions. First, was step one a search for congressional intent or textual clarity? Second, was the search at step one to be broad and include a review of legislative history, statutory purpose, and other sources of statutory meaning, or was it to be narrow and focus primarily, if not exclusively, on the text? *Chevron* was indecisive on this question. When the Court created its two-step approach, the Court did not explain clearly how ambiguity should be resolved at step one. Justice Stevens described this step as a search for congressional intent that "employ[s] traditional tools of statutory construction," but he did not explain which tools of statutory construction were appropriate and "traditional." *Id.* at 843 n.9. Moreover, the opinion contained textualist language: "[If] the statute is silent or ambiguous with respect to the specific issue, the question for the court is whether the agency's answer is based on a permissible construction of the statute." *Id.* at 843. Finally, the Court approached the interpretive process in a decidedly non-textualist way, by starting with the legislative history, then turning to the text. *Id.* at 851.

As you should know by now, throughout history, the appropriate tools and approaches have changed as different theories of statutory interpretation have held favor. Because Justice Stevens used an intentionalist approach in *Chevron*, and because he referenced the traditional tools of statutory construction, it seemed that he anticipated step one to be intentionalist. Indeed, many of the Justices on the bench when *Chevron* was decided were intentionalists or, at least, were willing to look at legislative history and purpose to find meaning. This fact helps explain why Justice Stevens began his analysis in the majority opinion by pursuing the legislative history. He turned to the text only after finding this history inconclusive. Today, such an approach would seem odd indeed.

In the years immediately following *Chevron*, the Court remained true to the intentionalist direction set forth by Justice Stevens. But with time and a change in the composition of the Court, *Chevron*'s first step was narrowed:

step one transformed from a search for congressional intent into a search to resolve textual ambiguity. This change started in 1986 when President Reagan
appointed Justice Scalia to the Supreme Court. Coming from the D.C. Circuit
Court, which handles many challenges to federal agency action, and having
been a teacher of administrative law before his appointment to that court, Justice Scalia was particularly interested in agency issues. And, as a committed
textualist, Justice Scalia must have felt compelled to "reformulate the two-step
inquiry to purge it of these intentionalist elements." Thomas W. Merrill, *Textualism and the Future of the* Chevron *Doctrine*, 72 WASH. U. L.Q. 351, 353
(1994). By 2006, *Chevron*'s first step was routinely described and applied as a
search to resolve ambiguity, using moderate textualist methods. Linda D. Jellum, *Chevron's Demise: A Survey of Chevron from Infancy to Senescence*, 59
ADMIN. L. REV. 725, 761 (2007). A search to find and resolve ambiguity is not
the same as a search to determine whether Congress has directly spoken to the
precise issue before the court. While there is evidence that textualism has not
completely won the battle (for many of the current Justices will still consider
legislative history and unexpressed purpose in some cases), there can be no
doubt that Justice Scalia has, at a minimum, altered the discourse.

When *Chevron* was decided, it appeared to streamline deference analysis
into two straightforward steps: first, a court looked to see if Congress had resolved this issue (or whether the text was ambiguous); if not, the court adopted
the agency's interpretation so long as it was reasonable. But not long after
Chevron was decided, the Court began to move away from *Chevron's* sweep-
ing grant of delegation for some types of agency decision-making. *Chevron*
addressed the degree of deference to be given to legislative rulemaking. After
Chevron was decided, the Court initially applied its two-step framework to all
agency interpretations. In subsequent decisions, however, the Court retreated
from the strong deference rhetoric it espoused in *Chevron* and resurrected *Skidmore's* less deferential "power-to-persuade" test for non-legislative rulemaking. *Chevron* no longer applied in every case involving an agency interpretation.
We turn next to the question of when *Chevron* applies.

E. Deference Post-*Chevron*

1. *Chevron* Step Zero

Not all agency interpretations are entitled to *Chevron* deference. Rather, before a court can apply *Chevron*, the court must make sure that the interpreta-

tion is one deserving of *Chevron*. This step has become colloquially known as "*Chevron* Step Zero," and it is exceedingly complex. But if you break the analysis into its sub-questions, the analysis is at least approachable. Here are the sub-questions: (1) *What* did the agency interpret?; (2) *Which* agency interpreted the statute?; (3) *How* did the agency interpret the statute?; and (4) *Can* this agency interpret the statute? Below, each question is explored in more detail.

a. What Did the Agency Interpret?

Chevron deference is applicable only when an agency interprets a specific type of legal text. To illustrate, *Chevron* does not apply when agencies interpret the Federal Constitution, court opinions, and legal instruments such as contracts. Similarly, *Chevron* does not apply when agencies interpret other agencies' regulations. Indeed, in these situations, courts do not defer at all.

When an agency interprets its own regulation, a different form of deference applies: *Auer* deference. While judicial deference to agency interpretations of statutes has varied widely through time, judicial deference to an agency's interpretation of its own regulations has remained relatively constant. Traditionally, courts defer almost completely to an agency's interpretation of its own regulation. This high level of deference

> Under *Auer*, courts defer to an agency's interpretation of its own *regulation* unless the interpretation is "plainly wrong."

should come as no surprise; after all, it was the agency that drafted the regulation in the first place. Thus, in 1945, the Supreme Court held that an agency's interpretation of its regulation has "controlling weight unless it is plainly erroneous or inconsistent with the regulation." *Bowles v. Seminole Rock & Sand Co.*, 325 U.S. 410, 414 (1945). The Court reasoned that when Congress delegates the authority to promulgate regulations, it also delegates authority to interpret those regulations; such power is a necessary corollary to the former. This substantial level of deference is generally known as either *Seminole Rock* or *Auer* deference. The latter term refers to the Supreme Court case of *Auer v. Robbins*, 519 U.S. 452 (1997), which came after *Chevron* and confirmed that *Seminole Rock* deference had survived *Chevron*. *Id.* at 461-63.

There is at least one limit on when an agency will receive this high level of deference. When an agency does little more than parrot statutory language in its regulation and then claims that it is interpreting the regulation rather than the statute, the agency is not entitled to *Auer* deference. When an agency does no more than parrot a statute (meaning it simply copies the language Congress used), the agency will not receive *Auer* deference because the agency is interpreting Congress's language, not its own. *Gonzales v. Oregon*, 546 U.S. 243, 257 (2006). In *Gonzales*, the Supreme Court refused to defer to the Attorney General's decision that physician-assisted suicide was not a legitimate medical purpose for prescribing medication. The Attorney General had issued an interpretative rule stating that " 'assisting suicide [was] not a 'legitimate medical purpose' within the meaning of [the regulation].' " *Id.* at 254 (quoting 66 Fed. Reg. 56607, 56608 (Nov. 9, 2001)). An Attorney General regulation stated that prescriptions must be issued " 'for a legitimate medical purpose.' " *Id.* at 256 (quoting 21 C.F.R. § 1306.04 (2005)). Under the Attorney General's interpretation of its regulation interpreting the Federal Controlled Substances Act, if a physician prescribed medication for assisted suicide, the physician violated the Act. *Id.* at 257–69. When challenged, the United States Government argued that the interpretive rule was entitled to *Auer* deference because the Attorney General was simply interpreting its own regulation. The Court rejected that argument, stating that *Auer* deference is appropriate when agencies interpret regulations bringing "specificity" to the statutes they are enforcing. When the agency interprets a regulation that simply repeats or paraphrases statutory text, the interpretation does not warrant *Auer* deference because the agency is interpreting Congress's language, not its own. *Id.* at 257. Additionally, the Court refused to give *Chevron* deference to the interpretive rule because it was not promulgated as a legislative rule, which we will discuss in more detail below. *Id.* at 258–65. Ultimately, the Court applied *Skidmore* deference and found the agency's interpretation entirely unpersuasive. *Id.* at 269.

In summary, *Chevron* applies only when an agency (1) *interprets a statute.*

b. Which Agency Interpreted the Statute?

But it is not enough that an agency interprets the correct type of legal text, a statute. *Chevron* applies only when the agency that interprets the statute "administers" that statute. Agencies often interpret and apply statutes, including statutes that the agency does not administer. While the Supreme Court has never clearly articulated what it means to "administer" a statute, lower court cases that have addressed this issue suggest that agencies administer a statute when they have a special and unique responsibility for that statute. *Wagner Seed Co. v. Bush*, 946 F.2d 918, 925–26 (D.C. Cir. 1991) (Williams, J., dissenting). Moreover, when more than one agency administers a statute, *Chevron* is inappropriate. *Rapaport v. U.S. Dep't of the Treasury*, 59 F.3d 212, 216-17 (D.C. Cir. 1995). So, for example, although multiple agencies must interpret the Internal Revenue Code, it is only the Internal Revenue Service (IRS) that actually administers those statutes; thus, only the IRS should receive *Chevron* deference for its interpretations of the federal tax code.

Agencies also must interpret generally applicable statutes, such as the Administrative Procedure Act, the Regulatory Flexibility Act, and the Freedom of Information Act. For generally applicable statutes, no agency's interpretation is entitled to *Chevron* deference.

In summary, *Chevron* applies only when an agency (1) interprets a statute (2) *that the agency administers.*

c. How Did the Agency Interpret the Statute?

But it is not enough that an agency interpret a statute that it administers. As you learned in the last chapter, agencies act in a variety of ways. Some of these ways require more procedural formality and deliberation than others. For example, an agency might interpret a statute as part of a notice and comment rulemaking process, like the EPA did in *Chevron*. Also, an agency might interpret a statute during a formal adjudication. Or, an agency might interpret a statute when drafting an internal policy manual or when writing a letter to a regulated entity. With the former processes (adjudication and notice and comment rulemaking), Congress has given the agency the authority to act with the force of law, and the agency has used that authority to implement change. With the latter processes (non-legislative rulemaking), Congress has not given the agency the authority to act with the force of law. For these reasons, the former processes are considered more formal, or procedurally prescribed, while the latter processes are thought to be less formal, or less procedurally prescribed.

In *Chevron*, the Supreme Court did not indicate, expressly or implicitly, whether the deliberateness of an agency's procedures affected the applicability of the two step analysis. Before the Court decided *Chevron*, however, the Court factored the deliberative nature of the agency's interpretive process into the analysis. Under *Skidmore* deference, interpretations that are made through a more deliberative process, such as notice and comment rulemaking, are considered more persuasive than interpretations made through a less deliberative process, such as non-legislative rulemaking. But when the Court decided *Chevron*, the Court did not distinguish between deliberative agency decision-making and non-deliberative agency decision-making. Indeed, not long after *Chevron* was decided, the Court applied its two-step analysis to all types of agency interpretations, regardless of the deliberative nature of the procedure involved. So, for example, in *Reno v. Koray*, 515 U.S. 50 (1995), the Court held that *Chevron* should apply to an interpretation contained in an agency's internal guideline, a non-legislative rule. *Id.* at 61. And in *NationsBank of North*

Carolina v. Variable Annuity Life Insurance Co., 513 U.S. 251 (1995), the Court applied *Chevron* to an agency's decision to grant an application to act as an agent and sell annuities, an informal adjudication. *Id.* at 256–57, 263. But, with time, the formality of the procedure has gained importance.

Beginning in 2000, the Supreme Court decided a trilogy of cases that limited *Chevron*'s application based on the procedures the agency used to make the interpretation. In *Christensen v. Harris County*, 529 U.S. 576 (2000), *United States v. Mead Corp.*, 533 U.S. 218 (2001), and *Barnhart v. Walton*, 535 U.S. 212 (2002), the Court substantially checked *Chevron*'s applicability based, in part, upon the formality of the procedure the agency had used to reach the interpretation being challenged. Let's start with *Christensen*.

i. Christensen v. Harris County

You will remember that *Chevron* involved notice and comment rulemaking. Yet, agencies also interpret statutes more routinely and less formally in non-legislative rulemaking and informal adjudication. For example, an agency may send a letter in response to a question from a regulated entity. Assuming this interpretation is part of a legitimate, non-legislative rule or informal adjudication, the agency need not use formal or informal rulemaking procedures under section 553 of the APA.

Agencies routinely advise regulated entities in informal ways. The question for the Supreme Court in *Christensen v. Harris County*, 529 U.S. 576 (2000), was whether the Court should apply *Chevron* deference to an agency interpretation of a statute reached in such an informal manner. In *Christensen*, Harris County (the "County") was concerned about the fiscal consequences of having to pay its employees for accrued and unused compensatory time ("comp time") pursuant to the Fair Labor Standards Act of 1938 ("FLSA"). *Id.* at 578. The County asked the U.S. Department of Labor's Wage and Hour Division ("Division") whether the County could require its employees to take comp time. *Id.* at 580. In an opinion letter, the Division stated its interpretation of FLSA that absent an employment agreement to the contrary, an employer could not require an employee to use comp time. This letter did not go through notice and comment or formal rulemaking procedures. *Id.* at 581.

> Under *Christensen's* "force of law" test, an agency's interpretation is entitled to *Chevron* deference when arrived at through a more procedurally prescribed process and to *Skidmore* deference when arrived at through a less procedurally prescribed process.

Despite receiving this letter, the County forbade its employees from accumulating more than a certain maximum amount of comp time, thus forcing the employees to take the time once the maximum had been reached. *Id.* The employees sued, alleging that the County's policy violated the FLSA. The issue for the Court was whether the Division's interpretation of the FLSA should be given *Chevron* deference. A majority of the Court held that the agency's interpretation contained in the opinion letter was not the sort of interpretation that was entitled to *Chevron* deference. *Id.* at 587. In reaching its decision, the majority divided agency interpretations into interpretations made during a process using *force of law* procedures and those that did not. *Id.* A process includes "force of law" procedures when "Congress has delegated legislative power to the agency and [] the agency intended to exercise that power in promulgating the rule." *Am. Mining Cong. v. Mine Safety & Health Admin.*, 995 F.2d 1106, 1109 (D.C. Cir. 1993). According to the majority in *Christensen*, agency actions having the force of law include more formal actions such as formal adjudication, formal rulemaking, and notice and comment rulemaking. Agency actions lacking the force of law include less formal actions such as "opinion letters ... policy statements, agency manuals, and enforcement guidelines[.]" *Christensen*, 529 U.S. at 587. The Court stated that *Chevron* deference is warranted only when the agency makes interpretations using force of law procedures. *Id.* Those interpretations made without force of law warrant the lesser, *Skidmore* power-to-persuade deference. *Id.* Applying *Skidmore* to the facts in *Christensen*, the majority did not find the agency's interpretation to be persuasive. *Id.*

Perhaps surprisingly, Justice Breyer dissented. According to Justice Breyer, *Chevron* and *Skidmore* deference are not different deference standards. Instead, the two cases simply articulated different reasons for affording deference to agency interpretations:

> *Skidmore* made clear that courts may pay particular attention to the views of an expert agency where they represent "specialized experience," even if they do not constitute an exercise of delegated lawmaking authority. The Court held that the "rulings, interpretations and opinions of" an agency, "while not controlling upon the courts by reason of their authority, do constitute a body of experience and informed judgment to which courts and litigants may properly resort for guidance." As Justice Jackson wrote for the Court, those views may possess the "power to persuade," even where they lack the "power to control."

Chevron made no relevant change. It simply focused upon an additional, separate legal reason for deferring to certain agency determinations, namely, that Congress had delegated to the agency the legal authority to make those determinations.

Id. at 596 (Breyer, J., dissenting). According to Justice Breyer, *Skidmore* indicated why courts might choose to defer to agency interpretations when agencies act without formal process, while *Chevron* indicated why courts should choose to defer to agency interpretations when agencies act with formal process.

Also dissenting, but for different reasons, Justice Scalia maintained that *Chevron* had signaled *Skidmore's* end. *Christensen*, 529 U.S. at 589 (Scalia, J., dissenting). Justice Scalia rejected the majority's force of law dichotomy and explained that deference should be determined by whether an agency's interpretation was "authoritative" and reasonable, not by what process was used. To Justice Scalia, deference and no deference were the only two possible choices. He believed that *Chevron* had eliminated limited deference altogether. But the majority disagreed, preferring to have two deference doctrines (*Skidmore* and *Chevron*), which would save courts from the stark choice of electing either full deference or no deference at all.

ii. United States v. Mead Corporation

After *Christensen*, it seemed that courts applied *Chevron* deference when an agency interpreted a statute using relatively formal procedures (including formal adjudication, formal rulemaking, and notice and comment rulemaking) and that *Skidmore* deference applied to all other actions (interpretive rules, policy statements, ruling letters, informal adjudications). This test would have been relatively simple to apply: simply look to the agency action and apply the appropriate deference standard, *Chevron* or *Skidmore*.

But alas, nothing remains so simple, and the Court refined *Christensen's* force of law test a year later in *United States v. Mead Corp.*, 533 U.S. 218 (2001). The issue in *Mead* was whether the U.S. Customs Service's ("Customs") informal ruling letters (which do not go through notice and comment or other formal procedures) were entitled to *Chevron* or *Skidmore* deference. The plaintiff imported day planners. Although Customs had classified the planners as duty-free "day planners" for several years, it changed its interpretation and issued a ruling letter classifying them as "bound diaries." *Id.* at 225. Ruling letters were issued without any preliminary procedure, were not published, and were non-binding. The letters simply described the goods being imported and identified the amount of tariff to be paid. *Id.* at 223. The decision had financial consequences to both parties because bound diaries were subject to tariff, while day planners were not.

The majority held that *Skidmore* deference was appropriate, which should not be surprising or confusing given the absence of any formalized procedures. *Id.* at 227. In reaching its holding, the majority reaffirmed *Christensen* by explaining that *Chevron* applies when an agency acts with the "force of law," which occurs "when it appears that Congress delegated authority to the agency generally to make rules carrying the force of law and that the agency interpretation claiming deference was promulgated in the exercise of that authority." *Id.* at 226–27. Had *Mead* stopped at this point, it would not even warrant a footnote. Unfortunately, the Court did not stop at this point. The Court added a wrinkle to *Christensen*'s force of law test by saying that "[d]elegation of such authority may be shown in a variety of ways, as by an agency's power to engage in adjudication or notice-and-comment rulemaking, *or by some other indication of a comparable congressional intent.*" *Id.* at 227 (emphasis added). The Court added, "[A]s significant as notice-and-comment is in pointing to *Chevron* authority, the want of that procedure here does not decide the case, for we have sometimes found reasons for *Chevron* deference even when no such administrative formality was required and none was afforded." *Id.* at 231 (citing *NationsBank of N.C.,* 513 U.S. at 256–57, 263). The Court did not explain what these reasons were. But the Court did find that there were no such reasons in *Mead* because (1) the face of the statute gave no indication that Congress intended to delegate authority to Customs to issue classification rulings with the force of law, (2) Customs regarded the classification decisions as conclusive only between itself and the importer to whom it was issued, and (3) forty-six different Customs' offices issued 10,000 to 15,000 classifications each year. *Id.* at 233. There were simply too many classification rulings each year for Customs to be able to carefully consider the issue. Hence, the Court held that *Skidmore* deference, not *Chevron*, was appropriate.

Prior to *Mead*, the test was bright-lined: *Chevron* applied when the agency acted with more procedure, and *Skidmore* applied when the agency acted with less procedure. Now, the bright-line was blurring. The Court in *Mead* stated, without elaborating, that some agency actions might qualify for *Chevron* deference even though the agency used less formal procedures. Exactly what types of "other indications" would be sufficient to trigger *Chevron* was not readily apparent from this case alone. However, in the following year, the Court explained when *Chevron* deference should apply to agency interpretations arrived at without force of law procedures.

iii. Barnhart v. Walton

In *Barnhart v. Walton*, 535 U.S. 212 (2002), the Court explained what types of "other indications" might be sufficient to warrant *Chevron* deference. *Id.* In that case, the Social Security Administration (SSA) determined that the plaintiff, who was unable to work for eleven months, was not eligible for disability benefits. *Id.* at 215. The SSA enacted a regulation, using notice and comment procedures, (apparently in response to the pending litigation) which stated that a claimant was not disabled if that claimant could engage in "substantial gainful activity." In doing so, the SSA codified an existing, non-legislative rule. In addition to codifying the non-legislative rule, the SSA subsequently interpreted this new regulation to mean that the claimant was not disabled if "within 12 months after the onset of an impairment ... the impairment no longer prevent[ed] substantial gainful activity." *Id.* at 217 (quoting 65 Fed. Reg. 42772 (2000)). All parties agreed that the second regulation, as an interpretation of the new regulation, was entitled to *Auer* deference. However, the parties disagreed about whether the new regulation governed because it was enacted in response to the litigation. If so, *Chevron* deference would be the appropriate deference standard under *Mead* and *Christensen*.

Writing for the majority, Justice Breyer held that the regulation controlled and thus *Chevron* deference was appropriate. *Id.* at 217. Given the level of procedure that was used (notice and comment rulemaking), that result should not be surprising. But once again, Justice Breyer did not stop when he should have; instead, and *in dicta*, he resurrected his *Christensen* dissent in which he argued that *Skidmore* and *Chevron* are simply different articulations of the rationale for judicial deference to agency interpretations. Justice Breyer rejected the formality dichotomy by saying that "the fact that the [SSA] previously reached its interpretation through means less formal than 'notice-and-comment' rulemaking does not automatically deprive that interpretation of the judicial deference otherwise its due." *Id.* at 221. *Mead* made clear that there was no bright-line deference dichotomy based on how the agency made its interpretation. *Id.* Thus, *Barnhart* reaffirmed *Mead*, which had said that some interpretations contained in non-legislative rules might receive *Chevron* deference.

Justice Breyer explained that *Chevron* applies whenever Congress intended the courts to defer to an agency's interpretation. To determine whether Congress intended for courts to defer, a court must consider the following five factors: (1) the interstitial nature of the legal question, (2) the relevance of the agency's expertise, (3) the importance of the question to administration of the statute, (4) the complexity of the statutory scheme, and (5) the careful consideration the agency had given the question over a long period of time. *Id.* at 222. In other words, the more difficult the issue and the regulatory scheme are, the more experience the agency has in the particular area, the more important resolution of the issue is to the agency's ability to administer the program, and lastly, the more carefully the agency considers the interpretation, the more likely that Congress would have intended for courts to defer to the agency using *Chevron* deference.

After *Barnhart*, at least one thing is clear; the appropriate level of deference rests on congressional intent. If Congress intends that an agency receive judicial deference for interpretations, then courts should apply *Chevron* regardless of how the agency reached the interpretation. In these situations, *Chevron* is appropriate because Congress intended for the agencies, not the courts, to develop this area of law. In contrast, if Congress does not so intend, then the agency is deserving of only *Skidmore* deference. In this situation, Congress intended the courts to be the final arbiters of these legal issues, but an agency's expertise can inform a court's decision.

Despite this five factor test, since *Barnhart* was decided, the Supreme Court has not applied *Chevron* deference to an agency interpretation that was made without force of law procedures. However, some lower courts have done so. *Compare Schuetz v. Banc One Mortg. Corp.*, 292 F.3d 1004, 1011–13 (9th Cir. 2002) (holding that *Chevron* applied to a HUD Statement of Policy), *and Kruse v. Wells Fargo Home Mortg., Inc.*, 383 F.3d 49, 61 (2d Cir. 2004) (same), *with Krzalic v. Republic Title Co.*, 314 F.3d 875, 879 (7th Cir. 2002) (holding that *Chevron* did not apply to an HUD Statement of Policy).

In summary, *Chevron* applies only when an agency (1) interprets a statute (2) that the agency administers (3) *while using force of law, or procedurally prescribed procedures.*

d. Can the Agency Interpret the Statute?

i. FDA v. Brown & Williamson

But it is not enough that an agency interpret a statute that the agency administers while using force of law procedures. In the midst of deciding the *Christensen/Mead/Barnhart* trilogy, the Supreme Court issued another trilogy of cases in this area that would add to the complexity. Remember that in *Chevron*, the Court rationalized deference to an agency's interpretation by suggesting that when Congress enacts gaps and creates ambiguities, Congress *implicitly* intends to delegate interpretive authority to the agency. But in three cases, *FDA v. Brown & Williamson Tobacco Corp.*, 529 U.S. 120

(2000), *Gonzales v. Oregon*, 546 U.S. 243 (2006), and *Hamdan v. Rumsfeld*, 548 U.S. 557 (2006), the Court rejected, or at least narrowed, this rationale for some situations. In each of these cases, the Court reasoned that in some instances, despite ambiguity, Congress does not intend to delegate authority to the agency at all.

> Deference under *Chevron* to an agency's construction of a statute that it administers is premised on the theory that a statute's ambiguity constitutes an implicit delegation from Congress to the agency to fill in the statutory gaps. In extraordinary cases, however, there may be reason to hesitate before concluding that Congress has intended such an implicit delegation.

Brown & Williamson, 529 U.S. at 159 (internal citations omitted).

Brown & Williamson is interesting historically. The Food and Drug Administration (FDA) knew for years that tobacco was deadly. The FDA was authorized to regulate "drugs" and "devices," but chose not to regulate tobacco because it feared that Congress would reject its action. The tobacco companies had, and still have, an extremely powerful lobby in Washington. ESKRIDGE ET AL., CASES AND MATERIALS ON LEGISLATION, *supra*, at 798–99. Moreover, Presidents Reagan and Bush would not have supported the FDA's attempt to regulate tobacco. In 1993, Bill Clinton assumed the office of president. President Clinton was anti-tobacco. He appointed Dr. David Kessler to head the FDA and indicated a willingness to support the FDA's attempt to regulate tobacco. Armed with Clinton's support, the FDA interpreted cigarettes and tobacco products to be "drugs." In response, the tobacco companies sued.

In *Brown & Williamson*, the majority rejected the FDA's decision to regulate tobacco. The FDA was authorized to regulate "drugs," "devices," and "combination products." *Brown & Williamson*, 529 U.S. at 126 (citing 21 U.S.C. §§ 321(g)–(h) (1994 and Supp. III)). The statute defined these terms as "articles ... intended to affect the structure or any function of the body." *Id.* (quoting 21 U.S.C. § 321 (g)(1)(C)). The FDA interpreted this language as allowing it to regulate tobacco and cigarettes. *Id.* at 125. Despite the fact that the language of the statute alone should have been broad enough to support the agency's interpretation, the majority concluded "that Congress ha[d] directly spoken to the issue here and precluded the FDA's jurisdiction to regulate tobacco products." *Id.* at 133. The majority supported its holding by noting that Congress had: (1) created a distinct regulatory scheme for tobacco products, (2) squarely rejected proposals to give the FDA jurisdiction over tobacco, and (3) acted repeatedly to preclude other agencies from exercising authority in this area. *Id.* at 155–56. In this case then, the majority held that while Congress may not have spoken to the precise issue when enacting the relevant statute, Congress had spoken broadly enough on related questions to prevent the agency from acting at all. *Id.* The Court afforded no deference whatsoever, not even *Skidmore* deference, to the agency's interpretation even though the agency had used force of law procedures.

ii. Gonzales v. Oregon

Six years later, in *Gonzales*, the Supreme Court again held that Congress had not delegated interpretive authority to an agency despite an obvious gap in the statute. The issue before the Court was "whether the Controlled Substances Act allowed the United States Attorney General to prohibit doctors from prescribing regulated drugs for use in physician-assisted suicide, notwithstanding a state law permitting the procedure." *Gonzales*, 546 U.S. at 248–49. The Justices disagreed over what deference standard to apply to the Attorney General's interpretative rule (a non-legislative rule), which interpreted a regulation enacted pursuant to notice and comment procedures. Because the regulation simply parroted the language in the statute, the majority refused to apply *Auer* deference to the interpreting regulation. *Id.* at 244.

> Under *Brown & Williamson* and *Gonzales*, when Congress does not intend to delegate a specific issue to an agency, then the agency's interpretation is entitled to either no deference or to *Skidmore* deference.

Additionally, the majority refused to apply *Chevron* deference to both the notice and comment regulation and the interpretive regulation. The majority reasoned that because Congress did not intend for the Attorney General to have interpretative power in this area, Congress had not delegated interpretive power to the agency: "The idea that Congress gave the Attorney General such broad and unusual authority through an implicit delegation in the [Controlled Substances Act] registration provision is not sustainable." *Id.* at 267. However, unlike the majority in *Brown & Williamson*, the majority in *Gonzales* applied *Skidmore* deference to the Attorney General's interpretation. *Id.* at 268. Applying *Skidmore*, the majority reasoned that this issue was critically important to the nation and was, therefore, skeptical of what it viewed as the Attorney General's attempt to backdoor an overly broad interpretation into the statute. *Id.* at 272. Ultimately, the majority rejected the Attorney General's interpretation under *Skidmore*, affording the Attorney General's interpretation no deference at all.

iii. Hamdan v. Rumsfeld

The final case in the trilogy came that same year. In *Hamdan*, the Court rejected an interpretation contained within former President George W. Bush's executive order, which created military commissions to prosecute illegal enemy combatants. 548 U.S. at 567. The commissions were established after the tragic events of 9/11. First, Congress adopted a joint resolution, granting the President the power to "use all necessary and appropriate force against those nations, organizations, or persons he determines planned, authorized, committed, or aided the terrorist attacks." *Id.* at 568 (quoting Authorization for Use of Military Force, Pub. L. No. 107-40, 115 Stat. 224 (2001) (codified at 50 U.S.C. § 1541 (2006)). Second, acting pursuant to this resolution, President Bush issued the "Detention, Treatment, and Trial of Certain Non-Citizens in the War Against Terrorism" executive order, which provided that any noncitizens determined to be members of al Qaeda or of another terrorist group would be tried by a military commission. *Id.* (citing 66 Fed. Reg. 57,833 (Nov. 13, 2001)). The relevant issue for the Court was whether, and to what extent, the Uniform Code of Military Justice ("UCMJ") authorized a president to establish procedures for military commissions that were different from the procedures for traditional courts-martial. The UCMJ explicitly provided that the procedures for the two proceedings should be the same "insofar as practicable." *Id.* at 640 (Kennedy, J., concurring in part) (quoting 10 U.S.C. § 836 (2006)) (internal quotation marks omitted). This ambiguous language should have given any president broad flexibility to determine what procedures were appropriate; however, the Court concluded that the procedures President Bush used violated the UCMJ. *Id.* at 622–23. In so doing, the majority failed to apply either *Chevron* or *Skidmore* deference, leaving uncertain the appropriate deference level to apply to interpretations in executive orders. In a related case, *Hamdi v. Rumsfeld*, 542 U.S. 507 (2004), the Court similarly refused to apply either *Chevron* or *Skidmore* deference to evaluate the correctness of the President's interpretation of another section of Congress's joint resolution.

In the *Brown & Williamson* trilogy, the Court significantly limited the implied-delegation rationale. In all three cases, the Court held that Congress did not implicitly delegate interpretive power to the agency despite statutory ambiguity. Notably, in none of the applicable statutes did Congress expressly say that it was not delegating to the agency. Rather, the Court inferred Congress's intent not to delegate based on other factors, including the existence of other legislation (*Brown & Williamson*), the importance of the issue (*Gonzales*), and the failure to explain a choice that affected "a fundamental protection" (*Ham-*

dan). Moreover, in *Brown & Williamson* and *Hamdan*, the Court reviewed the agency's interpretation *de novo*; while, in *Gonzales,* the Court applied *Skidmore* deference, but rejected the agency's interpretation as unpersuasive. The holdings in these cases are at odds with *Chevron's* implicit-delegation rationale, which states that "[d]eference under *Chevron* to an agency's construction of a statute that it administers is premised on the theory that a statute's ambiguity constitutes an implicit delegation from Congress to the agency to fill in the statutory gaps." *Brown & Williamson,* 529 U.S. at 159. Perhaps these cases are simply extraordinary, but for now, their guidance must still be considered.

Recapping, when *Chevron* was decided, many thought it applied to all agency interpretations. *Christensen* limited *Chevron's* reach by holding that *Chevron* applied only when the agency acted using force of law procedures. *Mead* and *Barnhart* then expanded *Christensen* to hold that *Chevron* applied when Congress intended for *Chevron* to apply. *Brown & Williamson, Gonzales,* and *Hamdan* then limited *Chevron's* reach. Prior to these cases, courts assumed that when Congress left a gap or drafted ambiguously, Congress intended, albeit implicitly, to delegate the power to interpret the statute to the agency. After these cases, a court now needs to ensure that Congress *actually* intended to delegate interpretive power: gaps and ambiguities are no longer enough.

In summary, *Chevron* applies only when an agency (1) interprets a statute (2) that the agency administers (3) while using force of law procedures, (4) *so long as Congress intended to delegate interpretive power to the agency.* You have now mastered the sub-steps of *Chevron* step zero.

2. Applying *Chevron*'s Step Zero

At this point, you may well be wondering how to apply *Chevron*'s step zero. Let me suggest the following process: First, ask whether the agency is interpreting a statute and whether the agency has the sole or primary authority to administer that statute. If the agency is interpreting its own regulation, *Auer* deference is appropriate; if the agency is interpreting anything else, no deference is due.

Second, ask whether Congress intended to delegate the specific issue to the agency at all. If the issue is one of such major importance that Congress would never have intended to delegate authority, then the agency likely has no power to interpret the statute. Such a finding should be rare. This step is based on the holdings in *Brown & Williamson, Gonzales,* and *Hamdan.*

If Congress did not intend to delegate, then, *Skidmore* deference should apply regardless of the procedure the agency used. While *Brown & Williamson* and *Hamdan* both implied that even *Skidmore* deference would not be applicable in these cases, the majority in *Gonzales* did apply *Skidmore* deference.

Gonzales is the better approach to these issues for two reasons; first, it appears that the Justices in *Brown & Williamson* and *Hamdan* did not consider whether *Skidmore* deference would be appropriate. Second, because *Skidmore* deference requires a court do little more than consider an agency's interpretation, the court can relatively easily reject that interpretation if the interpretation is inconsistent with the regulatory scheme. Indeed, the Court in *Gonzales* did just that. 546 U.S. at 275. Because agencies have expertise, have access to data and information, and are politically accountable, their input should be relevant even if not decisive.

Third, if Congress intended to delegate interpretive authority to an agency, you should determine whether Congress intended courts to defer to that particular agency's interpretation. To do so, look first to the type of agency action at issue; in other words, look to see if the agency acted with the force of law. If the agency interpreted the statute during notice and comment rulemaking, formal rulemaking, or formal adjudication, then *Chevron* deference would be appropriate. This step is based on *Christensen*'s holding.

Fourth, you should determine whether *Chevron* deference is appropriate even though force of law procedures were not used. To do so, determine whether Congress intended *Chevron* to apply as shown by the *Barnhart* factors. Those factors include the following: (1) the interstitial nature of the legal question, (2) the relevance of the agency's expertise, (3) the importance of the question to administration of the statute, (4) the complexity of the statutory scheme, and (5) the careful consideration the agency has given the question over a long period of time. If these factors suggest that Congress did not intend for courts to defer, then *Chevron* is inapplicable. If *Chevron* is inapplicable, then you should apply *Skidmore*'s power-to-persuade test. This step is based on the holdings from *Mead* and *Barnhart*. But if the *Barnhart* factors suggest that Congress did intend for the courts to defer, you should apply *Chevron* deference.

Fifth, apply the deference standard that you determined was appropriate. If you determined at step three or four that *Chevron* should apply, then, using traditional tools of statutory interpretation, ask whether Congress has spoken to the precise issue before the court. This is *Chevron*'s first step. If Congress has so spoken, then your analysis is complete, for Congress has the authority to interpret its own statutes when it so chooses. But, if Congress has not directly spoken to the precise issue, or if Congress has left a gap or impliedly delegated to the agency, then proceed to *Chevron*'s second step: Ask whether the agency's interpretation is reasonable in light of the underlying statute. Compare the interpretation with the language of the statute, the legislative history, and the purpose of the statute. If the agency's interpretation is unreasonable when compared to these sources, then no deference is due. If the agency's interpretation is reasonable, then full deference is due.

If, instead, you determined at step four that *Skidmore* deference should apply, then apply *Skidmore*'s power-to-persuade factors to the agency's interpretation. An agency's interpretation is entitled to deference based on the following factors: (1) the consistency in the agency interpretation over time; (2) the thoroughness of the agency's consideration; and (3) the soundness of the agency's reasoning. Deference under this standard is earned, not automatic.

Understanding the difference between *Chevron* and *Skidmore* in application is not always so easy. Professor Gary Lawson has offered a way of thinking of the difference, which he defines as the difference between legal deference and epistemological deference. Gary Lawson, *Mostly Unconstitutional: The Case Against Precedent Revisited*, 5 AVE MARIA L. REV. 1, 2–10 (2007). Legal deference is deference earned solely based on the identity of the interpreter and the method of interpretation. *Id.* at 9. For example, lower courts must defer to interpretations of higher courts within the same jurisdiction, but need not defer to interpretations from courts in other jurisdictions. The decision of whether to defer depends entirely on the identity of the interpreter. *Chevron* deference is a form of legal deference: agencies earn deference simply because they are agencies that interpreted statutes using a particular process. In contrast, epistemological deference is deference earned because of the persuasiveness of the reasoning. *Id.* at 10. Courts in neighboring jurisdictions need not follow each other's opinions but can choose to do so because the reasoning is persuasive. The decision of whether to defer depends entirely on the persuasiveness of the reasoning; the identity of the interpreter is irrelevant. *Skidmore* deference is a form of epistemological deference: agencies earn deference based on the soundness of their reasoning, not because they are agencies interpreting statutes.

Not all academic administrative law experts would agree that this simplified, five step process completely or even accurately captures *Chevron* Step Zero analysis. Rightly, they would note that the interaction of these cases is extremely complex. To illustrate, during listserv discussions, one scholar stated that the "force of law" phrase is one of the most confusing in administrative law. Another stated that *Mead* is not particularly coherent and raises tough issues regarding when *Chevron* should apply. These comments show that even the experts disagree on exactly how to understand and reconcile these cases. *Chevron*'s Step Zero is a mess.

F. Agency Interpretations that Conflict with Judicial Interpretations

All of the cases above addressed what level of deference, if any, a court should give to an agency interpretation when there are no pre-existing judicial interpretations of the same statute. The next obvious question is: what if there is a prior judicial opinion? Should a court defer to an agency interpretation of a statute that varies from an existing judicial interpretation? Prior judicial interpretations exist when a court defers to an agency interpretation or interprets the meaning of a statutory provision when an agency has not yet interpreted it. The question is whether thereafter an agency is bound to follow this prior judicial interpretation or whether the agency is free to make its own interpretation. At issue is flexibility—the ability for an agency to adjust policy and statutory interpretations. On the one hand, flexibility is essential to the effective operation of administrative agencies as technology and economics advance and administrative priorities change with time and with a new administration. If agencies were unable to alter their interpretations over time, flexibility would be significantly hindered and agencies would be less effective at responding to changes. On the other hand, too much change can lead to unpredictability, uncertainty, and, potentially, unfairness. Similarly situated litigants expect the government to treat them similarly.

The Supreme Court addressed this issue in *National Cable & Telecommunications Ass'n. v. Brand X Internet Services*, 545 U.S. 967 (2005). In that case, the Court chose flexibility over certainty by holding that, if a prior court had determined that the statute was clear under *Chevron's* first step, the agency would be bound by that judicial interpretation. *Id.* at 985. But, if the court did not decide that the statute was clear under *Chevron's* first step, then the prior interpretation would not bind the agency. *Id.* In other words, a prior judicial interpretation does not eliminate a pre-existing ambiguity. The prior interpretation merely reflects a determination that either there is no ambiguity or that there is ambiguity. If there is no ambiguity, then Congress has spoken and the agency, as well as the courts, must follow Congress's intent. But if there is ambiguity, then regardless of whether a court issues the first interpretation of an ambiguous statute or an agency does, the interpretation does not bind the agency.

This approach is intuitively appealing; however, judges have not always been so clear about whether an adopted interpretation rests on a finding that Congress was ambiguous at *Chevron's* first step, especially for cases that predate *Brand X*. Justice Scalia eloquently summarized this point in a recent case:

In cases decided pre-*Brand X*, the Court had no inkling that it *must* utter the magic words "ambiguous" or "unambiguous" in order to (poof!) expand or abridge executive power, and (poof!) enable or disable administrative contradiction of the Supreme Court. Indeed, the Court was unaware of even the utility (much less the necessity) of making the ambiguous/nonambiguous determination in cases decided pre-*Chevron*, before that opinion made the so-called "Step 1" determination of ambiguity *vel non* a customary (though hardly mandatory) part of judicial-review analysis. For many of those earlier cases, therefore, it will be incredibly difficult to determine whether the decision purported to be giving meaning to an ambiguous, or rather an unambiguous, statute.

United States v. Home Concrete & Supply, 132 S. Ct. 1836, 1846 (2012) (Scalia, J., concurring in part). In *Home Concrete*, the Court had to resolve the meaning of a tax statute. The statute allowed the IRS to assess a deficiency against a taxpayer within "3 years after the return was filed." *Id.* at 1839 (quoting 26 U.S.C. §6501(a)(2000). The statute further provided that the three-year period would be extended to six years when a taxpayer "omit[ed] from gross income an amount properly includible therein which is in excess of 25 percent of the amount of gross income stated in the return." *Id.* (quoting 26 U.S.C. §6501(e)(1)(A)). The question for the Court was "whether this latter provision applied (and extended the ordinary 3-year limitations period) when the taxpayer overstated his basis in property that he had sold, thereby understating the gain that he received from its sale." Basis in property is generally the purchase price of an asset or its value. *Id.* In an earlier case, the Court had held that taxpayer statements overstating the basis in property did not fall within the scope of the statute. *Colony, Inc. v. Comm'r*, 357 U.S. 28, 32 (1958). Long after *Colony* was decided, the IRS enacted a regulation interpreting the relevant language in the statute to include basis misstatements. *Id.* at 1843.

When challenged in court, the IRS argued that it was entitled to *Chevron* deference for its interpretation pursuant to *Brand X* because the *Colony* Court had stated that the tax statute was "not unambiguous," meaning it was ambiguous. The majority disagreed. It observed that *Colony* had been decided long before *Chevron* and suggested that the *Colony* Court was not thinking in first step/second step terms. The *Home Concrete* Court noted that the *Colony* Court had said that the taxpayer had the better textual argument, had found that the legislative history supported the interpretation, concluded that the government's interpretation would create a patent incongruity in the tax law, and believed its interpretation to be in harmony with the 1954 Tax Code. *Id.* at 1843–44. For the majority, these findings resolved any ambiguity.

Not surprisingly, Justice Scalia vehemently disagreed. Because the *Colony* Court had stated that the statute was "not unambiguous," Scalia argued that the majority could only reject the agency's later interpretation under *Brand X* if the interpretation were unreasonable. *Id.* at 1847 (Scalia, J. dissenting). Calling for *Brand X*'s death, Scalia lamented, "*Colony* said unambiguously that the text was ambiguous, and that should be an end of the matter.... Rather than making our judicial-review jurisprudence curiouser and curiouser, the Court should abandon the opinion that produces these contortions, *Brand X*." *Id.* at 1848.

G. Mastering This Topic

Return to the hypothetical ordinance provided in Chapter 1 on page 9. You may recall that the Commissioner of Parks ("Commissioner"), an agency, promulgated a regulation interpreting the PPSO regarding whether certain vehicles were permitted in Pioneer Park. How does the agency's regulation affect your determination of whether an ambulance is a vehicle?

First, you should know that *Chevron* and its progeny apply only to interpretations made by federal agencies, not state agencies or local agencies. For educational purposes, however, let's ignore that fact and assume that this chapter identifies the applicable law that your jurisdiction would follow. The relevant regulation (33 C.F.R. § 2300(1)) defines a motor vehicle as follows:

> "Motor vehicle" in the PPSO means a road vehicle driven by a motor or engine used or physically capable of being used upon any public highway in this state in the transportation of persons or property, except vehicles operating wholly on fixed rails or tracks and electric trolley buses.

Would a court defer to this agency's interpretation? Let's apply *Chevron*'s step zero process to see whether a court would defer to this interpretation and, if so, which deference standard would apply, *Chevron* or *Skidmore*.

First, you should confirm that the Commissioner interpreted an ordinance— for our purposes the equivalent of a statute—that the agency administers. Second, you should ask whether the City Council intended to delegate the specific issue to the Commissioner at all. If the issue is one of such major importance that the Council would never have intended to delegate, then the Commissioner likely has no force of law power to interpret the statute. In this case, it is unlikely that the City Council would consider this issue too important for the Commissioner's interpretation.

Second, ask whether the City Council intended to delegate interpretive authority to the Commissioner. To do so, look first to the type of agency action at issue; in other words, look to see if the Commissioner acted with the force of law. If the Commissioner interpreted the statute during notice and comment rulemaking, formal rulemaking, or formal adjudication, then *Chevron* deference is appropriate. In this case, the Commissioner promulgated a regulation, though we do not know whether it was by notice and comment procedures or by formal procedures. We do not need to resolve the latter question because either type of procedure is considered force of law and, thus, the Commissioner would be entitled to *Chevron* deference.

Third, note that step four above is inapplicable because the Commissioner acted with force of law procedures. Hence, you have determined that the applicable deference standard is *Chevron*, so you will apply that standard. Using traditional tools of statutory interpretation, ask first whether the City Council has spoken to the precise issue — what the term "motor vehicles" means. You have already resolved this question as you have worked though this hypothetical in preceding chapters. For example, in Chapter 4, you determined whether the text was ambiguous. In Chapters 5 and 6, you applied the grammar and linguistic canons to see if the ambiguity was resolved. In Chapter 9, you considered the legislative history and the purpose of the ordinance. Perhaps at one of these steps, you concluded that the City Council had spoken, intending the term motor vehicles to include or not include ambulances. If so, then your analysis is complete, for the Council has the authority to determine what its ordinances mean.

But if you did not conclude that the City Council had definitively resolved this issue and that ambiguity remained, then you would proceed to *Chevron*'s second step and ask whether the Commissioner's interpretation is reasonable in light of the ordinance. To do so, you must compare the interpretation in the regulation with the language of the ordinance, with its legislative history, and with its purpose. When we compare the text of the ordinance to the interpretation in the regulation, we would see that the text of the ordinance and the interpretation are compatible. The ordinance prohibits motor vehicles from entering the park, and the regulation defines motor vehicles broadly to include all vehicles that typically are driven on roads.

When we compare the interpretation in the regulation to its legislative history and the regulation itself, we would see that these two are also consistent. The City Council members seemed concerned about safety and wished to ban all vehicles that could injure people. The interpretation in the regulation is consistent with this intent.

Finally, when we compare the interpretation in the regulation to the purpose of the ordinance—to increase safety and decrease noise pollution—we see that they are similarly consistent. Likely, you would find that the Commissioner's interpretation in its regulation is reasonable compared to these factors; hence, full deference is due and you would apply the interpretation to the ambulance. Does the interpretation aid your decision of whether an ambulance is a vehicle? Perhaps. The Commissioner's definition is broadly inclusive of all motor vehicles that operate on the roads and an ambulance is a vehicle that operates on the road. Likely, this result is unsettling to you. Perhaps the facts of the case make a difference. After all, this driver did not simply drive the ambulance through the park; rather, he drove into the park to pick up an individual who needed medical attention. Likely, though we do not know for sure, the ambulance driver drove slowly and carefully. Now what? Because this next step involves a question of law application, which we have not studied in detail, we will stop here. But remember that the appropriate standard to apply to mixed questions of law and fact is currently unclear. Some courts accept an agency's decision if it has "warrant in the record" and a reasonable basis in law. Other courts break the mixed question into its component parts—questions of law and questions of fact. Questions of fact are reviewed under different standards pursuant to the section 706(2) of the APA. For agency findings of fact made during informal rulemaking, the relevant standard is whether the agency's findings are arbitrary and capricious. 5 U.S.C. § 706(2)(A). Applying the arbitrary and capricious standard, a court would determine whether the agency's findings were based on a consideration of irrelevant factors or whether the agency made a clear error of judgment. For agency findings of fact made during formal rulemaking the standard is whether the agency's findings are supported by substantial evidence. 5 U.S.C. § 706(2)(E). Applying the substantial evidence standard, a court would determine whether the record contains "such evidence as a reasonable mind might accept as adequate to support a conclusion." *Consol. Edison Co. v. NLRB*, 305 U.S. 197, 229 (1938).

For educational purposes, let's assume that the Commissioner had issued this interpretation via a non-legislative, interpretive rule. Would the result be different? Return to the *Chevron* step zero process, but this time at the third step, and note that you would conclude that the Commissioner did not use force of law procedures. Hence, *Chevron* deference is not automatic. Instead, you must now determine whether *Chevron* deference is appropriate even though force of law procedures were not used. To do so, determine whether the City Council intended *Chevron* to apply as shown by the *Barnhart* factors. Those factors include the following: (1) the interstitial nature of the legal question, (2) the relevance of the agency's expertise, (3) the importance of the question to administration of the statute, (4) the complexity of the statutory scheme, and (5) the careful consideration the agency has given the question over a long period of time. You will remember that the more difficult the issue and the regulatory scheme are, the more experience the agency has in the particular area, the more important resolution of this issue is to the agency's ability to administer the program; and finally, the more carefully the agency considered the interpretation, the more likely that the lawmaking body would have intended for courts to defer to the agency's interpretation using *Chevron* deference. In this case, the issue and regulatory scheme are not complex and do not seem to need special expertise to resolve. Further, there is no indication that the Commissioner considered the issue carefully or that the Commissioner needed to resolve this issue to take care of the parks. Thus, because the *Barnhart* factors suggest that the City Council did not intend for courts to defer, *Chevron* would be inapplicable. Instead, you should apply *Skidmore*'s power-to-persuade test.

Under *Skidmore*, the Commissioner's interpretation would be entitled to some deference based on the following factors: (1) the consistency in its interpretation over time; (2) the thoroughness of its consideration; and (3) the soundness of its reasoning. In this case, this is the first time the Commissioner has interpreted this ordinance; there is no indication regarding how thoroughly the Commissioner considered the issue; and, there is no reasoning offered for the interpretation. Applying *Skidmore* deference, you might conclude that the Commissioner's interpretation is not persuasive. Alternatively, you might conclude that the interpretation is consistent enough with the ordinance to be persuasive. If you decide the former, then you must determine whether the ordinance applies to the ambulance without regard to the Commissioner's definition. If you decide the latter, you must determine whether the ordinance as refined by the regulation applies to the ambulance.

Did you notice that the Commissioner's interpretation did not significantly help you resolve the ambulance hypothetical? Does this mean that agency interpretations are generally unhelpful? Not at all. Consider whether the Commissioner's interpretation would help you reseolve the other hypothetical questions, notably the helicopter and airplane questions.

Checkpoints

- Under *Auer*, courts defer to an agency's interpretation of its own *regulation* unless the interpretation is "plainly wrong."

- Under the *Brown & Williamson* trilogy, a court must first decide whether Congress intended to defer the specific issue to an agency before determining whether to give an agency's interpretation of a statute any deference.

- Assuming Congress intended to defer the specific issue to the agency, then courts will look at two things to determine whether Congress intended courts to defer: the interpretive process used and the nature of the question at issue.

- Under *Christensen's* "force of law" test, an agency's interpretation is entitled to *Chevron* deference when arrived at through a more procedurally-prescribed process and to *Skidmore* deference when arrived at through a less procedurally-prescribed process. Additionally, under *Barnhart's* "other-factors" test, an agency's interpretation is entitled to *Chevron* deference when the nature of the question at issue shows that Congress likely wanted the courts to defer to the agency's interpretation.

- *Chevron* established a two-step test. At step one, a court should determine "whether Congress has directly spoken to the precise question at issue." At step two, if Congress has not so spoken, then a court must accept any "permissible" or "reasonable" agency interpretation.

- Under *Skidmore's* power-to-persuade test, an agency's interpretation of a statute is entitled to deference when (1) the agency consistently interprets the language over time, (2) the agency thoroughly considers the issue, and (3) the agency offers sound reasoning to support the interpretation.

Chapter 13

Canons Based on Policy-Based Considerations: Constitutional & Prudential

---

Roadmap

- Identify the canons based on the Constitution and on prudential considerations.
- Understand the Constitutional Avoidance Doctrine.
- Learn the rule of lenity and its role in penal cases.
- Understand when clear statements are necessary.
- Explore the canons regarding remedial statutes and statutes in derogation of common law.
- Understand implied causes of action and implied remedies.

A. Introduction to This Chapter

We have finished examining the intrinsic and extrinsic sources. We turn now to the third and final source: policy-based sources of meaning. The canons we cover next are presumptions based on constitutional and prudential considerations.

B. Policy-Based Sources

Remember that policy-based sources are those sources that are extrinsic both to the statute and to the legislative process. They reflect important social and legal choices derived from the Constitution or prudential ideals. These canons protect fundamental constitutional rights, such as due process, and advance particular policy objectives, such as requiring Congress to be clear when it impacts federalism.

Unlike the canons we have looked at so far, these canons do not claim to be neutral; rather, they value one consideration at the expense of another. For example, the rule of lenity directs judges to adopt the least penal interpretation of an ambiguous criminal statute or civil statute with a penal component. In this example, fair notice trumps imposing a penalty on bad behavior.

Because these canons are non-neutral, their use may seem activist to an outsider. Consider, for example, the 2000 Bush versus Gore election debacle; a Florida canon, derived from that state's constitution, directed Florida judges to construe election statutes so that the right of Florida voters to participate fully in the federal electoral process would be protected. *Palm Beach Cnty. Canvassing Bd. v. Harris*, 772 So. 2d 1220, 1237 (Fla. 2000). Hence, the court ordered the Florida Secretary of State to accept some amended returns. *Id.* at 1240. To some, this outcome appeared activist, favoring Democrat Al Gore over Republican George Bush.

The use of a particular policy-based source changes over time and over jurisdictions. For example, the rule of lenity, which arises from constitutional due process concerns about providing adequate notice of penal conduct, has been relegated to a rule of last resort in many states as a result of society's current focus on penalizing criminals. Indeed, some state legislatures, such as California's, have attempted to abolish the rule of lenity entirely; however, because the rule of lenity flows from constitutional procedural due process concerns, the California courts have had difficulty discarding it, despite a statute directing them to do so. While one jurisdiction might reject the rule of lenity, another may, by statute or common law, embrace it.

Thus, policy-based sources can play a fundamental role in interpretation. Your education in statutory interpretation would be incomplete without a discussion of these sources and the canons developed to further them. While you will gain an overview of these canons in this chapter, it is critical for you as a lawyer to research the role these canons play within your particular jurisdiction, for jurisdictions vary in their willingness to embrace or reject these sources. We begin our discussion with the more critical of the two: constitutionally based canons. Then, we will move onto the prudentially based canons.

C. Canons Based on the Constitution

Before we detail the various canons based on the Constitution, we first need to review the legal structure of the United States. There is a hierarchy of law in the United States. This hierarchy has an important impact on statutory interpretation. As you are no doubt aware, the U.S. Constitution is the highest source of law. No statute passed by Congress or any state legislature can conflict with the U.S. Constitution. Statutes that do so are unconstitutional. Thus, one canon that we will discuss in more detail addresses this issue: To avoid declaring statutes unconstitutional, courts try to avoid interpreting statutes in a way that would raise a constitutional issue.

The second highest source of law are federal statutes (and cases). The historical development of statutes is informative. While parliament enjoyed almost unlimited power in early England, that power appeared to shift in 1610 with *Dr. Bonham's Case*. In that case, a "physician" was jailed for practicing medicine without a license. *The Case of the College of Physicians*, 8 Co. Rep. 107a, 77 Eng. Rep. 638 (C.P. 1610). He sued for false imprisonment. In defense, the Royal College of Physicians pointed to a statute that allowed it to imprison and fine the doctor. The Chief Justice, Sir Edward Coke, held for the doctor and said in dicta, "[W]hen an Act of Parliament is against common right or reason, or repugnant, or impossible to be performed, the common law will controul it and adjudge such Act to be void." *Id.* at 118a, 77 Eng. Rep. at 652. Despite what some thought at the time, *Bonham's Case* did not actually make English common law supreme over statutory law. "[N]otwithstanding what was attributed to Lord Coke in *Bonham's Case* ... the omnipotence of parliament over the common law was absolute ... for English liberty against legislative tyranny was the power of a free public opinion represented by the commons." *Hurtado v. California*, 110 U.S. 516, 531 (1884).

But Coke's dictum set the stage for the acceptance of judicial review of legislation in America by "providing an early foundation for the idea that courts might invalidate legislation that they found inconsistent with a *written* constitution." *Seminole Tribe v. Fla.*, 517 U.S. 44, 162 n.56 (1996) (Souter, J., dissenting). Judicial review was, of course, adopted in this country in *Marbury v. Madison*, 5 U.S. (1 Cranch) 137 (1803). As a result, federal statutes fall below the U.S. Constitution, and the judiciary is charged with determining whether such statutes are constitutional.

On par with federal statutory law is federal common law. While you may have heard that there is no federal common law, this statement is not quite accurate. It is true that there is no federal common law in areas traditionally under the authority of state courts, such as torts and contracts. But, there are two basic areas where federal common law does exist. The first area of federal common law includes those areas in which Congress has given federal courts the power to develop substantive law (for example, in admiralty, antitrust, bankruptcy, interstate commerce, and civil rights). The second area of federal common law includes those areas in which a federal rule of decision is necessary to protect interests that are uniquely federal. In *Clearfield Trust Co. v. United States*, 318 U.S. 363 (1943), the Court identified a three-step test for determining whether a federal common law rule was necessary to protect a significantly important federal interest:

- First, ask if there is federal competence to create law in this area—in other words, would Congress be able to adopt a law in such an area?
- If so, then, second, ask whether state or federal law should govern the area?
- If federal law should govern, then, third, ask whether courts should borrow state law or create an entirely new federal rule.

Thus, federal common law does exist, but it exists only so long as Congress allows it to exist.

Next on the hierarchy are federal regulations. As you saw in Chapter 11, federal regulations are legislative rules that federal administrative agencies promulgate. Congress enacts a statute granting an agency the power to regulate—the enabling statute. This enabling statute defines the parameters of the administrative agency's regulatory power. So long as the agency stays within those parameters, judges generally afford agencies wide deference. So, for example, the Environmental Protection Agency (EPA) has the power to regulate all matters regarding environmental issues. When an agency steps outside of its parameters, however, any regulations are invalid. Thus, the EPA could not issue a regulation related to international trade.

Federal law of any kind trumps state law. The U.S. Constitution explicitly places federal law above state law, even state constitutions. Under the Supremacy Clause of the Constitution, federal law "preempts" state laws that conflicts with federal law. Thus, for example, if a federal statute required gasoline to be lead-free, a state law that permitted the sale of leaded gasoline would conflict with federal law, would be preempted, and would be unconstitutional.

Although occupying the lowest tier of our legal hierarchy, state law is the overwhelming source of most rights and obligations. Virtually all tort law, contract law, and property law comes from state statutes and state common law. State law comes in four forms: constitutions, statutes, regulations, and common law. Each state has its own constitution. Many of them differ in important respects from the U.S. Constitution, often by providing for greater protection than the federal Constitution. State constitutions can legitimately provide more protection to its state citizens than the U.S. Constitution; however, states cannot provide less protection.

Just as all state law must be constitutional under the U.S. Constitution, each statute a state legislature passes must also be constitutional under that state's constitution. A state statute that violates its state constitution is unconstitutional. Accordingly, state courts endeavor to interpret state statutes to be constitutional, just as federal courts do the same with respect to the Federal Constitution. And, similar to federal agencies, state agencies have the power to enact regulations. State law creates one additional issue that seldom arises in connection with construing federal statutes: State statutes can conflict with state common law. Thus, courts must determine how to interpret state statutes that conflict with state common law.

This section explores how courts interpret statutes in light of these hierarchies, starting with the constitutional avoidance doctrine.

1. The Constitutional Avoidance Doctrine

The *constitutional avoidance doctrine* is a statutory canon that respects this hierarchy. This canon directs that, when there are two reasonable interpretations of statutory language, one which raises constitutional issues and one which does not, the statute should be interpreted in a way that does not raise the constitutional issue. *Murray v. The Charming Betsy*, 6 U.S. (2 Cranch) 64, 118 (1804). Simply put: "A statute or rule is construed, if possible, to: ... avoid an unconstitutional ... result." UNIF. STATUTE & RULE CONSTR. ACT, §18(a3) (1995). When the court faces a question about the constitutionality of a statute, even if serious constitutional doubt is raised, the court will first ascertain whether another construction of the statute is *fairly possible* so that the constitutional question can be avoided.

This canon serves two purposes: first, it protects separation of powers. The court avoids declaring an act of Congress unconstitutional unless the court must. The rationale here is simple and reflects judicial respect for the legislature. Judges presume that Congress intended to enact a constitutional statute. They further presume that Congress did not intend to enact a statute that would raise questions about constitutional boundaries absent clear evidence that Congress meant to challenge those boundaries. Second, this canon furthers judicial economy. If the court need not determine whether a statute is constitutional, why should it bother? Note that this canon does not require a court to first find that an interpretation violates the constitution before adopting another interpretation; rather, this canon requires a court to find only that one interpretation would require the court to consider the constitutionality of the statute in question.

> [W]here a statute is susceptible of two constructions, by one of which grave and doubtful constitutional questions arise and by the other of which such questions are avoided, our duty is to adopt the later." This "cardinal principle," which "has for so long been applied by the Court that it is beyond debate," requires merely a determination of serious constitutional *doubt*, and not a determination of *unconstitutionality*. That must be so, of course, for otherwise the rule would "mea[n] that our duty is to first decide that a statute is unconstitutional and then

proceed to hold that such ruling was unnecessary because the statute is susceptible of a meaning, which causes it not to be repugnant to the Constitution."

Almendarez-Torres v. United States, 523 U.S. 224, 250 (1998) (internal citations omitted). Thus, a judge need not first, indeed should not first, reach the constitutional question. Rather, the constitutional issue need simply appear and then be avoided. This distinction is fundamental and often confuses judges.

How exactly does this canon work? In *United States v. Marshall*, 908 F.2d 1312, 1335 (7th Cir. 1990) (en banc), *aff'd sub nom Chapman v. United States*, 500 U.S. 453 (1991), the court had to interpret the federal sentencing guidelines, which set mandatory minimum terms of imprisonment for individuals who were caught selling drugs. According to the guidelines, anyone selling more than ten grams of a "mixture or substance containing a detectable amount" of a drug would be sentenced to a minimum of ten years, while those selling less than ten grams would be subject to a minimum of five years. The defendant was convicted of selling more than ten grams of LSD and was sentenced to twenty years. *Id.* at 1314. The issue for the court was whether the language of the statute—"mixture or substance containing a detectable amount of"—meant that the weight of a carrier mixed with the drug was included. Unlike other drugs such as cocaine, LSD is sold in a very heavy carrier such as orange juice or gelatin cubes. If the weight of the carrier were included, then LSD dealers would be subject to the higher penalty even if they sold a smaller total amount of the drug than other drug dealers. In fact, LSD dealers would be sentenced entirely based on the weight of the carrier because the weight of LSD itself is so small in comparison to its carrier. *Id.* at 1315.

The defendant argued that this interpretation of the statute would raise two constitutional questions: (1) whether the statute violated substantive due process because it penalized individuals without regard to the severity of the crime, and (2) whether the statute violated equal protection because it treated drug dealers differently based on a nonsensical distinction. *Id.* at 1320, 1322. The majority refused to apply the constitutional avoidance doctrine because the language of the statute was clear: "mixture" did not mean pure drug. *Id.* at 1318. Because the majority did not find that another interpretation was fairly possible, the majority adopted the interpretation that raised the constitutional questions.

In contrast, the dissent argued that the majority should have avoided the constitutional questions altogether by interpreting the language to exclude the carrier. Although admitting that his interpretation was not the *best* interpretation of the language, the dissent concluded that Congress likely did not understand how LSD was sold and, thus, probably did not intend to raise the constitutional issues that the majority's interpretation raised. *Id.* at 1331 (Posner, J., dissenting). Thus, the dissent believed that another interpretation was within a fair reading of the statute.

This case raises an important point. In theory, the constitutional avoidance canon should apply only if there are two *reasonable* and *fair* interpretations of a statute. Limiting the choice to interpretations that are fair and reasonable prevents the judiciary from rewriting the statute to mean something the legislature did not intend. This limit confines the judiciary to its proper constitutional role of construing statutes so as to give effect to congressional intent and words. But in reality judges often "do interpretive handsprings to avoid having even to *decide* a constitutional question." *Id.* at 1335.

In many cases, judges actually seem to accept any possible interpretation to avoid the constitutional issue, not just fair interpretations. For example, in *NLRB v. Catholic Bishop*, 440 U.S. 490 (1979), the majority refused to adopt an interpretation of the National Labor Relations Act that might violate the Constitution "if any other *possible construction* remain[ed] available." *Id.* at 500 (emphasis added). In this case, the Court was asked to determine whether the National Labor Relations Board, an agency, had jurisdiction over lay teachers who taught at church-operated schools. By its terms, the Act applied to all "employer[s]," defined as "any person acting as an agent of an employer, directly or indirectly...." *Id.* at 510 (Brennen, J., dissenting) (quoting 29 U.S.C. § 152(2)). Refusing to adopt the ordinary meaning of "employer" to include the church-operated schools, the majority required "a clear expression of Congress' intent to [raise Constitutional questions involving] the First Amendment Religion Clauses." *Id.* at 507. Finding no such showing, the majority concluded that "employer" must mean all employers *except* church-operated schools. *Id.* at 499. In sum, the majority refused to reach the constitutional question absent clear direction from Congress that it wanted the question addressed; hence, the majority adopted an interpretation that strained the fair meaning of the statute's text.

Critics of the constitutional avoidance canon suggest that when judges fail to adopt fair and reasonable interpretations, judges can be accused of rewriting the statute rather than interpreting it. This problem prompted Judge Easterbrook, a textualist, to write that the canon "is a closer cousin to invalidation than to interpretation," because a court can significantly alter a statute's meaning by applying it. *Marshall*, 908 F.2d at 1318. Yet, despite the criticism of this canon, it remains a powerful tool for avoiding the ordinary meaning of a statute.

2. The Rule of Lenity & Penal Statutes

While the constitutional avoidance doctrine is based on concerns about the Constitution as a whole, the next canon, the rule of lenity, is based on concerns about one particular provision in the Constitution: the Fifth (and Fourteenth) Amendment's guarantee of procedural due process—specifically, the right to notice. Pursuant to the *rule of lenity*, judges should strictly interpret penal statutes, which are statutes that impose a fine or imprisonment to punish citizens. Why? Historically, the rule of lenity flourished in seventeenth and eighteenth century England as a result of regulatory and statutory proliferation. Citizens grew nervous about the expansion of parliamentary power. English judges took on the role of guardian of individual liberty against legislative intrusions. One way judges could limit this expansion was by narrowly construing the language of criminal statutes.

In this country, the U.S. Constitution (and all state constitutions for that matter) requires notice before the government can deprive a person of a protected interest involving life, liberty, or property. If a statute does not clearly and unambiguously target specific conduct, an individual should not be penalized because that individual would not have had notice prior to the deprivation. Thus, the rule of lenity furthers the Constitution's promise that people should have fair warning of crimes before they are penalized. "[I]ndividuals should not languish in prison unless the legislature has clearly articulated precisely what conduct constitutes a crime." *United States v. Gonzalez*, 407 F.3d 118, 125 (2d Cir. 2005). Although ignorance of the law is no defense, in this country, Americans believe that those accused of crimes should have notice of what is illegal.

The rule of lenity also furthers a second consideration; one that relates to the power distribution between the judiciary and the legislature. Congress defines crimes in statutes; judges have no power to determine that an activity not clearly criminalized by statute should be penalized. In other words, if judges included activity not clearly covered in the statutory language, they would be expanding the statute's reach. "[L]egislatures and not courts should define criminal activity." *United States v. Bass*, 404 U.S. 336, 347–48 (1971). Thus, the rule of lenity furthers separation of powers and respects the constitutional power distribution.

Like the constitutional avoidance doctrine, this canon also requires that the two interpretations be *fair* or *reasonable* constructions of the statute. "[A]n appellate court should not strain to interpret a penal statute in defendant's favor if it can fairly discern a contrary legislative intent." *People v. Avery*, 38 P.3d 1, 6 (Cal. 2002). In the past, the rule of lenity was applied relatively often in criminal cases. For example, in *McNally v. United States*, 483 U.S. 350 (1987), the majority relied on the rule of lenity to reverse convictions of the defendants, who allegedly violated the federal mail fraud statute. That statute prohibited individuals from using the mail for "any scheme or artifice to defraud [individuals of] money or property...." *Id.* at 352 (quoting 18 U.S.C. § 1341). The government claimed that the defendants' alleged participation in a self-dealing patronage scheme defrauded the citizens and the state of the right to have the state's affairs conducted honestly. *Id.* The issue for the Court was whether the mail fraud statute, which explicitly protected money and property, also protected an intangible right of the citizenry to good government. Applying the rule of lenity, the majority held that it did not: "[W]hen there are two rational readings of a criminal statute, one harsher than the other, we are to choose the harsher only when Congress has spoken in clear and definite language." *Id.* at 360 (citing *Bass,* 404 U.S. at 347; *United States v. Universal C.I.T. Corp.,* 344 U.S. 218, 221–22 (1952)).

The dissent strongly disagreed. Arguing that the purpose of the mail fraud statute resolved any ambiguity, the dissent claimed that the rule of lenity was inapplicable. *Id.* at 375 (Stevens, J., dissenting). Because there was no ambiguity, the rule of lenity should not be applied. Oddly, in a footnote, the dissent implied that the rule of lenity might apply differently to educated defendants because they would be more likely to read statutes accurately. *Id.* at 375 n.9. While Justice Stevens might be correct that educated defendants are better able to understand the meaning of statutes, judges should not determine criminality based on class or education.

The rule of lenity applies to both criminal statutes and civil statutes that have a penal component. But in civil cases, judges are more reluctant to rely too heavily on the canon. For example, in *Babbitt v. Sweet Home Chapter,* 515 U.S. 687 (1995), the Court rejected the plaintiffs' rule of lenity challenge. In that case, the Court interpreted the Endangered Species Act, which penalized the "taking" of an endangered species. *Id.* at 690 (quoting 16 U.S.C. § 1532(9)(a)(1)). The term "take" was defined in the statute to mean "harass, *harm,* pursue, hunt, shoot, wound, kill, trap, capture, or collect, or to attempt to engage in any such conduct." *Id.* at 690-91 (quoting 16 U.S.C. § 1532(9)(a)(1)) (emphasis added). The Secretary of the Interior, the head of the agency in charge of implementing the Act, promulgated a regulation defining "harm" to include "significant habitat modification or degradation where it actually kills or injures wildlife." *Id.* at 691 (quoting 50 C.F.R. § 17.3 (1994)).

Logging companies and landowners in the Northwest sued, alleging that the Secretary's interpretation of the word "harm" was unlawful. They argued that the rule of lenity should apply because the civil statute imposed criminal penalties for violations. If the rule of lenity were applied, the plaintiffs contended

that the Court would find that the word "harm" was ambiguous and conse-
quently adopt the plaintiffs' interpretation; one that would minimize criminal penalties. The majority rejected this argument and held that the rule of
lenity should not apply in this case. "We have never suggested that the rule of
lenity should provide the standard for reviewing facial challenges to administrative regulations whenever the governing statute authorizes criminal enforcement." *Id.* at 704 n.18.

Notice also that a different result would have eviscerated another bedrock
of statutory interpretation you studied in Chapter 12: *Chevron* deference. Pursuant to *Chevron's* two step analysis, administrative agencies have the power to
interpret ambiguous statutes. In this case, the plaintiffs were asking the Court
to change that balance such that agencies could interpret ambiguous statutes
only if the statute did not include a penal element. This limitation would have
added even more complexity to agency deference, an already challenging area
of law. In any event, the Court rejected the proposed limit.

The question of exactly when to apply the rule of lenity is subject to some
controversy. Should a defendant "win" from the start if ambiguity appears on
the face of the statute or should all evidence of intent be explored first? In other
words, should the canon be a rule of first or last resort? While the canon may
have been applied as a rule of first resort in the past, today other sources of
meaning are usually explored before the canon is applied. The canon "is not
a catch-all maxim that resolves all disputes in the defendant's favor — a sort of
juristical 'tie goes to the runner.'" *United States v. Gonzalez*, 407 F.3d 118, 125
(2d Cir. 2005). Instead, many courts apply the canon, not when the statutory
text is ambiguous, but only when the ambiguity remains after the court has
examined all other sources of meaning, including legislative history and statutory purpose. *Reno v. Koray*, 515 U.S. 50, 65 (1995). The canon is reserved
"for those situations in which a reasonable doubt persists about a statute's intended scope even *after* resort to the language and structure, legislative history, and motivating policies of the statute." *Moskal v. United States*, 498 U.S.
103, 108 (1990). For example, in *Modern Muzzleloading, Inc. v. Magaw*, 18 F.
Supp. 2d 29 (D. D.C. 1998), the defendant manufactured and distributed
30,000 Knight Disc Rifles without a license, believing that the Gun Control
Act excluded them as "antique firearms." The agency charged with interpreting the Act determined that the rifles were not antique firearms. Modern Muzzleloading sued for a declaratory judgment that the rifles were exempt antiques.
The court denied the relief, reasoning that the statute was not "*grievously ambiguous.*" *Id.* at 33. The plaintiff argued that, because the statute was penal in
nature, the rule of lenity required that any ambiguity should be resolved in its
favor. The court disagreed and refused to apply the rule of lenity at all. Ac-

cording to the court, the plaintiff overstated the canon. *Id.* The point at which a judge should turn to the rule of lenity is when all other sources fail to resolve the ambiguity. In this case, the court resolved the ambiguity by using *in pari materia* and by looking at the statute as a whole. *Id.*

This case illustrates the difficulty with applying the canon solely as a method of last resort. Had the statute in *Modern Muzzleloading* been clear, the plaintiff would likely have complied: Why incur unnecessary fines? If the basis for the canon is fair notice, it appears disingenuous to require criminal defendants to read legislative history and determine statutory purpose to understand the meaning of the language used.

Judges and legislatures are less enthusiastic about the rule of lenity today than was true in the past. The rule of lenity has fallen so out of favor that some state legislatures, such as New York and California, have attempted to abrogate it by statute. For example, California's statute provides, "The rule of the common law, that penal statutes are to be strictly construed, has no application to this Code." CAL. PENAL CODE § 4 (West 2013). But because the rule of lenity rests on constitutional concerns, courts are understandably reluctant to eliminate it entirely. Thus, in New York, the Court of Appeals cautioned that "[a]lthough [the anti-lenity statute] obviously does not justify the imposition of criminal sanctions for conduct that falls beyond the scope of the Penal Law, it does authorize a court to dispense with hypertechnical or strained interpretations...." *People v. Ditta*, 422 N.E.2d 515, 517 (N.Y. 1981). Similarly, the California courts have explained that "while ... the rule of the common law ... has been abrogated ... it is also true that the defendant is entitled to the benefit of every reasonable doubt, whether it arises out of a question of fact, or as to the true interpretation of words or the construction of language used in a statute." *People v. Superior Court*, 926 P.2d 1042, 1056 (Cal. 1996) (internal citations omitted). In one famous case, in *Keeler v. Superior Court*, 470 P.2d 617 (Cal. 1970), the California Supreme Court applied the rule of lenity in a murder case, despite an earlier statute from 1871 that directed state courts not to construe criminal states narrowly. *Id.* at 623. Applying the rule in a case where the defendant kicked his wife in the stomach after learning she was pregnant, the court refused to interpret the term "human being" to include fetuses.

In contrast, the South Carolina Supreme Court refused to apply the rule of lenity to the word "child" in a child abuse and endangerment statute. *Whittner v. State*, 492 S.E.2d 777 (S.C. 1977). The mother had been convicted for smoking crack in her third trimester. The statute criminalized neglect of a "child," which was defined in another section of the children's code as "a person under the age of eighteen"; thus, the issue for the court should have been whether a fetus was a "person" under age eighteen. The majority focused on the word "child" instead, found it to be clear and unambiguous after a thorough analysis, and, therefore, refused to apply the rule of lenity. *Id.* at 784. Disagreeing by saying that the language was ambiguous, the dissent noted that the majority should have applied the rule of lenity: "I cannot accept the majority's assertion, that the child abuse and neglect statute unambiguously includes a 'viable fetus.' If that is the case, then why is the majority compelled to go to such great lengths to ascertain that a 'viable fetus' is a 'child?'" *Id.* at 787–88 (Fine, C.J., dissenting).

The rule of lenity generally remains viable in the federal arena although Congress attempted in at least one instance to limit its reach. The federal Racketeer Influenced and Corrupt Organization Act specifically directs that its "provisions ... be liberally construed to effectuate [the bill's] remedial purposes...." Pub. L. No. 91-452, § 904(a), 84 Stat. 922 (1970). Like the state courts, the federal courts have refused to apply this "anti-lenity" provision broadly, instead limiting its application to the civil aspects of the Act. *Keystone Ins. Co. v. Houghton*, 863 F.2d 1125, 1128 (3d Cir. 1988) ("[A]pplicability of the liberal construction standard has been questioned in *criminal* RICO cases in view of the general canon of interpretation that ambiguities in criminal statutes are to be construed in favor of leniency....") (emphasis added). Thus, at least in the criminal context, the rule of lenity can provide some powerful arguments for a criminal defendant. But a good prosecutor should be aware of the rule's limitations and current use as a canon of last resort.

3. Ex Post Facto Laws

We turn now to another policy-based constitutional consideration, the prohibition against *ex post facto*, or retrospective, laws. Like the rule of lenity, this canon is based on one specific section of the U.S. Constitution: Congress shall pass "[no] ... ex post facto law." U.S. Const. art. I, § 9, cl. 3. In Chapter 8, we discussed retroactivity in regard to civil cases. This section addresses retroactivity in regard to criminal cases.

Ex post facto is Latin for "something done afterwards." An *ex post facto* law is impermissible if it is both retroactive and disadvantageous to a defendant. An *ex post facto* statute is a statute that changes the legal consequences of an action after the action has occurred, specifically, by redefining criminal conduct or by increasing the penalty for criminal conduct. There are four types of *ex post facto* statutes: (1) those criminalizing actions that were legal when committed; (2) those altering the nature of a crime so that it is categorized more severely than it was when committed; (3) those increasing the punishment prescribed for a crime; and (4) those altering the rules of evidence to make conviction easier. *Calder v. Bull*, 3 U.S. (3 Dall.) 386 (1798). The two purposes behind the *ex post facto* prohibition are to prevent legislatures from enacting vindictive laws to punish individuals and to ensure that statutes give fair notice of their legal effect. The canon shares this latter purpose with the rule of lenity.

Retroactive effect is not enough to make a law unconstitutional. A law may have *retroactive* effect and still not be an impermissible *ex post facto* law. To be an impermissible *ex post facto* law, the statute must punish defendants for prior actions. For example, the Adam Walsh Child Protection and Safety Act of 2006, Pub. L. No. 109-248, 120 Stat. 587 (2006), requires convicted sex offenders to register in a database. When enacted, it applied retroactively. In *Smith v. Doe*, 538 U.S. 84 (2003), the Supreme Court held that the Act did not violate the *ex post facto* clause because compulsory registration was not a punishment. *Id.* at 105.

Similarly, the Domestic Violence Offender Gun Ban of 1996, 18 U.S.C. § 922(g)(9), prohibits persons who are convicted of misdemeanor domestic violence and who are subject to a restraining order from owning guns or ammunition. When enacted, it also applied retroactively. Persons convicted of violating the Act could be sentenced to up to ten years for possessing a firearm, regardless of whether they legally possessed the weapon at the time the law was passed. In *United States v. Brady*, 26 F.3d 282 (2d Cir. 1994), *cert. denied*, 513 U.S. 894 (1994), the court denied an *ex post facto* challenge because the Act was considered regulatory, not punitive—in other words, violation of the Act was a status offense, not a punishment.

You can see that determining whether a statute is an *ex post facto* law, meaning it has punitive effect, is challenging. Even judges do not always agree. In *People v. Leroy*, 828 N.E.2d 786 (Ill. App. Ct. 2005), the Illinois Court of Appeals addressed this issue in determining whether a statute that limited where convicted sex offenders could live was an *ex post facto* law. As a child, the defendant had been convicted of a sexual offense. He later pled guilty for failing to register as a sex offender and was sentenced to one year's probation. While on probation, he lived in his mother's house, which was located near an elementary school. A statute, which was enacted after his underlying criminal conviction, prohibited convicted sex offenders from "knowingly resid[ing] within 500 feet of a playground or a facility providing programs or services exclusively directed toward persons under 18 years of age." *Id.* at 533 (quoting 720 Ill. Comp. Stat. 5/11-9.4(b-5)). The State sought to revoke his probation because he violated this statute.

The defendant admitted violating the statute but argued that the statute was an unconstitutional *ex post facto* law because the statute increased the penalty he received for his underlying conviction. The appellate court disagreed, holding instead that (1) the legislature intended to enact a regulatory scheme, not to punish individuals, and (2) the effect of the law was not so punitive that it prevented the State from creating civil restrictions. Therefore, the statute was not an impermissible *ex post facto* law. *Id.* at 469. Disagreeing, the dissent claimed that "a punitive effect unquestionably flow[ed] from this enactment [and violated the] constitutional guarantee against the imposition of *ex post facto* punishment." *Id.* at 475 (Kuehn, J., dissenting).

A question arises when courts change their prior interpretation of a criminal statute. Does doing so violate the *ex post facto* clause? In *Michigan v. Schaeffer*, 703 N.W.2d 774 (Mich. 2005), the Michigan Supreme Court tackled this question. In that case, the defendant struck and killed an eleven-year-old girl while he was driving drunk. He was charged with driving while intoxicated *"by the operation of that motor vehicle caus[ing] the death of another person."* *Id.* at 781 (quoting MICH. COMP. LAWS § 257.625(4)). In an earlier case, the Michigan Supreme Court had held that "the people must establish that the particular defendant's decision to drive while intoxicated produced a change in that driver's operation of the vehicle that caused the death of the victim." *Id.* at 781–82 (quoting *People v. Lardie*, 551 N.W.2d 656, 668 (Mich. 1996)). At the preliminary hearing in *Schaeffer*, the prosecutor's expert testified that it was irrelevant that the defendant was drunk because the accident was unavoidable. *Id.* at 779. Thus, the defendant moved to dismiss the charges against him. In response, the State argued that *Lardie* should be overruled. The majority agreed, finding that the language of the statute clearly stated that "the defendant's *operation* of the motor vehicle ... must cause the victim's death, not the defendant's 'intoxication.'" *Id.* at 783. Despite changing the interpretation, the majority did not find an *ex post facto* concern because the court concluded that it was merely correcting its prior, erroneous interpretation. The corrected interpretation should have been clear from the statute's face. "[I]t is not 'indefensible or unexpected' that a court would ... overrule a case that failed to abide by the express terms of a statute." *Id.* at 790 n.80.

The concurring judge disagreed. He argued that the court had already interpreted the statute in such a way that the majority's new interpretation criminalized behavior that was not criminal when performed. *Id.* at 793 (Cavanagh, J., concurring in part and dissenting in part). Thus, the new interpretation violated the *ex post facto* clause. The concurrence argued that if the legislature had responded to *Lardie* by enacting a statute that mirrored the majority's interpretation and had done so after the defendant hit the child, the statute would be an impermissible *ex post facto* law. Thus, because the legislature could not change the law without violating the *ex post facto* clause, the court should similarly not be able to do so. *Id.* at 794. But few courts feel so bound.

Hence, the legislature cannot enact statutes that have retroactive punitive effects without violating the *ex post facto* clause of the U.S. Constitution. The challenge, of course, is determining exactly when a statute has a punitive, rather than regulatory, effect.

4. Clear Statement Rules

Where a statute can be interpreted to abridge long-held individual or states' rights, or when it appears that a legislature has made a large policy change, courts will generally not interpret the statute to abridge those rights or make that change unless the legislature was clear about its intention. The requirement of a clear, or plain, statement is based on the simple assumption that a legislature would not make major policy changes without being absolutely clear about doing so. Thus, courts require clear statements to encourage the legislature to explicitly indicate that it wants a change in the status quo.

Courts tend to require clear statements to maintain under-enforced constitutional traditions. Above, we saw two examples of when courts require clear statement rules: the constitutional avoidance doctrine and the rule of lenity. Below, we turn to four additional areas of important concern: federalism, preemption, American Indian rights, and sovereign immunity. We will look at each in turn. You should be aware, however, that clear statement rules have a role in many areas of statutory interpretation. We are looking at just a few of those areas so that you understand what a court means when the court requires the legislature to be clear about what the legislature intends.

a. Federalism

Our nation is made up of one federal government and fifty state governments. At times, the laws of the two sovereigns conflict. The principle of federalism respects the sovereignty of each state from federal intrusion. Judges will not interpret statutes to burden state sovereignty unless Congress clearly expresses the intent to do so. The requirement of a clear statement respects federalism because Congress must be clear when it wishes to impact areas of traditional state power, such as land management and taxation.

> Federal statutes impinging upon important state interests "cannot ... be construed without regard to the implications of our dual system of government.... [W]hen the Federal Government takes

over … local radiations in the vast network of our national economic enterprise and thereby radically readjusts the balance of state and national authority, those charged with the duty of legislating (must be) reasonably explicit."

BFP v. Resolution Trust Corp., 511 U.S. 531, 544 (1994) (quoting Felix Frankfurter, *Some Reflections on the Reading of Statutes*, 47 COLUM. L. REV. 527, 539–540 (1947)).

For example, "[r]egulation of land [and water] use … is a quintessential state and local power." *Rapanos v. United States*, 547 U.S. 715 (2006). If Congress wants to encroach on this traditional and primary state power, then Congress should say so very clearly. In 1972, Congress enacted the Clean Water Act, which made it illegal to discharge dredged or fill material into "navigable waters" without a permit. "Navigable waters" are defined as "the waters of the United States, including the territorial seas." *Id.* at 760 (quoting 33 U.S.C. §§ 1362(7) & (12)). The Army Corps of Engineers had interpreted "the waters of the United States" very broadly to include not only waters that were navigable but also "[t]ributaries of such waters" and "'wetlands' adjacent to such waters and tributaries." *Id.* at 724 (quoting 33 CFR §§ 328.3(a)(5) & (7)). In essence, the Corps interpreted the language broadly to include any waters that might ultimately enter navigable waters. In *Rapanos*, the Supreme Court had to consider whether four Michigan wetlands, which lay near ditches and man-made drains that would eventually empty into traditional navigable waters constituted "waters of the United States" within the meaning of the Act. The majority rejected the Corps's interpretation as unreasonable. The Court in *Rapanos* noted that it ordinarily required a "'clear and manifest'" statement from Congress to authorize an unprecedented intrusion into traditional state authority. [And t]he phrase 'the waters of the United States' hardly qualifie[d]." *Id.* at 738.

b. Preemption

Clear statements are also required in the area of preemption. Judges presume that state law is not preempted absent a clear statement from Congress to this effect. Preemption is the displacing effect that federal law has on conflicting or inconsistent state law. Preemption occurs because the Supremacy Clause in the Constitution states that "[t]he Laws of the United States, (which shall be made in Pursuance to the Constitution), shall be the supreme Law of the land." U.S. CONST. art. VI, § 2. Thus, if there is a conflict between state and federal law, federal law preempts state law.

Preemption is an enormously complicated area of law, which we need not delve into too deeply here. It is sufficient for you to know that there is a presumption in favor of the applicability of state law and against preemption. Courts presume that Congress generally does not intend to preempt state law when a enacting federal law; thus, Congress must provide a clear statement that it intended to preempt state law:

> "In all pre-emption cases, and particularly in those in which Congress has 'legislated ... in a field which the States have traditionally occupied,'... we 'start with the assumption that the historic police powers of the States were not to be superseded by the Federal Act unless that was the clear and manifest purpose of Congress.'"

Medtronic, Inc. v. Lohr, 518 U.S. 470, 485 (1996) (quoting *Rice* v. *Santa Fe Elevator Corp.*, 331 U.S. 218, 230 (1947)).

Sometimes, Congress includes a specific preemption clause in the act at issue, which makes the preemption question relatively easy. For example, the Supreme Court held that the Medical Device Amendments Act of 1976 preempted state common-law claims challenging the safety and effectiveness of any medical device approved by the Federal Drug Administration. *Riegel v. Medtronic, Inc.*, 552 U.S. 312 (2008). The Act contained a clause that expressly preempted state requirements that differed from federal law. *Id.* at 330 (citing 21 U.S.C. §360k(a)(1)).

But Congress is not always so clear about its intent. What if Congress is not clear? When possible, courts generally try to reconcile seemingly inconsistent state and federal laws. But reconciliation is not always possible. For example, in *Wyeth v. Levine*, 555 U.S. 555 (2009), the Supreme Court had to determine whether the federal Food, Drug, and Cosmetic Act ("FDCA"), which did not include a preemption provision, impliedly preempted state tort law. *Id.* at 560–61. The plaintiff in the case had lost her arm after she was injected with the defendant's anti-nausea drug. Although the label warned of this risk, the plaintiff argued that under state tort law the defendant should not have allowed the drug to be used intravenously, even with the labeling. The FDCA outlined a comprehensive process for approving drug labels. The drug manufacturer-defendant argued that the FDCA's labeling process preempted state tort law for two reasons. First, the defendant raised the issue of "impossibility preemption" and argued that it was impossible to comply with both the labeling requirements and state tort law. The Court rejected this argument, noting that the defendant "failed to demonstrate that it was impossible for it to comply with both federal and state requirements." *Id.* at 574–75.

Second, the defendant argued that the state tort claims were preempted because allowing state tort claims to apply would interfere with "Congress's purpose to entrust an expert agency to make drug labeling decisions that strike a balance between competing objectives." *Id.* at 574. The Court similarly rejected this argument, in part, because Congress had enacted a preemption provision in a related area, the Medical Device Amendments Act:

> "The case for federal pre-emption is particularly weak where Congress has indicated its awareness of the operation of state law in a field of federal interest, and has nonetheless decided to stand by both concepts and to tolerate whatever tension there [is] between them."

Id. at 575 (quoting *Bonito Boats, Inc. v. Thunder Craft Boats, Inc.*, 489 U.S. 141, 166–67 (1989) (internal quotation marks omitted). In sum, the Court held that the FDCA's regulatory approval process did not preempt state tort law.

Disliking this second analysis, Justice Thomas wrote separately to criticize the majority for routinely invalidating state laws based on perceived conflicts with broad federal policy objectives, legislative history, and statutory purposes that are not contained within the text of federal law. *Id.* at 582 (Thomas, J., concurring). For Justice Thomas, preemption can be implied only through a textual analysis.

Lastly, even in the absence of any clear statement that Congress intended to "occupy the field" of a particular area, courts will be more likely to find that federal law preempts state law if the state law touches upon an area that has historically implicated a strong federal interest, such as banking, interstate commerce, or foreign affairs.

c. American Indian Treaty Rights

Clear statements are also required when Congress impacts American Indian treaty rights by diminishing native lands. Not only are we a nation with various sovereigns, we are a nation within a nation. American Indian lands should be protected from unnecessary federal intrusion and diminishment. The *diminishment doctrine* was established to distinguish between those statutes that removed lands from a reservation from those statutes that merely made surplus lands available for settlement within a reservation. Courts require a clear statement when Congress "diminishes" reservation boundaries by statute. *Hagen v. Utah*, 510 U.S. 399, 411 (1993).

Further, when a statute has two possible interpretations, the non-diminishment interpretation should govern. Courts presume that Congress would not have wanted to diminish the reservation boundaries without being explicit. Thus, in *Solem v. Bartlett*, 465 U.S. 463 (1984), the Supreme Court held that there was no such clear statement to reduce the Cheyenne River Sioux Reservation in the Cheyenne River Act, despite language describing opened areas as being in "the public domain" and describing unopened areas as comprising "the reservation thus diminished." *Id.* at 475–76. This language simply was not clear enough to imply diminishment. Additionally, the Act had been enacted at a time when the word "diminished" was not yet a term of art in American Indian law. *Id.* at 476 n.17. Finally, the Court found that there was no clear congressional purpose to reduce the reservation. *Id.* at 476.

d. Sovereign Immunity

Clear statement rules are also used to protect sovereign immunity. Sovereign immunity is a judge-made doctrine that dates from the beginning of our nation's birth. The doctrine is fairly straightforward: the federal government, or sovereign, may not be sued without its consent. To further this doctrine, federal courts developed two statutory interpretation principles to determine whether a statute waives immunity. The first principle is that a statutory waiver of sovereign immunity must be definitely and unequivocally expressed. In other words, Congress must provide a clear statement that Congress intended to waive sovereign immunity. The second principle is that if a waiver is found, a court must construe the waiver narrowly in favor of the government.

These presumptions are so strong that they can trump other canons. For example, in *Burch v. Secretary of Health & Human Services*, No. 99-946V, 2001 WL 180129 (Fed. Cl. Feb. 8, 2001), the court refused to give the word "received" its ordinary meaning because the language at issue came from a statute implicating sovereign immunity. In that case, a child was allegedly injured when her mother received a vaccine while the child was *in utero*. A statute allowed anyone who had "received" a vaccine and been injured as a result to sue the federal government. Although the parties stipulated that the vaccine could have caused the child's injuries, the court denied the claim. Despite the fact that Congress waived immunity very clearly for anyone injured as a result of receiving a vaccine, the court interpreted the term "received" in the statute very narrowly. *Id.* According to the court, the narrow interpretation was warranted pursuant to the second principle of this doctrine: Statutes that waive sovereign immunity must be interpreted narrowly in favor of the government.

Thus, when a statute could be interpreted to abridge federalism, to preempt state law, to diminish American Indian lands, or to waive sovereign immunity, courts generally require the statute to express clearly the legislature's intention to impact these rights. Additionally, courts require clear statements in other situations not explored here. Clear statement rules place the burden on Congress to be clear in its drafting, but such rules can also frustrate Congress's intent by requiring such meticulousness. It is questionable whether the Supreme Court has the power to demand clear statements when the Constitution does not require Congress to write laws in this way.

D. Canons Based on Prudential Considerations

We move now away from the constitutional-based considerations and into the prudential-based considerations. Here, the constitution is not the star; rather, concerns about the interplay between the common law and statutes are center-front. We will begin with two related canons: (1) courts should strictly construe statutes in derogation of the common law, and (2) courts should broadly construe remedial statutes. These rules sound easy in theory, but it can be difficult to tell whether a statute is remedial or in derogation of the common law. These two canons have particular force in states because there is limited federal common law.

1. Statutes in Derogation of the Common Law

Courts should strictly construe statutes in derogation of the common law. A statute is in derogation of the common law when the statute partially repeals or abolishes existing common law rights or otherwise limits the scope, utility, or force of that common law right. BLACK's LAW DICTIONARY 476 (8th ed. 2004).

For example, statutes that alter existing property rights are in derogation of the common law. Another example is wrongful death statutes. Before wrongful death statutes existed, the common law did not recognize the existence of a wrongful death claim because any claim died with the victim, and there is no way to compensate a dead victim. Thus, under the common law, no surviving family members could seek damages from the person who caused the victim's death. But this common law rule led to odd results—a tortfeasor would be off the hook if the victim died, but not if the victim lived. For this reason, England enacted Lord Campbell's Act in 1846: the first "wrongful death statute" that allowed relatives who were damaged by the death of the victim to sue the tortfeasor despite the victim's death. American states quickly followed suit. But these wrongful death statutes were in derogation of the common law; thus, the early thought was that they should be strictly construed. In *Boroughs v. Oliver*, 64 So. 2d 338 (Miss. 1953), the Mississippi Supreme Court narrowly construed the word "parent" in its wrongful death statute to prevent adoptive parents from suing for the negligent death of their son. *Id.* at 314. Shortly after that case, the Mississippi legislature corrected this absurdly narrow reading. MISS. CODE ANN. § 11-7-13 (2004) ("Any rights which a blood parent or parents may have under this section are hereby conferred upon and vested in an adopting parent or adopting parents surviving their deceased adopted child, just as if the child were theirs by the full blood and had been born to the adopting parents in lawful wedlock.")

But a bigger question is why should statutes in derogation of the common law be strictly construed? Basically, the answer to this question is power. Before the 1900s, common law was more prevalent than statutory law. Hence, statutes were viewed with suspicion:

> Statutes then were not created from common law methodology. Indeed, 18th century judges felt them rather subject to tyrannical majorities and shifting whims. England had suffered through the civil wars of the Seventeenth Century and the abuses of unchecked majorities in Parliament. The beheading of Charles I was followed by the post-restoration instability leading to the Glorious Revolution in 1685. [Judges] viewed the common law as a source of social stability, cast from the wisdom of the ages and forged in cases evolving over the long sweep of history. Statutes often emerged from ephemeral, narrow and parochial interests, but the common law was eternal and universal.

Blankfeld v. Richmond Health Care, Inc., 902 So. 2d 296, 305 (Fla. Dist. Ct. App. 2005) (Farmer, J., concurring).

Not only were statutes viewed with suspicion, but those statutes that did exist were either very narrow, were limited exceptions to existing common law, or were narrow corrections of common law. Hence, judges developed the canon that statutes in derogation of the common law should be strictly construed. A common articulation of the canon from that time is as follows: "No statute is to be construed as altering the common law, farther than its words import." *Shaw v. Merchants' Nat. Bank*, 101 U.S. (11 Otto) 557, 565 (1879). Thus, the derogation canon is best understood as reflecting the early reluctance of American courts to allow legislatures to restrict common law rights. Because there is very little federal common law, this canon is generally implicated only when state statutes modify state common law.

But in the twentieth century, a power struggle ensued. Wishing to increase its lawmaking power, legislatures enacted more statutes. Wishing to maintain the power it had, the judiciary limited the breadth of those statutes with the derogation canon. If the legislature failed to clearly address an issue, then that issue fell into the judiciary's jurisdiction. Eventually, the legislature won this battle; today, statutes create most rights and responsibilities, while common law acts as the gap filler. As a consequence, the usefulness of the derogation rule of statutory construction has waned.

But one area in which it has, at least briefly, reemerged is in tort reform, which, by definition, is in derogation of common law tort rights and remedies. For example, early wrongful death statutes limited recovery to actual damages. Should more modern wrongful death statutes be limited similarly? This was the issue in two similar cases: *Behrens v. Raleigh Hills Hospital, Inc.*, 675 P.2d 1179 (Utah 1983) and *Cohen v. Rubin*, 460 A.2d 1046 (Md. Ct. Spec. App. 1983). The courts in these cases reached opposite results based on their decisions to either apply or not apply the derogation canon. In *Behrens*, the Utah Supreme Court rejected the canon and allowed the award of punitive damages in a wrongful death case even though the statute did not specifically provide for punitive damages. 675 P.2d at 1179. In contrast, in *Cohen*, the Maryland Court of Appeals applied the canon and prohibited the damages, despite a virtually identical statute. 460 A.2d at 1046. Application of the canon was, therefore, outcome determinative.

Today, many states have abolished the derogation canon. For example, a Kentucky statute provides: "All statutes of this state shall be liberally construed with a view to promote their objects and carry out the intent of the legislature, and the rule that statutes in derogation of the common law are to be strictly construed shall not apply to the statutes of this state." KY. REV. STAT. ANN. § 446.080(1) (West 2008). Thus, this canon is less useful to litigants than it once was. In contrast, the remedial canon, which we will address next, remains more firmly a factor.

2. Remedial Statutes

One purpose of the derogation canon was to prevent a legislature from unintentionally abrogating rights the common law granted. Remember, prior to the twentieth century, legislatures focused on running the government, not making law. So, when a legislature did enact statutes, many of those statutes were designed to remedy errors in the common law. These statutes were specific, narrow, and limited in application. A statute passed to repair the common law was not *in derogation* of the common law, but rather was *in aid* of the common law. Hence, courts did not view such statutes with suspicion because common law remained supreme. Courts interpreted these "remedial statutes," as they were known, liberally, not narrowly, to achieve the statutory purpose. *Chrisom v. Roemer*, 501 U.S. 380, 403 (1991); *Smith v. Brown*, 35 F.3d 1516, 1525 (Fed. Cir. 1994).

In addition to corrective statutes, remedial statutes include those statutes that create new rights or expand remedies that were otherwise unavailable at common law. For example, a tax statute would not be remedial, while a statute intended to protect civil rights would be. While this definition seems clear, in reality the distinction between remedial and non-remedial is more elusive. "[I]t is not at all apparent just what is and what is not remedial legislation; indeed all legislation might be thought remedial in some sense — even massive codifications." *Ober United Travel Agency, Inc. v. U.S. Dep't of Labor*, 135 F.3d 822, 825 (D.C. Cir. 1998). For example, if we return to the wrongful death cases above, a wrongful death statute may be remedial as to a plaintiff because it adds a cause of action or measure of damages otherwise lost, but non-remedial as to the defendant, who would have been exempt from liability under common law. Thus, some states consider wrongful death statutes to be remedial, such as Wyoming and Rhode Island. *See, e.g., Corkill v. Knowles*, 955 P.2d 438, 442 (Wyo. 1998); *O'Sullivan v. Rhode Island Hosp.*, 874 A.2d 179, 183 (R.I. 2005). Other states, such as Arkansas and Maryland, consider wrongful death statutes to be in derogation of the common law. *See, e.g., Cockrum v. Fox*, 199 S.W.3d 69, 73 (Ark. 2004) (Thornton, J., dissenting); *Cohen v. Rubin*, 460 A.2d 1046, 1056 (Md. Ct. Spec. App. 1983).

Many statutes today are remedial in nature, enacted to solve a problem the legislature identified, so this canon has particular force. Yet, interpreting remedial statutes broadly may conflict with the plain meaning canon or other canons. For example, in *Burch v. Secretary of Health & Human Services*, No. 99-946V, 2001 WL 180129 (Fed. Cl. Feb. 8 2001), the court rejected the ordinary meaning of the word "received" and refused to interpret the statute broadly despite the remedial nature of the act at issue because another canon urged a narrow reading of the statute. In that case, the plaintiff-mother had been given a vaccine through injection while she was pregnant that allegedly injured her child. The court acknowledged that pursuant to the ordinary meaning of "received," the child had received the vaccine. Moreover, the court concluded that the statute was remedial. *Id.* Despite these two findings, the court denied the claim, narrowly construing the statute because it implicated sovereign immunity. *Id.*

3. Implied Causes of Action & Remedies

Our next topic is, in many ways, at the cutting edge of statutory interpretation. Implied causes of action and remedies are just that, implied. Because neither is explicitly set forth in the statute, their existence confounds textualists. As such, the current movement is to deny the existence of new implied actions and restrict the reach of those already in existence, as we will see below.

a. Implied Causes of Action

An implied cause of action exists when a court determines that even though a statute does not expressly grant private parties the right to sue, the statute implicitly does so. In early English common law, private lawsuits were the primary method of enforcing common law and statutes. WILLIAM ESKRIDGE, JR. ET AL., CASES AND MATERIALS ON LEGISLATION: STATUTES AND THE CREATION OF PUBLIC POLICY 1110 (3d ed. 2001). Early American courts adopted this presumption. When Congress drafted a statute protecting important interests, courts readily assumed private individuals had the ability to enforce those rights in court.

But after the New Deal, agencies were delegated the responsibility of enforcing many of these rights; thus, private rights of action became less necessary and, over time, were implied from statutes less often. Over the past half century, the Supreme Court has taken three different approaches to implied causes of action; each approach has more severely limited the availability of implied causes of action.

The most liberal approach is illustrated by *J.I. Case Co. v. Borak*, 377 U.S. 426 (1964). In that case, the Court had to decide whether the Securities Exchange Act of 1934 allowed a private right of action when none was expressly provided in the Act. Examining the Act's legislative history and purposes, the Court held that a private right of action should be implied. The Court believed that it was "the duty of the courts to be alert to provide such remedies as are necessary to make effective the congressional purpose." *Id.* at 433. This case was decided long before new textualism refocused attention on text. The case also offered a somewhat simplistic rationale, "for it assume[d] that more enforcement is always better." ESKRIDGE ET AL., CASES AND MATERIALS ON LEGISLATION, *supra*, at 1111. Beginning in 1975, the Court began to retreat from this simplistic approach to implied remedies.

More than ten years after *Borak*, the Court rejected the idea that a private cause of action was always necessary to further the purposes of a statute. In *Cort v. Ash*, 422 U.S. 66 (1975), the Court retreated from the broad language of *Borak*. The issue in *Cort* was whether a civil cause of action existed under a criminal statute prohibiting corporations from making contributions to a presidential campaign. The Court held that a civil action should not be implied. In doing so, the Court identified four factors to consider when deciding whether a statute implicitly included a private cause of action. *Id.* at 78. These factors included the following:

1. Whether the plaintiff was within the class of persons "for whose especial benefit" the statute was enacted,
2. Whether the legislative history showed that Congress intended to create or deny a private cause of action,
3. Whether an implied cause of action would be consistent with the underlying purposes of the statute, and
4. Whether the issue would be one that is traditionally left to state law.

THE
CORT
FACTORS

Cort is easily distinguishable from *Borak* because *Cort* involved a criminal statute. Criminal statutes are generally drafted to protect the rights of the general public rather than the rights of individuals, so choosing not to imply a civil cause of action made sense.

For several years after *Cort*, the Supreme Court applied its four-part test and generally refused to create implied causes of action. A notable exception was the case of *Cannon v. University of Chicago*, 441 U.S. 677 (1979), in which the Court recognized an implied private cause of action for intentional actions under Title IX of the Education Amendments of 1972, which prohibited sex discrimination in federally funded programs. *Id.* at 695. However, Justice Powell, in dissent, criticized the majority's decision and the idea of implied causes of action in general. Powell believed that the Court's test for implied causes of action violated separation of powers. *Id.* at 730 (Powell, J., dissenting). Congress, not the judiciary, had the power to create causes of action. Therefore, absent evidence that Congress intended to create a private cause of action, none should be implied. "Absent the most compelling evidence of affirmative congressional intent, a federal court should not infer a private cause of action." *Id.* at 731.

Despite Powell's heartfelt dissent, *Cannon* was reaffirmed in *Jackson v. Birmingham Bd. of Education*, 544 U.S. 167 (2005), in which the Court allowed a private individual to sue for sex-based *retaliation* under Title IX, which prohibits discrimination based on "sex." One might question whether the Court created a new implied cause of action or simply expanded an existing one because the cause of injury was different. In *Cannon*, the plaintiff was discriminated against because of her sex. In *Jackson*, the plaintiff, a male, was discriminated against because *other people*, the members of the women's basketball team, were discriminated against because of their sex. Apparently, the majority believed that it was merely exploring the contours of an existing cause of action, for the majority never discussed *Cort* or *Alexander*. Justice Thomas, in dissent, criticized the majority's choice to contradict the text of the statute: "[The majority's] holding is contrary to the plain terms of Title IX, because retaliatory conduct is not discrimination on the basis of sex." *Id.* at 184 (Thomas, J., dissenting).

Soon after *Cannon* was decided, the Court adopted a new approach to implying causes of action in *Touche Ross & Co. v. Remington*, 442 U.S. 560 (1979). The issue before the Court was whether another section of the Securities Exchange Act of 1934 had an implied cause of action. The Court apparently agreed with Justice Powell's *Cannon* dissent. While the Court mentioned all of the *Cort* factors, it suggested that the first three were relevant only because they showed legislative intent. "The ultimate question is one of congressional intent, not one of whether this Court thinks that it can improve upon the statutory scheme that Congress enacted into law." *Id.* at 576. Thus, the *Cort* factors were relevant, but only to the extent that they illustrated congressional intent. This case was decided when many of the Justices were intentionalists.

Then, after Justice Scalia's ascendancy to the bench, the Court refined the implied rights doctrine once more. In *Alexander v. Sandoval*, 532 U.S. 275 (2001), the Court held that there was no private cause of action to enforce disparate-impact regulations promulgated under Title VI of the Civil Rights Act of 1964. *Id.* at 285. Justice Scalia, writing for the majority, reiterated *Touche's* focus on legislative intent; however, he added his own twist: "We therefore begin (and find that we can end) our search for Congress's intent with the text and structure of Title VI." *Id.* at 288. In other words, even though the statute at issue had been enacted during a time when the Court easily implied private rights of action (the *Borak* era), even though the enacting Congress might thus have anticipated that the Court would imply a cause of action in this statute, and even though implied rights are by their very nature *non-explicit*, Justice Scalia used a textualist approach to determine whether Congress intended the act in question to allow private causes of action. In essence, Justice Scalia obliterated the concept of *implied* private causes of action. In dissent, Justice Stevens noted: "[T]oday's decision is the unconscious product of the majority's profound distaste for implied causes of action rather than an attempt to discern the intent of the Congress that enacted Title VI of the Civil Rights Act of 1964." *Id.* at 317 (Stevens, J., dissenting).

The current tension amongst Justices in this area is demonstrated in *CBOCS West, Inc. v. Humphries*, 533 U.S. 442 (2008). In this case, the plaintiff alleged that he was fired after he complained that another employee was fired because of race. Section 1981 of the Civil Rights Act provides that all persons "shall have the same right in every State and Territory to make and enforce contracts ... as is enjoyed by white citizens...." 42 U.S.C. § 1981(a). Employment is considered a contract, so the employee who was fired because of his race would have been covered under the Act. This case raised the question of whether an employee who was fired for whistleblowing could bring a claim for *retaliation* under Section 1981. Relevantly, the Court had held, in an earlier case, that a companion statute to section 1981, 42 U.S.C. §1982 ("section 1982"), included a prohibition against retaliation for advocating for the rights of those section 1982 protects. *Sullivan v. Little Hunting Park, Inc.*, 396 U.S. 229, 237 (1969). Because sections 1981 and 1982 were enacted together, the plaintiff argued that the statutes should be interpreted similarly. The majority agreed and held that Section 1981 did encompass retaliation claims. Not surprisingly, the textualists on the Court, Justices Thomas and Scalia, dissented from the majority decision finding an implied cause of action. *CBOCS West*, 553 at 456–47. (Thomas, J., dissenting). Indeed, Justice Scalia stated at oral argument: "We inferred that cause of action [for section 1982] in the bad old days, when we were inferring causes of action all over the place." Transcript of Oral Argument at 45, *CBOCS West, Inc. v. Humphries*, 553 U.S. 442 (2008).

It is unclear whether the Supreme Court will continue to apply such a strict approach to implied causes of action. With the renewed focus on the text of the statute, however, it is likely that implied actions will not become more common.

b. Implied Remedies

"[A] right without a remedy is not a right at all." *Doe v. Cnty of Centre*, 242 F.3d 437, 456 (3d Cir. 2001). Thus, once a cause of action has been implied, courts must determine which, if any, remedies are available. After *Cannon* was decided, the Supreme Court addressed the issue of whether the remedy for Title IX's implied cause of action included recovery of money damages or was limited to injunctive relief. In a later case, the Court held that monetary damages were recoverable. *Franklin v. Gwinnett Cnty. Pub. Sch.*, 503 U.S. 60, 66 (1992). The Court indicated that it would "presume the availability of all appropriate remedies unless Congress has expressly indicated otherwise." *Id.* (internal citations omitted). It might be hard to find that "Congress has expressly indicated otherwise" when Congress does not expressly grant a private cause of action!

The plaintiff in *Franklin*, a student at the public high school, was the subject of inappropriate and unwanted sexual advances by one of her teachers. According to the student, the school failed to take any action other than discouraging her from filing charges. *Id.* at 64. By the time the case was heard, both the student and the teacher had left the school. Hence, injunctive relief would not have benefited this particular student. In holding that all forms of relief were available unless Congress had indicated otherwise, the *Franklin* majority was quick to distinguish its evolving test for finding implied remedies. "[T]he question whether a litigant has a 'cause of action' is analytically distinct and prior to the question of what relief, if any, a litigant may be entitled to receive." *Id.* at 69 (internal quotation marks omitted). Because the Court had implied a cause of action in its *Cannon* decision, the legislative silence surrounding available remedies did not trouble the *Franklin* majority. "Since the Court in *Cannon* concluded that this statute supported no express right of action, it is hardly surprising that Congress also said nothing about the applicable remedies for an implied right of action." *Id.* at 71.

The Court turned to another source to resolve the issue: subsequent legislative acts. In two subsequent, related acts (the Rehabilitation Act Amendments of 1986 and the Rehabilitation Act of 1973), Congress had eliminated the states' Eleventh Amendment immunity from suit. In doing so, Congress broadly defined the available remedies to include all forms of damages. *Id.* at 73. The *Franklin* majority and concurrence saw Congress's subsequent legislation as "a validation of *Cannon's* holding" and "as an implicit acknowledgment that damages are available." *Id.* at 78 (Scalia, J., concurring). Even Justice Scalia, a firm critic of implied causes of action, was willing to grant all available remedies once the cause of action was implied. Thus, if the Court is willing to imply a cause of action, it will likely be willing to award both equitable and legal remedies. For example, relying on the *Franklin* presumption—that all remedies are available absent congressional intent to the contrary—the Fourth Circuit held that a plaintiff could seek punitive damages under Section 504 of the Rehabilitation Act. *Pandazides v. Virginia Bd. of Educ.*, 13 F.3d 823, 830-32 (4th Cir. 1994).

There is a different, but related, issue regarding implied remedies. When a statute expressly provides a private cause of action, are the explicitly identified remedies in the statute exclusive? We addressed this issue earlier when we talked about wrongful death statutes and punitive damages. If a statute does not specifically say that punitive damages are recoverable, should a court interpret the statute to allow them? What about equitable relief? Should a statute that provides for monetary damages be interpreted to provide equitable relief as well?

As you might imagine, the decision of whether to expand a statute to include remedies not specifically identified in the statute turns on the judge's particular approach to statutory interpretation. Judges who follow a purposivist approach to this issue consider whether the identified remedy will further the purpose of the statute. For example, in *Orloff v. Los Angeles Turf Club, Inc.*, 180 P.2d 321 (Cal. 1947), the court held that equitable relief should be implied. In that case, the plaintiff was repeatedly kicked out of a horse racing track because of his race. A state statute provided that anyone who was denied access to a public facility would be entitled to recover either actual damages or one hundred dollars. Because he was not hurt, plaintiff would have been limited to an award of one hundred dollars. Because of the inadequacy of the available damages, the plaintiff sought equitable relief, specifically an injunction. *Id.* at 322. The court held that injunctive relief was necessary to effectuate the purpose of the statute: to prevent the exclusion of persons from certain places based on their race. *Id.* at 325. This is a very old case.

With the emerging hostility towards implied remedies and the refocus on the text of the statute, it is unlikely that a court today would expand remedies beyond those explicitly provided in the statute. Indeed, in *Snapp v. Unlimited Concepts, Inc.*, 208 F.3d 928 (11th Cir. 2000), the court held that the Fair Labor Standards Act's anti-retaliation provision for general damages did not include punitive damages. The Act allowed "such *legal* or equitable *relief* as may be appropriate to effectuate the purposes of section 215(a)(3) of this title, including without limitation employment, reinstatement, promotion, and the payment of wages lost and an additional equal amount as liquidated damages." *Id.* at 933 (quoting 29 U.S.C. §216(b)) (emphasis added). Because the types of damages specifically enumerated in this section and in other sections of the Act were all "meant to *compensate* the plaintiff," the court determined that punitive damages were inappropriate. *Id.* at 935.

These two areas of law — implied causes of action and implied remedies — are at the forefront of statutory interpretation. Over time, with changes in the composition of the Supreme Court, the doctrines have completely reversed course in ways that make little sense. How will it ever be possible to find an implied cause of action using textualism? If Congress is to be clear and only the text can be consulted, then unless Congress expressly includes such a cause of action, one will not be implied. This tension between the power of the legislature to say what the law is, and the power of the judiciary to say what the law means, underscores every aspect of statutory interpretation, but it is most visible in this area. The two most recent additions to the Supreme Court, Justice Sotomayor and Justice Kagan, will play a huge role in shaping the Court's doctrine and approach to statutory interpretation. Sit back and relax. It should be an interesting show!

E. Mastering This Topic

Return to the hypothetical ordinance provided in Chapter 1 on page 9. Let's apply the canons you learned in this chapter. First, the ordinance does not raise a constitutional avoidance issue. However, the ordinance has penal implications, so the rule of lenity is definitely implicated. Remember that the rule of lenity directs that when there are two or more fair and reasonable interpretations of a penal statute, the interpretation that is less penal should be favored. Alternatively, you might say that penal ordinances should be strictly construed. In this case, there are two reasonable interpretations: ambulances are either motor vehicles, or they are not. Hence, by applying the rule of lenity in this case, you would likely find that the ambulance driver did not have fair enough notice that driving the ambulance into the park to rescue someone would be criminal. However, you should remember that the rule of lenity is disfavored in some jurisdictions, and other jurisdictions required a court to exhaust all other sources of meaning before adopting the less penal alternative.

Turning to the other topics, you should note that the ordinance does not raise *ex post facto* issues. The ordinance did not criminalize or increase the penalty on prior behavior. If the city council were to amend the statute to require anyone who in the future, or *had in the past* been convicted of violating the statute to surrender their driver's license, then the *ex post facto* issue would be raised.

The ordinance does not raise federalism, federal preemption, American Indian, or sovereignty immunity issues, so the clear statement canon is not applicable. However, if there was a state statute that specifically permitted emergency vehicles to travel wherever necessary to aid injured individuals (as suggested in the hypothetical analysis in Chapter 8), then the statute and ordinance would conflict. In this scenario, the state statute would essentially "preempt" the local ordinance, although we don't typically use preemption language in this situation. While the state statute likely did not contain a clear statement that it preempted all local conflicting laws, preemption would be implied given the irreconcilable conflict.

Additionally, the ordinance is neither in derogation of the common law — there is no common law right to drive on public land — or remedial — the ordinance does not create new rights or expand remedies.

Finally, for the hypothetical offered, there are no issues involving implied causes of action and implied remedies. But assume that someone was hurt by an ambulance while it was driving through the park. Could the individual successfully argue that this ordinance included an implied cause of action allowing victims to sue drivers who violated the ordinance (for purposes of this hypothetical, ignore the likelihood that state tort law would be applicable)? The current test for implying causes of action is to look for legislative intent by considering the *Cort* factors. The first factor — whether the victim was within the class of persons "for whose especial benefit" the ordinance was enacted — seems to be met here. The ordinance was enacted to further safety and protect individuals in the park from getting hurt. The second factor — whether the legislative history showed that the city council intended to create or deny a private cause of action — seems not to be met. The city council did not address the issue in any way. Because it would be unusual to add a cause of action for this type of ordinance, likely the city council would have at least discussed the issue (the "dog does not bark" canon). The third factor—whether an implied cause of action would be consistent with the underlying purposes of the statute—seems to be met. Imposing civil liability on top of criminal liability in this situation would likely discourage individuals from driving in the park and promote safety. Finally, the fourth factor—whether the issue would be one that is traditionally left to "local" law—also seems not to be met. Tort liability is generally a matter of state rather than local law.

Assuming a court implied a cause of action, what remedies would a court imply? Generally, courts will presume the availability of all appropriate remedies unless the legislating body has expressly indicated otherwise.

Checkpoints

- Reminder: policy-based sources are those sources that are extrinsic both to the statutory act and to the legislative process. They reflect important social and legal choices derived from the Constitution or prudential ideals.

- The constitutional avoidance doctrine directs that when there are two reasonable interpretations of statutory language, one of which raises constitutional issues and one of which does not, the statute should be interpreted in a way that does not raise the constitutional issue.

- Pursuant to the rule of lenity, judges should strictly interpret penal statutes, those statutes that punish citizens by imposing a fine or imprisonment.

- An *ex post facto* law is one that redefines criminal conduct or increases the penalty for criminal conduct. *Ex post facto* laws violate the U.S. Constitution.

- Where a statute could be interpreted to abridge federalism, to preempt state law, to impact American Indian rights, or to waive sovereign immunity, courts generally require the legislature to be clear about its intention. The requirement of a clear statement is based on the simple assumption that a legislature would not make such important changes without being absolutely clear about doing so.

- Statutes in derogation of the common law should be strictly construed. A statute is in derogation of common law when it partially repeals or abolishes existing common law rights or otherwise limits the scope, utility, or force of that law.

- Remedial statutes, those that create new rights or expand remedies, are to be liberally, not narrowly, construed to achieve their statutory purpose.

- Implied causes of action are not expressly provided for in the statute; rather, they are implied by a court. The ultimate question is one of congressional intent. Once a cause of action is implied, generally all statutory rights will similarly be implied.

Conclusion

While there are many ways to approach interpretation today, the linear (or moderate textualist) approach appears to be gaining ground. For this reason, the outline below provides one possible step-by-step approach to convincing a court to interpret a statute in a way that would benefit your client. Because of the uncertainty in this area, however, it is not the only approach to try. Remain flexible and realize the depth of possible arguments that may be available to you.

The Linear Approach

- Step 1: Identify the language of the statute at issue
  - What do you want the language to mean?
  - What does your opponent want the language to mean?

- Step 2: Determine the ordinary or technical meaning of that language
  - Determine whether ordinary or technical meaning is appropriate
    - "words and phrases shall be construed according to the commonly approved usage of the language"
      - Ordinary meaning differs from definitional meaning
        - Dictionaries offer evidence of broad, definitional meaning
        - Consider which dictionary to use
    - "technical words and phrases as have acquired a peculiar and appropriate meaning shall be construed accordingly"
      - Technical meaning is rarely intended

- Step 3: Determine whether the ordinary meaning is ambiguous
  - Ambiguity
    - Commonly defined: two or more reasonable people disagree
    - More accurately defined: two or more equally plausible meanings

- Step 4: Determine whether there is a reason to avoid the ordinary meaning
  - Absurdity
    - Narrow definition: would frustrate purpose/intent
    - Broad definition: would shock the general moral/common sense

- Scrivener's error, or
- Constitutional avoidance doctrine
- Step 5: See if other intrinsic sources are relevant to meaning
  - Grammar & Punctuation
    - Grammar and punctuation matter unless they contradict the ordinary meaning
    - Doctrine of last antecedent
  - Linguistic Canons
    - *In pari materia*
      - Whole act rule
      - Related code rule
      - The presumption of consistent usage and meaningful variation
      - The rule against surplusage, or redundancy
      - *Noscitur a sociis*
      - *Ejusdem generis*
      - *Expressio unius est exclusio alterius*
  - Textual Components
    - Titles
    - Preambles, findings, purpose clauses
    - Provisos
- Step 6: See if extrinsic sources are relevant to meaning
  - Other Laws
    - Conflicting statutes canons
      - Harmonize if possible, if not
        - Specific statutes trump general statutes
        - Later-enacted statutes trump earlier-enacted statutes
        - Repeal by implication is disfavored
    - Borrowed & modeled statutes
  - Timing
    - Pre-enactment context
      - Legislative history
        - The legislative process
          - Bicameral passage
          - Presentment
        - Legislative record
          - Bill drafts
          - Committee reports & hearings
          - Floor debates
          - Conference committee reports
          - Presidential messages

- Purpose, or spirit
- Post-enactment context
  - "Subsequent" legislative history
  - Super-strong *stare decisis* & legislative acquiescence
  - Deference to Agency Interpretation
    - Regulations
      - *Auer* = plainly wrong
    - Statutes
      - *Skidmore* = power-to-persuade test, or
      - *Chevron* = 2 step
        - Is the text silent or ambiguous?
        - If so, is the agency interpretation reasonable?

- Step 7: See if policy-based sources are relevant to meaning
  - Canons based on the constitution
    - Penal Statutes
      - The rule of lenity
      - *Ex post facto* rule
    - Clear Statement Rules
      - Federalism
      - American Indian lands
      - Preemption
      - Sovereign Immunity
  - Canons based on prudential considerations
    - Statutes in derogation of the common law are narrowly construed
    - Remedial statutes are broadly construed
    - Implied causes of action & remedies

Master Checklist

The following outline reflects the topics covered in each chapter. A good understanding of the overall material requires detailed knowledge of each of these topics.

Chapter 1 — Preliminary Matters
- ❑ What statutory interpretation is
- ❑ The relevance of separation of powers to interpretation
- ❑ How Constitutional interpretation differs

Chapter 2 — The Art of Statutory Interpretation: Sources & Theories
- ❑ The three sources of meaning: intrinsic, extrinsic, and policy-based
- ❑ The most common theories of interpretation, including textualism, intentionalism, and purposivism
- ❑ The relevance of theory to meaning

Chapter 3 — The Legislative Process
- ❑ How a bill becomes a law: bicameralism and presentment.
- ❑ The role of legislators, staffers, lobbyists, and the executive

Chapter 4 — Canons Based on Intrinsic Sources: The Words
- ❑ The plain and technical meaning rules
- ❑ Ambiguity
- ❑ How to avoid the ordinary meaning using absurdity, scrivener's error, and the constitutional avoidance doctrine

Chapter 5 — Canons Based on Intrinsic Sources: Grammar & Punctuation
- ❑ The general grammar rule and exceptions
- ❑ The punctuation rules and exceptions

Chapter 6 — Canons Based on Intrinsic Sources: The Linguistic Canons
- ❑ *In pari materia*
- ❑ The presumption of consistent usage and meaningful variation
- ❑ The rule against surplusage, or redundancy

Chapter 13 — Canons Based on Policy-Based Considerations: Constitutional & Prudential

❑ The constitutional avoidance doctrine
❑ The rule of lenity & penal statutes
❑ Clear statement rules
❑ Statutes in derogation of the common law and remedial statutes
❑ Implied causes of actions and their remedies

Appendix A

Selected Bibliography

Selected Books

1. RONALD BENTON BROWN & SHARON JACOBS BROWN, STATUTORY INTERPRETATION: THE SEARCH FOR LEGISLATIVE INTENT (2002).
2. GUIDO CALABRESI, A COMMON LAW FOR THE AGE OF STATUTES (1982).
3. JACK DAVIES, LEGISLATIVE LAW AND PROCESS IN A NUTSHELL (3d ed. 2007).
4. REED DICKERSON, THE INTERPRETATION AND APPLICATION OF STATUTES (1975).
5. EINER ELHAUGE, STATUTORY DEFAULT RULES: HOW TO INTERPRET UNCLEAR LEGISLATION (2008).
6. WILLIAM N. ESKRIDGE, JR. ET AL., LEGISLATION AND STATUTORY INTERPRETATION (2d ed. 2006).
7. WILLIAM ESKRIDGE, JR. ET AL., CASES AND MATERIALS ON LEGISLATION: STATUTES AND THE CREATION OF PUBLIC POLICY (3d ed. 2001).
8. WILLIAM N. ESKRIDGE, JR. & PHILIP P. FRICKEY, INTRODUCTION TO HENRY M. HART, JR. & ALBERT M. SACKS, THE LEGAL PROCESS (1994) 1374 (William N. Eskridge, Jr. & Philip P. Frickey, eds., 1994).
9. KENT GRENAWALT, LEGISLATION: STATUTORY INTERPRETATION: 20 QUESTIONS (1999).
10. JABEZ GRIDLEY SUTHERLAND STATUTES AND STATUTORY CONSTRUCTION (6th ed. 2000 Norman Singer ed.) (often cited as "Sutherland Statutory Construction").
11. HENRY HART & ALBERT SACKS, THE LEGAL PROCESS: BASIC PROBLEMS IN THE MAKING AND APPLICATION OF LAW (1958).
12. SAMUEL ISSACHAROFF, PAMELA KARLAN & RICHARD PILDES, THE LAW OF DEMOCRACY: LEGAL STRUCTURES OF THE POLITICAL PROCESS (1998).
13. LINDA D. JELLUM & DAVID C. HRICIK, MODERN STATUTORY INTERPRETATION: PROBLEMS, THEORIES, AND LAWYERING STRATEGIES (2d ed. 2009).
14. NANCY P. JOHNSON, SOURCES OF COMPILED LEGISLATIVE HISTORIES: A BIBLIOGRAPHY OF GOVERNMENT DOCUMENTS, PERIODICAL ARTICLES, AND BOOKS (Rothman ed., 1979 & Supps.).

15. ABNER MIKVA & ERIC LANE, LEGISLATIVE PROCESS (1995).
16. EUGENE NABORS, LEGISLATIVE REFERENCE CHECKLIST: THE KEY TO LEGISLATIVE HISTORIES FROM 1789 TO 1903 (1982).
17. WILLIAM D. POPKIN, MATERIALS ON LEGISLATION: POLITICAL LANGUAGE AND THE POLITICAL PROCESS (2d ed. 1997).
18. WILLIAM D. POPKIN, STATUTES IN COURT; THE HISTORY AND THEORY OF STATUTORY INTERPRETATION (1999).
19. WILLIAM D. POPKIN, A DICTIONARY OF STATUTORY INTERPRETATION (2007).
20. BERNARD D. REAMS FEDERAL LEGISLATIVE HISTORIES: AN ANNOTATED BIBLIOGRAPHY AND INDEX TO OFFICIALLY PUBLISHED SOURCES (Greenwood Press 1994).
21. ANTONIN SCALIA & BRYAN A. GARNER, READING LAW: THE INTERPRETATION OF LEGAL TEXTS (2012).
22. ANTONIN SCALIA, A MATTER OF INTERPRETATION: FEDERAL COURTS AND THE LAW (1997).
23. MICHAEL SINCLAIR, GUIDE TO STATUTORY INTERPRETATION (2000).
24. LAWRENCE M. SOLAN, THE LANGUAGE OF STATUTES (2010).
25. PETER L. STRAUSS, AN INTRODUCTION TO ADMINISTRATIVE JUSTICE IN THE UNITED STATES (2d. ed. 2002).

Selected Articles

1. Barak, Aharon, *Foreword: A Judge on Judging: The Role of a Supreme Court in a Democracy*, 116 HARV. L. REV. 16 (2002).
2. Breyer, Stephen, *On the Uses of Legislative History in Interpreting Statutes*, 65 S. CAL. L. REV. 845 (1992).
3. Bell, Bernard, *"No More Vehicles in the Park:" Reviving the Hart-Fuller Debate to Introduce Statutory Construction*, 48 J. LEGAL EDUC. 88 (1988).
4. James J. Brudney & Corey Ditsler, *Canons of Construction and the Elusive Search for Neutral Reasoning*, 58 VAND. L. REV. 1 (2005)
5. Chomsky, Carol, *Unlocking the Mysteries of Holy Trinity: Spirit, Letter, and History in Statutory Interpretation*, 100 COLUM. L. REV. 901 (2000).
6. Dougherty, Veronica M., *Absurdity and the Limits of Literalism: Defining the Absurd Result Principle in Statutory Interpretation*, 44 AM. U. L. REV. 127 (1994).
7. Easterbrook, Frank H., *Statutes' Domain*, 50 U. CHI. L. REV. 533 (1983).
8. Easterbrook, Frank H., *The Role of Original Intent in Statutory Construction*, 11 HARV. J. L. & PUB. POL'Y 59 (1988).

9. Easterbrook, Frank H., *What Does Legislative History Tell Us?* 66 Chi-Kent L. Rev. 441 (1991).
10. Eskridge, William, Jr. & Frickey, Philip P., *The Supreme Court, 1993 Term-Foreword: Law as Equilibrium,* 108 Harv. L. Rev. 26 (1994).
11. Frankfurter, Felix, *Some Reflections on the Reading of Statutes,* 47 Colum. L. Rev. 527 (1947).
12. Frickey, Philip P., *From the Big Sleep to the Big Heat: The Revival of Theory in Statutory Interpretation,* 77 Minn. L. Rev. 241 (1992).
13. Fuller, Lon, L., *The Case of the Speluncean Explorers,* 62 Harv. L. Rev. 616 (1949).
14. Fuller, Lon, L., *Positivism and Fidelity to Law—A Reply to Professor Hart,* 71 Harv. L. Rev. 630 (1958).
15. Holmes, Oliver W., *The Theory of Legal Interpretation,* 12 Harv. L. Rev. 417 (1898–1899).
16. Jellum, Linda D., *But that is Absurd! Why Specific Absurdity Undermines Textualism,* 76 Brook. L. rev. 917 (2011).
17. Jellum, Linda D., *Chevron's Demise: A Survey of Chevron from Infancy to Senescence,* 59 Admin. L. Rev. 725 (2007).
18. Krotoszynski, Ronald J., *On the Danger of Wearing Two Hats: Mistretta and Morrison Revisited,* 38 Wm. & Mary L. Rev. 417 (1997).
19. Llewellyn, Karl N., *Remarks on the Theory of Appellate Decision and the Rules or Canons About How Statutes Are to be Construed,* 3 Vand. L. Rev. 395 (1950).
20. Llewellyn, Karl N., *Remarks on the Theory of Appellate Decisions and the Rules or Canons About How Statutes Are to be Construed,* 3 Vand. L. Rev. 395 (1949).
21. Magill, M. Elizabeth, *The Real Separation in Separation of Powers Law,* 86 Va. L. Rev. 1127 (2000).
22 Manning, John F., *Continuity and the Legislative Design,* 79 Notre Dame L. Rev. 1863 (2003–2004).
23. McCutchen, Peter B., *Mistakes, Precedent, and The rise of the Administrative State: Toward a Constitutional Theory of the Second Best,* 80 Cornell L. Rev. 1 (1994).
24. McGreal, Paul E., *Slighting Context: On the Illogic of Ordinary Speech in Statutory Interpretation,* 52 U. Kan. L. Rev. 325 (2004).
25. Mullins, Morrell E. Sr., *Tools Not Rules: The Heuristic Nature of Statutory Interpretation,* 30 J. Legis. 1 (2003).
26. Posner, Richard A., *Statutory Interpretation—In the Classroom and the Courtroom,* 50 U. Chi. L. Rev. 800 (1983).

27. Pound, Roscoe, *Spurious Interpretation*, 7 COLUM. L. REV. 379 (1907).
28. Radin, Max, *Statutory Interpretation*, 43 HARV. L. REV. 863 (1930).
29. Radin, Max, *A Short Way with Statutes*, 56 HARV. L. REV. 388 (1942).
30. Redish, Martin H. & Cisar, Elizabeth J., *"If Angels Were to Govern": The Need for Pragmatic Formalism in Separation of Powers Theory*, 41 DUKE L.J. 449 (1991).
31. Ross, Jeremy L., *A Rule of Last Resort: A History of the Doctrine of the Last Antecedent in the United State Supreme Court*, 39 Sw. L. Rev. 325 (2010).
32. Shapiro, David L., *Continuity and Change in Statutory Interpretation*, 67 N.Y.U. L. REV. 921 (1992).
33. Shumsky, Michael D., *Severability, Inseverability, and the Rule of Law*, 41 HARV. J. ON LEGIS. 227 (2004)
34. Smith, Glen, *Solving the Initiatory Construction Puzzle (and Improving Direct Democracy) by Appropriate Refocusing on Sponsor Intent*, 78 U. COLO. L. R. 257 (2007).
35. Vermeule, Adrian, *Legislative History and the Limits of Judicial Competence: The Untold Story of Holy Trinity Church*, 50 STAN. L. REV. 1833 (1988).
36. Walker, John M. Jr., *Judicial Tendencies in Statutory Construction: Differing Views on the Role of the Judge*, 58 N.Y.U. ANN. SURV. AM. L. 203 (2001).
37. Weinberg, Louise, *Dred Scott and the Crisis of 1860*, 82 CHI.-KENT L. REV. 97 (2007).

Appendix B

Glossary

Absurdity doctrine — when interpreting a statute according to its ordinary meaning would lead to absurd results, courts can avoid the ordinary meaning

Act — a bill that Congress has passed and the president has signed; an enacted bill

Adjudication — agency action that is similar to civil litigation; can be very informal

Administrative Procedures Act — the statute that governs the procedural activities of federal agencies

Agency — "each authority of the Government of the United States ... not includ[ing Congress, the courts, state governments, etc.]"

Ambiguity — when reasonable people understand words to have more than one meaning

Amendment by Implication — when the legislature does not indicate expressly that it is amending a statute, but the judiciary assumes that the legislature intended to amend the existing statute

Appropriations Bill — a bill that authorizes the government to spend money

Auer (*Seminole Rock*) Deference — judicial deference to agency interpretations of regulations; the standard is plainly wrong

Bargaining Theory — a legislative process theory that focuses on furthering the compromises that lead to a bill's passage

Bicameral Passage — the Constitutional requirement that both chambers of Congress pass a bill in identical form before it can become law; also required in almost all states

Bill — a law that Congress or the President has or is considering but is not yet an act

Borrowed Statutes — statutes that are taken, in whole or in part, from another jurisdiction

Cabinet — the collective heads of the Departments, who have served to guide the president in years past

Canons of Interpretation—rules of thumb, or guides, judges use when interpreting statutes

Chevron's **two step deference**—judicial deference to agency interpretations of a statute; requires that the court look first to see if Congress has spoken on the issue, and then if not, to defer to any reasonable agency interpretation

Clear Statement Rules—when courts require the legislature to make a clear or plain statement when a statute will impact important rights such as federalism because the court assumes that a legislature would not make such a major change without being absolutely clear

Cloture—the process in which sixty senators agree to defeat a filibuster

Codification—the process of consolidating statutes into subjects, forming a legal code

Committee of the Whole—the largest committee in the House, which is made up of all representatives and was formed to debate proposed bills

Conference Committee—an ad hoc committee of select senators and representatives who try to resolve differences in bills the House and Senate pass

Conflicting statutes—statutes that cannot exist harmoniously

Contextualism—the process of using the context to determine why the legislature acted or to determine what a statute means

Delegation Doctrine (the)—the doctrine by which the Supreme Court determines whether intelligible principles sufficiently constrain the power delegated to agencies from Congress to be constitutional

Derogation of the Common Law—a statute that partially repeals or abolishes existing common law rights or otherwise limits the scope, utility, or force of that law

Dog-Does-Not-Bark Doctrine—the canon that directs that silence in the legislative history about a particular subject is generally not a good guide to meaning

Dynamic Interpretation—a theory of interpretation that encourage judges to be flexible and consider what the enacting legislature would have wanted given common day realities

Ejusdem Generis—the linguistic canon that general words should be limited to include only things similar in nature to the specific words near the general words

Enacting Clause—a section of a bill that is statutorily required. Components following enacting clauses are codified. Components preceding enacting clauses are not codified.

Engrossed Bill—a bill that one chamber of Congress has passed and forwarded to the other chamber

Enrolled Bill—a bill that both chambers of Congress have passed in identical form and have forwarded to the president for signature

Enrolled Bill Rule—the rule that once a bill is filed, it is conclusively presumed to have been validly adopted

Ex Post Facto **Law**—a law that redefines what is criminal conduct or increases the penalty for criminal conduct; the *Ex Post Facto* Clause of the U.S. Constitution prohibits such laws

Executive Agency—an agency that is very much subject to presidential control for the head serves at the pleasure of the president

Executive Order—statements from a president or governor directing agencies and officials in the execution of legislatively granted authority

Expressio Unius Est Exclusio Alterius—the linguistic canon of negative implication such that the inclusion of one thing means the exclusion of another

Extrinsic Sources of Meaning—materials outside of the official act, but within the legislative process that created the act

Filibuster—a delaying tactic used in the Senate to prevent a vote on a bill

Formalism—an approach the Supreme Court uses in separation of powers cases to maintain three distinct branches of government with constitutionally defined powers

Functionalism—an approach the Supreme Court uses in separation of powers cases to balance the inevitable overlap among the branches

Funnel of Abstraction—a v-shaped diagram Professors Eskridge and Frickey generated that depicts the sources of interpretation on one side of the v and the concreteness of that source on the other side of the v to explain pragmatic theory

General Assemblies—the name for state legislatures

Germaneness Rule—the rule in the house that permits amendments to bills only if the amendments are germane

Golden Rule Exception—the absurdity doctrine; the idea that if interpreting a statute according to its ordinary meaning would lead to absurd results, a court can avoid the ordinary meaning

Imaginative Reconstructionism—a theory of interpretation in which a judge would try to imagine what the enacting legislature would have intended had the precise factual problem before the court been raised during the enactment process

Implied Causes of Action and Remedies—causes of action and remedies that are not expressly provided for in the statute, but that the court implies based on the goals of the legislature

In Pari Materia—a linguistic canon that identifies the statutory material that judges can legitimately look at to discern meaning, including the entire act and other statutes with similar purposes

Independent Agency—a type of agency that is more independent from the president because it is headed by a multi-member, bi-partisan board, serving terms

Initiative Process—a form of direct democracy in which a certain minimum number of registered voters sign a petition to force a public vote on a proposed issue

Inseverability Provision—a provision in a bill or act that indicates a legislature's expectation that if any provision in the act is unconstitutional, the act as a whole must fail

Intentionalism—a theory of statutory interpretation that focuses on finding the specific intent of the enacting legislature

Intrinsic Sources of Meaning—sources of meaning from the official act being interpreted, also called textual sources

Journal Entry Rule—a rule in states that allows judges to determine whether constitutional enactment requirements were met by looking at the bill's journal entry

Last Antecedent, Doctrine of—a grammar canon that directs that a limiting or restrictive clause in a statute is generally construed to restrict the immediately preceding clause unless a comma separates the two

Last Enacted Rule—the doctrine that when two statutes conflict and cannot be harmonized, the last in time controls

Legislative Acquiescence—the reasoning that the legislature's failure to take action in response to a judicial interpretation of a statute means that the legislature agreed with or acquiesced to the judicial interpretation

Legislative History—the written record of deliberations surrounding and preceding a bill's enactment, including committee reports and hearing transcripts, floor debates, recorded votes, conference committee reports, presidential signing and veto messages, etc.

Legislative Inaction—when the legislature takes no action in response to a judicial interpretation of a statute

Legislative Intent, General—the purpose of the enacting legislature for enacting a bill

Legislative Intent, Specific—the intent of the enacting legislature on the specific issue before the court

Legislative Rules—rules an agency enacted via informal or formal rulemaking processes (legislative rulemaking is the process of enacting legislative rules)

Lenity, Rule of—a canon of interpretation based on due process concerns that judges should strictly interpret penal statutes

Lobbyists—individuals who are generally paid to represent a particular point of view for a specific industry or organization

Mischief Rule—the idea that statutes should be interpreted to further their purpose or to limit the mischief the statute was designed to remedy

Model Acts—proposed acts that the National Conference of Commissioners on Uniform State Laws or the American Law Institute developed to address multijurisdictional issues; uniformity is not central

New Textualism—a form of textualism credited to Justice Antonin Scalia

Non-legislative Rule—a rule an agency enacted without using informal or formal rulemaking procedures (non-legislative rulemaking is the process of issuing a non-legislative rule)

Noscitur a Sociis—the linguistic canon that that when a word has more than one meaning, the appropriate meaning should be gleaned from the words surrounding the word being interpreted; generally used when the statute contains a list of words

Notice and Comment Rulemaking—another name for informal rulemaking required under the Administrative Procedures Act; an agency publishes notice of a proposed rule, then seeks public comment on the rule

Ordinary Meaning—the commonly understood meaning of a word or phrase often arrived at by consulting a dictionary

Override—Congress's ability to overcome a president's veto of a bill, requires 2/3 positive vote from each chamber of Congress

Penal Statute—a statute that has a punitive effect

Plain Meaning Rule—a canon that allows judges to presume that words in a statute have their "plain" or "ordinary" meaning

Pluralist Theories—theories of legislative process that focus on the role special interest groups play in setting legislative policy, such as bargaining theory and public choice theory

Pocket Veto—if the president does not sign an enrolled bill for ten days during which Congress adjourns, the bill is vetoed

Policy-Based Sources of Meaning—sources of meaning that are extrinsic to both the statutory act and the legislative process; generally based on the Constitution or policy considerations

Preambles—a component in a bill that often precedes the enacting clause and explains the reason the statute is being enacted

Preemption—the displacing effect that federal law has on conflicting or inconsistent state law

Presentment — the Constitutional requirement that a bill be presented to the president and be signed before it becomes law

President *Pro Tempore* — usually the most senior senator in the majority party

Proviso — a clause in a statute that creates an exception to or otherwise limits the effect of another provision; provisos often start with "provided that," "except for," and "provided however"

Public Choice Theory — a legislative process theory that statutes are the result of compromises among legislators and various competing private interest groups

Purpose — the reason the statute was enacted, the mischief that was designed to be remedied, also called the spirit of the law

Purposivism — a theory of statutory interpretation that focuses on the purpose of the statute and looks at all sources of meaning

Recodification — to codify again

Referendum — a popular form of democracy that allows voters to approve or reject legislation a legislature pass

Regulation — a rule an agency enacted via its rulemaking procedures

Remedial Statutes — statutes that are *in aid* of the common law or create new rights and remedies rather than being in derogation of the common law

Repeal by Implication — when the legislature does not indicate expressly that it is repealing a statute, but the judiciary assumes that the legislature intended to repeal the existing statute because it cannot exist in harmony with a conflicting statute

Retroactive — statutes that govern both past and future conduct; generally statutes only govern future conduct

Rules Committee — the committee in the House or Senate that determines the rules governing debate on proposed bills

Scrivener's Error — a doctrine that permits judges to correct obvious clerical or typographical errors

Separation of Powers — the notion that the powers of government should be split among the various branches of government

Session Laws — legislative enactments for an annual period that have been bound chronologically. Federal session laws can be found in the *Statutes at Large*

Severability Provision — a provision in a bill or act that indicates a legislature's expectation that if any one section of an act is unconstitutional, then it shall be severed so that the rest of the act may be saved

Signing Statements — statements a president or governor issues when a bill is passed, often to impact the law in some way

Single Subject Rule—the rule in most state constitutions that bills may only include one subject

Skidmore **Deference**—judicial deference to agency interpretations that do not receive *Chevron* deference; agency interpretations receive deference to the extent that they have the power-to-persuade the court

Slip Laws—a legislative enactment that is published separately and promptly after passage, which can be used and cited in temporary form until it is published in a more permanent form by the Government Printing Office or state equivalent.

Sovereign Immunity—a judge-made doctrine that a government or sovereign may not be sued without its consent

Speaker of the House—the leader of the House of Representatives

Spirit of the Law—the purpose of the statute

Stare Decisis—the policy of the court to respect prior precedent

Statute—a written law enacted by a legislative body and the executive, a section or piece of an act,

Statutes at Large (U.S.)—a chronological compilation of all enacted acts

Strict Construction—a theory of interpretation similar to textualism that strictly construes words in the statute

Super-Strong *Stare Decisis*—a heightened form of *stare decisis* the Supreme Court (and occasionally lower courts) uses for its statutory interpretation decisions

Technical Meaning Rule—a corollary to the plain meaning rule: the technical meaning rule is a canon that a word or phrase that has acquired a technical or particular meaning in a particular context has that meaning if it is used in that context

Textualism—a theory of statutory interpretation that focuses on the text and intrinsic sources of meaning

Unicameral—a legislature like Nebraska's that has only one chamber

Uniform Acts—proposed acts the National Conference of Commissioners on Uniform State Laws or the American Law Institute developed to address multijurisdictional issues; uniformity is central across jurisdictions

Uniform Statute & Rule Construction Act—a uniform act the National Conference of Commissioners on Uniform State Laws drafted to unify statutory interpretation

Veto—the president's rejection of a bill

Vetogate—a term Professors Eskridge and Frickey coined to describe the chokepoints in the legislative process that can prevent a bill from becoming law, such as committee votes

Whip—legislators who try to ensure that the party's members vote as the party leadership desires

Whole Act Rule—a component of the *in pari materia* canon that a court may look to the entire act when construing a statute

Whole Code Rule—a component of the *in pari materia* canon that a court may look to the entire code, so long as the statutes have similar purposes, when construing a statute

Appendix C

Bibliography: Where to Find Federal Legislative History On-Line

Compiled by Denise Gibson, J.D., M.L.S.
Mercer University School of Law
Assistant Law Librarian for Research Services

Bill Versions and Status

THOMAS: http://thomas.loc.gov/
  Contains the full text of bills and resolutions from **1989** (**101st Congress**) to the current Congress; bill summaries and status for legislation introduced from **1973** (**93rd Congress**).
GPO Federal Digital System (FDsys): http://www.gpo.gov/fdsys/
  Contains all published versions of bills in PDF and full text from **1993** (**103rd Congress**), and the "History of Bills and Resolutions" section of the Congressional Record Index from **1983** (**98th Congress**).
ProQuest Congressional: (basic subscription) http://cisupa.proquest.com
  Contains the full text of bills from **1989** (**101st Congress**) and selected earlier materials from **1983** (**98th Congress**). A full subscription to ProQuest Congressional includes the full text digital collection of all U.S. bills and resolutions from the first Congress in **1789** to the current Congress.
Lexis: http://lexisnexis.com/lawschool
  Contains the full text of bills from **1989** (**101st Congress**) in BTX, and bills from the current Congress are included in BLTEXT.
Westlaw Classic: http://www.lawschool.westlaw.com/
  Contains the full text of bills from **1991** (**102nd Congress**) in BILLTXT-ALL and bills from the current Congress are in CONG-BILLTXT; bill history and tracking are included in US-BILLTRK, and BILLTRK-OLD.

<u>WestlawNext</u>: http://www.lawschool.westlaw.com/
Contains bill texts and resolutions introduced in the current session of Congress and historical bills from **1995** (**104th Congress**).

<u>A Century of Lawmaking</u>: http://memory.loc.gov/ammem/amlaw/lwhbsb.html
Historical—Contains bills and resolutions for selected sessions of Congress, beginning with the 6th Congress in the House of Representatives, the 16th Congress in the Senate, and the 18th Congress for Senate Joint Resolutions.

Hearings

<u>GPO Federal Digital System (FDsys)</u>: http://www.gpo.gov/fdsys/
Contains select House and Senate hearings from **1985** (**99th Congress**) forward.

<u>ProQuest Congressional</u>: (basic subscription) http://cisupa.proquest.com
Contains selected testimony transcripts from **1988**, and published hearing abstracts and indexing from **1970**. A full subscription to ProQuest Congressional includes a digital collection of hearings (published and unpublished) from **1823** to present.

<u>HeinOnline</u>: (subscription) http://www.heinonline.org
Contains committee hearings from 71st Congress (**1927**) through the 112th Congress (**2011**) in the U.S. Congressional Documents Library. HeinOnline will be releasing hearings each month with plans to bring the collection up to date through the current Congress.

<u>Lexis</u>: http://lexisnexis.com/lawschool
The CQ Congressional Testimony (CNGTST) database contains written statements of witnesses from **July 28, 1993** (**103rd Congress**) before Committees of the U.S. House of Representatives, the U.S. Senate, and Joint Committees of the House and Senate. The CQ Transcripts (POLTRN) database contains the transcripts of hearing of witnesses and "Q&A" sessions between witnesses and members of Congress, and also contain LINKS™ to the BLTRCK file when a transcript pertains to a bill pending in Congress.

<u>Westlaw Classic</u>: http://www.lawschool.westlaw.com/
Contains most prepared statements in USTESTIMONY from **1996**, and selected transcripts of hearings from **1993** (**103rd Congress**) forward.

<u>WestlawNext</u>: http://www.lawschool.westlaw.com
Contains selected transcripts of testimony in the CONGTMY database from **11/2004**.

<u>Law Library of Congress</u>: http://www.loc.gov/law/find/hearings.php
A collaborative pilot project between the Law Library of Congress and Google, Inc. began in 2011 to provide a digital collection of Congressional

hearings in PDF. Included on the website are hearings regarding the U.S. Census, Freedom of Information/Privacy, and Immigration.

House, Senate, Conference Committee Reports; House and Senate Documents

THOMAS: http://thomas.loc.gov/
Contains House, Senate, and conference reports from 1995 (104th Congress) in PDF.

Federal Digital System (FDsys): http://www.gpo.gov/fdsys/
Contains House, Senate, conference and executive reports from 1995 (104th Congress) in PDF.

ProQuest Congressional: (basic subscription) http://cisupa.proquest.com
Contains selected full text House and Senate Committee Reports from 1990, and selected full text House and Senate Documents from 1995.

Lexis: http://www.lexisnexis.com/lawschool
Contains selected full text House and Senate Committee reports from 1990 in CMTRPT file, and complete coverage from 1993 (103rd Congress).

Westlaw Classic: http://www.lawschool.westlaw.com
The LH database contains selected congressional committee reports from 1948 (80th Congress) forward. From 1990, the database contains all congressional committee reports, including reports on bills that did not become law.

WestlawNext: http://lawschool.westlaw.com
Contains all congressional committee reports, including reports on bills that did not become law, from 1990. Also sets out the legislative history of public laws as reprinted in U.S. Code Congressional and Administrative News (USCCAN), from 1948 through 1989, as well as the legislative history of securities laws beginning with 1933.

A Century of Lawmaking: http://memory.loc.gov/ammem/amlaw/lwss.html
Historical — Contains the U.S. Serial Set with full-text of selected House and Senate documents and reports beginning with the 23rd Congress (1833–35) through the 64th Congress (1915–17). Bills and resolutions begin in the House with the 15th Congress (1817) and in the Senate with the 30th Congress (1847). Documents before 1817 may be found in the American State Papers at http://memory.loc.gov/ammem/amlaw/lwsp.html.

Committee Prints

<u>Federal Digital System</u>: http://www.gpo.gov/fdsys/
   Contains committee prints from **1991** (**102nd Congress**) in PDF and full
   text; some prints can also be found on web pages maintained by individual
   House and Senate committees.
<u>ProQuest Congressional</u>: (basic subscription) http://cisupa.proquest.com
   Contains committee prints from **1993** (**103rd Congress**) through **2004**.
<u>Open CRS</u>: http://www.opencrs.com/
   Contains reports, including congressional committee prints, from the Con-
   gressional Research Service, that previously were distributed only to members of Congress.

Congressional Record — Floor Debates

<u>THOMAS</u>: http://thomas.loc.gov
   Contains the daily Congressional Record from **1989** (**101st Congress**) forward. Search by keyword, member of Congress, section, date or session,
   and index subject.
<u>Federal Digital System (FDsys)</u>: http://www.gpo.gov.fdsys/
   Contains the daily Congressional Record from **1994** (**103rd Congress**) forward, and Congressional Record volumes from 140 (**1994**) to the present.
   The current year's Congressional Record database is usually updated daily
   by 11 a.m. Contains the Bound Permanent Congressional Record from **1999-
   2001** in PDF.
<u>HeinOnline</u>: (subscription) http://www.heinonline.org
   HeinOnline's U.S. Congressional Documents Library contains the **daily** edition of the Congressional Record from **1990** (**101st Congress**) in PDF, its
   predecessors in PDF from **1789–1913**, and the **bound official edition** from
   1873–2006. There is also a "Congressional Record Daily Edition Locator" to
   the permanent bound version of the Congressional Record from **Jan 25, 1994**.
<u>Westlaw Classic / WestlawNext</u>: http://www.lawschool.westlaw.com
   Contains the daily Congressional Daily Record from **1985** (**99th Congress**)
   forward.
<u>Lexis</u>: http://www.lexisnexis.com/lawschool
   Contains the daily Congressional Daily Record from **1985** (**99th Congress**)
   forward.
<u>ProQuest Congressional</u>: (basic subscription) http://cisupa.proquest.com
   Contains Congressional Daily Record from **1985** (**99th Congress**) forward;
   updated daily when Congress is in session.

Congressional Record — Floor Debates — Historical

A Century of Lawmaking: http://memory.loc.gov/ammem/amlaw/lwcr.html.
This collection from the Library of Congress includes The Debates and Proceedings in the Congress of the United States (**1789–1824**), the Register of Debates in Congress (**1824–1837**), and the Congressional Globe (**1833–1873**).

HeinOnline (historical) (subscription): http://www.heinonline.org
Contains the Annals of Congress, the Register of Debates, and the Congressional Globe in HeinOnline's U.S. Congressional Documents Library.

ProQuest Congressional (historical) (full subscription): http://cisupa.proquest.com
Subscription to ProQuest's Congressional Record Permanent Digital Collection includes the Congressional Record (**1873–to date**), the Annals of Congress (**1789–1824**), the Register of Debates (**1824–1837**), and the Congressional Globe (**1833–1873**).

Presidential Documents and Signing Statements

GPO Federal Digital System (FDsys): http://www.gpo.gov.fdsys/
Contains the Federal Register from **1994**, the Daily Compilation and its predecessor, the Weekly Compilation of Presidential Documents, from **1993**, and Public Papers of the President (presidential documents and photographic portfolios) from **1991** in PDF.

Lexis: http://www.lexisnexis.com/lawschool
Contains presidential statements from **March 1979**. Search: Legal tab > Federal Legal-U.S. > Executive Branch Materials > Public Papers of the Presidents.

Westlaw Classic: http://www.lawschool.westlaw.com/
Contains presidential statements in the USCCAN database (USCCAN-MSG) from **1986**, in the PRES-DAILY database from **1993**, and from **1995** in the Weekly Compilation of the Presidential Documents.

WestlawNext: http://www.lawschool.westlaw.com/
Contains presidential signing statements reprinted in USCCAN from **1986**, and executive orders from **1936** and other documents from **1984** in the Presidential Documents database.

HeinOnline: (subscription) http://www.heinonline.org
HeinOnline's U.S. Presidential Library includes such titles as Messages and Papers of the Presidents, Public Papers of the Presidents beginning with Herbert Hoover—Barack Obama (1931-2009) in PDF, CFR Title 3 (Presidents), Weekly Compilation of the Presidential Documents from **1965** to

2009 in PDF, Daily Compilation of Presidential Documents from **Jan. 20, 2009 to date,** and other documents related to the president.

The American Presidency Project: http://www.presidency.uscb.edu/sign ingstatement.php
Contains signing statements from **1929.**

Additional Sources of Legislative Information

Graphical Statutes on Westlaw Classic/WestlawNext and Lexis Advance — integrated source for legislative history documents.

HeinOnline: (subscription) http://www.heinonline.org
Contains a Federal Legislative History Library that includes the legislative histories of significant pieces of United States legislation. Hein also publishes an online edition of Sources of Compiled Legislative Histories.

Westlaw Classic: http://www.lawschool.westlaw.com/
Contains thirty-one legislative histories of significant pieces of United States legislation compiled by the Arnold & Porter law firm.

Congressional Research Service (CRS Reports):
http://digital.library.unt.edu/govdocs/crs/index.tkl
The University of Texas Libraries provides an integrated, searchable source to many of the full-text CRS reports that have been available at a variety of different web sites since **1990.** Searchable by keyword, title, author, subject and report number, or browse by subject. The Open CRS Network: http://www.opencrs.com/ also provides convenient access to select CRS reports. ProQuest Congressional (subscription) has an index and selected CRS Reports in PDF from **1916** to present.

Westlaw Classic / WestlawNext: U.S. GAO Federal Legislative Histories http://www.lawschool.westlaw.com/
Contains comprehensive legislative histories for most U.S. Public Laws enacted from **1921 to 1995,** and **PL 104–191,** as compiled by the U.S. Government Accountability Office, including the text of laws, bills, committee reports, Congressional Record documents, transcripts of hearings, and other documents in PDF format.

Appendix D

House Bill 916

Union Calendar No. 88

110TH CONGRESS   H. R. 916
1ST SESSION

[Report No. 110-148]

To provide for loan repayment for prosecutors and public defenders.

———

IN THE HOUSE OF REPRESENTATIVES
FEBRUARY 8, 2007

Mr. SCOTT of Georgia (for himself, Mr. GORDON of Tennessee, Mr. LEWIS of Georgia, Mr. PAYNE....) introduced the following bill; which was referred to the Committee on the Judiciary

MAY 14, 2007

Additional sponsors: Mr. LINCOLN DAVIS of Tennessee, Mr. COOPER, Mr. CHANDLER, Mr. UDALL of Colorado....

MAY 14, 2007

Reported with an amendment, committed to the Committee of the Whole House on the State of the Union, and ordered to be printed

———

A BILL

To provide for loan repayment for prosecutors and public defenders.

Be it enacted by the Senate and House of Representatives of the United States of America in Congress assembled,

SECTION 1. SHORT TITLE.

This Act may be cited as the "John R. Justice Prosecutors and Defenders Incentive Act of 2007".

SEC. 2. LOAN REPAYMENT FOR PROSECUTORS AND DEFENDERS.

Title I of the Omnibus Crime Control and Safe Streets Act of 1968 (42 U.S.C. 3711 et seq.) is amended by adding at the end the following:

"PART JJ—LOAN REPAYMENT FOR PROSECUTORS AND PUBLIC DEFENDERS

"SEC. 3111. GRANT AUTHORIZATION.

"(a) PURPOSE. — The purpose of this section is to encourage qualified individuals to enter and continue employment as prosecutors and public defenders.

"(b) DEFINITIONS. — In this section:

"(1) PROSECUTOR. — The term 'prosecutor' means a full-time employee of a State or local agency who —

"(A) is continually licensed to practice law; and

"(B) prosecutes criminal or juvenile delinquency cases (or both) at the State or local level, including an employee who supervises, educates, or trains other persons prosecuting such cases.

"(2) PUBLIC DEFENDER. — The term 'public defender' means an attorney who —

"(A) is continually licensed to practice law; and

"(B) is —

"(i) a full-time employee of a State or local agency who provides legal representation to indigent persons in criminal or juvenile delinquency cases (or both), including an attorney who supervises, educates, or trains other persons providing such representation;

"(ii) a full-time employee of a non-profit organization operating under a contract with a State or unit of local government, who devotes substantially all of such full-time employment to providing legal representation to indigent persons in criminal or juvenile delinquency cases (or both), including an attorney who supervises, educates, or trains other persons providing such representation; or

"(iii) employed as a full-time Federal defender attorney in a defender organization established pursuant to subsection (g) of section 3006A of title 18, United States Code, that provides legal representation to indigent persons in criminal or juvenile delinquency cases (or both).

"(3) STUDENT LOAN. — The term 'student loan' means —

"(A) a loan made, insured, or guaranteed under part B of title IV of the Higher Education Act of 1965 (20 U.S.C. 1071 et seq.);

"(B) a loan made under part D or E of 20 title IV of the Higher Education Act of 1965 (20 U.S.C. 1087a et seq. and 1087aa et seq.); and

"(C) a loan made under section 428C or 23 455(g) of the Higher Education Act of 1965 (20 U.S.C. 1078-3 and 1087e(g)) to the extent that such loan was used to repay a Federal Direct Stafford Loan, a Federal Direct Unsubsidized Stafford Loan, or a loan made under section 428 or 428H of such Act.

"(c) PROGRAM AUTHORIZED.—The Attorney General shall, subject to the availability of appropriations, establish a program by which the Department of Justice shall assume the obligation to repay a student loan, by direct payments on behalf of a borrower to the holder of such loan, in accordance with subsection (d), for any borrower who—

"(1) is employed as a prosecutor or public defender; and

"(2) is not in default on a loan for which the borrower seeks forgiveness.

"(d) TERMS OF LOAN REPAYMENT.—

"(1) BORROWER AGREEMENT.—To be eligible to receive repayment benefits under subsection (c), a borrower shall enter into a written agreement with the Attorney General that specifies that—

"(A) the borrower will remain employed as a prosecutor or public defender for a required period of service of not less than 3 years, unless in voluntarily separated from that employment;

"(B) if the borrower is involuntarily separated from employment on account of misconduct, or voluntarily separates from employment, before the end of the period specified in the agreement, the borrower will repay the Attorney General the amount of any benefits received by such employee under this section; and

"(C) if the borrower is required to repay an amount to the Attorney General under subparagraph (B) and fails to repay such amount, a sum equal to that amount shall be recoverable by the Federal Government from the employee (or such employee's estate, if applicable) by such methods as are provided by law for the recovery of amounts owed to the Federal Government.

"(2) REPAYMENT BY BORROWER.—

"(A) IN GENERAL.—Any amount repaid by, or recovered from, an individual or the estate of an individual under this subsection shall be credited to the appropriation account from which the amount involved was originally paid.

"(B) MERGER.—Any amount credited under subparagraph (A) shall be merged with other sums in such account and shall be available for the same purposes and period, and subject to the same limitations, if any, as the sums with which the amount was merged.

"(C) WAIVER.—The Attorney General may waive, in whole or in part, a right of recovery under this subsection if it is shown that recovery would be against equity and good conscience or against the public interest.

"(3) LIMITATIONS.—

"(A) STUDENT LOAN PAYMENT AMOUNT.—Student loan repayments made by the Attorney General under this section shall be made subject to the availability of appropriations, and subject to such terms, limitations, or conditions as may be mutually agreed upon by the borrower and the Attorney General in an agreement under paragraph (1), except that the amount paid by the Attorney General under this section shall not exceed—

"(i) $10,000 for any borrower in any calendar year; or

"(ii) an aggregate total of $60,000 in the case of any borrower.

"(B) BEGINNING OF PAYMENTS.—Nothing in this section shall authorize the Attorney General to pay any amount to reimburse a borrower for any repayments made by such borrower prior to the date on which the Attorney General entered into an agreement with the borrower under this subsection.

"(e) ADDITIONAL AGREEMENTS.—

"(1) IN GENERAL.—On completion of the required period of service under an agreement under subsection (d), the borrower and the Attorney General 7 may, subject to paragraph (2), enter into an additional agreement in accordance with subsection (d).

"(2) TERM.—An agreement entered into under paragraph (1) may require the borrower to remain employed as a prosecutor or public defender for less than 3 years.

"(f) AWARD BASIS; PRIORITY.—

"(1) AWARD BASIS.—The Attorney General shall provide repayment benefits under this section—

"(A) subject to the availability of appropriations; and

"(B) in accordance with paragraph (2), except that the Attorney General shall determine a fair allocation of repayment benefits among prosecutors and defenders, and among employing entities nationwide.

"(2) PRIORITY.—In providing repayment benefits under this section in any fiscal year, the Attorney General shall give priority to borrowers—

"(A) who, when compared to other eligible borrowers, have the least ability to repay their student loans (considering whether the borrower is the beneficiary of any other student loan repayment program), as determined by the Attorney General; or

"(B) who—

"(i) received repayment benefits under this section during the preceding fiscal year; and

"(ii) have completed less than 3 years of the first required period of service specified for the borrower in an agreement entered into under subsection (d).

"(g) REGULATIONS.—The Attorney General is authorized to issue such regulations as may be necessary to carry out the provisions of this section.

"(h) REPORT BY INSPECTOR GENERAL.—Not later than 3 years after the date of the enactment of this section, the Inspector General of the Department of Justice shall submit to Congress a report on—

"(1) the cost of the program authorized under this section; and

"(2) the impact of such program on the hiring and retention of prosecutors and public defenders.

"(i) GAO STUDY.—Not later than one year 1 after the date of the enactment of this section, the Comptroller General shall conduct a study of, and report to Congress on, the impact that law school accreditation requirements and other factors have on the costs of law school and student access to law school, including the impact of such requirements on racial and ethnic minorities.

"(j) AUTHORIZATION OF APPROPRIATIONS.—There is authorized to be appropriated to carry out this section $25,000,000 for each of the fiscal years 2008 through 2013."

Appendix E

Companion Senate Bill to H.R. 916

John R. Justice Prosecutors and Defenders Incentive Act of 2007
(Reported in Senate)

S 442 RS

Calendar No. 113
110th CONGRESS
1st Session
S. 442
[Report No. 110-51]
To provide for loan repayment for prosecutors and public defenders.

IN THE SENATE OF THE UNITED STATES
January 31, 2007

Mr. DURBIN (for himself, Mr. SPECTER, Mr. LEAHY, Mr. SMITH, Mr. KERRY, Ms. COLLINS, Ms. LANDRIEU, Ms. SNOWE, Mr. BIDEN, Mr. COCHRAN, Mr. KENNEDY, Mr. FEINGOLD, Mrs. FEINSTEIN, Mr. SCHUMER, Mr. WHITEHOUSE, Mr. COLEMAN, Mr. KOHL, and Mr. HARKIN) introduced the following bill; which was read twice and referred to the Committee on the Judiciary

April 10, 2007

Reported by Mr. LEAHY, with amendments
[Omit the part struck through and insert the part printed in italic]

———

A BILL

To provide for loan repayment for prosecutors and public defenders.
Be it enacted by the Senate and House of Representatives of the United States of America in Congress assembled,

SECTION 1. SHORT TITLE.

This Act may be cited as the "John R. Justice Prosecutors and Defenders Incentive Act of 2007".

SEC. 2. LOAN REPAYMENT FOR PROSECUTORS AND DEFENDERS.

Title I of the Omnibus Crime Control and Safe Streets Act of 1968 (42 U.S.C. 3711 et seq.) is amended by adding at the end the following:

"PART JJ—LOAN REPAYMENT FOR PROSECUTORS AND PUBLIC DEFENDERS

"SEC. 3111. GRANT AUTHORIZATION.

"(a) Purpose—The purpose of this section is to encourage qualified individuals to enter and continue employment as prosecutors and public defenders.

"(b) Definitions—In this section:

"(1) PROSECUTOR—The term "prosecutor" means a full-time employee of a State or local agency who—

"(A) is continually licensed to practice law; and

"(B) prosecutes criminal *or juvenile delinquency* cases at the State or local level*(including supervision, education, or training of other persons prosecuting such cases).*

"(2) PUBLIC DEFENDER—The term "public defender" means an attorney who—

"(A) is continually licensed to practice law; and

"(B) is—

"~~(i) a full-time employee of a State or local agency or a nonprofit organization operating under a contract with a State or unit of local government, that provides legal representation to indigent persons in criminal cases; or~~

"(i) a full-time employee of a State or local agency who provides legal representation to indigent persons in criminal or juvenile delinquency cases (including supervision, education, or training of other persons providing such representation);

"(ii) a full-time employee of a nonprofit organization operating under a contract with a State or unit of local government, who devotes substantially all of his or her full-time employment to providing legal representation to indigent persons in criminal or juvenile delinquency cases, (including supervision, education, or training of other persons providing such representation); or

"(ii)*(iii)* employed as a full-time Federal defender attorney in a defender organization established pursuant to subsection (g) of section 3006A of title 18, United States Code, that provides legal representation to indigent persons in criminal *or juvenile delinquency* cases.

"(3) STUDENT LOAN—The term "student loan" means—

"(A) a loan made, insured, or guaranteed under part B of title IV of the Higher Education Act of 1965 (20 U.S.C. 1071 et seq.);

"(B) a loan made under part D or E of title IV of the Higher Education Act of 1965 (20 U.S.C. 1087a et seq. and 1087aa et seq.); and

"(C) a loan made under section 428C or 455(g) of the Higher Education Act of 1965 (20 U.S.C. 1078-3 and 1087e(g)) to the extent that such loan was used to repay a Federal Direct Stafford Loan, a Federal Direct Unsubsidized Stafford Loan, or a loan made under section 428 or 428H of such Act.

"(c) Program Authorized—The Attorney General shall establish a program by which the Department of Justice shall assume the obligation to repay a student loan, by direct payments on behalf of a borrower to the holder of such loan, in accordance with subsection (d), for any borrower who—

"(1) is employed as a prosecutor or public defender; and

"(2) is not in default on a loan for which the borrower seeks forgiveness.

"(d) Terms of Agreement—

"(1) IN GENERAL—To be eligible to receive repayment benefits under subsection (c), a borrower shall enter into a written agreement that specifies that—

"(A) the borrower will remain employed as a prosecutor or public defender for a required period of service of not less than 3 years, unless involuntarily separated from that employment;

"(B) if the borrower is involuntarily separated from employment on account of misconduct, or voluntarily separates from employment, before the end of the period specified in the agreement, the borrower will repay the Attorney General the amount of any benefits received by such employee under this section;

"(C) if the borrower is required to repay an amount to the Attorney General under subparagraph (B) and fails to repay such amount, a sum equal to that amount shall be recoverable by the Federal Government from the employee (or such employee's estate, if applicable) by such methods as are provided by law for the recovery of amounts owed to the Federal Government;

"(D) the Attorney General may waive, in whole or in part, a right of recovery under this subsection if it is shown that recovery would be against equity and good conscience or against the public interest; and

"(E) the Attorney General shall make student loan payments under this section for the period of the agreement, subject to the availability of appropriations.

"(2) REPAYMENTS—

"(A) IN GENERAL—Any amount repaid by, or recovered from, an individual or the estate of an individual under this subsection shall be credited to the appropriation account from which the amount involved was originally paid.

"(B) MERGER—Any amount credited under subparagraph (A) shall be merged with other sums in such account and shall be available for the same purposes and period, and subject to the same limitations, if any, as the sums with which the amount was merged.

"(3) LIMITATIONS—

"(A) STUDENT LOAN PAYMENT AMOUNT—Student loan repayments made by the Attorney General under this section shall be made subject to such terms, limitations, or conditions as may be mutually agreed upon by the borrower and the Attorney General in an agreement under paragraph (1), except that the amount paid by the Attorney General under this section shall not exceed—

"(i) $10,000 for any borrower in any calendar year; or

"(ii) an aggregate total of $60,000 in the case of any borrower.

"(B) BEGINNING OF PAYMENTS—Nothing in this section shall authorize the Attorney General to pay any amount to reimburse a borrower for any repayments made by such borrower prior to the date on which the Attorney General entered into an agreement with the borrower under this subsection.

"(e) Additional Agreements—

"(1) IN GENERAL—On completion of the required period of service under an agreement under subsection (d), the borrower and the Attorney General may, subject to paragraph (2), enter into an additional agreement in accordance with subsection (d).

"(2) TERM—An agreement entered into under paragraph (1) may require the borrower to remain employed as a prosecutor or public defender for less than 3 years.

"(f) Award Basis; Priority—

"(1) AWARD BASIS—Subject to paragraph (2), the Attorney General shall provide repayment benefits under this section on a first-come, first-served basis, and subject to the availability of appropriations.

"(2) PRIORITY—The Attorney General shall give priority in providing repayment benefits under this section in any fiscal year to a borrower who

"(f) Award Basis; Priority—

"(1) AWARD BASIS—Subject to paragraph (2), the Attorney General shall provide repayment benefits under this section—

"(A) giving priority to borrowers who have the least ability to repay their loans, except that the Attorney General shall determine a fair allocation of repayment benefits among prosecutors and public defenders, and among employing entities nationwide; and

"(B) subject to the availability of appropriations.

"(2) PRIORITY—The Attorney General shall give priority in providing repayment benefits under this section in any fiscal year to a borrower who—

"(A) received repayment benefits under this section during the preceding fiscal year; and

"(B) has completed less than 3 years of the first required period of service specified for the borrower in an agreement entered into under subsection (d).

"(g) Regulations—The Attorney General is authorized to issue such regulations as may be necessary to carry out the provisions of this section.

"(h) Study—Not later than 1 year after the date of enactment of this section, the Government Accountability Office shall study and report to Congress on the impact of law school accreditation requirements and other factors on law school costs and access, including the impact of such requirements on racial and ethnic minorities.

"(h)(i) Authorization of appropriations—There are authorized to be appropriated to carry out this section $25,000,000 for fiscal year 2008 and such sums as may be necessary for each succeeding fiscal year."

Calendar No. 113

Appendix F

Senate Report 110-051

VIII. ADDITIONAL VIEWS

ADDITIONAL VIEWS OF SENATORS KYL AND HATCH

While the bill reported by this Committee will help reduce the burden of the heavy law-school student loans borne by many young prosecutors and public defenders, this legislation treats only the symptoms, not the source, of this problem. The source of the problem—the cause of the excessive cost of becoming eligible to practice law in the United States today—was identified in testimony before this Committee by George B. Shepard, an associate professor of law at Emory University School of Law. In his testimony on February 27, Professor Shepard endorsed the John R. Justice Act, but went on to note that:

> [W]e need to recognize that passage of the Act is necessary partly because of the [law-school] accreditation system; without the accreditation system, many more students would graduate from law school with no loans or much smaller ones, so that they would not need to use the benefits that the Act provides. With the accreditation system, the Act will, in effect, transfer much taxpayers' money from the federal government to overpriced law schools.

Professor Shepard went on to describe exactly how the American Bar Association's law-school accreditation rules substantially and unnecessarily increase the cost of becoming eligible to practice law:

> The ABA's accreditation requirements increase the cost of becoming a lawyer in two ways. First, they increase law school tuition. They do this by imposing many costs on law schools. For example, accreditation standards effectively raise faculty salaries; limit faculty teaching loads; require high numbers of full-time faculty rather than cheaper part-time adjuncts; and require expensive physical facilities and library collections. The requirements probably cause law schools' costs to more than double, increasing them by more than $12,000 per year,

with many schools then passing the increased costs along to students by raising tuition. The total increase for the three years of law school is more than $36,000.

The impact of the increased costs from accreditation can be seen by comparing tuition rates at accredited schools and unaccredited schools. Accredited schools normally charge more than $25,000 per year. Unaccredited schools usually charge approximately half that amount. One example of the many expensive accreditation requirements is the ABA's requirement that an accredited school have a large library and extensive library collection. Insiders confirm that the ABA requires a minimum expenditure on library operations and acquisitions of approximately $1 million per year. This is more than $4,000 per student in an averaged-sized school.

The second way that the ABA requirements increase students' cost of entering the legal profession is as follows. The ABA requires students to attend at least six years of expensive higher education: three years of college and three years of law school. Before the Great Depression, a young person could enter the legal profession as an apprentice directly after high school, without college or law school. Now, a person can become a lawyer only if she can afford to take six years off from work after high school and pay six years of tuition.

The requirement of six years of education is expensive. The sum of the tuition payments and foregone income can easily exceed $300,000, or more. For example, a conservative estimate is that attending a private college and law school for six years would cost approximately $25,000 per year for a total of $150,000. In addition, let's assume conservatively that a student who could qualify for college and law school would have earned only $25,000 per year if the student had not attended college and law school. The amount of income that the student sacrifices for six years to become a lawyer is $150,000. The total is $300,000.

In addition to the John R. Justice Act, there are two other means by which the problem of the excessive cost of becoming eligible to practice law in this country could be addressed. First, the states themselves could liberalize their law-school accreditation requirements. This would directly reduce the cost of becoming a lawyer in all cases, not just for prosecutors and public defenders. In his February 27 testimony, Professor Shepard recommended that:

> [T]he accreditation system's restrictions should be loosened. For example, law schools might be permitted to experiment with smaller li-

braries, cheaper practitioner faculty, and even shorter programs of two years rather than three, like business school. Or the requirements might be eliminated completely; students without a degree from an accredited law school would be able to practice law.

Removing the flawed, artificial accreditation bottleneck would not in fact be a drastic change, and it would create many benefits but few harms. The current system's high-end qualities would continue, while a freer market for variety would quickly open up. To Rolls-Royce legal educations would be added Buicks, Saturns, and Fords. The new system would develop a wider range of talent, including lawyers at $60, $40, and even $25 an hour, as well as those at $300 and up. This would fit the true diversity of legal needs, from simple to complex. With cheaper education available to more people, some lawyers for the first time would be willing and able to work for far less than at present.

The addition of many more lawyers would produce little additional legal malpractice or fraud, and the quality of legal services decline little, it at all. Private institutions would arise within the market for legal services to ensure that each legal matter was handled by lawyers with appropriate skills and sophistication. For example, large, expensive law firms would continue to handle complicated, high-stakes transactions and litigation. However, law companies that resembled H&R Block would open to offer less-expensive legal services for simple matters. Accounting and tax services are available not only for $300 per hour at the big accounting firms, but also for $25 per hour at H&R Block. The new law companies would monitor and guarantee the services of their lawyer-employees.

Elimination of the accreditation requirement is a modest, safe proposal. It merely reestablishes the system that exists in other equally-critical professions, a system that worked well in law for more than a century before the Great Depression. Business and accounting provide comforting examples of professions without mandatory accreditation or qualifying exams. In both professions, people may provide full-quality basic services without attending an accredited school or passing an exam. Instead, people can choose preparation that is appropriate for their jobs. A person who seeks to manage a local McDonald's franchise or to prepare tax returns need not attend business school or become a CPA first. Yet there is no indication that the level of malpractice or fraud is higher in these fields than in law. Likewise, there is no indication that malpractice and fraud were any more frequent during the century before accreditation and the bar exam, when lawyers like Abraham Lincoln practiced. Lincoln never went to law school.

Second, in response to those who have turned to Congress to address this problem, I would note that Congress already *has* acted. It acted in 1868, by

enacting the Privileges and Immunities Clause of the Fourteenth Amendment.
That Clause was understood at the time of the nation's founding 'to refer to those
fundamental rights and liberties specifically enjoyed by English citizens and, more
broadly, by all persons.' *Saenz v. Roe,* 526 U.S. 489, 524 (Thomas, J., dissenting)—a meaning that carried over to the Fourteenth Amendment as well, see
Id. 526–27. Legal scholars and civil-rights organizations such as the Institute
for Justice have in the past presented compelling arguments that the fundamental rights and liberties protected by the Privileges and Immunities Clause
include a right to pursue a career or profession. And that right is in clear tension with the apparently protectionist nature of the current accreditation regime.
As Professor Shepard noted in his testimony:

> Strict accreditation requirements are a relatively recent phenome-
> non, having begun in the Great Depression. What seems normal now
> after 70 years was in fact a radical change from a much more open
> system that had functioned well for more than a century before then.
> Until the Great Depression, no state required an applicant to the bar
> to have attended any law school at all, much less an accredited one. In-
> deed, 41 states required no formal education whatsoever beyond high
> school; 32 states did not even require a high school diploma. Simi-
> larly, bar exams were easy to pass; they had high pass rates.

* * * * * * *

During the Depression, state bar associations attempted to eliminate so-
called 'overcrowding' in the legal profession; they felt that too many new lawyers
were competing with the existing ones for the dwindling amount of legal business. They attempted to reduce the number of new lawyers in two ways. First,
they decreased bar pass rates. Second, they convinced courts and state legislatures to require that all lawyers graduate from ABA-accredited law schools.

The protectionist nature of the current accreditation regime not only is at
odds with the Privileges and Immunities Clause; it also has a disproportion-
ate impact on the very minority groups that the Fourteenth Amendment was
originally designed to protect. Several of the witnesses who testified before the
Committee emphasized the negative effects that escalating tuition costs have
on minority participation in the legal profession and on access to legal services in minority communities. Jessica Bergeman, an Assistant State's Attorney
for Cook County, Illinois, stated:

> I truly believe that it is good for the communities of Chicago to see As-
> sistant State's Attorneys of color. Unfortunately, it is often we who are
> most burdened with educational debt. People like me who are forced

to leave the office because they cannot afford to stay cannot be categorized as just a personal career set-back, but rather it has the potential to further the divisions between the prosecutors and so many of the people they prosecute.

Professor Shepard seconded this point in his testimony, noting that 'the system has excluded many from the legal profession, particularly the poor and minorities. It has raised the cost of legal services. And it has, in effect, denied legal services to whole segments of our society.'

Simple legal planning plays an important role in individuals' efforts to provide for their families, start businesses, and plan for their economic futures. Lower and middle-income citizens' lack of access to legal services makes it more difficult for them to make the informed choices that will improve their lives. And existing law-school accreditation requirements play a significant role in driving up the cost of legal services. Recognizing the significance of these phenomena, the Committee adopted an amendment to this legislation that will require the Government Accountability Office to report to Congress on the impact that law-school accreditation requirements have on law-school tuition, including the effect that the elevated cost of legal services has on members of minority groups.

The bill reported by this Committee addresses a real problem. It is a problem, however, that should also be addressed by other, more direct means.

JON KYL.
ORRIN G. HATCH.

Index